JUSTICE INTERRUPTED

JUSTICE INTERRUPTED

*The Struggle for Constitutional Government
in the Middle East*

ELIZABETH F. THOMPSON

HARVARD UNIVERSITY PRESS
Cambridge, Massachusetts
London, England
2013

Library of Congress Cataloging-in-Publication Data

Thompson, Elizabeth, 1959– author.
Justice interrupted : the struggle for constitutional
government in the Middle East / Elizabeth F. Thompson.
pages ; cm
Includes bibliographical references and index.
ISBN 978-0-674-07313-5 (hardcover : alk. paper)
1. Middle East—Politics and government—20th century.
2. Middle East—Politics and government—19th century.   I. Title.
DS62.8.T46 2013
320.956—dc23   2012039279

In memory of my mother

RUTH STANTON THOMPSON

(1928–2010)

CONTENTS

III

STRUGGLES FOR JUSTICE IN THE ABSENCE
OF A POLITICAL ARENA, SINCE 1965

PREFACE

This book began with a generous grant from the Carnegie Corporation of New York's program to promote literature on the Islamic world for nonspecialists. In that spirit, I have written this text with a minimum of scholarly jargon for the audience that so eagerly read Albert Hourani's *A History of the Arab Peoples* a few years ago and who have since followed news of the turbulent political transitions in the region. For the ease of the ordinary reader, I have omitted the usual diacritical marks used in the transliteration of Ottoman Turkish, Arabic, Persian, and modern Turkish. Those names are consequently printed in an altered form, and I trust that scholars will recognize the original spellings. I have provided an annotated, selected bibliography to guide readers more deeply into the historical trends raised.

The book took shape in the course of my engagement with journalists, activists, and policymakers at two research centers in Washington, DC: the United States Institute of Peace and the Woodrow Wilson Center for International Scholars. I thank both programs for their financial support and for sharing my belief that a historical perspective is critical to understanding the contemporary Middle East. Many of the movements described here are only scantily known outside of academia and have hardly been described in English from the viewpoint of the activists themselves.

I am especially grateful to two colleagues at the University of Virginia who have supported me through the six years of writing, William Quandt and Melvyn Leffler. I also thank the University of Virginia's dean of the College and Graduate School of Arts and Sciences,

Center for International Studies, and Corcoran Department of History for support in starting and finishing the book.

A work of synthesis like this book cannot be the product of an individual mind. I have drawn upon the research of many fine scholars who have worked in obscurity and under personal stress in Middle Eastern archives. Their research provides rich context for understanding the political movements profiled here. They are remembered in the chapter notes. I am especially grateful to those who read drafts of chapters: Osama Abi Mershed, Abdulrahim Abuhusayn, Yiğit Akin, Margot Badran, Linda Darling, Lerna Ekmekcioglu, Ellen Fleischmann, Fatma Halim, Tareq Ismael, Ussama Makdisi, Farzaneh Milani, Shira Robinson, Ariel Salzmann, Aziz Sbahi, Samer Shehata, John Voll, Radwan Ziadeh, and the CCAS graduate seminar at Georgetown University. I have learned much from them, and I am, of course, responsible for any and all errors that remain in the text.

This book also benefited from the informal advice and insight given by many others, including Mustafa Aksakal, Gamal al-Banna, Ahmed al-Rahim, Seda Altug, Lisa Anderson, Orit Bashkin, Susan Beckman-Brindley, Joel Beinin, Hamit Bozarslan, Nathan Brown, Linda Butler, Ipek Çalişlar, Helena Cobban, John Milton Cooper, Selim Deringil, Sibel Erol, Selcuk Esenbel, Haleh Esfandiari, Khalid Fahmy, Israel Gershoni, Steve Heydemann, Samir Khalaf, Rashid Khalidi, Dina Khoury, Erol Köroğlu, Joshua Landis, Sami Moubayed, Soli Özel, Abdul Karim Rafeq, Ruhi Ramazani, Rowaida Saad-El-Din, Hanan Sabea, Abdulaziz Sachedina, Kaya Shahin, Nader Sohrabi, Barbara Slavin, Ron Suny, Selim Tamari, Suhail Kader Tarazi, Zafer Toprak, John Voll, Keith Watenpaugh, and Peter Wien. Edhem Eldem was exceptionally generous in sharing his photo collection with me. My thinking was also sharpened by discussions with students in my seminars "Seeking Justice in the Middle East," "World War I in the Middle East," and "Roots of the Arab Spring" taught at the University of Virginia. I also benefited tremendously from conversations held at the University of Michigan's Eisenberg Institute for Historical Studies, with Mark Mazower and the seminar on partial sovereignties at Columbia University, at Georgetown University's Center for Contemporary Arab Studies, and at George Washington University's Institute for Middle East Studies. For their help in research and translation, I thank Huseyin Aydin, Meagan Bridges, Suad Jafarzadeh, Rana Khoury, Leila Piran, and Leila Tawfiq Aranki Tarazi.

Writing this book was also inspired by those closest to me. Many of these pages were composed at Open City, a café with real soul in Washington, DC. Week after week, the good coffee and good company gave me creative energy. My two sons, Dylan and Benjamin, gave me much comfort and more patience than they should have been asked to give. My husband, David Waldner, was my guiding star, leading me through every difficulty and inspiring me to finish. I dedicate this book to my mother, Ruth Stanton Thompson, because its deepest roots lie in my childhood in the rebellious 1960s. She introduced me to the courageous men and women who struggled for justice in my own country. She continued to inspire me as I wrote this book at the end of her life. May this book be a testament to life lived passionately in the pursuit of principle.

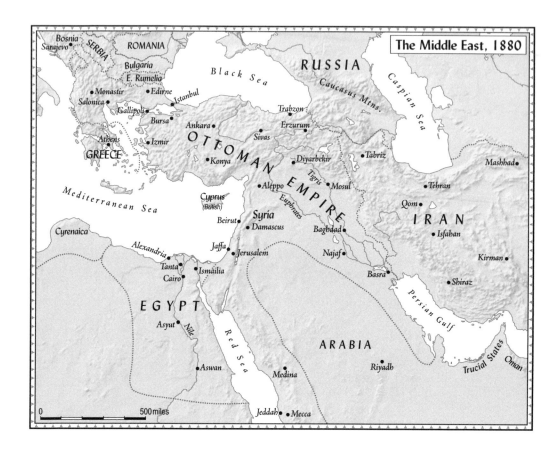

The Middle East, 1880

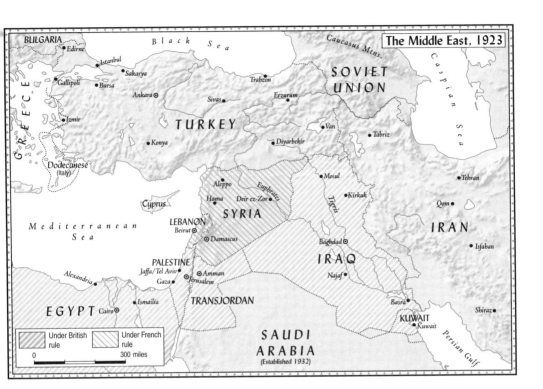

The Middle East, 1923

BULGARIA
Black Sea
Caucasus Mtns.
Edirne
Istanbul
Sakarya
Gallipoli • Bursa
Trabzon
SOVIET UNION
Caspian Sea
Ankara ⊙
Sivas
Erzurum
Izmir
TURKEY
Van
Tabriz
Konya
Diyarbekir
Tehran
Dodecanese (Italy)
Mosul
Qom
Cyprus
Aleppo
Euphrates
Kirkuk
IRAN
Hama
Deir ez-Zor
Mediterranean Sea
SYRIA
Tigris
LEBANON
Beirut ⊙
Baghdad ⊙
Isfahan
Damascus ⊙
IRAQ
PALESTINE
Jaffa/Tel Aviv
Amman ⊙
Najaf
Alexandria
Gaza • Jerusalem ⊙
Basra
Shiraz
EGYPT
Cairo ⊙ • Ismailia
TRANSJORDAN
KUWAIT
Kuwait
Persian Gulf

Under British rule   Under French rule

0   300 miles

SAUDI ARABIA
(Established 1932)

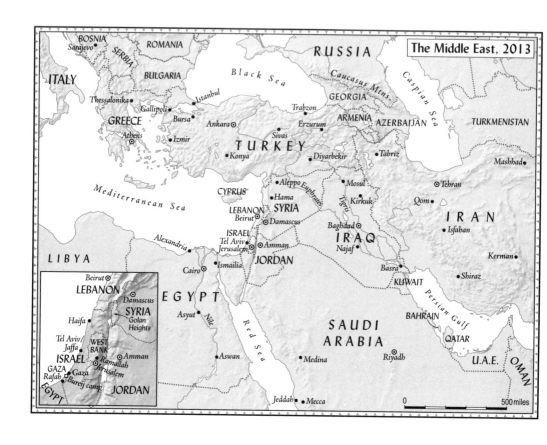

INTRODUCTION

In 1599, an Ottoman bureaucrat named Mustafa Ali returned to Cairo with fond memories of the city he had visited a quarter century before. "But in the course of time the state of the world had changed," he reported. "The various classes of mankind had become distressed in the matters of livelihood, and peace and order had been chased from the face of the earth."[1] He urged the sultan to restore justice by imposing stricter Ottoman rule and Islamic law over the Land of the Nile.

Mustafa Ali uncannily detected the beginnings of fundamental change in the Middle East's position in the world economy and the global balance of power. The Ottomans had once ruled over the heart of the world economy. Now, as the rise of capitalism in Europe diverted trade and disrupted the Ottoman economy, patrimonial ideals of harmony collapsed. By 1770, the once-awesome Ottoman army could no longer defend the realm. Mustafa Ali's royal reports had by then launched a tradition of jeremiad among reform minded bureaucrats. They warned of imperial decline unless the sultan revived the empire's forgotten principles of justice. Finally, they inspired an Ottoman bill of rights in 1839, when the sultan decreed that a citizenry with equal rights under the law would replace the paternalistic hierarchy of ruling class and subjects.

Since then, Middle Eastern peoples have mobilized against injustices caused by global economic change and growing state power. By the time of World War I, Ottoman, Egyptian, and Iranian citizens united in movements to demand constitutional government as a new model of justice. They hoped that constitutions—which would limit

1

the monarch's power and grant legislative power to a representative assembly—would assure full sovereignty against the encroachments of European imperialism. They also hoped that constitutions would assure all citizens equality under the law. Their constitutional governments collapsed, however, in the wake of foreign invasion. Faith in constitutionalism also collapsed, because it had not lived up to its promise to protect sovereignty.

After World War I, the Ottoman and Iranian dynasties fell, ceding political space to a new array of movements that embraced new models of justice. Liberals now confronted mass movements that often rejected their role as a ruling elite. Mass movements rallied popular support through local vernaculars of justice, promising equality and security. Constitutionalism remained an end-goal, but no longer was it the preferred means. To attain sovereignty—the prerequisite to constitutional justice—the new movements demanded revolt and national unity, voicing deep suspicion of the liberal ideals that Europeans used to justify their occupation and colonization of the Middle East after the war.

The consequences of World War I went beyond the rejection of elitist liberalism. The extreme violence on the war's killing fields ushered in a new era of political violence. To populations devastated by death, disease, and hunger, the new mass movements prioritized collective security over individual rights, a strong state over freedom, in agendas variously labeled nationalist, socialist, communist, and Islamist. Rejection of liberal ideals was not due to Islamic culture, but rather to historical circumstance. In the name of unity, some of the new movements vaunted one ethnic or religious group over others, in a brutal and violent politics of exclusion. Other movements, like Iraqi communism, promoted political inclusion of lower classes and minorities.

In World War II and the Cold War, these rival visions of justice exploded into conflict. While many Arabs, Turks, and Iranians embraced the victory of democracy, the Middle East again became a primary battleground between world powers—this time, the United States and Soviet Union. Fearful of communism, the United States supported coups against popularly elected governments in Syria, Iraq, and Iran that promised to unite citizens across religious, ethnic, and class lines. Soviet- and American-backed dictators suppressed the region's most popular movements: the Egyptian Muslim Brothers, the Iraqi communists, and the Syrian socialists.

In the wake of the Cold War, ethnic violence surged again. The already fraught issue of partitioning British Palestine into independent Jewish and Arab states became a flashpoint of Cold-War and postcolonial politics, laying the ground for the region's longest conflict. By 1965, the political arena in Iran and the Arab countries had virtually collapsed. With little or no legal space to organize opposition movements, some Palestinians and Islamists turned to the methods of Third Worldist guerrilla warfare and terror.

The dawn of the twenty-first century, like that of Mustafa Ali's seventeenth century, has ushered in a new era of global transformation. Constitutionalism has returned as the dominant model of justice in the Middle East. Turks elected an opposition government that has eased the military out of politics. In Iran, the Green Movement rose up in 2009 against religious elites' control of government. Two years later, the Arab Spring broke out against the petty and pervasive tyranny of governments in Tunisia, Libya, Egypt, Syria, Yemen, and Bahrain.

These new revolutions do not represent, as the press often claims, the Middle East's discovery of democracy. The roots of constitutionalism in the Middle East are deep; faith in universal ideals of justice was interrupted—but not broken—in World War I. As a result, the liberal politics of Cairo's Tahrir Square are historically linked to the politics of terror in al-Qaeda. Political violence in the Middle East is neither a persistent pathology of backward or Eastern cultures nor a recent product of Third World radicalism. Rather, it is intimately related to the frustrated engagement of local liberal movements with European (and later American) power since the mid-nineteenth century.

ON BIOGRAPHY AS HISTORY

Justice Interrupted tells the history of the modern Middle East as it has never been told before—from the perspective of those who struggled for justice against invasion, tyranny, and economic inequality. Much of the writing in Middle Eastern history has focused on diplomatic maneuvers and wars waged by heads of state. The common people have often remained an abstraction. Each of the following chapters tells the story of an activist (sometimes more than one) who inspired or led a movement with a new ideal of justice.

The result is a history of ideas in action that reveals the complex lineages of political violence and political idealism in the Middle East today. The focus on individual activists does not suggest that individuals (or Great Men) are agents of change in history. Most of those profiled here failed in their missions: several were executed or assassinated, others faced exile, and only a few lived to taste victory. Their life stories are noteworthy because they refract and synthesize the larger historical processes that have determined the course of politics in the Middle East.

Biography is also an important mode of political discourse in the Middle East. As an Iranian friend reminded me, *Justice Interrupted* resembles an old genre in Middle Eastern literature, the biographical dictionary. It is rooted in the seventh century, with the first efforts to retell the life story of the Prophet Muhammad as a model for Muslims. Like a *Who's Who,* the dictionaries list notables and scholars of a certain town or region. They detail their lives as exemplars of struggle for justice in the Islamic path. Collective biographies still circulate in the Middle East, published often to inspire patriotism or social reform. Most remarkable has been the publicizing of women's lives as models for emulation.[2] Historical memory for many in the Middle East is grounded in the life stories of outstanding individuals. The memoir remains the most popular form of history book.

And so it is appropriate that *Justice Interrupted* mirrors the indigenous form. This book collects the stories of the Middle East's modern political heroes, leaders of the largest political movements in the past 200 years. In their day, all of the activists profiled here were well known—if not universally loved. I use speeches and memoirs to evoke how they presented their stories as life lessons, and as inspiration, to their political followers. I preserve their subjective visions as a valuable window on the values that motivated masses to join the movements. In this way, subjectivity and the deliberate distortion of memory can be yoked to the historian's effort to write "objective" history.

Scholars may quibble with the choices I have made. Some will suggest that there were other, more important, leaders who have been omitted. This is undoubtedly true. A dozen life stories cannot encapsulate two centuries of history. The selection is intended, however, to be representative: all of the activists led the largest movements in modern Middle Eastern history. While the memory of some activists has been suppressed or forgotten by ordinary citizens today, they are all familiar to contemporary activists and to modern Middle East historians. Scholars may also question the fact that the chapters rely on activists' own narratives. Most of the narratives used here were published. They have become part of a public and collective memory. The tales they tell may not be factual, but they have been influential in shaping people's sense of past injustices and the fight for the future.

In order to capture that dynamism, I have avoided the stories of rulers, who tend to rewrite the past with the heaviest overlay of propaganda and who impose their version of history through mechanisms of coercion. I have instead favored the stories of the second-in-command or the runners up. Their stories tend to be told from the perspective of an activist who is not yet in power, and so needs to earn the faith of followers. They also tap observations made of leaders at a critical distance. And so we begin with a disgruntled Ottoman bureaucrat who pens reports to the sultan and an Egyptian colonel who briefly installed a revolutionary government in 1882. Halide Edib's story of the birth of modern Turkey casts a critical look on that country's George Washington, Mustafa Kemal Ataturk. I chose Akram al-Hourani for the chapter on Arab socialism and the Baath Party because he wrote his memoir as a defense against the victorious, military wing of the Syrian Baath Party. Abu Iyad, second-in-command in the Palestine Liberation Organization (PLO), wrote his memoir with little mention of Yasser Arafat. He aimed to convince an international public of the righteousness of the PLO's cause. Their memoirs partly reflect the genre of memoir as personal confession and redemption. Some are written more in the mode of jeremiad, a call to readers to halt society's decline and to return to a mythical golden age or to a forgotten ideal.

Other activists left no personal memoir. I have found, for example, the voice of Tanyus Shahin, a semiliterate blacksmith who challenged feudal elites in Lebanon, in letters, speeches, and reports by contemporaries. Likewise Comrade Fahd, founder of Iraqi Communist Party, lived a life deep in the underground. We have only a few letters and some important articles and manifestos written by him. The personal papers of Hasan al-Banna, founder of the Muslim Brotherhood, have been carefully guarded, if they exist at all. However, Banna published a highly stylized "memoir" in serial form intended to set an example for his followers. It cannot be read as a factual autobiography, but it offers valuable clues to what Banna saw as injustices in his life, how he envisioned a more just society, and what inspired the hundreds of thousands who followed him.

ON JUSTICE AS HISTORY

Why choose "justice" as the subject of this book? Because it was the dominant term used by all Middle Eastern activists. It defined the norms and rules they believed should determine righteous behavior in state and society. "Justice" is a buzzword in Middle Eastern politics much as "freedom" is in American politics. Freedom endures as a political value, argues American historian Eric Foner, because it works as both a cultural bond and a political fault line. Freedom's meaning was revised and contested by each generation.[3] So too, in the Middle East, definitions of justice have varied according to time, place, and political circumstance. This book traces the evolution of the meaning of justice, in the face of historical change and as a motivational tool in building political movements.

Justice is also used in this book as a method of inquiry. As political philosopher Judith Shklar argues, aggrieved people are not inspired by theories of justice; rather, they derive their visions of justice from feelings of injustice.[4] Each chapter, accordingly, locates the origins of a vision of justice in the life stories of activists, as revealed in their memoirs, speeches, and letters. The chapters ask why activists decided their suffering was an injustice, not merely misfortune. This was the "personal" sense of justice. Each chapter also analyzes how activists constructed a political or public meaning of justice, recruited followers, built an organization, and developed a strategy to fight injustice. They adapted the repertoires of action and ideological frameworks of previous movements to conditions. In so doing, the meaning of justice was modified to meet new needs.

This book also contributes to current conversations about international norms of justice. Shklar's book, *The Faces of Injustice*, anticipated the arguments of the philosopher Michael Sandel and the Indian economist Amartya Sen. Sandel has criticized idealist models of justice, like that of John Rawls, in favor of what he calls a dialectic of reason and experience. "Moral reflection," Sandel writes, "needs some engagement with the tumult of the city."[5] *Justice Interrupted* looks at the largest political movements in the Middle East's modern history as just such a series of engagements between reflection and the city. These popular movements mobilized support precisely because they tapped deeply held values among citizens. They give us evidence, then, of what common people believed justice to be. They also give us a record of how ideals of justice evolved as they engaged in political tumult.

Likewise, Sen argues that justice is a process, not an institution. "What moves us, reasonably enough, is not the realization that the world falls short of being completely just—which few of us expect—but that there are clearly remediable injustices around us which we want to eliminate," he writes. "Most who fight for justice don't fight as crusaders for a static ideal, but as citizens and neighbors for something a bit better."[6] When considered this way, justice can be seen as a product of history, not a product of static cultural values. It can be studied in comparative terms, across nations and cultures. Sen's book *The Idea of Justice* sought to decenter Western, liberal models of justice by arguing that we must understand justice in practice, not just theory. His goal was not so much to criticize the West, but to rescue history from the rhetoric of empire and global rivalry, where Europe and the United States have stood in judgment over other peoples. Self-serving rhetoric of the past has distorted our understanding of contemporary politics in much of the world.

Following Sen, *Justice Interrupted* seeks to recoup a mutual understanding lost in the past two centuries, when the Middle East became ensnared in European rivalries for world empire. Clichés about the clashes between Western and Eastern civilization have demeaned and even demonized values held by Muslims, Christians, and Jews. Exotic quotes from the Quran on television news are, indeed, a misleading indicator of Middle Eastern peoples' values. The struggles for justice portrayed in these chapters reveal that Middle Easterners' dearest values—the ones that large numbers of them took risks to fight for—are not as exotic as readers of this book might suppose.

In his landmark book *Orientalism* Edward Said exposed the historical fallacy of viewing the Orient as the antithesis of the West, as a despotic society that threatens our democracy.[7] He rejected the idea of a cultural line between East and West. He called for understanding the peoples of the Middle East on the terms fully lived by the people themselves, in their complexity as Arabs, Turks, Kurds, and Persians; Christians, Muslims, and Jews; Asians, Levantines, and Africans; colonial subjects and national citizens; peasants and landlords; bureaucrats and freedom fighters.

By examining ideas in action, *Justice Interrupted* offers a new—and less pessimistic—way of thinking about politics in today's Middle East. The life stories retold here show that there have long been democrats in the region and that some Islamists today are heirs to political traditions that support peaceful, liberal, and capitalist values. The roots of Islamism lie in the history it shares with other mass movements that arose earlier in the twentieth century. The stories also show how Middle Eastern history has long been intertwined with European and American history. This history was not known to Americans who asked in true bafflement, "Why do they hate us?" after the terrorist attacks of September 11, 2001. Contrary to portrayals of Islamists as soldiers in an age-old clash of civilizations, *Justice Interrupted* reveals them as players in a game of mass politics that emerged only recently and in dialogue with—not in opposition to—the West.

In practice there has been no essential conflict between democratic values and Islam. While some Islamists have supported essentialist ideas of East and West, others have insisted that individual rights and freedoms are inherent in Islam's message. Liberal reforms were carried out mainly by pious Muslim bureaucrats, not secularists. Even communists viewed socialism as the Prophet's message adapted to the modern era. Islam was, in fact, integral to the liberal, constitutional, and socialist movements that dominated Middle Eastern politics through the mid-twentieth century.

The stories in *Justice Interrupted* suggest that Islamism and political violence are rooted not just in Middle Eastern culture, but also in global politics. Since the nineteenth century, Middle Eastern activists have eagerly borrowed political ideas and strategies from foreign models. Similarly, their success or failure was determined not just locally, but also by foreign powers. Because the Middle East is located so close to the seats of European empire, the region has one of the most highly penetrated systems of politics in the world.[8] Since the nineteenth century, Europeans—and later Americans—have intervened repeatedly in Turkish, Arab, and Iranian politics, and their consuls often determined the rise and fall of local rulers.

Justice Interrupted recalls the title of another book, *Justice Interruptus*, by Nancy Fraser, written for American citizens at a time of transition between two frames of justice, that of social equality and that of identity recognition. She suggested ways in which the interruption of an idea may be productive.[9] Her book influenced me as I studied how Middle Eastern politicians responded to the interruption of World War I.

The Great War emerges in these pages as a pivotal moment, a traumatic interruption of Middle Eastern history. While the collective terror of the trenches in Europe has been much written about, the war's traumatic impact on Middle Eastern peoples and politics has been less studied. Civilians arguably suffered more than their European counterparts, as the Allies blocked food supplies and as the Ottoman state resorted to mass murder and mass expulsion.

World War I had as much impact on Middle Eastern politics and society as the Civil War did in the United States. Before the war, liberal constitutionalism was the hegemonic model of justice. It inspired the broadest political coalitions and it provided the ideological glue among would-be political rivals. Ottoman defeat in World War I caused the defeat of constitutionalism. The peace treaties negotiated at Paris were seen as a profound betrayal by liberal European powers, who embarked on an aggressive program of colonization in the region.

The feeling that justice was betrayed in World War I has haunted Middle Eastern politics ever since. It has fueled decades of antiliberal movements and suspicion of Western governments. Constitutionalism lay dormant, as a postponed goal, until the recent wave of revolts in the early twenty-first century. Today's activists view constitutionalism not as a European import, but as the revival of a past Middle Eastern political experience.

I have therefore arranged the book in three parts, reflecting this interruption. Part I traces the nineteenth-century roots of constitutionalism. Beginning with elite Ottoman reforms in 1839, activists converged around a new, constitutional model of justice to replace the paternalistic justice of the sultan. Part II features the movements that arose from the cinders of World War I: the effort to retool liberalism as a popular movement in Turkey, the turn to nationalism in Palestine, the Muslim Brotherhood's movement for religious justice in Egypt, Iraqi communism, and finally a movement of peasants and socialists in Syria. These movements, the most powerful of the postwar period, emphasized collective security and local culture against constitutionalism's language of universal and individual rights. They feared and resisted Western influence, but they rarely rejected constitutionalism as an ultimate goal. Part III examines the fate of politics in an era of growing tyranny and the Cold War. Without free political arenas in which to mobilize, activists turned to other forms and forums of protest—international violence and the mosque.

The concluding chapter places the Arab Spring of 2011 in this historical context. Activists in Egypt's Tahrir Square consciously called for the destruction of their Cold War-era dictatorship. They sought to reclaim the popular revolution interrupted by Gamal Abdel Nasser and other army officers who staged a coup in 1952. The Arab Spring expresses three enduring principles of justice in Middle Eastern politics: that sovereignty is a prerequisite for the rule of law; that constitutional government is an Islamic ideal; and that foreign intervention has done more harm than good. The revolts were built upon a new common ground between Islamic and secular models of justice. The question remains whether the political violence of states and their militant opposition will be contained enough to permit the revival of political arenas.

I offer this book as a contribution and challenge to current public discourse in the United States and Europe about violence, Islam, and democracy in the Middle East. The stories of these Middle Eastern activists suggest ways in which American policy might be revised in the post-Cold War era to break cycles of political violence and dictatorship: through respect for Middle Easterners' sovereignty, for their memory of rights stolen and faith betrayed, and for their long struggle for rule of law and equality.

I

THE RISE OF A CONSTITUTIONAL MODEL OF JUSTICE, 1839–1920

1

MUSTAFA ALI

Ottoman Justice and Bureaucratic Reform

Mustafa Ali of Gallipoli was a curmudgeonly old man. Disappointed, but not yet defeated by life, he boarded a ship in July 1599 to cross the Mediterranean from Istanbul to Egypt. His career had begun so brilliantly back home in Gallipoli, a small seaside town on the European side of the Dardanelles. As a young poet and star student from a family of religious scholars, he had won entrance at age fifteen to an imperial school in the Ottoman capital of Istanbul. Those were the glorious days of Sultan Suleyman the Lawgiver (1520–1566).

Now past his prime, at age fifty-eight, Mustafa Ali was about to take up the latest in a string of midlevel posts in the Ottoman financial administration. These duties had led him across the empire, to Damascus, Aleppo, Baghdad, Anatolia, Bosnia, and Istanbul. Now he had accepted the post of governor of Jeddah, the important Arabian port. But as his ship crossed the sea, Mustafa Ali still harbored ambition for the office that he had long coveted: governor of Egypt. To remind Sultan Mehmed III (1595–1603) of his talents, he planned to stop for a few months in Cairo and write a report on the state of the province.

Some of Mustafa Ali's peers ridiculed him for his self-promotion, flowery writing, and tendency to inflate personal disappointment into apocalyptic warnings of Ottoman decline. He compared himself to a phoenix rising above "the shackles of the Chancellery."[1] To modern readers, Mustafa Ali resembles the pompous courtier Polonius in

Hamlet, penned by a greater bard of the same era. He routinely sent poems to sultans to dazzle them with his rhetoric. He also admitted to the bad habit of "revealing others' faults."

Mustafa Ali's self-promotion did not obstruct his sharp social and political perception. His personal sense of injustice, piqued by the advancement of men he considered less skilled and more corrupt, triggered his desire to report on the suffering of the sultan's poorest subjects.[2] His lamentation of imperial injustice would inspire a new literary genre called *nasihatnameler,* or advice books to princes. This bureaucratic movement for justice used the pen and access to power as its repertoire of action. The bureaucrats framed their mission to restore justice (unsurprisingly) in terms of administrative reform. Their books, passed on to successive generations of bureaucrats, led circuitously and contentiously to the triumphant declaration of imperial reform in the 1839 Rose Garden decree. Called the Tanzimat, the reform program sought to turn subjects of the sultan into Ottoman citizens and so mobilize them to save the empire.

Bureaucrats' reports were responses to the vast changes in the Ottoman empire in the seventeenth and eighteenth centuries. Economic change came as Western Europeans diverted trade from Asia away from Ottoman land routes to sea routes around Africa, and as their conquistadors opened the Atlantic trade with the Americas. Political and military change came as Peter the Great and Catherine the Great expanded Russia into an empire in repeated wars on Ottoman territory. These changes sparked unrest and revolts around the empire. This pressure from below motivated bureaucrats to write their reports and ultimately to act upon them, culminating in what subjects viewed as an Ottoman bill of rights in 1839.

Mustafa Ali's *Description of Cairo*

To Egyptians, Cairo was the "Mother of the World." To Ottomans like Mustafa Ali, it was the empire's second capital. In 1599 it housed more than 200,000 residents, a population exceeded only by Istanbul's half million. Monumental mosques, imperial villas, and vast markets clustered around the magnificent Nile River. Merchants amassed fortunes by transporting foodstuffs grown in Egypt and luxury goods imported from the East to Istanbul and Europe.[3] Mustafa Ali lingered in Cairo, before heading across the Red Sea to Jeddah, not only to write his report, but also to conduct research. He knew Arabic from his youthful religious education and he was completing his magnum opus, a world history called *The Essence of History,* begun in the year of the Islamic millennium (1591–1592). Cairo's numerous private libraries and bookshops near the prestigious al-Azhar mosque held knowledge that Ottoman elites thirsted for.[4]

The city that Mustafa Ali found in 1599, however, was not the same as the one he had visited thirty years before. Local people were less friendly. Food was less abundant, and soldiers were an unruly menace in the streets. Mustafa Ali's candid observations constitute what historians call the first modern bureaucratic report, written without "zeal and bias" and with "shortness and precision." The introduction proclaims his mission to rescue not just Egypt, but also the whole empire, from crisis:

> I had previously visited the land of Egypt around the year [1568] and become thoroughly acquainted with the prosperity of the country.... But in the course of time the state of the world had changed, the various classes of mankind had become distressed in the matter of livelihood, and peace and order had been chased from the face of the earth. Not only in Egypt, also in other provinces, the means of ease and prosperity had become scarce.[5]

Mustafa Ali's *Description of Cairo* combines his favorite themes of Ottoman glory and imminent decline with practical advice about how to restore just and efficient rule. He divided his report into three parts: the praiseworthy features of Egypt, its blameworthy aspects, and an epilogue on how to reverse the corruption of Ottoman rule. "Egypt is God's treasure-house on earth" and its people are open-hearted, generous, pious, and clean, he notes. But they still suffer from bad traits that predated Ottoman rule: they are "rarely beautiful"; the women are immodest compared to Turkish women and wear gems on their turbans; and the poor and African slaves wear so few clothes they are practically naked. Worse, these poor and uncouth Egyptians have taken jobs in government and the military and so the local regiments have become unruly.

Why had bountiful Egypt sunk so low? Corruption. "The managers of the treasury of Egypt resemble hungry wolves and jackals who have broken into a flock of sheep," Mustafa Ali explained. The government had ceased to guarantee order and equity: prices are no longer regulated, bribery is the rule, and brokers tyrannize the market. The solution: direct rule from Istanbul. Only the Ottoman dynasty can restore Islamic law and justice. The sultan must appoint only Ottoman Turks—not Egyptians—as governors and soldiers in the province.

Mustafa Ali illustrates his model of just government with praise for former Ottoman governors, like Ibrahim Pasha. Appointed in 1584, he was "dedicated to justice, interested in the study of the past, moderate in his acts and manners" and "a merciful friend of the poor." His successor, Uveys Pasha, was even greater "in regard to absolute justice, rectitude in the collection of revenues, and in showing consider-

Mustafa Ali of Gallipoli (1541–1600) was a midlevel bureaucrat and historian in the Ottoman empire, who launched a tradition of reform-writing known as the *nasihatname*. Drawing by Carolyn Brown based on a sixteenth-century miniature.

(From Cornell H. Fleischer, *Bureaucrat and Intellectual in the Ottoman Empire*. © 1986 Princeton University Press. Reprinted by permission of Princeton University Press.)

ation for both sides." With strict honesty he still managed to increase tribute paid to Istanbul. By contrast, Governor Mustafa Pasha mismanaged revenues and ruled through extortion. "Finally, they [Egyptians] could not bear his behavior [any longer]," Mustafa Ali wrote. "When he set out to kill certain beys they had him shot and killed with a rifle."[6]

Just rule, in Mustafa Ali's view, resembles a circle of interlocking and mutual interests. A prosperous peasantry is the bedrock of good government, because peasants provide tax revenues to support courts and the military. Such a revenue stream is assured only when taxes are legally gathered by honest imperial servants. When the sultan failed to discipline his officers, the "Circle of Justice" broke in Egypt. Despotic governors had siphoned off tribute needed in Istanbul and left troops unpaid. Overtaxed peasants fled from the land. As a result, Mustafa Ali warned, enemies are now poised to grab the Ottomans' "most essential province."[7]

Mustafa Ali closed his report on an optimistic note, assuring Sultan Mehmed III that the flow of truth upward from an honest bureaucrat may yet rescue Egypt from injustice: "Awareness is one of the marks of statesmanship."[8] Mustafa Ali sent off his report and crossed the Red Sea in November 1599. After making a pilgrimage to Mecca, however, he fell ill in Jeddah. Before the sultan could respond to his report, Mustafa Ali passed away in the spring of 1600.

THE OTTOMAN CIRCLE OF JUSTICE

While Mustafa Ali never attained his coveted post in Cairo, his plea for justice reached the highest halls of government. His reports circulated for decades among bureaucrats who shared his anger that honest men were not justly rewarded. They read them not just out of empathy, but also for inspiration. Mustafa Ali became the father of a scholarly movement that elaborated a vision of the just social order as a Circle of Justice.[9] If every element of the empire plays its proper role, they believed, then harmony would reign. "Justice," wrote Mustafa Ali, "means putting things in the places where they belong." ←

The Circle of Justice originated among Greek philosophers and was passed on to Ottomans by medieval Persian and Arab scholars. Ottoman bureaucrats adapted it to the structure of their empire by arranging each social estate around the circumference with an assigned function. One version went:

> The world is a garden, its walls are the state
> The Holy Law orders the state
> There is no support for the Holy Law except through royal authority
> There can be no royal authority without the military
> There can be no military without wealth
> The subjects produce the wealth
> Justice preserves the subjects' loyalty to the sovereign
> Justice requires harmony in the world.[10]

This version of the Circle of Justice proclaims Ottoman royal authority as the guarantor of Islamic justice. While earlier Islamic dynasties had ruled solely through Islamic law (sharia), the Ottomans introduced a Central Asian tradition of imperial decree *(yasa)* to Middle Eastern statecraft. This gave the state greater legislative power and enabled it to regulate a more complex bureaucracy. When Mustafa Ali was young, Suleyman the Lawgiver attempted to align the two legal traditions by codifying imperial law *(kanun)*. He institutionalized legal justice by incorporating a hierarchy of the ulama (Islamic scholars) into the Ottoman bureaucracy.[11]

The Ottomans' powerful machinery of rule was viciously depicted by their rivals, the Venetians, as Oriental despotism.[12] If despotism is unlimited rule by whim, then the Ottoman sultan was no despot. In the Ottoman view, God had granted the sultan the power to assure the reign of justice on Earth. Divine duty bound the sultan to honor and enforce Islamic law.[13] "The sultan is God's shadow, all oppressed take refuge with him," Mustafa Ali remarked, quoting the Prophet Muhammad.[14]

In his major treatise, *The Counsel for Sultans,* Mustafa Ali used the word justice *(adalet)* twenty-one times in the preface alone. Its root meaning in Arabic *(adadl)* is that of equality, balance, and moderation. Its opposite was tyranny *(zulm),* the extreme imbalance of wealth and power. "To condone the darkness of tyranny is equal to cause the eclipse of the sun of justice," Mustafa Ali wrote.[15]

Justice was no mere rhetorical ideal. It was the basis of the Ottoman dynasty's legitimacy. Descended from Central Asian migrants, the Ottomans could make no dynastic claim to rule as descendants from the Prophet. Instead, they claimed rule as defenders of the faith, whose army and law would establish Islamic justice throughout the realm.[16] Sultans performed justice by issuing decrees (adaletnameler) that set out a code of conduct for bureaucrats. In 1595, for example, the new sultan Mehmed III issued a justice decree ordering tax collectors to stop forcing villagers to board them and to condemn underpaid soldiers for pillaging villages. A 1609 justice decree reminded bureaucrats: "The object in appointing you . . . is so that the holy law and the government's laws be respected, so that no one be allowed to tyrannize."[17]

The Ottomans also promoted Islamic courts as a pillar of their justice. The sultan's top religious official, the Sheikhulislam, appointed judges to every major town in the empire. Judges saw themselves as soldiers of justice sent out into a barbaric, tribal hinterland. Contrary to images current today of Islamic law as rigidly oppressive, they used Islamic law to rescue the weak from tribal custom: women, children, the poor, and non-Muslim minorities. Ottoman courts became arenas to appeal against the abuse of power and to assert egalitarian moral standards.[18] In court, subjects "expressed their resistance to the hierarchy of social and moral worth," according to historian Leslie Peirce. The courts eventually established a uniquely Ottoman model of justice, combining imperial law, sharia, and custom.[19]

The Ottoman criminal justice system may seem brutal by today's standards, but punishments were comparable to those in Christian Europe of the time.[20] In both regions, imprisonment was a rare punishment, reserved mainly for debt. Public shaming and servitude in naval galleys were most common. The Ottomans tended to substitute fines for traditional corporal punishments. A Muslim caught stealing a chicken could pay a fine of one akce in place of every two strokes of the whip ordered by a judge. Suleyman's criminal code prescribed fines for adultery, against those who read the Quran literally to advocate stoning. More serious crimes called for corporal punishment: stealing livestock was punished by amputation of the hand. Only a few crimes warranted the death penalty: arson, theft of a prisoner of war, libel of the sultan, crimes against public security, heresy, and apostasy.[21]

Law did not, of course, guarantee the enforcement of justice. Mustafa Ali complained that underpaid judges took bribes and political officials ignored proper police procedure.[22] Accused criminals were often whipped on the spot, before arrest or a trial.[23] Despite shortcomings, however, European visitors in the sixteenth through eighteenth centuries often remarked upon the efficiency and fairness of Ottoman criminal justice.[24]

Justice also ordained economic protection. In the Circle of Justice, the imperial garden may have been protected by judges and soldiers, but it was cultivated by simple gardeners. Peasants were the foundation of the political order, and their welfare was critical. Mustafa Ali repeatedly cited the plight of overtaxed peasants in his 1599 report. Mistreatment of peasants, he warned, would leave Egypt "depopulated and in ruins."[25] Mustafa Ali laid responsibility for social justice, like legal justice, at the sultan's feet.[26]

But Mustafa Ali's concern for the poor did not make him a democrat. His justice was hierarchical and paternalistic. He readily identified himself as a slave of the sultan: liberty and equality were not ideals in his worldview. Racialism and sexism are evident in his Egypt report: the primary cause of injustice was failure to keep lowly subjects in their place—especially unruly women and ambitious African eunuchs who gained power over (white) men. Ottoman subjects deserved care, but not equality with ruling elite.[27]

While Mustafa Ali's unabashed elitism appears antiquated, his insistence on human responsibility for injustice seems quite contemporary. Personal misfortune was a consequence of human error, not a fate ordained by the stars:

> This wound from an arrow of malice comes from a human fist!
> It is neither from the bow in the hand of Destiny
>   nor was it ordained [by God].
> Everybody has in his hand his individual freedom of will.
> Do not talk of preordained fate! Regard [all acts]
>   as actions of an autonomous actor![28]

Likewise, peasants' suffering was an injustice, not merely a misfortune. The choices of corrupt officials and the sultan—not fate—had caused the crisis that seemed to engulf the empire.[29] Government officials, like all Muslims, have the free will to embrace God's message or not, to promote just rule or not.

As a member of the ruling elite, Mustafa Ali believed it was his duty to "spread what is good and to fight what is harmful."[30] With law, reason, and the inspiration of Islam, he concludes, the Ottomans might defy cycles of dynastic decline and so maintain the harmony of the Circle of Justice.[31]

THE *NASIHATNAMELER* AND POPULAR PROTEST

Mustafa Ali concluded his *Counsel for Sultans* with a call to bureaucrats to take up the mission for justice: "All persons of Islamic faith, the entire population of the time, are called by the command of the Sacred Fight, and are obliged to serve with all their power in the promotion of the sublime word."[32] This general summons is noteworthy. Historically, the injunction upon Muslims to uphold good and forbid evil was regarded mainly as the duty of ulama. They scolded individual believers to uphold Islamic morals like avoiding wine. Only occasionally did groups of rebels embrace the command to justify revolt.[33] It was unusual—and significant—for Mustafa Ali to make the command collectively upon the Ottoman ruling elite.[34]

It was this sense of common duty that inspired the reformist tradition of writing *nasihatname*. Bureaucrats wrote and read their treatises as jeremiads, reminders to fellow Ottoman officials of the sacred mission of government. Like the jeremiads of American Puritans who recalled their flocks to the ideal of the City on the Hill, bureaucrats sought to rally Ottomans to their founding ideal of justice.[35] The Ottoman *nasihatnameler* (plural) were influenced by Greek, Persian, and Arab traditions of writing advice books for princes. Unlike their predecessors, however, the Ottomans did not write theoretical books. They focused on the practical details of daily governance.[36] Writers of *nasihatnameler* were men of government, not secluded scholars. Their tradition of reform writing might therefore be understood as a form of political activism.

The *nasihatnameler* were inspired also by popular protest—and increasing stress upon the Circle of Justice caused by both shifts in world trade and military aggression. The seventeenth century was a time of profound economic change, as Northern European merchants flooded the Indian Ocean basin, interrupting trade routes and cutting into merchants' income. The Spanish conquerors of the Americas brought back much silver, causing currency inflation that devalued the salaries of soldiers and bureaucrats. As in the Europe of the seventeenth century, the Ottomans experienced frequent palace coups and provincial revolts. Banditry and bribery flourished and state revenues fell. The cash-strapped Ottoman military confronted new threats from Iran in the east and from Peter the Great's Russia in the north. The Ottomans were forced to accept limits to their imperial ambition. In 1683, they tried—and failed—to take Vienna for the last time. In 1699, they permanently lost territory (Hungary) for the first time.

Meanwhile, Ottoman subjects mobilized through their tribes, guilds, religious fraternities (Sufi *tarikat*), and neighborhood networks. Most continued to appeal to the sultan as the guarantor of justice.[37] Against their suffering of high taxes, unemployment, food shortages, and crime, they demanded that the sultan restore the reciprocity, stability, and harmony promised in the Circle of Justice.[38] As hard times stressed families, women brought cases against oppressive fathers and husbands to court. Judges and legal scholars (muftis) generally supported their Islamic right to choose their husbands and to expect financial support from them.[39] When local courts failed to redress their feelings of injustice, Ottoman subjects routinely directed petitions to Istanbul, seeking *adaletnameler* to condemn official abuses. The sultan's imperial council, at Topkapi Palace, became an important vehicle for promoting trust in Ottoman justice in troubled times. The palace's Tower of Justice soared above the divan, visible from afar to the residents of the capital.

Imperial courts could not, however, contain all dissent. A wave of uprisings crossed Anatolia and Syria, mounted by unemployed soldiers and discontented local officials who had lost faith in Istanbul's promise of justice. As Mustafa Ali had presciently warned, coffeehouses became a new nexus of political dissent. In 1599, he had complained of the unruly soldiers who gathered in Cairo's coffeehouses. Coffee arrived in Cairo about the time of the Ottoman conquest, in the early sixteenth century, probably brought by students from Arabia and Yemen who attended the city's prestigious al-Azhar university. Pious Egyptians loved a morning cup because "its slight exhilaration strengthens them for their religious observance and worship," Mustafa Ali noted. But, he warned, "dissolute" persons who lounged too long in coffeehouses were dangerous. "Their talk is mostly lies, their nonsensical speeches are either gossip and backbiting or slander and calumny."[40]

As a novel gathering place—in a society where mosques were often the only other public space—coffeehouses soon played a role in the

The Tower of Justice rises above Topkapi Palace in Istanbul, visible to residents of the city and intended as a symbol of the Ottomans' promise of just rule.
(© José Luiz Bernardes Ribeiro/CC-BY-SA-3.0)

revolts in Anatolia and Syria. Wandering dervishes took up residence in coffeehouses of small towns and villages, stirring up millenarian visions and demands for justice.[41] They joined unemployed students and underpaid soldiers in banditry and brigandage to support themselves.[42] Soon governors, too, joined them. Demanding autonomy, they stopped sending taxes to the capital. Istanbul elites dubbed them the "Jelali revolts" to discredit the rebels. *Jelali* means "heretic."

In this uneasy era, bureaucratic jeremiads proliferated. Bureaucrats debated how the sultan should respond to the revolts. Writing just after Mustafa Ali's death, Mustafa Safi agreed with him that sultans possessed unique God-given powers to assure the reign of justice on Earth. But, he argued, their law-and-order aspect of justice should be tempered with generosity.[43] Kocu Bey, on the other hand, emphasized Mustafa Ali's hard-line view that the sultan must discipline his subjects sternly.[44] "If in any of the lands of Islam an atom of injustice is done to any individual," he warned, "then on the Day of Judgment not ministers, but Kings will be asked for a reckoning."[45]

The debate between hard-liners and soft-liners continued in writings of the later seventeenth century. When Sultan Osman II appeared too conciliatory toward rebels and Arabs of the east, a coalition led by Janissaries overthrew him in 1622.[46] His successor, Sultan Murad IV (1623–1640) then waged a brutal war against the Jelalis to restore the power of Istanbul there.

Murad IV was in part inspired by a reform movement led by Kadizade Mehmed, a leader of the religious bureaucracy in Istanbul. As a preacher in the capital's top imperial mosques, Kadizade Mehmed promoted his own version of jeremiad to a popular following of artisans and workers. He blamed Ottomans' moral deviance as the cause of the Jelali revolts and military defeat. (Iran occupied Baghdad between 1624 and 1638.) The Ottomans could restore their glory only by embarking on a collective morals campaign to "enjoin right and forbid wrong." In the 1630s, their campaign inspired Murad IV to crack down on Sufi mysticism, to ban coffee and tobacco, and to shut down coffeehouses as dens of treason.[47] Kadizade's followers, called Kadizadelis, practiced a puritanism based on a strict reading of Islamic law, not on the Circle of Justice. With little of Mustafa Ali's compassion for the poor, they sought the return of the sultan as "ghazi," holy warrior. Kadizadeli pressure inspired the ill-fated siege of Vienna in 1683.

On the other end of the political spectrum, Evliya Chelebi (ca. 1610–1683) was an important proponent of tolerance in the *nasihat-nameler* tradition. Chelebi was the son of a royal goldsmith, raised in the Ottoman palace. After working variously as a secretary, messenger, and customs clerk, in 1640 he embarked on a life of travels. As he crossed Anatolia, he wrote detailed reports on local conditions, taking much interest in local customs and dialects. He sympathized with rebels at Erzerum, where a relative of his had just been dismissed as governor, and joined a revolt of another ex-governor against the whims of Sultan Mehmed IV (1648–1687).

While Chelebi was fiercely loyal to the Ottoman dynasty, he condemned fanaticism of all kinds, and especially the Kadizadelis'. He also condemned the view of Ottoman "justice" that entailed a daily quota of heads. In 1659, he witnessed Sultan Mehmed IV and his grand vezir conduct a bloody purge in Western Anatolia, where, he claimed, hundreds of men were beheaded with little heed to whether they were truly Jelalis. The sultan sat in a "pavilion of justice" to witness the carnage. Chelebi called Ottomans back to their former ideals of justice to reverse the empire's decline. Like Mustafa Ali, he urged the sultan to root out corruption, promote honest men, and improve trade and military defense. In 1672, Chelebi retired in Cairo, after making the pilgrimage to Mecca.[48] His *Book of Travels* became one of the most quoted sources on Ottoman history.

As the eighteenth century dawned, the debate continued. In 1703, a Kadizadeli mufti claimed the religious bureaucracy's highest post, that of Sheikulislam. He and the sultan were overthrown by another faction of bureaucrats who opposed their puritanism and military adventurism. Sympathetic to the anti-Kadezadeli revolt was court historian and finance minister Mustafa Naima. Naima self-consciously wrote in the *nasihatname* tradition. He defended Sultan Murad IV's brutal suppression of the Jelalis as necessary to reassert state authority. Naima believed justice flowed from the elite's unique access to orthodoxy and truth. He admitted no possibility of loyal dissent from below, and therefore condemned the Kadizadeli movement for its violence, intolerance, and disruption of order.[49]

Naima continued to uphold the Circle of Justice as the ideal that would save the Ottoman empire from decline. Like Mustafa Ali, he called on bureaucrats to stop corruption among officials and assure prosperity among subjects.[50] But his view of justice showed the effects of change over the century since Mustafa Ali's death. In his version of the Circle of Justice, Naima deemphasized law *(kanun)* in favor of practical economics:

1. There is no property *(mulk)* and no state *(devlet)* without the military and without manpower.
2. Men are to be found only by means of wealth *(mal)*.
3. Wealth is only to be garnered from the peasantry.
4. The peasantry is to be maintained in prosperity and only through justice.
5. And without property and the state there can be no justice.[51]

Naima's views reflect popular pressure from below. While he guarded the prerogative of the bureaucratic elite, he also admitted that the empire must acknowledge the merit of talented subjects. His contemporary, Sari Mehmed Pasha, was more egalitarian. He urged the sultan to fight tyranny and corruption with "justice and equity" and to treat "with equality the humble and the noble, the wealthy and the poor, the learned and the unlearned." Citing Suleyman the Lawgiver, Sari Mehmed continued, the "benefactors [of mankind] are the rayas (peasants) who, in their agriculture and husbandry make repose and comfort unlawful to themselves and feed us with the blessings which they have earned."[52]

The new social views of the bureaucratic elite transformed the Ottoman state in the eighteenth century. Instead of promoting war, the palace promoted social justice. The sultan's image as "khan," or military conqueror, gave way to that of "padishah," guarantor of Islamic justice.[53] Istanbul also shared more power and resources with the provinces. Instead of building magnificent imperial mosques in the capital, the palace built bridges, caravanserais, and roads to promote trade. To promote social welfare, it constructed mosque complexes in major cities, with schools, markets, soup kitchens, and even clinics and mental hospitals.

Generally speaking the empire did not decline until after 1750. Only after then did trade and standards of living decline relative to earlier years. And only after defeat by Russia in 1774 did military weakness become critical.[54] Some historians credit the empire's stability to its relatively egalitarian distribution of land and to its robust internal trade. Others give credit to savvy bureaucrats, who were able to co-opt new ambitious elites into the ruling oligarchy.[55]

With economic decline after 1750 came new social inequity. A new provincial elite arose in the eighteenth century that profited from the empire's new federalism to exploit weaker citizens.[56] These elites claimed control over local religious posts, tax farms, and the military. Large plantations arose in the Balkans and in Egypt to feed Istanbul's appetite and Europeans' demand for imports of food and cotton. The plantations violated old *kanun* limits on farm size and increased taxes on peasants. Peasants suffered in what historians call a new feudalism, as this 1785 report on Egypt describes:

> The rice and corn they gathered are carried to the table of their masters, and nothing is left for them but dourra or Indian millet, of which they make bread without leaven. . . . This bread is eaten with water and raw onions, their only food throughout the year; and they esteem themselves happy if they can sometimes procure a little honey, cheese, sour milk, and dates.[57]

Unprecedented numbers of peasants began fleeing to the cities, abandoning their meager huts and family plots, just as Mustafa Ali had warned 200 years before.

Another downside of this vernacular federalism was that imperial coffers ran low, and local government officials became corrupt. A comparison to eighteenth-century France demonstrates the problem. In 1789, both the Ottoman sultan and the French king ruled a comparable population of 25–30 million. However, the sultan collected only one-eighth the amount of tax revenue as Louis XVI collected. Bureaucrats lost the capacity not only to raise large armies, but also to regulate social justice in the provinces. Governors and judges sent from Istanbul resorted to bribery and tax abuses to make up for their declining authority. Under fiscal pressure, the Circle of Justice broke down.[58]

Once again, revolt broke out across the empire. But now rebels used a new language of dissent, one that challenged the sultan's authority with a direct appeal to Islamic law.[59] They also made new claims to egalitarianism against the Circle of Justice's social hierarchy. Two of the most significant examples of Islam-framed protest occurred in the Ottoman empire's most prestigious Arab provinces, Arabia and Egypt.

In the 1740s, the Wahhabi movement arose near the current Saudi capital of Riyadh. Under the banner of a puritanical doctrine of Islam, it united tribes to conquer much of the Arabian peninsula. The movement's leaders were Muhammad Ibn Abd al-Wahhab, a scholar, and Ibn Saud, a local tribal chief (shaykh). Urban Sunnis of the Ottoman empire regarded Wahhabis with contempt, as desert zealots who threatened their cosmopolitan, and tolerant, civilization. The Wahhabis smashed the Prophet's tomb as a site of false idolatry, murdered hundreds they called infidels, and attempted to invade Syria.

Wahhabi ideology was not, however, an exotic product of the remote desert. Muhammad Ibn Abd al-Wahhab was educated in top religious schools of Medina and Basra (Iraq) by mainstream urban teachers. These schools taught new methods of interpreting sacred texts and new reformist religious ideas from India that emphasized purity against the empire's tolerance of diversity.[60] Wahhab based his vision of justice on the Prophet Muhammad's first Muslim community in the seventh century, not on the Ottomans' golden age of the sixteenth century.

Wahhabis' egalitarian vision of justice completely rejected the Circle of Justice and the validity of *kanun*, imperial law. Only Islamic law is valid, they argued. Like Protestants in Europe, they rejected monarchs' claim as God's representatives and religious clergy's claim as spiritual mediators. They insisted that all Muslims were equal before God and that they should consult scripture for themselves.[61]

In 1803 and 1806, the Wahhabis dealt a heavy blow to the sultan's prestige: they occupied the holy city of Mecca. It would take the Ottomans another decade to defeat the Wahhabi movement, with the help of the Egyptian army.

The Egyptian army was itself the product of another popular challenge to Ottoman authority. In 1805, rebels in Cairo had forced the sultan to recall his governor in preference to a locally popular leader, Mehmed Ali. He had asserted autonomy from Istanbul to build his own powerful and reformed army.

Egypt's 1805 revolt was rooted not only in the social distress that affected the rest of the empire, but also in the invasion of Egypt by Napoleon Bonaparte in 1798. A powerful oligarchy had emerged in Egypt in the late eighteenth century, built upon rice and cotton plantations in the Nile Valley and the coffee trade from Yemen.[62] Cairo grew to a population of 250,000, second in the empire to Istanbul's 600,000 residents. The city was controlled by Mamluks, wealthy lords who controlled militias and rivaled one another for control over economic resources. They grew independent of Istanbul; few learned Turkish. Indeed, Egyptians resented the glass ceiling that blocked their advancement to high imperial posts in the capital.[63] Despite Mustafa Ali's warnings, tribute paid to Istanbul trickled to perhaps only 10 percent of local tax revenues.[64]

Meanwhile, artisans joined with religious leaders to protest high taxes. They typically proclaimed revolt with drums, to recruit members of guilds and Sufi fraternities to march under their banner. To pressure elites, they closed down markets and threw up barricades to block entrances into their neighborhoods.[65] Peasants across Egypt rebelled against unfair taxes in the late eighteenth century. In one revolt, they traveled to Cairo and won support for their tax protest from the shaykhs of al-Azhar, the preeminent religious college.[66]

Egyptians were well prepared to rebel when Napoleon invaded in 1798. Historian Abd al-Rahman al-Jabarti recorded their reactions when French ships appeared off the coast of Alexandria. At first, they blamed the disaster on the Mamluks' corruption. They had siphoned off tax revenues for their personal profit, rather than use them to maintain defenses at the port.[67] When the Mamluks escaped to the south, commoners began looting their houses, as if to correct the imbalance of wealth that had accrued.

Anger turned against the French in October 1798. The French-run governing council cut pensions and bread rations at the same time that the French imposed new property taxes. The people "raised an uproar," Jabarti wrote. Some religious clerics organized the masses to rebel, preaching, "O Muslims, the *jihad* is incumbent upon you. How can you free men agree to pay the poll tax *(jizya)* to the unbelievers?"[68]

The revolt against Napoleon in October 1798 invoked a new language of protest. It blamed injustice on non-Muslim foreigners and the elites (like Jabarti) who collaborated with them. Jabarti's text showed his own discomfort with the revolt. At first he wrote in elitist terms, criticizing the "great rabble" for attacking shops and killing the French commander, Dupuy, as they yelled, 'May God give victory to the Muslim."[69] But Jabarti's tone shifted when he described how Napoleon turned his cannons on the city and bombed al-Azhar mosque. "The French entered the city," Jabarti wrote, "like demons of the Devil's army." Outraged at the desecration of Cairo's holiest mosque, Jabarti dropped his elitist criticism and joined the popular lament at the assault on Islam: "The injustice and obduracy of the unbelievers continued and they achieved their evil intentions toward the Muslims."[70]

This first invasion by a European power set a paradigm for the nineteenth century. European rule, in Jabarti's eyes, was an inversion of Islamic justice, a moral void. He devoted much space in his history to exposing the hypocrisy and atheism of Napoleon, mocking France's proclamation that it had come to save Egypt from tyranny. Europeans would justify their colonial occupation of Algeria in 1830 and Egypt in 1882 on the same grounds.

In 1801, the French were forced to withdraw from Egypt by the British fleet, in an early chapter of the Napoleonic Wars. This opened a window of opportunity to establish a new moral order. Urban groups mobilized against a return to the tyranny of the Mamluks and the corrupt Ottoman governor. In May 1805, al-Azhar shaykhs issued a fatwa (religious edict) asserting their authority to appoint the next governor. They chose Mehmed Ali, leader of a contingent of Albanian troops posted in the city. Umar Makram, a popular leader, rallied support for Mehmed Ali in terms that would have shocked Mustafa Ali. "It's the tradition from time immemorial that the people *(ahl al-balad)* depose the governor *(vali)* if he be unjust," Makram told an Ottoman messenger.[71] Civil war broke out. Makram led 40,000 workers, greengrocers and butchers, leaders of guilds, to lay siege to the Citadel, the Ottoman military fortress. In July, Istanbul capitulated and agreed to appoint Mehmed Ali governor.[72]

Like the Wahhabis, the urban rebels of Cairo asserted a new egalitarian vision of the just social order, based on more populist traditions of Islam. Their movement challenged the moral hierarchy of the ruling elite over subjects that had long been enshrined in the Ottoman Circle of Justice. They also exposed the weakness of the Ottomans' claim to rule—with their inability to defend the Muslim community from invasion. The 1805 Egyptian revolt helped to pressure bureaucrats to advance their most radical reform yet: a virtual bill of rights for Ottoman citizens.

THE GULHANE DECREE OF 1839

The Ottoman empire plunged into deep crisis after Napoleon's invasion, the 1805 revolt in Egypt, and the Wahhabis' occupation of Mecca. Sultan Selim III (1789–1807) had, as one historian put it, come to accept "a revised perception of the Ottoman place in the world." He sent embassies to Europe and quietly began to curtail tax farming that had enriched provincial families.[73] And he had built the New Order Army, more disciplined and more modern that the unruly Janissaries. But it was still too small to confront Napoleon or the Wahhabis. Worse, Balkan leaders took advantage of the transfer of Ottoman troops to Egypt to stage revolts, especially in Serbia.

Even worse for Selim III, the Janissaries and religious leaders organized a crowd of 50,000 to gather outside of Topkapi Palace in 1807. They condemned the New Order Army and demanded Selim III's deposition. They specifically condemned the army's European-style uniforms—and all of Selim's reforms—as violations of Islam and its tradition. As in Egypt, populist rebels deployed their own brand of Islamic justice against the prerogatives of the ruling elite. They blamed

Ottoman inequality and injustice on European influence. Foreign invasion, it seems, raised the political ambitions of conservative hardliners in the Middle East.

The struggle for power forced Selim III to abdicate in favor of Sultan Mustafa IV (1807–1808). This started a factional war. In July 1808, a group of Balkan leaders tried to restore Selim to the throne, but Mustafa IV ordered Selim murdered. In revenge, Selim's supporters forced Mustafa to abdicate. This bloody episode launched reforms that upended the Circle of Justice.

Sultan Mahmud II (1808–1839) secured his rule first through compromise with the provincial elites and then brutal suppression of opponents. The 1808 Charter of Alliance granted provincial elites limited autonomy in exchange for promises to support imperial reforms. The charter fundamentally recast the terms of their relationship. "In exchange for mutual defense, past privileges were elevated to permanent rights," observes historian Ariel Salzmann. The elites promised to guarantee the sultan's justice in their provinces. "Signatories were obliged to protect the state-mandated rights of all subjects, Muslim, Christian and Jew."[74]

By the 1820s, Mahmud II was secure enough to reprise Selim III's reforms to centralize the state. In 1826 he destroyed the Janissaries and built a new army called the "Victorious Soldiers of Muhammad" to fend off religious opponents. For a time, clerics supported his reforms and became the sultan's emissaries to the people. But Mahmud II's drive to centralize power soon targeted them as well. He confiscated the religious endowments that paid clerics' salaries and funded their schools. Meanwhile, he assassinated opponents in government and brutally massacred Muslim rebels in the Balkans. Intent on saving the empire at any cost, Mahmud II alienated many Muslims, who called him the "Infidel Sultan."[75]

Mahmud II's son, Abdulmecid I (1839–1861), came to the throne at the height of the Ottomans' rivalry with Egypt and at the nadir of the sultan's prestige. With the pen of an esteemed bureaucrat, Mustafa Reshid Pasha (1800–1858), he aimed to restore Muslims' belief in Ottoman justice. The Imperial Decree of Gulhane (Rose Garden decree) was promulgated at Topkapi Palace on November 3, 1839. The decree proclaimed a new era of just government to an assembly of Ottoman officials and European diplomats. The state would hereafter respect the "life, honor and property" of all its subjects. Later called the Ottoman bill of rights, Gulhane inaugurated a decades-long project of political reform called the Tanzimat (Reorganization).[76]

Reshid Pasha was, at the time, foreign minister of the empire. Born thirty-nine years before in Istanbul, he had been Mahmud II's ambassador to Paris in the mid-1830s.[77] Like Mustafa Ali, he believed that skillful policy could arrest the empire's decline. Unlike Mustafa Ali, he believed bureaucrats were more capable than the sultan to enact reform. Justice, for Reshid Pasha, lay in the law and practice of government, not in the virtue of the monarch. He and the new generation of Tanzimat statesmen proposed to save the empire by promoting "civilization," a set of cultural values that they believed Ottomans shared with Europeans. Their belief in a universal idea of civilization contrasted with populist calls to defend Islam against foreign culture. Reshid Pasha and the men of the Tanzimat did not reject Islam, but they believed that Islam shared traits with a common human civilization that would lead Ottoman peoples to progress.

This belief in Islam's similarity to other civilizations enabled Reshid Pasha to publicize the Tanzimat as a return to past Ottoman glory. He penned the opening lines of Gulhane with the familiar tropes of the *nasihatname* tradition, which couched reform in the language of jeremiad. They alerted Ottomans to their decline and promised a return to a mythical golden age:

> All the world knows that since the first days of the Ottoman state, the lofty principles of the Quran and the rules of the *shari'a* were always perfectly preserved. Our mighty sultanate reached the highest degree of strength and power, and all its subjects, of ease and prosperity.
>
> But in the last 150 years, because of a succession of difficulties and diverse causes, the sacred *shari'a* was not obeyed, nor were the beneficent regulations followed; consequently, its former strength and prosperity have changed into weakness and poverty. . . . Thus, full of confidence in the help of the Most High, and certain of the support of our Prophet, we deem it necessary and important from now on to introduce legislation in order to achieve effective administration of the Ottoman government and provinces.[78]

The decree declares the goal of reform to promote prosperity, strengthen the military, and restore loyalty to the Ottoman regime. It lays out

Mustafa Reshid Pasha (1800–1858) authored the 1839 Gulhane decree, known by many as the Ottoman bill of rights. He was heir to the bureaucratic reform tradition launched by Mustafa Ali of Gallipoli.
(*L'Illustration*, November 22, 1856)

four avenues of legal reform: 1) guarantees of life, honor and fortune (greater security against violence and crime and an end to state confiscation of officials' property); 2) a regular system of assessing and levying taxes (abolition of tax farms in favor of a central tax bureaucracy); 3) a regular system for military conscription (with shorter duration of service); and, most radically, 4) equality under the law for all subjects (Muslim and non-Muslim).

The decree effectively proposed a new relationship between ruler and ruled, one rooted in legal rights, not paternal protection, and in the equality of subjects, not hierarchy. Gulhane did not use the word "citizen," but it suggested such a contract in explaining that security would ensure people's loyalty to the government and concern for common welfare. It referred not to a ruling military class, but rather to a popular army recruited on the basis of patriotism, the "duty of all the people to provide soldiers for the defense of the fatherland." In return for the people's service, the state would reduce the term of service to four or five years, so that family farms and businesses would not be disrupted. And in return for their tax payments, the state assured them that the funds would be spent in the public interest, mainly military defense. The decree even promised popular participation in government. Laws assuring security and prosperity would be promulgated by the majority vote of a quasi-legislative Council of Justice, where everyone "will express his ideas and give his advice freely."

The seeming contradictions of the Gulhane text have given rise to debate about its origin and intent. Older scholars viewed the decree as an imitation of European political ideas.[79] They assumed that Ottoman culture was stagnant and tradition-bound by Islam; all reform, therefore, had to be borrowed from Europe.

Scholars have recently cast doubt on that view, however. Ottomans did not blindly adopt European ideas; rather, they embraced liberal concepts precisely because they resonated with their own values. Gulhane was both a time-honored Ottoman claim to just government and a radical break with older models of justice. "The Tanzimat can be seen, in part, as the synthesis of a two-hundred year sequence of experiments and ad hoc solutions," writes one historian. "There was no consensus within the ruling class on the course to be taken."[80]

Gulhane's arguments were made within the Ottoman political tradition. Reshid Pasha and the Tanzimat reformers embraced Naima's elitist centralism over Chelebi's decentralized tolerance. Like Mahmud II, they rejected the Ottomans' eighteenth-century experiment in federalism because they believed only centralization could strengthen the military defense of the empire.[81]

Gulhane was also inspired by popular conceptions of justice. Reformist Sufi movements were quite influential in early nineteenth-century Istanbul. They called for strong government, the restoration of Sunni orthodoxy and Islamic law, and the reform of deviant forms of Sufi mysticism. Most influential was the Naqshbandiyya-Mujaddidiyya movement. Sultan Mahmud II had relied on support from them when he destroyed the old Ottoman army in 1826. The Sufi reformers' support ensured that he did not suffer the fate of Selim III when he built a new army.[82]

Reshid Pasha and Sultan Abdulmecid were both taught by followers of the Naqshbandiyya-Mujaddidiyya about virtue in governance.[83] Two weeks after ascending to the throne (at age sixteen), Abdulmecid directed his ministers to "follow the law of justice and equity in all matters" and to apply "the honoured *sheri'at* [Islamic law] in all affairs of the exalted sultanate."[84] He used his reformist Sufi lessons to undo the absolutism of his father.

This religious context convinces historians that Ottoman reform was not inspired primarily by Europe. Nor was it derived from a secularist or alien tradition. Rather, the Tanzimat reforms came largely from indigenous roots in order to address indigenous protest against injustice. "The Tanzimat, as a whole, was an era during which translations into Turkish of Islamic literature reached unprecedented proportions," historian Serif Mardin observed, while "no translations from European thinkers . . . were undertaken in the first half of the nineteenth century."[85]

Yet the meaning of Gulhane was not immediately clear. Many Ottomans welcomed it as a "declaration of justice"[86] in the same spirit as the justice decrees *(adaletnamler)* issued by new sultans since the sixteenth century. But soon they recognized that it portended much broader change and stirred political controversy. Some officials, and subjects, understood Gulhane to imply legal equality among all subjects, Muslim and non-Muslim, under a rational system of law. Such a promise of legal equality would potentially dismantle the imperial hierarchy, challenge prevailing views of Islamic doctrine, and challenge privileges enjoyed by Muslims for centuries.

Gulhane unloosed democratizing movements across the empire, all invoking the language of the Tanzimat to justify their claims to equal rights, fair taxes, and representation in government. Reshid Pasha, however, insisted that he never intended to introduce full equality or European-style constitutionalism.[87] His true goal, he claimed, had been merely to secure the rights of bureaucrats against the sultan. Bureaucrats did indeed assert a newly powerful status in the Tanzimat era, expressed in their new uniform of a red tarbush and black frock coat.[88]

Yet unclear to Reshid Pasha, however, was the deathblow he had dealt to Mustafa Ali's paternalistic Circle of Justice and to the privileges of the ruling elite. Gulhane was initially an imperial response to the displacement of the Ottoman empire in the new capitalist world economy. Its guarantees of property rights and fair taxation aimed to fill the state's need for cash to modernize its army. However, Reshid Pasha's embrace of market economics effectively jettisoned the old

Ottoman model of the shepherd state that protects its flock. It also jettisoned the idea that Muslims were bound in loyalty to the Ottoman dynasty as God-given guarantors of Islamic justice, in favor of a new political contract between ruler and citizen.

In sum, Reshid Pasha's effort to assure the power of a bureaucratic ruling class instead laid the groundwork for the abolition of all privilege. Writing a century later, historian Bernard Lewis compared the door opened by Gulhane to the American Civil Rights era of the 1950s: "To give up this principle of inequality and segregation required of the Muslim no less great an effort of renunciation than is required of Westerners who are now called upon to forgo the satisfactions of racial superiority."[89] As in the United States, the dislodgement of privilege was not quickly or peacefully accomplished. For the Ottomans, the process would lead, circuitously, in unforeseen and unintended ways, to the rise of constitutionalism as a new model of justice.

2

TANYUS SHAHIN OF MOUNT LEBANON
Peasant Republic and Christian Rights

In 1858, something extraordinary happened on Mount Lebanon, some 600 miles southeast of Istanbul. Christian peasants in a dozen villages united to protest against heavy taxes and brutal treatment by their landlords. They targeted the Khazin family, landowners in thirty villages, whose power was recently shaken by drought, European trade, and by political rivalries of other elite factions. As one eyewitness wrote, "Terror was instilled by the Khazin family into the people of Kisrawan. For they no longer took any account of their subjects."[1]

Revolts spread across the region that year, but this one took a different path. The peasants chose as their leader a blacksmith and muleteer named Tanyus Shahin. He expanded complaints about unfair taxes into demands for legal and political reform. The peasants demanded not only repayment of the illegal taxes imposed on them, but also a return to rule of law. Most remarkably, Shahin cited the sultan's Gulhane promise of the equality of all Ottoman citizens to justify revolt. In early 1859, the peasants invaded the Khazins' estates. Waving muskets and their own flag, they expelled the feudal lords and established a virtual peasant republic.

The revolt reveals a shift in common peoples' view of their place in the Ottoman empire. Mountain people living hundreds of miles from Topkapi Palace had not only heard Sultan Abdulmecid's decrees promising equality, but they also took enforcement into their own hands. They exceeded the sultan's intentions by demanding the abolition of feudalism and claiming the right to elect representatives to local government. In short, these Lebanese Christian peasants turned the Tanzimat on its head. In the eyes of Muslim elites, they breached the strict divide between ruling class and subject and threatened the empire's hierarchy of Muslim over non-Muslim.

The story of the peasant republic reveals how volatile new concepts of justice were. Shahin, likely under influence of Maronite Church officials and foreign consuls, exaggerated the condition of Christians, likening them to slaves. In April 1860, he called for the abolition of slavery in all of Mount Lebanon: "I have a [decree] from the Seven Sovereigns for the emancipation of all the Christians, who are no longer to be in bondage to anyone; if you want to be emancipated from your slavery, no one can prevent you."[2] Then Shahin sent his Christian troops into another district, where Christian peasants had rebelled against their Druze (Muslim) landlords.

The battle for legal equality between peasants and lords transformed into a broader battle for Christian equality with Muslims in the empire. It is difficult to unthread the complex politics of 1860, due to the scarcity and bias of sources. Shahin's declaration abolishing slavery appeared to ally Ottoman Christians with foreign (Christian) powers against Ottoman sovereignty. His audacity turned to tragedy, as the Druze landlords crushed Christian peasants' revolt in their districts. Antifeudal revolt turned into sectarian war. In May and June 1860, the better-armed Druze massacred 4,000 or more Christians.[3]

The massacres in Mount Lebanon signaled that the state's project to turn subjects into equal citizens was a politically dangerous proposition. No privileged elite—whether defined by religion, race, or class—willingly cedes its status, as Americans in 1860 knew too well. While slavery in the United States was of a very different character from what Shahin termed the slavery of Christians to Muslims and of peasants to landlords, the simultaneity of the conflicts begs comparison. Much as the abolitionists' campaign to end white privilege over black slaves would ignite the American Civil War, the peasant revolt in Lebanon ignited a fury of violence on a scale unseen ever before in the Middle East.

Historians are still unraveling the mystery of how things went so wrong. It appears that the entanglement of local and imperial agendas of reform, of religious and class identity, and of foreign and local interests made Mount Lebanon a bellwether for the challenges of reform in the wider Ottoman empire. The conflict in Lebanon was a battle over the meaning of the Tanzimat, notes historian Ussama Makdisi.[4] Tanzimat reformers desperately advocated equality for Christians in order to maintain the loyalty of their wealthy European provinces. But equality threatened the very essence of the empire's foundational character, as guarantor of Islamic justice. At the same time, the Mount Lebanon revolt shattered conservatives' hopes of preserving the old social order against reform. There seemed to be no way back to the stable hierarchy idealized by Mustafa Ali in 1599. The Tanzimat had opened the door to popular movements in politics. Consensus on a model of justice was lost, and so was the power of elites to enforce it. The Middle East remains embroiled today in the ensuing conflict over what model of justice might replace the old paternalism and so restore stability.

THE EVENTS OF 1858–1860

When the peasants first raised protest in 1858, trouble was brewing across the empire. Two years before, Grand Vezir Mehmed Emin Ali Pasha had issued a second Tanzimat decree, which expanded promises of equality for non-Muslims. It assured freedom of belief and no discrimination against non-Muslims in access to government schools, jobs, and courts. It also promised that Christians would pay taxes at an equal rate to Muslims, and in exchange Christians were obligated to perform military service just as Muslims did. The decree overturned the Ottoman hierarchy of ruling class and subject and threatened privileges enjoyed by Muslims since the founding of the first Muslim state in the seventh century.

Ali Pasha had issued the decree under pressure from Britain, an ally in the Crimean War at the time. This angered his mentor and Gulhane-author, Mustafa Reshid Pasha. The 1856 decree made no conciliatory gestures toward Muslims as Reshid's 1839 decree had done: no mention of the Quran, Islamic law, or the plight of poor Muslims in the empire. Indeed, Reshid called it a "ferman of concessions" that undermined Ottoman sovereignty.[5] Rumors flew around Istanbul that the British ambassador had a direct hand in writing it. Conservatives who might have gone along with the 1839 edict now viewed Muslim–Christian equality as a kind of treason, an illegal intervention of

Europeans in internal affairs. Backlash fueled a conspiracy in Istanbul to overthrow the government in 1859.

The political errors made in 1856 set an inauspicious precedent for future European efforts to protect minorities in the Ottoman empire. They also tainted good-faith efforts from within the empire to advance equality among citizens.

Meanwhile, in Mount Lebanon, social and economic tensions rose to a new pitch. The roots of the 1858 revolt go back to the 1830s, when Mehmed Ali of Egypt sent his new army to occupy Lebanon and Syria. The populace rose up against the Egyptians' harsh rule, and many Muslims protested Egypt's apparent preference for local Christians and permission to let Christian missionaries enter the territory. In 1840, the Ottomans allied with Britain to oust the Egyptians—at a price. Britain demanded the right to market the cheap textiles churned out by England's Dickensian factories. The flood of imports harmed local weavers. Meanwhile, the French built silk-spinning factories in Lebanese villages. They exported the silk thread back to France. By 1858, the economy of the region was hitched to the interests of industrializing Europe. Beirut boomed as a port that served new steamships that crossed the Mediterranean. And the French had begun building a highway between Beirut and Damascus, to replace the dirt tracks used by pack animals.

All of these economic developments changed Mountain society. Merchants profited, as did landlords who could afford to plant the mulberry trees needed to feed silkworms. Peasants were marginalized in the new cash economy. They began borrowing from Beirut banks to pay their feudal dues. With a poor grain harvest in 1858, peasants grew desperate. The European financial crisis of 1858 made conditions worse, because the district also relied heavily on silk exports to France. That year, 5,000 left Mount Lebanon in pursuit of work. It was the start of a decades-long diaspora that took Lebanese peasants to the Americas, Africa, and Asia.[6]

Kisrawan, the epicenter of the peasant revolt, had been producing silk since the sixteenth century. Located northeast of Beirut, the district embraced 50 villages perched on rocky peaks between steep chasms. Some 35,000 peasants and village notables—nearly all Christian—lived there in small stone houses. They tilled carefully terraced orchards fed by winter rains that had once assured them a relatively good living. But as the population grew, their tiny plots were no longer big enough to feed their families. They increasingly depended on wages earned from landowners of larger estates.

Landowners, too, faced a crisis. The Khazins were the most prominent in the district. But they had subdivided the family wealth among too many heirs in each new generation. Ottoman governors squeezed them for more tax revenue, while denying them former political privileges. And French companies skimmed profits from local spinners by diverting crops to their factories located south of Kisrawan.

The Khazins resorted to the dangerous practice of oppressing peasants more even as their own power declined. They extracted gifts of coffee, sugar, and other luxuries on holidays and demanded free labor on roads and the use of daughters as housemaids. Recently, they had imposed new taxes on land sales and deprived peasants' of income from cultivation of extra crops alongside the mulberry trees. To add insult to injury, family leaders reasserted their status by insisting that peasants kiss their hands. Facing hunger themselves, the peasants reacted sharply to every new demand by the Khazins. In the peasants' eyes, the Khazins were violating the implicit patriarchal bargain that obliged their lords to assure them basic sustenance.[7]

Three other factors contributed to the outbreak of revolt in 1858. The Maronite Church became a locus of organized dissent against the Khazins. The Church, which was affiliated with the Catholic Church in Rome, had its headquarters in the Kisrawan village of Bkirki. Patriarch Bulus Masad, said to sympathize with the plight of peasants, turned the church into a competitor with Khazins. He aimed to displace the feudal lords as the preeminent authority in Mount Lebanon. A second factor favoring revolt was education. Since the 1830s, hundreds of Jesuits, monks, and nuns had settled in Kisrawan. They opened schools for children, and the district's humble priests and villagers.[8] The Church and Catholic teaching offered peasants an alternate frame of morality from the paternalistic norms that governed their feudal relations with the lords. Third, because local government was weak, conflicts escalated easily. Since 1840 Ottomans had still not re-established firm rule over local feudal lords. Neither did the state block imports of cheap Belgian guns, which emboldened peasants. Observers reported a brisk trade in weapons in Mount Lebanon by 1859 and speculated that the French and the Church helped peasants buy them.[9]

In early 1858, Kisrawani peasants made their first collective complaints against the Khazins to the Ottoman governor in Beirut, Khurshid Pasha. In March, peasants turned a meeting convened by the Khazins (to rally support for their choice of district governor) into a forum of dissent against them. In October, representatives of several villages united "in a spirit of unmalicious love" to denounce tyranny. Two months later, they elected Shahin as their commander.

Revolt broke out in January 1859, when Shahin and 800 peasants surrounded a meeting of the Khazin lords in the town of Ghusta. The Khazins fled and the peasants raided their property. They moved on to other towns, and by July 1859 the peasants had ousted all of the Khazins, some 500 family members, from their various estates. The raids were methodical and relatively bloodless. The peasants collected silk and wheat from Khazin storehouses not as loot, but for redistribution to peasants. There were no casualties until July, when a mother and daughter were killed during a house raid.

Shahin, meanwhile, established a rebel government ruled by a council of village delegates *(wakils)*; it is unclear whether they were elected or appointed by him. He issued decrees in the name of the people *(jumhur)*, disciplined renegades who might betray the revolt, collected weapons, and assured law and order on the roads. Negotiations with the Khazins reached a stalemate. In 1860, Shahin expanded his field of action to promote the emancipation of Christians in neighboring districts. In late May he led 300–500 soldiers across the Dog River to capture the silk crop in the district of Metn.

As many as 50,000 Maronites confronted 12,000 Druze in a series of clashes that lasted for a month and destroyed some 200 villages. In addition to the 4,000 Christian dead, up to 100,000 Christians fled as refugees. Fighting finally ended as European gunboats arrived off Beirut. Fuad Pasha arrived from Istanbul soon afterward to negotiate the peace. In 1861 international powers signed the Reglement, which established Mount Lebanon as an autonomous district under a Christian governor, abolished feudalism, and inaugurated the freest system of elections and political representation in the empire.[10]

THE MORAL ECONOMY OF REVOLT

Political and economic factors cannot fully explain what motivated peasants of multiple villages to unite and to maintain a common government for more than two years, from January 1859 to July 1861. It is notoriously difficult to recover the views of rebellious peasants. They are generally illiterate; and their revolts are often spontaneous.

In the case of the Kisrawan revolt, for example, we have only the sketchiest biographical details about the leader, Tanyus Shahin. He was born in 1815 in a village twelve miles northeast of Beirut. He worked as a blacksmith and a muleteer, carrying goods—and making contacts—among Kisrawan's densely packed villages. As an artisan and entrepreneur, he may have been literate, but he was certainly nothing of the poet that Mustafa Ali or other bureaucrats were. He was more a man of spoken word than the pen, famous for powerful, sermon-like speeches at village meetings. His tall muscular build, even at the age of forty-four, apparently contributed to his charisma.[11]

Eyewitness reports offer ambiguous and highly partisan evidence of Shahin's motivation and actions. Some describe him as a shrewd strategist, who used rumor, intrigue, and murder to gain leadership of the movement. Foreign consuls called him a "ruffian" and a "profoundly dishonest man." Even Church clergy who cooperated with Shahin viewed his tactics as deceitful. But peasants rallied to Shahin as their "redeemer," according to an eyewitness. "In every village he entered, the people would prepare a grand reception for him amid joy and celebration and continuous firing of rifles, as if it were the visit of a ruler to his subjects."[12] Peasants' letters addressed Shahin as his "respected Excellency." After the revolt, even landlords addressed Shahin as "the respected agent."[13] After relinquishing the republic in 1861, Shahin worked as a judiciary official in his home village. He left no personal testimony of the revolt when he died in obscurity in 1895.

Fortunately, a few letters between Shahin, peasants, and Church officials survive. They offer a glimpse of how the peasants felt injustice, how they envisioned a more just society, and how they organized their revolt. Five letters were apparently written by Shahin himself; fifteen more by groups of peasants. Dating from December 1858 to July 1860, the letters hint at competing moral frameworks for peasant actions and

Tanyus Shahin, leader of the 1858 peasant revolt, was a muleteer like these men. He carried supplies and information among Lebanon's mountainous villages and so was well-positioned to organize villagers into a peasant revolt. (Library of Congress)

document the evolution of goals from specific, economic complaints to a program for political and social revolution.

The first letters concern a December 1858 meeting of peasants from six villages. They drew up a list of demands and submitted it to their "spiritual father," the Maronite patriarch, requesting his mediation "to secure the return of our rights to us." Pledging loyalty to the Ottoman state and its laws, Article 2 of the petition declared that shaykhs must pay their fair share of taxes, and they must pay back excesses collected in the past:

> Whereas oppressions, wrongdoings, exaction of extras from travelers and servants, and the money transfers *(hawalat)* taken from the people by the dissimulations of Their Excellencies the Shaikhs [landlords], are contrary to the laws of the Sublime State and the benevolent decrees, when these deeds are ascertained by whatever body is designated, whether the present (judicial) council or another, the doer of these offenses and of violations

of the law, after confirmation, must return and repay what he has taken in its entirety.

The petition's fifth article invoked the Tanzimat to claim equality before the law:

Whereas the Sublime State—may the Lord of Creation preserve it!—has granted us universal equality and complete freedom, so that there should be no distinctions or degradations in addressing persons, and so that all the old principles should be changed in regard to the (tax) registers, and whereas new taxes have been levied on all, we pray that this may be kept in mind by Your Beatitude.

The fourth and sixth articles claimed a right to fair representation in government:

As for the question of the office of the ma'mur, which is of the greatest importance, having to do with governing the people and removing grievances and violations, the ma'mur must govern in accordance with justice and law so that there shall be no further disputes between us and Their Excellencies the Shaikhs. . . . The authority of the ma'mur [must] be effective on everyone without exception in accordance with the reform measures taken, so that from now on no one will be set apart and distinguished from the general public except for the ma'mur himself.[14]

In essence, the peasants called for the transfer of the feudal landlords' authority to an administrator nominated by the patriarch and ratified by the people. The administrator (mamur) would then be assisted by representatives chosen by each village.

At about the same time, peasants in other villages sent Patriarch Masad a letter appealing for intervention against the "devious" factionalism of the Khazins, who bullied them to take sides. The letter used strikingly new language of collective action, suggesting self-consciousness about building a political movement:

We have found no sure way to ward off the said evils from us as a group and individually, except to bind ourselves together in a spirit of love free from deceit, and to stand aside from all provocations. Upon the occurrence of oppression in any village, a petition shall be presented to

> whomever is in authority on behalf of all of us as a group. . . . We have drawn up a list of our grievances to clarify our compact.[15]

Reference to union in a "spirit of love free from deceit" suggests influence of the moral teaching of Maronite clergy. Priests likely played a role in formulating rebel demands, as they were often the only educated people that villagers knew.

Some letters show that individual priests cooperated with the peasants. Some spoke at peasant meetings and cosigned documents. Father Yohannes Habib addressed several letters to Shahin with the alias "Amigo." Habib apparently acted as an advocate for the peasants. He wrote to Maronite and French authorities in October 1959 to argue that only Shahin could ensure peace in Kisrawan: "If the Amigo became the mamur (representative) he would try to consolidate his position by doing justice and settling problems," he wrote. But these elites rejected the idea that a public official might be drawn from the "ignorant" class of commoners.[16]

Patriarch Masad had in fact pressured peasants to make peace with the Khazins. The peasants refused, arguing that the Khazins were not sincere in seeking reconciliation and that their thugs had beaten up peasant activists. They instead asked the patriarch to intercede for them with the Khazins, for the restitution of expenses and abolition of illegal taxes. Despite their disobedience, they concluded their letter deferentially: "We shall be satisfied with laying our wishes and our obedience in all humility under your command."[17]

Other letters directly challenged Church authority. One threatened the patriarch that if he did not expel the Khazins who had taken refuge with him in Bkirke, they would send "a large band of men." Another warned the patriarch not to choose an administrator without consulting the people: "It is not expected that you will destroy the rights of your poor children."[18] The language used in this letter juxtaposed the dual systems of social order at work on Mount Lebanon: the patriarchal order of the Church, and a political order based on rights.

This mixed language of paternal duty and citizens' rights appeared in Shahin's own letters. His earliest surviving letter accompanied a petition to the patriarch on March 6, 1859. Shahin expressed deference even as he refused the patriarch's invitation to a private meeting. He insisted on discussing the appointment of the mamur in an open council:

Most Holy Father,

After kissing the earth upon which Your Beatitude's pure feet have trod, seeking your Apostolic blessing, and offering prayers to God to prolong your life forever, we submit the following petition:

We were honored to receive Your Beatitude's letter and praised God that you are pleased. You wrote for us to come to kiss your footprints in order to deal with the matter. What we understand from the wakils [peasant delegates] is that you spoke to them of three ma'murs [administrators], that is, ma'murs for each district (*'uhda*). But after the debate in the council concerning the previous dispute, and since Shaikh 'Abdullah Khattar arranged in Beirut that on Monday, the fast day, they will come to the council, for that reason we refused to deal with matters until they came to the council. This is what we must lay before you. We repeat the kissing of your fingertips, and may God perpetuate the pleasure of your life forever.

Your son,
Tanyus Shahin

Enclosure: The Petition of March 6, 1859

The items demanded by us from the Khazins:

Article 1. General claims shall be settled by two elected individuals, one elected to represent us and the second elected to represent the shaikhs [Khazins]. Whatever amount it is decided that they owe shall be paid immediately.

Article 2. The shaikhs shall pay the expenses that we have incurred because of them, our payment of the money exacted from us, and the fees of the wakils.

Article 3. The ranks of the shaikhs shall be the same as ours in all matters without any exception whatsoever.

Article 4. None of the shaikhs shall be appointed as a ma'mur over us.

Article 5. The donation taxes which they are imposing upon us on the basis of receipts given at the time of their sale to us of places belonging to them, whereas they have been exacted by force, shall be null and void for the past, the present, and the future.[19]

These demands depart radically from the language of revolt seen in Chapter 1. While rebels in Cairo in 1805 intervened exceptionally to advance their choice for governor, Shahin and his delegates *(wakils)* proposed to change the political rules of the game. They rejected the right of landlords to appoint their administrative representatives and insisted on electing them. They also insisted that their representative be a peasant. The peasants' vision of justice based on equality was a direct challenge to the feudal order that had reigned in Lebanese villages since the eighteenth century.

By May 1859, Shahin commanded a government with an "army" of 800 men that ruled over dozens of villages. But support wavered with a poor harvest. The price of silkworms rose high. Some peasants abandoned cultivation and migrated to Beirut. When Shahin tried to collect taxes, five villages resisted payment. By autumn, however, Shahin managed to expand his support. He won over reluctant villages of the northwest that had formerly preferred to rely on the Church's mediation. A letter from a previously hostile village said, "We thank you for your goodness in improving the welfare of the common people, and especially for your desire to deal with the question of Kisrawan."[20]

The extent of Shahin's authority is suggested by a letter signed by him, which ensured any traveler safe passage on Kisrawan's roads. He also wielded authority over village priests, whom he scolded in a January 1860 letter for permitting too much public drinking on a holiday. He warned the priests to heed the republican council's regulations on disorderly conduct.[21]

Shahin did not apparently intend the republic to be an independent state. Peasants continued to pledge loyalty to the Ottomans' "Sublime State," even as they continued to resist the authority of local landlords. Shahin's commitment to the empire is evidenced by his demand to be appointed as the peasants' sole representative to the Ottoman government. A July 1859 letter also reveals that Shahin and his men "harbored hope that Ottoman troops would side with them in a battle with landlords."[22]

But even as the peasant republic invoked the principles of the Tanzimat, it was unable to win the full endorsement of the Ottoman state, or the Maronite Church. It remained in a liminal legal space, suspended between the competing ideals of paternalism and rights.

It is this ambiguity, perhaps, that best explains Shahin's surprising decision to take the revolution beyond Kisrawan. The last letters we have from Shahin, written in the spring of 1860, shifted dramatically in tone. The first, dated April 3, urged the people of Jubail, north of Kisrawan, to reject the new Ottoman-appointed governor, Emir Yousef, in favor of unity with the republic. Signed "Your Brother," the letter appealed to a common Christian fraternity:

> Do not accept, for I have a bouyourouldi [order] from the Seven Sovereigns for the emancipation of all Christians, who are no longer to be in bondage to anyone; if you desire to be emancipated from your slavery no one can prevent you, neither the Mushir nor the Kaimakam. I enclose an order to the Emir Yousef to return to his place: deliver it to him without delay and do not fear anything. If you require a body of men let me know, and I will come myself with all my men.[23]

Previous letters had also appealed to fraternal bonds that bound the republic. Letter writers routinely referred to one another as "brother."

Fraternity was a concept commonly used in republican discourses, but the April letter makes it clear that in 1860 Lebanon it was used as a religious code of solidarity, perhaps to complement the language of filial bonds between the peasants and their Church. Shahin wrote not as a fellow peasant combating their landlords, but as a Christian in solidarity with all Christians who lived beyond the boundaries of Kisrawan. Indeed, the "seven sovereigns" he refers to were likely foreign, Christian powers whom he believed backed the liberation of Christians from Muslim rule. The battle was now aimed against the enslavement of Christians, not merely the feudal abuse of peasants.

The April 1960 letter also challenged Ottoman authority more directly than before. Formerly, Shahin presented his mission as restoring balance and rule of law to the existing political system. Here, his tone was revolutionary and warlike.

A June 1, 1860, letter to two other villages reinforced this shift: "Since it has been agreed that we all rise with our people to the aid of our brother Christians, to defend them and protect our homes, it is necessary that you send men to carry supplies," Shahin wrote. And in a postscript: "It is necessary to have the priests come, since this is an undertaking of Christian zeal."[24]

Historians have puzzled over the change in aims of the Kisrawan peasants. Some have argued that the frenzy of revolt launched Shahin into a kind of maniacal excess of rhetoric and ambition. In this view, the sectarian war was a tragic deviation from the peasants' class-based struggle.[25] Similarly, some historians argue that the expansion of revolt set a tinderbox on fire. The revolt turned bloody because of latent Muslim jealousy of Christians who profited more from trade with Europeans. Shahin's invasion coincided with a period of lawless violence and murders of individual Christians and Druze. In this view, the revolt presented an unexpected opportunity for Muslims to restore the status quo ante.[26] Others, however, view the revolt as an intentional and early battle in the Maronite Church's campaign for hegemony in Mount Lebanon. They blame the Church and foreign consuls for exploiting the peasant revolt in an effort to expel the Druze from the Mountain. In later decades, the Church would guard Mount Lebanon's autonomy as a Christian enclave to the point of opposing representation in the Ottoman parliament.[27]

Could Shahin have imbibed elites' sectarian identity alongside his peasant, class identity? Ussama Makdisi argues that Lebanese peasants appropriated the sectarian language of missionaries and the Church along with the language of equality of Ottoman reformers. "Religiosity was from the outset inscribed, and actually enabled, Shahin's social struggle," writes Makdisi. "Shahin's transgression was to conflate the equality between religious communities that was mandated by the Tanzimat with equality within the religious communities."[28]

While Ottoman Tanzimat reformers promoted equality of all subjects before the law, they had not intended to promote social equality. They viewed themselves as a ruling elite in solidarity with provincial elites around the empire. Shahin and the peasants recast the language of Tanzimat to claim a more robust social and political equality. In elective government, landlords and peasants would act as equal citizens. Solidarity, or fraternity, demanded that Maronite landlords treat Maronite peasants as equals, not as an inferior social class.

Foreign missionaries likely accelerated the shift toward sectarianism, at least among the upper ranks of the peasantry that attended school. They taught that Eastern Christianity had been corrupted by Islamic influences, and that Maronites could purify their faith only through social segregation from Muslims. They implicitly discouraged social ties between Maronite landowners and Muslim elites and promoted solidarity across Maronite classes. A most compelling link between missionary views and Shahin's actions is that missionaries viewed Christians' inferior status in the Ottoman empire as a kind of slavery. That may be the source of Shahin's ideas of Christian enslavement.[29]

Christian rhetoric of solidarity was suited to a homogeneous district like Kisrawan, where religious fraternity easily melded with Tanzimat principles of equal rights and representation. Such melding was evident in the dualist rhetoric of letters that offered kisses to the patriarch's hand while insisting upon equal rights and elected representatives. But in mixed districts, Christian fraternity was explosive. South of Kisrawan, where Shahin rallied his army in May-June 1860, Christian solidarity sounded like a battle cry against Druze landowners.

It is not clear, however, that Shahin and his followers deliberately waged sectarian war. Letters written before April 1860 did not privilege Christian identity as the foundation of the peasants' community. References to Christian morals coexisted with the rhetoric of equal rights and class interest. Moreover the vast majority of peasants did not attend missionary schools. They continued to live at a social distance

In the late spring of 1860, the peasant revolt of Mount Lebanon veered into sectarian warfare, as Maronite Christian peasants rebelled against their Druze landlords. In the mixed-sect town of Deir al-Qamar, Druze fighters massacred 2,000 Christians, as imagined in this engraving published in *Harper's Weekly*. (*Harper's Weekly*, September 2, 1860—Widener Library, Harvard University, P207.6)

from educated elites, and their petitions and actions in redistributing property demonstrate class-based motives.

A comparison of the Kisrawan revolt with other peasant revolts suggests reasons for the slippage from class-based revolt into sectarian violence. In 1858–1860, Lebanese peasants acted according to multiple frames of justice at the same time: religion, paternalism, and the Tanzimat. Their mixture of paternalism and rights was common in other precapitalist peasant societies, according to anthropologist James Scott. The need for subsistence and norms of reciprocity represent universal standards of justice. The duty of the landlord is to assure them food and shelter. In what Scott calls the class dialectic of paternalism, that duty is in fact "a guarantee of minimal social rights in the absence of political or civil rights." The landlord's assistance in times of famine or family crisis is not charity, but a right. If the landlord neglects his paternal duty, then the peasants have the right to rebel. This sense of rights violated accounts for the shared, collective outrage typically expressed in peasant revolts: "To speak of righteous anger is, in the same breath, to speak of standards of justice."[30] The identity of duty and right also accounts for peasants' conservative agenda. Rebels whom Scott studied in Southeast Asia typically insisted that the landlords honor the paternalistic contract; that is, that landlords shun capitalist practices that undercut reciprocal responsibilities with a cash nexus and property laws.

Kisrawan's peasants expressed a similar tension between subordination/deference and rights/duties in their relationship with the Khazins. They, too, saw that contract strained by the introduction of capitalist markets and practices in the silk industry. They, too, began their revolt with calls for a return to old social obligations and an end to new burdens introduced by the landlords. However, the rebels broke with tradition by inverting Scott's dialectic, to claim political rights in absence of social rights. This inversion occurred when peasants displaced their deference to landlords onto the Church. Nowhere in the letters is there any expression of fealty to the Khazins; instead, the letters are filled with voluptuous gestures of deference to the patriarch and his clergy. This displacement appears to have opened a space for a second frame of justice to enter into the peasants' vision. They transformed rights/duties derived from a hierarchical relationship of patron to peasant into rights derived from the basic equality of all believers before God and also the equality of all citizens before Ottoman law.

The peasants did not merely borrow terms from the Tanzimat; they also adapted local vocabulary to assert rights in the name of the people. For example, the word they used for the people, *al-jumhur*, was an old word meaning "the masses," or "the popular majority." Shahin justified his decrees as being by the power of popular government *(bi-quwat al-hukuma al-jumhuriya)*. Another word was used in Lebanese peasant revolts, one that also expressed a consciousness that rose above individual sect: *ammiyya* (common folk). Maronite rebels also used a word borrowed from Islamic law: *al-maslaha* (public interest) to justify revolt. And they borrowed a word used by Maronite elites, *wakil* (delegate/representative), for an intermediary appointed by them to represent their interests to the peasants. Peasants turned the meaning of *wakil* around, to mean a representative chosen from among themselves. In 1859 they refused to be protected; that is, they broke the paternal bargain with their landlords. Likewise, the protracted negotiations over the choice of mamur expressed peasants' attempt to wrest the office from elites.[31]

The 1858 revolt is a window on how vernacular visions of social justice were changing by the mid-nineteenth century. The peasants' claim to social and political equality is most remarkable. As we saw earlier, an egalitarian spirit had long animated revolts in the Ottoman empire. But never had lowly subalterns articulated so forcefully the demand to remake the empire's hierarchical structure. A half century earlier, in Egypt, Cairenes had rebelled against French rule as a violation of proper hierarchies, of Muslim over Christian. Their chants called for the defense of Islam. And the Egyptian historian Abd al-Rahman al-Jabarti scoffed at Napoleon's proclamation that all men are created equal.

In 1860, Ottoman elites no longer scoffed at equality. Their response to the Lebanon events was shaped in part by the realization that old privileges must be abandoned if the empire were to survive.

RESPONSES TO THE 1860 REVOLT

An essential part of the story about Mount Lebanon's peasant revolt is that these Tanzimat reformers did not welcome vernacular movements for equality. Officially and publicly, they responded to the revolt and massacres by blaming the backwardness of Lebanon. In fact, the violent end of the peasant republic was understood as an omen for the entire Tanzimat project.

Reformers in Istanbul had privately embraced Christian equality as the key to the empire's future. In 1856 the empire ruled over 36 million subjects in provinces from Bosnia to Iraq, Arabia, and Algeria. Of these, 15 million (about 40 percent) were non-Muslim, mostly Greek Orthodox Christians.[32] European powers, goaded by public opinion, had demanded the 1856 decree as part of the peace settlement after the Crimean War. Ottoman reformers understood that only the dramatic elevation of Christian status might keep Europeans from meddling in the empire's affairs and keep Balkan Christians in the empire. By that logic, they had seated non-Muslims on the Supreme Council and Council of State in Istanbul. They also enforced provisions of the 1856 decree that guaranteed non-Muslims equal access to schools and the civil service, taxation, military service, and in courts.

Readers today would view the proclamation of equality for 40 percent of a state's population as natural and just. But in the political context of the nineteenth-century Ottoman empire, it was as radical and provocative as Abraham Lincoln's proclamation to free slaves in the United States. The 1856 decree violated principles of sacred Islamic law that forbade the testimony of non-Muslims against Muslims in court and that placed non-Muslims under Muslim military protection in exchange for a poll tax. In essence, the decree abolished the institution of a Muslim ruling class that had characterized Islamic polities since the seventh century. Some Ottoman dissidents publicly mourned the loss of Muslims' right to rule won by the blood of their forefathers.[33] Others criticized it as a dangerous capitulation to European interference—a tragic sacrifice of sovereignty.

Istanbul expected a backlash to the 1856 decree, but reaction was magnified by economic stress. In response to the 1858 European fiscal crisis, bankers called in their loans and local elites around the empire resorted to imposing extraordinary taxes. Christian peasants in Crete and Bosnia rebelled against their Muslim landlords. In early 1859 the Sublime Porte (office of the grand vezir, or prime minister) transferred thousands of Ottoman troops from Beirut and Syria to the Balkans, leaving a security breach that would slow the empire's response to Mount Lebanon's violence in 1860.[34]

Meanwhile, in September 1859 Istanbul police arrested forty ringleaders in an underground plot to depose Sultan Abdulmecid and the leading Tanzimat ministers, Ali Pasha and Fuad Pasha. The group of religious clergy and students and soldiers was likely motivated to rebel by the state's delay in paying their scholarships and salaries during the fiscal crisis. They focused their discontent, however, on the promise of equality to non-Muslims. That violated Islamic law, they claimed, and the sultan was bound by sacred duty to uphold that law. Public opinion in the capital sympathized with the rebels. In May 1860, the grand vezir toured the Balkans in an effort to restore calm and reassure Christians. In the city of Nish alone, he received 4,000 petitions from Christians, mostly complaining that Christians were still blocked from testifying in court.[35]

The "cat" of equality was let out of the bag. Nearly a century before the United Nations would promulgate a universal declaration of human rights, Ottoman justice already could no longer operate in isolation from new international norms. That such norms were tied to European imperialism, however, aggravated efforts to gain acceptance of them.

And so news of violence in Lebanon and Damascus in June and July 1860 shook Istanbul: the Porte forbade citizens to talk about it on the street.[36] Opponents of equality seized upon the revolts as evidence of Christians' disloyalty and the need to put them back in their place. There were even rumors that the sultan's brother, Abdulaziz, had supported the massacre of Lebanese and Syrian Christians.

Fuad Pasha rushed to Beirut. His primary concern was to preserve Ottoman sovereignty against the claims of French troops who arrived to restore order. He meted out draconian punishments in Damascus, where eight days of pillage and murder had left perhaps 5,000 Christians dead. Fuad ordered hundreds of Muslims arrested; 167 were executed on the spot, in public, as a lesson. Later that year, 181 more Muslims were executed and another 146 exiled. Most of them were of the lower classes.[37] Investigations, hearings, trials, and punishment took nearly a year in Lebanon.

Ottoman and Church officials in Beirut pressured Shahin and village representatives to resolve their differences with the Khazin shaykhs. Shahin was forced, along with representatives of twenty-three villages, to sign a document that blamed the revolt on "certain masters of corruption" who "induced us into rebellion against the commands of the government." It explained that the bishop of Beirut advised Shahin and his representatives to respect "the orders and laws of the gracious Sublime State . . . and to put an end to this disagreement prevailing between us and the aforesaid Shaikhs, so that they may return to their homes." The document also obliged the peasants to meet the Khazins "to make amends and to exchange forgiveness and absolution from them."[38] In effect, the agreement used the myth of unnamed instigators as a means of absolving Shahin and his cosigners from punishment. Shahin remained in control of the district for another year, as the Khazins returned to their property. Shahin finally stepped down as commander in Kisrawan in 1861.

Meanwhile, European powers and the Ottomans established a new international regime on Mount Lebanon. It required that the governor be a Christian from the empire and that the choice be approved by an international council. To the ultimate satisfaction of the rebels, the Reglement of 1861 also abolished feudal privileges and established an elected council to oversee the government administration. Electoral districts were drawn so that they each contained a mix of Christians and Muslims. This ensured that only moderates would win elections. While the Reglement did little to address economic inequalities, it contributed to decades of peace on Mount Lebanon, until World War I.[39]

Ottoman damage control denied the complex causes of the sectarian violence in Lebanon. By blaming ignorant commoners, the state repressed popular claims to justice and equality. Meanwhile in Istanbul, Tanzimat reformers Ali Pasha and Fuad Pasha did not repeal the 1856 decree. They quietly secured support in the army but kept a tight lid on public criticism. Recruitment of non-Muslims into the bureaucracy stalled in an atmosphere of fear.

But a new generation of reformers resumed the project to build a polity of equal Ottoman citizens. In 1867, dissident bureaucrats and intellectuals formed an opposition group called the Young Ottomans.

They condemned Ali and Fuad's tyranny, their capitulation to European interference, and their public disregard of Islamic culture. They called for representative government and the protection of individual rights as the key to reconciling Muslims and non-Muslims in the empire. As one member argued: "There are no Christian politics or Moslem politics, for there is only one justice and politics is justice incarnate."[40]

The Young Ottomans embraced ideas of representative government similar to those that had emerged from commoners in Lebanon. But they aimed their ideas at fellow Muslims. In their view, "the establishment of a constitutional system in Turkey was equated with a return to the rule of law as embodied in the practice of the Seriat (Islamic law)."[41] Their most outstanding member, Namik Kemal, was a poet and playwright who is still read and revered in Turkey. He was among the first to advocate Islamic liberalism. "The real source of sovereignty," he declared, rests in "the inviolability of the private person of the citizen."

The Young Ottomans found sympathy in one of the empire's most able governors, Midhat Pasha. In 1876 he led a coup d'état against Sultan Abdulmecid's successor, Abdulaziz, and forced his successor, Sultan Abdulhamid II (1876–1909), to agree to a constitution and parliament.

Midhat Pasha drafted the 1876 constitution as war loomed with Russia, backer of Christian separatists in the Balkans. The constitution guaranteed the eligibility of non-Muslims for office, their proportional representation in the legislature, and their equality under the law. He arrested opponents and won support for the constitution among officials by arguing that it was the only bulwark left against invasion. The constitution was proclaimed publicly on December 23, 1876, as a guarantee of "equal rights and constitutional liberties to all subjects of the Empire alike."[42]

Parliament opened in March 1877 with a prayer for the welfare of the Ottoman state and the Sultan.[43] Gathered in the chamber were 130 deputies from around the empire: seventy-one Muslims, forty-four Christians, and four Jews. Christians, Greeks, Anatolia, and Syria were overrepresented in proportion to the population. (Egypt was not represented because it was ruled by Mehmed Ali's

The Ottoman Constitution, proclaimed on a rainy day in December 1876, was an effort by Midhat Pasha and the Young Ottomans to strengthen sovereignty by incorporating Christians of the empire into a parliament that would also limit the sultan's tyranny.
(*London Illustrated News*, January 6, 1877).

semiautonomous dynasty. Lebanon was not represented because the Maronite Church feared parliament would undercut its autonomous authority.)[44] Christian deputies in Istanbul declared their faith in the constitution and denounced Russian aggression. But tensions rose when some Muslim deputies objected to the nomination of a Christian as presiding president of the chamber.[45]

The 1876 constitution set an important precedent in Middle East politics. It attracted support for constitutionalism through the belief that only representative government could secure the state's sovereignty. Constitutional government would make a stronger state, by pulling nationalist Christians back into the empire. Midhat expressed these views in an article published in a British magazine in 1878:

Turkey, in a word, ought to be governed by a constitutional regime, if it is desired that serious reforms be carried out, that a fusion be effected of the different races, and that out of this fusion should spring the progressive development of the population to whatever nationality and whatever religion they may belong; it is the only remedy for our ills and the sole means we have of struggling with advantage against enemies at home and abroad.[46]

But Midhat's article did not save constitutionalism. Facing defeat by the Russians, Sultan Abdulhamid had declared a state of emergency and dissolved the parliament. The article asked the British to pressure Russia to return territory and Abdulhamid to reinstate the constitution and parliament. The British would not. Public opinion in London militated against support for an Oriental despot who massacred Christians. Midhat's effort to share the Ottoman view of those events made little impression. He was crushed and soon forced from power.

The events in Lebanon demonstrated that Tanzimat principles of equality and rights were embraced by common subjects within two decades of the Gulhane decree. Popular pressure once again prompted bureaucrats to push reform, now formulated in terms of constitutional monarchy. The failure of both Shahin's peasant republic and Midhat's constitution epitomized the acute political dilemma facing Ottoman state and society in the late nineteenth century: How might a weakened state, under threat from foreign aggression, orchestrate a fundamental political transformation? In contrast to European states, notes historian Ariel Salzmann, Ottoman rulers telescoped the transition to a regime of equal citizens into a few short decades.[47] State officials groped for ways to appease both Christians seeking equality and Muslims anxious about European influence. They bought peaceful coexistence in Lebanon at the price of lost sovereignty, under the 1861 Reglement. Political repression, in turn, undermined the transition to equality. The absence of a parliament and a free press in Istanbul severely limited necessary political discussion between Christians and Muslims, even as Sultan Abdulhamid increasingly invoked Islamic symbols to justify state reform.[48] Suspicions of Christian disloyalty festered and would resurface in another constitutional revolution in 1908.

Meanwhile, grassroots constitutionalism spread around the Middle East among subject-citizens as well as disgruntled bureaucrats among the ruling elite. Constitutionalism's broad appeal was due in part to its promise to build stronger government, to protect sovereignty, and to assure the rule of law. However, constitutionalists in other countries also grappled with reconciling claims to Muslim privilege with the principle of equality under the law and claims to elite privilege with popular claims to political participation. The reverberations of the Ottomans' failed experiment were felt most immediately in the constitutional revolution in Egypt in 1882.

3

AHMAD URABI AND NAZEM AL-ISLAM KERMANI
Constitutional Justice in Egypt and Iran

On October 29, 1882, Colonel Ahmad Urabi sat in a jail cell in Cairo and composed a testimonial for the trial for his life. Six weeks before, he had been commander of the Egyptian army and leader of a revolutionary government. The revolutionaries had stood up to Britain's bombardment of Alexandria and declared their monarch, Tawfiq Pasha, unfit to rule. They elected a people's government in Cairo. In September, however, British troops easily defeated Urabi's peasant army. In his testimonial, Urabi defended himself against charges of treason:

> My sole objective was the emancipation of my country and the prosperity its people would enjoy under a just, truly representative government. Such a government would give the people their proper rights without distinction between civilians and foreigners, so that all inhabitants of Egypt would be as one, regardless of differences of religions and beliefs, since all men belonged to the same common humanity.[1]

Urabi's movement embraced liberal principles of popular sovereignty, representation, and equality under the law. Like peoples around the globe, Egyptian revolutionaries viewed liberalism as a universal model of justice, applicable in all cultures. There was as yet no single term in Arabic for "constitution," but Urabi's movement united a spectrum of political groups around the goal of obtaining a written document to limit the power of the monarch and set out the rights of citizens.

Between 1875 and 1920, constitutionalism inspired the largest political movements across the region. Turks, Iranians, Arabs, and others of varied political persuasions joined movements to demand elected representation, legislative control over state finances, and equality under the law. Thousands demonstrated in the streets in the belief that constitutional government would protect their national sovereignty. They also believed that sovereignty was the prerequisite to the rule of law and to equality of all citizens. And they believed that their monarchs were vulnerable to foreign manipulation; they needed the supervision of a legislature.

The popularization of constitutionalism followed initial top-down efforts by reforming bureaucrats, first in Tunisia in 1861 and then by Midhat Pasha in Istanbul in 1876. These reformers presciently recognized the need to rally subjects' loyalty to their regimes. Both were short-lived affairs, however, as other elite factions resisted the change.

Beginning with Egypt's revolution of 1881–1882, constitutionalism became a grassroots phenomenon: the Iranian mass revolution of 1906, a second Ottoman constitutional revolution in 1908, and a final wave of constitutionalism in Egypt and Syria in 1919–1920. The movements grew steadily larger, inspiring thousands to protest and dance in streets, and then to cast their first ballots in parliamentary elections. These popular movements tapped feelings of injustice felt by commoners who readily embraced the principles of equality and representation.

Popular constitutionalism was a reaction to foreign intervention and the social change it caused. Since the mid-nineteenth century, European governments had moved into the Mediterranean to build ports and railroads, market industrial goods, and ensure routes to other reaches of empire. European missionaries followed merchants, building schools to train middlemen and translators. By the 1860s European steamship and railroads transported crops from the hinterland to Europe and distributed European textiles and manufacturers throughout the Middle East. Egypt became a "Klondike on the Nile" when the American Civil War caused a cotton boom.[2] British textile firms sought Egyptian cotton as a replacement for supplies from the American South. Thousands of European profit-seekers settled in Alexandria and Cairo: Italians, Greeks, French, and British.

Foreign investment and settlement did not benefit everyone equally. Indeed, many constitutionalists believed only the aristocratic elite benefited. Their feelings of injustice focused on how foreigners created plural systems of law. The Great Powers imposed treaties on weaker Middle Eastern states that granted Europeans and their clients different courts and lower tax rates than ordinary citizens. A rising middle class of Muslim bureaucrats, soldiers, journalists, and educators expressed anger at the double standards. They remarked that most clients of the Europeans were Christians and Jews; as in Lebanon, sectarian tensions flared. In Iran, meanwhile, Europeans snapped up monopoly rights to the country's mines, to build its telegraph system, and to wholesale crops—to the disadvantage of indigenous businessmen.

Popular constitutionalism was also a response to the growing power of the state over citizens. The Ottoman Tanzimat and Egypt's reforms increased the number of bureaucrats and centralized power at Istanbul and Cairo. The central government reached directly into the everyday lives of citizens as never before. Tax collection and the military draft became more efficient. New legal codes extended state control in business, public health, and education. In the name of modernization, the states embarked on massive reforms in cities and forced peasants to work on projects like the Suez Canal for little compensation.

After the 1839 Gulhane decree, states no longer pretended to protect their *raya* (flocks). The Ottomans transformed their protective "garden" into a competitive market, in the hope that enterprising subjects would enrich the tax base. Foreign companies paid Egyptian workers lower wages than Italian, Greek, and Maltese immigrants. And the Egyptian state at first permitted the use of forced labor to build the Suez Canal, until workers rebelled. It is also no coincidence that revolts multiplied in the 1870s, when prices of crops and commodities collapsed during a global recession.[3]

Constitutional movements arose to restore the Circle of Justice but ended by replacing it with a new model of justice. Leaders came from the new Muslim middle class; they recruited educated artisans and village headmen, squeezed by the global marketplace, as the backbone of their movements. They believed that only a parliament could force monarchs to protect the welfare of the poorest citizens. They also believed that justice must be founded on the equality of all citizens under one law. Such an idea would have shocked Mustafa Ali;

it had deeply disturbed Mustafa Reshid Pasha. But by the 1870s, even state reformers like Midhat Pasha recognized that equal rights were crucial to maintaining support for states beleaguered in the international arena.

Middle Eastern constitutionalism reflected global trends that produced constitutional revolutions in Russia, Mexico, China, and elsewhere. In all of these countries, the industrializing world economy had encouraged the growth of new, educated middle classes. They provided the know-how and financial means to build sustained political movements.[4] And they combined ideas of representative government and the separation of powers—modeled on the French Revolution of 1789—with local political values. Middle Easterners infused constitutionalism with an Islamic spirit.[5]

Middle Eastern constitutional revolutions were distinctive, argues historian Juan Cole, because of the region's particular experience of informal imperialism. Opposition movements confronted a dual elite. On one side were a monarch and his court, who profited from close ties to foreign bankers, merchants, and rulers. On the other side was a rising indigenous elite, shut out of power and burdened by the profligate demands of the court. To ensure that tax revenues were spent for the people's benefit, this elite supported demands for an elected legislative assembly.[6]

The shift away from paternalistic government based on the Circle of Justice toward popular sovereignty took different paths. While this chapter cannot recapitulate the entire history of the constitutional wave, it will suggest the major trends through the comparison of two cases: 1881–1882 Egypt and 1906–1911 Iran. Both were popular, grassroots movements led by a new indigenous middle class that spread constitutional ideas in their newspapers, schools, and political clubs. Both revolutions began with specific economic complaints and then blossomed into a carnival of political invention. Both ended when foreign governments saw their interests threatened, and shifted support to the monarch.

Constitutionalism transformed political culture not in the quiet of a scholar's study, but in the messy process of mobilizing large numbers of people. Like the peasants in Mount Lebanon, Iranian and Egyptian leaders expressed their ideals in a mixed, contradictory, and sometimes ambivalent language. At times they appealed to the universality of human rights; at other times they insisted on differences between Eastern and Western civilization. Eventually, they forged a vernacular language of rights and equality against that of social hierarchy and privilege. Constitutionalism fused with a new collective identity of the people as a nation, and of the nation as the seat of sovereignty.

The transformation is revealed in the memoirs of Egyptian colonel Ahmad Urabi and the Iranian activist Nazem al-Islam Kermani. Urabi was a military officer of peasant background, one of several leaders of what Cole calls multiple, simultaneous revolutions in Egypt. Nazem al-Islam was a provincial religious scholar who migrated to Tehran and joined ranks with opposition leaders. The memoirs of these two men offer a window on motives and strategies of revolutionaries. But they are, by their very nature, also subjective and incomplete: Urabi was writing in his own defense about a revolution that encompassed multiple movements and leaders; Nazem al-Islam was a minor player in just one faction in the Iranian revolution. However, they both directed their memoirs toward a reading public and so by necessity invoked a revolutionary language that they imagined was shared. Critically read, their memoirs reveal how a common language about felt injustice became a language of future justice.

Finally, their memoirs reflect the differences in the two revolutions. Egypt's revolution pitted indigenous Arabic-speakers against a Turco-Circassian aristocracy allied with foreign capital. Class differences ultimately split the constitutional movement. The revolution ended, before constitutional government could be fully established, with a British invasion that defended the interests of the landed elite. Iran's revolution lasted longer and its constitution shifted power dramatically from the shah to the National Consultative Assembly. That shift, however, plunged Iran into a civil war that opened new cleavages between landed and religious elites on the one hand and a radicalized class of merchants, middle-class reformers, and workers on the other. Iran's revolutionary coalition ultimately split on religious–secular lines, and a Russian invasion secured the interests of the Shah, religious conservatives, and their landowning allies.

AHMAD URABI AND THE EGYPTIAN
REVOLUTION OF 1881–82

Urabi's defense statement and memoir were written without notes and contain factual errors and much hindsight. We must read them, as we read Mustafa Ali's reports and Tanyus Shahin's letters, as texts that reconstruct reality to suit the author's purpose. Their subjectivity is useful, however, in suggesting how Urabi came to question the norms of his society. He describes, in particular, how he viewed social hierarchy as an injustice only after exposure to the egalitarian policies of an earlier ruler. His narrative shows how the officers' revolt was inspired by an alternate vision of social justice, based upon equality before the law.[7]

Urabi opened his October 1882 defense statement by condemning the racial discrimination suffered by Egyptians in the army. He named his nemesis in the second line: Uthman Rifki Pasha, a member of the Turco-Circassian elite that had monopolized the officer corps and the royal court since Mehmed Ali took power as governor in 1805. Rifki Pasha had court-martialed Urabi in an 1879 conflict between Turco-Circassians and Arabic-speaking Egyptians. And in 1881 he had arrested Urabi for protesting against troop cuts that fell exclusively on Arab-Egyptian soldiers. "And so all promotions, decorations and rewards went to those of the Circassian race," Urabi wrote. "That is why, up to that date, not a single man born and bred Egyptian had attained in the army the rank of Pasha, or General."[8]

After twenty-five years of exile, Urabi opened his memoir on a different note. He had been tried and condemned for leading the revolution. Many Egyptians had blamed him for the failure. The bruise of humiliation showed as he introduced himself as a man of honorable lineage. He was born in 1841 to respectable parents and educated at the prestigious Islamic college in Cairo, al-Azhar, he advised his readers. The public has been given a false representation of the revolution, he continued. His memoir would correct the record.

The elderly Urabi wrote with less anger and more historical perspective about why he was provoked to fight injustice. His political education began, he wrote, "when I heard a speech by Said Pasha at the Kasr al-Nil [Nile Palace]." Said Pasha ruled Egypt from 1854 to 1863. He was a liberal and tolerant ruler who had opened a new program to enlist peasants into the officer corps. That was how Urabi had joined the army in 1854, at age fourteen. Now, years later at the Nile Palace, elite clerics and officials had gathered to hear Said Pasha: "O Brothers," he said, "see in the condition of the Egyptian people which has faced tyranny in history, the oppression of foreign countries. . . . I see myself as Egyptian and my duty is to nurture the sons of this people." Urabi portrayed Said Pasha as a benevolent ruler who guarded the welfare of his citizens. Said addressed citizens as "brothers" to emphasize common identity. While Turkish-speaking elites were unimpressed by the speech, Urabi remarked, Arabic speakers "left with faces filled with joy, at the first expression of the principle 'Egypt for the Egyptians.'"[9]

In Urabi's memory, Said Pasha's inclusive policy was a brief ray of justice soon clouded by the reigns of his successors, Ismail Pasha (1863–1879) and Tawfik Pasha (1879–1892). They marked their distance from common Egyptians by formally adopting the title of "Khedive," from a Persian word for prince. Turkish and French, not Arabic, remained the chief languages at the palace. It was this exclusion—felt as a reversal of justice—that caused the ache in Urabi's heart.

In the 1870s, Urabi was one of just four native Egyptian colonels in the army. Turkish and Circassian officers snubbed them and mistreated peasant conscripts.[10] They referred to the Arabic-speaking colonels, he recalled, as "lowly peasant fruit pickers."[11] The colonels shared fellow Egyptians' frustration at exclusion from Ismail Pasha's court. Unlike Said, Khedive Ismail's gaze turned toward Europe. He had courted the French empress at the opening of the Suez Canal in 1869 and he built an opera house to stage Verdi's *Aida* to advertise Egypt's embrace of European culture. These royal projects were funded by profits from the 1860s cotton boom. Little profit, however, trickled down to Egyptian-born peasants and workers. And then the boom went bust, as American cotton returned to international markets after 1865. Egypt sank into bankruptcy.[12]

Bankruptcy and war lit the spark of revolution. To repay the national debt, half of Egyptian tax revenues were now siphoned to European banks. And to ensure repayment, Europeans entered directly into Egyptian government. Then the Russo-Ottoman War broke out in 1877. Sultan Abdulhamid demanded that Egypt send troops (Egypt was still part of the Ottoman empire). But Ismail could not afford to raise the troops. After numerous tax hikes, Egyptian landlords resisted paying even higher taxes. Peasants rebelled, urban riots broke out, and soldiers protested for back pay. This set the context for Urabi's run-ins with Rifki Pasha.

In 1879, local Egyptian elites took the opportunity to demand a larger share in government. Under Sharif Pasha and with Khedive Ismail's blessings, the Council of Deputies issued a National Program to secure fiscal sovereignty and to draft a constitution. Europeans feared that the Egyptians intended to default on their debt. European consuls wielded tremendous political influence—as they had in 1850s Lebanon. They pressured Sultan Abdulhamid to depose Ismail. Sharif Pasha was forced to shelve his draft constitution. This was to be a dress rehearsal for a full-fledged constitutional movement in 1881.[13]

Urabi had meanwhile become leader of the Young Officers society, perhaps modeled on the Young Ottomans. The society responded to Arab-Egyptian exclusion from the highest ranks of government by promoting an Egyptian national identity. Other nationalist movements appeared at this time around the world, also mounted by local elites who had been denied promotion to the highest ranks of imperial government.[14] Nationalism dovetailed with new ideas about popular sovereignty and constitutional government.

The Egyptian colonels were provoked to political action by a new act of humiliation: Khedive Tawfik ordered them to perform unpaid hard labor, digging the Tawfikiyyah Canal. "We colonels were now once more with our regiments, and as native Egyptians subject to much oppression," Urabi told a British sympathizer.[15] When the colonels refused the discriminatory order, they crossed the line from victims of misfortune to soldiers for justice. This was the moment, in January 1881, when Rifki Pasha announced troop cuts aimed exclusively at native Egyptians.

The Young Officers took action by submitting a petition to the prime minister, Riyad Pasha. This was a risky move, they would discover, under a regime that recognized no loyal dissent. The petition demanded equality with Turco-Circassians in promotions, the "cessation of discrimination by race and the enactment of just laws that would ensure every man his rights." It also demanded a new war minister and reinstatement of Egyptian troops cut from army rolls. Finally, it demanded a nationalist war minister, who would run the military "in accord with the laws of justice-oriented nations."[16]

Riyad Pasha responded with an arrest order: he threw Urabi and the officers into prison. But unlike in 1879, Urabi was neither prosecuted nor demoted. Instead, other army officers came to support him, from the First Regiment and Sudan Regiment. They helped Urabi escape from prison.

On February 2, 1882, Urabi and his allies from the First and Sudan regiments surrounded Abdin Palace. In face of such force, Khedive Tawfik was forced to relent. He pardoned the officers and dismissed Rifki Pasha. Urabi's defense statement stressed that even though he had been the victim of an arbitrary and illegal arrest, he had acted legally and loyally toward the khedive. "I expressed the prayer that his reign would remain stable and secure, firmly based on the principles of justice and equality."[17]

Urabi's demand for equality, however, was a challenge to the regime. His views echoed those of prominent Egyptian intellectuals like Rifaa al-Tahtawi, an educator who had studied in France. In an 1875 textbook on citizenship, Tahtawi wrote that political equality is based on human beings' equality before God: "This equality cannot be suspended by human legislation."[18]

Muhammad Abduh, a leading religious reformer at al-Azhar, also shared Urabi's demand for the rule of law—and Urabi's belief in the justice of revolt. The Egyptian people must enact political change themselves, he argued, just as the French did when they established the Third Republic in 1870:

> The shift of government in France, for example, from an absolute monarchy to a restricted monarchy, then to a free republic, did not occur by the will of those in authority alone. Rather, the strongest contributing factors were the conditions of the people, the increase in their level of thought, and their new awareness of the need to ascend to a state higher than their present one.[19]

Abduh and other Egyptians were moving toward an idea of popular sovereignty, without yet calling for the overthrow of Egypt's monarchy.

Noteworthy is the frequent reference to politics in France and elsewhere in Egyptian political debate. Egyptians embraced constitutionalism as a *universal* model of justice—not as a foreign model. They insisted that politics in Egypt should rest on the same principles as those in Europe. They rejected Europeans' view that Islam was backward and despotic. Islam shared basic principles of justice with other great civilizations in Europe and Asia.

Universalist ideas were taught by Abduh's mentor, the international activist Sayyid Jamal al-Din al-Afghani. Born and educated in Iran, Afghani was living in India at the time of the 1857 Indian mutiny against the British. In the 1870s, he carried his mission to save Muslims from imperialism to Cairo, where he held forth in the city's cafes.[20] He called on Muslims to act on the principles of their religion, to cast off medieval superstition, and to unite against European domination. Most importantly, Muslims must depose tyrannical and weak rulers who opened the door to Europeans. Afghani inspired students to start political groups and publish political newspapers. Before Khedive Tawfik expelled him in 1879, Afghani gave a powerful sermon to a crowd of 4,000 gathered at Cairo's al-Husayn mosque, condemning British influence in Egypt.[21]

France's occupation of Tunisia in May 1881 shocked Egyptians. The "floodgates" of anti-regime politics opened that summer. Landowners, journalists, and intellectuals renewed their call for a constitution—now as a safeguard national sovereignty. They had no faith that Tawfik would defend Egypt from occupation. Urabi agreed. Tawfik was again maneuvering to transfer Urabi out of the capital, to Alexandria. The khedive was again blocking forces of change. Only with a constitution could the people force Tawfik to implement reforms needed to strengthen Egypt. That summer, Abduh, who had been working as a government censor, joined the constitutionalists. He met Urabi for the first time in August.[22]

The showdown came the next month. On September 9, in a scene immortalized in popular art, Urabi arrived at Abdin Palace on horseback, with some 4,000 soldiers. Only eighteen carried guns, Urabi later explained. They did not plan a military coup, but rather acted in self-defense: government forces had tried to arrest them earlier that day. Urabi dismounted, sheathed his sword, and confronted Khedive Tawfik in the palace courtyard. He made three demands: 1) dismiss the tyrannical cabinet of Riyad Pasha; 2) convene the Chamber of Deputies, which had been suspended in 1879; and 3) increase the army to 18,000 troops, to ensure national defense and return jobs to native Egyptians.[23]

Urabi's memoir recalled the encounter as a battle for sovereignty between monarch and people. "You have no right to make all of these demands. The sovereign rules this country for his sons," Tawfik replied, according to Urabi. "Who are you, but slaves?" Urabi said he responded that the army and the sultan would back him up. "We are God's creation and free. He did not create us as your property."[24]

Tawfik relented, and the crowd raised a cheer. He dismissed Riyad Pasha immediately and named Urabi's old ally, Sharif Pasha, as prime minister, and he promised to expand the army. In exchange, Urabi promised that the army would respect the civilian government's authority.[25]

Elections were held in November 1881, and the Chamber of Deputies convened in December. Deputies immediately called for "a just and lawful regime." Government must rest "on the basis of justice and freedom, so that everyone could enjoy security of life and property, freedom of thought and action and thus genuine happiness and prosperity."[26]

Sharif Pasha resurrected his draft constitution and opened debate. His 1879 draft had cast the Chamber of Deputies as an advisory council, much like the assembly in the Ottoman 1876 constitution. Like the sultan, the khedive would retain power over the cabinet and Europeans would control finances. In February 1882, however, Arab-Egyptian deputies demanded a constitution with real parliamentary power. Specifically, the Chamber of Deputies should control the half of Egypt's budget that was not automatically siphoned off to pay foreign debts. Sharif Pasha and his Turco-Circassian allies warned that European consuls would never accept such a transfer of fiscal power. But the deputies convinced Tawfik to approve their draft. Sharif resigned.

The Chamber of Deputies ratified Egypt's first written constitution on February 7, 1882. It established a constitutional monarchy with a parliamentary form of government. Most of its fifty-two articles outlined the Chamber of Deputies' rights and duties. They expanded its oversight of the budget, required its approval of treaties, and made ministers responsible to it.[27]

Urabi accepted the post of war minister in the new cabinet. He immediately reformed the military along the egalitarian lines that Said Pasha had long before promised. "The affairs of the army were put in good order and the deserving were now promoted rather than reduced in rank," he wrote.[28] He became famous in Egypt, known as "El Wahid" or "The Only One." Newspapers praised him as an Islamic hero who redeemed Egypt's honor and defended the people's rights. He toured the towns of the Nile Delta, where he gave speeches condemning Turkish privilege. In truth, he proclaimed, men come from one common stock, with equal rights.[29]

Urabi was, however, but one among many revolutionary leaders. Tensions soon surfaced on the question of equality. Urabi advocated comprehensive social reforms to abolish forced labor, distribute water fairly to small landholders, and to offer peasants loans at fair rates. Landowning deputies, however, resisted turning a political revolution into a social revolution. They guarded their status as elites and maintained contacts with the palace.

And Khedive Tawfik's inner circle had by no means accepted the constitution as a fait accompli. In May 1882, a plot by Circassian officers to murder Urabi was uncovered. Tawfik Pasha interfered to lighten the sentences of guilty officers. When Urabi accused him of double standards, Tawfik dismissed him from his post as war minister.[30] Huge crowds gathered in protest, forcing Tawfiq to reinstate Urabi.

Europeans, too, moved to undermine the constitutional regime. In late May, British and French consuls sent a joint note demanding dismissal of the government. They threatened to send warships to Egypt unless the Chamber of Deputies restored the political status quo; that is, rolled back constitutional reforms. They also demanded the exile of Urabi. The Chamber of Deputies refused. "Public opinion was united on their refusal to accept the note, and village mayors and notables began coming to Cairo asserting their rejection of it and those willing to accept it," Urabi recalled.[31] In effect, the Chamber of Deputies claimed the power of a true parliament.[32]

The Egyptian constitution was an ambitious attempt to assert true legislative power and popular control over state finances. It would fail not because Egyptian culture favored paternalistic monarchy, but because landed aristocrats allied themselves with the British to protect their profits.

On a false pretext of protecting Christians from Muslims, British warships appeared in Alexandria harbor in June 1882—almost exactly eighty-four years after Napoleon's fleet had arrived. The British press raised alarms that Urabi planned a Muslim massacre of

Christians—much as Ismail had falsely claimed in 1879 that Urabi intended to install a "Muslim theocracy." In fact, Urabi had no connection to the riots that broke out in Alexandria. Violence had started with a petty dispute between a Muslim and Christian. Mosques had actually opened their doors to rescue Christians and Jews.[33]

On July 11 and 12 the British ships bombarded Alexandria. Khedive Tawfik refused to accompany the Egyptian army as it retreated toward Cairo. He stayed under British protection in Alexandria, where he claimed to establish his capital. For the next two months, a rival, revolutionary government ruled in Cairo. On July 29, a national assembly of 400 notables, including Muslims, Jews, and Coptic Christians, convened. Delegates gave speeches only in Arabic, not Turkish. With the support of clerics, they voted to depose Tawfik, on the grounds that his alliance with Europeans against his own people was a violation of Islamic law. The assembly formed a common-law government, based on popular sovereignty, and elected Urabi head of government.[34] "All this transpired without my attendance," Urabi wrote in his testimonial, "until they themselves entitled me 'Protector and Guardian of all Egypt.'"[35]

The revolutionary government established a remarkable degree of public order, according to Cole. Civilian officials resettled refugees, distributed supplies, and protected property. The assembly attracted Egypt's young and talented journalists, religious scholars, teachers, and bureaucrats. Muhammad Abduh acted as its secretary. Meanwhile, thousands volunteered for military service and donated horses and food to the cause. Women as well as men helped to manufacture armaments for the coming battle.[36]

Debates continued about revolutionary goals. Abduh called for the rule of Islamic law and called for a new caliph who would be truly sovereign and who would lay an Islamic basis for modern life.[37] However, the national assembly also embraced Christians and Jews and demanded equality for all Egyptians, as brothers. Some delegates called for a social revolution. Guilds advocated the basic democratic values of the shop floor. Village headmen petitioned Urabi to redistribute land to the poor and to give them government jobs.

Peasants, too, mobilized in the summer of 1882, in actions that recalled Shahin's movement in Lebanon. They conducted "land invasions" of estates owned by the Turkish elites, attacked tax collectors, and refused to pay for the debts owed to Europeans. Some joined Urabi's army. Petitions demanding justice and freedom circulated among villages. As a comet appeared in the sky, political rhetoric turned millenarian. (The year 1300 in the Islamic calendar was to begin in November.)[38]

Urabi considered the British invasion immoral and called Muslims to defensive jihad. On July 2 he had written the British prime minister, William Gladstone: "Our Prophet in his Qur'an has commanded us not to seek war nor to begin it. He commanded us also, if war be waged against us, to resist."[39] War against the khedive and Britain was "lawful and legitimate," Urabi argued, because a representative council had ordered it. Justice, in Urabi's view, flowed from the people, not the monarch. "The Egyptian nation, for all its variety of religious affiliation, did indeed do its duty in defense of the homeland."[40]

On September 13, however, the British launched a surprise attack on Urabi at Tell el-Kebir, about 65 miles northeast of Cairo. He was awoken from sleep by the first shots. "I said my prayer and galloped," he recalled. But his peasant soldiers fled the battlefield. "I could see the day was lost."[41] Urabi took a train to Cairo in the vain hope of organizing a defense of the capital. But Cairenes were dispirited by news that Sultan Abdulhamid had condemned Urabi as a rebel.

The next evening, Urabi took a carriage to Abbasiya Square and surrendered to British officers.[42] Charged with treason, he was transferred on October 5 to a prison cell with only a blanket and a rug as furnishings.

Khedive Tawfik aimed to execute Urabi for raising rebellion. Sympathizers from Britain and in Egypt helped him avoid death, however. At Urabi's December 3 trial, he pleaded guilty to rebellion and his death sentence was commuted to exile. Urabi and several other constitutionalist leaders departed Egypt for Ceylon later that month. Urabi returned to Egypt in 1901 and died in Cairo ten years later.

In Urabi's absence, Gladstone appointed a veteran colonial administrator, Sir Evelyn Baring (later Lord Cromer) as consul-general in Egypt. Cromer viewed the revolution with contempt, as premature in a backward society. The policy of "Egypt for the Egyptians" was incapable of stable government, he wrote, because it would exclude "Europeans, with all their intelligence, wealth and governing power" and

Colonel Ahmad Urabi led the multifaceted 1882 Egyptian constitutional revolution. His government ruled in opposition to Khedive Tawfik for two months before British troops occupied the country. Urabi was convicted of treason and exiled to Ceylon. This image is taken from a commemorative stamp issued in 1981.

(Yay Images)

because it would replace the khedive with "some illiterate Egyptian, of the type of Arabi (Urabi)."[43]

The British ruled Egypt as a virtual colony, with a weak monarch and advisory councils packed with loyal elites. Cromer personally controlled Egypt's foreign policy, armed forces, and finances. From exile in 1884, Afghani and Abduh mocked Britain's claim to bring good government to Egypt, pointing to the turmoil the British had caused in Ireland and India. "Two years ago the English entered Egypt," they wrote, in a magazine they founded in Paris. "Blessed with English justice and improved by British administration, she is now, too, a land of discord. . . . Thousands of citizens have been tried in court and thrown out of their jobs in government."[44]

Abduh returned to become mufti of Egypt in the 1890s. Like other elites, he had by then lost his zeal for revolution. He preached that Egyptians needed much education and a deep spiritual revival before they could handle political independence.[45]

However, the 1881–82 revolution had planted the seeds of mass politics in Egypt. Workers continued to organize. They joined elites in a mass revolt against British rule in 1919, under the slogan "Egypt for the Egyptians!" But they won only partial independence.[46] Urabi was revived as a national hero in Egypt's 1952 revolution, which finally toppled the monarchy, ousted the British, and established a republic.[47]

The Iranian Constitutional Revolution of 1906–11

In Iran, constitutionalists also rebelled against a monarch under the financial yoke of foreigners. The Qajar dynasty had ruled Iran since 1785, but with only limited power over the landed aristocracy in the provinces beyond Tehran. Unable to collect taxes as Egyptian and Ottoman monarchs did, Qajar shahs resorted to selling monopolies to foreign companies to cover their palace finances.

In the quarter century after the Ottomans and Egyptians adopted constitutions, many Iranians also embraced constitutionalism as an ideal. They too consciously adapted universal principles to local practices, especially the model of the Circle of Justice. Bureaucrats, clerics, intellectuals, and workers united in 1906–1907 to wrest power from the shah. Their National Consultative Assembly briefly replaced the monarchy as the seat of popular justice.[48] As in Egypt, however, royal power was restored when landed elites and religious leaders dropped out of the revolutionary coalition, under pressure from foreign governments.

To a degree unseen in Egypt, however, Iran's revolution split into polarized secular and religious wings, pitting the language of rights and democracy against that of piety and loyalty. For the first three years of the revolution a majority of Iran's top clerics endorsed the constitution.[49] Only later did dissident factions invoke Islam to oppose constitutionalism. Islam was not, in itself, an obstacle to democracy. In these explosive five years, ideas moved quickly and fluidly; clear dichotomies emerged only later.[50]

Protests began in 1905, with the war victory of the small constitutional government of Meiji Japan over Tsarist Russia. Many Iranians argued that Japan was stronger because it had a constitution. The 1905 Russo-Japanese War also sparked revolution by aggravating economic stress. That year saw a bad harvest, and the price of wheat tripled. Revolutionary pamphlets and speeches accused the shah of neglecting his people's plight. Stories circulated of families forced to sell their daughters to pay taxes or buy food.[51] When the Tehran governor publicly beat sugar merchants for high sugar prices, rebels fanned the flames of protest.

Three groups that had previously protested the shah's injustice now revived their alliance: bureaucrat-intellectuals; high-ranking clerics, called mujtahids; and wealthy merchants. These groups had united in 1891 when Naser al-Din Shah (1848–1896) sold rights to the nation's entire tobacco crop to a British firm for his personal profit. They led a nationwide boycott of tobacco that forced the shah to cancel the concession.

The new shah, Mozaffar al-Din (1896–1907), had clearly not learned his father's lessons. He continued to grant foreign concessions. And in 1905 he committed a classic political error: even as he eased police repression, he adopted unpopular economic policies.

Revolutionary leaders knew, in December 1905, that the shah's tariff policy and the Russo-Japanese War—not the sugar merchants— made prices rise. Secret societies sprouted to renew protest. Some were founded by Marxists, especially in the northern city of Tabriz. Other groups were started by liberal intellectuals, merchants, and religious reformers in Tehran, Isfahan, Shiraz, Mashhad, Kerman, and other cities. They found common ground in an alternate model of justice, constitutionalism.[52]

In Tehran, the public face of the constitutional movement at first belonged to two top clerics: Sayyid Mohammad Tabatabai, a liberal known for his honesty and principles; and Sayyid Abdullah Behbahani, more traditional but also a good organizer and speaker. In December 1905, they organized a march against the Tehran governor who ordered the beating of sugar merchants. A general strike brought the capital to a standstill. The movement made three major demands: dismissal of a corrupt Belgian financial advisor, enforcement of Islamic law, and a House of Justice.

The House of Justice *(majles-e-adalat)* was a vaguely defined demand. The term was used for an advisory council convened by shahs earlier in the nineteenth century. As will be seen, the House of Justice quickly took on new meaning, as an elected (not appointed) assembly that did not merely consult with the shah, but promulgated law.

In a much-quoted sermon, Tabatabai reassured the movement that a House of Justice was ordained by Islam. And Islamic justice, he promised, meant equality under the law: "We want justice, we want a majles in which the shah and the beggar are equal before the law. We do not mean a constitution or a republic, we mean a majles, an Islamic [*mashru'a*] house of justice." Tabatabai stressed Islam because the shah's religious advisor condemned the protesters as heretics. In 1905 Iran legal matters were considered by most to be Islamic matters—in contrast to the Ottoman empire, with its tradition of *kanun* or imperial law. That the source of law might be an elected council, not the scripture, was a controversial idea.

Tabatabai did not play into royal clerics' hands, however. He subtly tried to expand his audience's imagination about the kind of government permitted in Islam. He assured them that Islam shares basic principles with other civilizations and argued that Islamic civilization should be open to modern and universal ideals:

> Nowadays the Infidels and foreign nations have established justice: we Muslims have departed from the path of justice. . . . You must study international laws, mathematics, and even foreign languages. . . . Were you informed about history, about the sciences of law, were you knowledgeable, then you would have understood the meaning of monarchy.

Tabatabai was not alone in his cultural openness: the highest religious scholars issued decrees (fatwas) in support of constitutional government. They did so in the confidence that Iranians would not distort or corrupt their own cultural identity. Tabatabai ended his sermon with a vow to fight for justice: "Should they kill me . . . my blood shall water [the tree of] justice."[53]

The shah remained unmoved. Months passed and he did nothing to fulfill his promises of the previous December. In June 1906 his troops killed a protester, who was quickly hailed as a martyr for the revolution.[54] Behbahani and Tabatabai called a second general strike. Rather than face the violence of royal troops, however, on July 15 they led thousands of their followers—some claim 100,000—to take sanctuary in the holy city of Qum. They now demanded not only the dismissal of the premier and elections for an assembly, but also a constitution.[55]

The departure of the mujtahids from Tehran left the political arena open to others. Some 14,000 merchants, students, and artisans took sanctuary in the British embassy's grounds in support of the clerics' demands. One-third of Tehran's workers were said to camp there, erecting one tent for each guild. Merchants provided the food.

As historian Nader Sohrabi has argued, the crowd quickly gained the ear of the populace and the shah. The traditional concept of House of Justice transformed into a constitutional assembly. The term *majles* (assembly) took on the meaning of an elected, representative legislature, not simply a traditional advisory council. The new majles would guard the shah's justice (a nod to the old Circle of Justice model), implement Islamic law, and inaugurate government reforms. The constitutional movement couched this innovation (as Ottoman reformers had done) in the deeply rooted practices of consultation and election in Iranian politics and guilds.[56]

Among those who camped in the 500 tents was Nazem al-Islam Kermani. He was a cofounder of the Secret Society, a revolutionary group linked to Tabatabai. Some historians call lower-ranking religious dissidents like Nazem al-Islam, and radicalized guild leaders, the heroes of the revolution. It was they who pushed the top mujtahids to protest and they who formulated the revolution's constitutional aims. They insisted on a real legislature with real power to appoint a cabinet, to adopt legislation, and to oversee the national budget.[57]

The diary kept by Nazem al-Islam gives an insider's view of motives in the revolution. The camp set up at the British embassy in August 1906, he wrote, was a veritable school for constitutionalism. Each night, by the light of lanterns, revolutionary speakers gave lessons to artisans and shopkeepers. In his view, the campers regarded constitutionalism as consonant with Islamic principles, not as an opponent of Islam.[58] The memoir demonstrates how pious people played a critical role in the revolution and that many religious leaders were willing to accept a secular government.

Nazem al-Islam was born in 1864 in Kirman, a southern city known for carpet making and for openness to religious reform. He traveled to Tehran at age twenty-seven to study philosophy and joined the Secret Society, a group of self-styled "freedom seekers." He became friends with Sadiq Tabatabai, the son of Sayyid Mohammad Tabatabai. Sadiq invited him to work as director of his "modern" Islam school. The name "Nazem al-Islam" means "director of the Islam [school]."

In his diary, Nazem al-Islam wrote that the Qajar state was hopelessly corrupt and despotic and that it was necessary to destroy it. The Secret Society believed that a constitution would impose rule of law and discipline corrupt officials.[59] It also argued that constitutional government would collect taxes fairly, build schools, and reorganize government bureaucracy as a meritocracy. In short, a constitution would bring progress. Like Tabatabai and Afghani, Nazem al-Islam believed that absolute monarchy caused social backwardness, making Iran fall behind Russia, India, and Japan.[60]

The Secret Society practiced the egalitarian democracy that it preached: while members took a vow on the Quran to respect the *ulama* and protect the group's secrecy, its membership was open to all Iranians, regardless of religion. It chose no leader, but rather recognized the Twelfth Imam, whom Shiite Muslims believe to be the messiah, as its sole leader. The Secret Society promoted active citizenship in religious terms: it urged members to pressure religious leaders to look after the people's welfare and to educate people to defend their fatherland. It also inspired members with religious stories about heroes who sacrificed for freedom.

Historian Mangol Bayat suggests that the Secret Society's Islamic rhetoric was more strategic than heartfelt: "Fear of *takfir* [being branded heretics] compelled them to enforce the practice of *taqiyya* [disguise] and adopt Islamic rhetoric, constantly referring to the holy texts to prove the validity of their views."[61] That did not necessarily make Nazem al-Islam a hypocrite. He was quite disturbed, for example, when organizers talked about manipulating the crowds with false religious symbols.[62]

Like Lebanese peasants in 1858, Iranian revolutionaries likely saw no contradiction in a constitutionalism that resonated with religious values and respected the authority of mujtahids. Constitutionalism, in their minds, was an extension of popular practices of justice in guilds and Sufi religious orders. Contrary to the claims of the shah's clerics, they did not apparently view constitutionalism as a foreign idea that would contaminate Islam.

The vernacular language used by the Secret Society had strategic value as well. It helped to unite the many different communities. Revolutionary committees expressed the belief that justice based on rights and representation was the truest message of the Quran and the Prophet. That solidarity of faith made the revolution possible.[63]

By the time he pitched his tent in August 1906, Nazem al-Islam had prepared to challenge political authority. He believed that change must come from the people: "Justice and national sovereignty must come about through and for the sake of the poor and oppressed people." "The foundation of a constitution, or a republic, or a house of justice, cannot be solid if brought about by the elite."[64]

In the fall of 1906, Mozaffar al-Din Shah finally permitted elections for a "national consultative assembly."[65] A quarter of the deputies elected were guild members, 15 percent were merchants, and 20 percent were clerics, including Tabatabai and Behbahani. For two months, the deputies debated and agreed upon a new constitution, which they called the Fundamental Law. On December 30, 1906, the shah signed it. A few days later, he died.

Iran's 1906 constitution, with 1907 amendments, established a more robust parliamentary regime than Egypt's. Articles 26 and 35 established that the powers of government "derive from the nation" and that the "monarchy is a trust given by the nation."[66] The shah could take no loans and sign no treaties without assembly approval. And ministers were responsible to the assembly, whose sessions were made public. The constitution also promised Iranians equality under the law, as wells as freedoms of speech and assembly. The assembly immediately used its new powers to block a new Russian loan and to plan a national bank.[67]

Some amendments to the constitution drew heated controversy. Conservative clerics—including Tehran's top mujtahid, Shaykh Fazullah Nuri—battled against compulsory schooling, a free press, and equal rights for all males, including non-Muslims. In the end they accepted these in exchange for the establishment of a clerical council to vet all laws for compliance with Islam. Nuri would serve along with Behbahani, Tabatabai, and two others. In the end, the clerical council never actually convened.[68]

Iranian citizens gather in a square in Tehran to celebrate the inauguration of a new parliament in 1910.
(*Ressimli Kitab*, June 1910)

Nazem al-Islam's diary entries from 1907 stress the importance of the assembly as representative of the entire Iranian nation and as guardian of its sovereignty. Now that the assembly's approval was required on contracts with foreigners, he noted, the shah could not violate national sovereignty at will.[69] The assembly also challenged the shah's role, in the old Circle of Justice, as guarantor of justice. It adopted "Adl-i Mozaffar" ("Justice Victorious") at its official emblem.

An early litmus test of the revolution was the much-publicized case of girls sold into slavery in 1905 because their family needed to pay high taxes to the governor of Khurasan, even in a time of drought. The girls' families petitioned the assembly to restore justice undone by the old regime. The public demanded equality of rich and poor under the law. "Until recently, it was impossible for a poor, weak man to confront an autocratic ruler or notable person," wrote a preacher about the governor's trial. "We lived and saw with our own eyes that [the governor of Khurasan is] equal with two poor Quchani peasant men and the Minister of Justice does not discriminate between them at all."[70]

(Secretly, however, officials worked to divert blame from the governor onto lower officials.)

Meanwhile, revolutionary societies and committees mushroomed across Iran. Hundreds of them were deputized as the administrative arm of the revolution. Many of them ran on the same system of personal clienteles that operated in Tehran. They used sit-ins, petitions, and general strikes to pressure local officials to adhere to the rule of law, to collect taxes fairly, and to uphold the authority of the assembly.

However, conflict flared in December 1907 when Nuri broke his promise to Behbahani and Tabatabai that he would accept the assembly. He staged a demonstration with chants like "We want the Qur'an, not the Constitution!" Nuri joined forces with Mozaffar al-Din Shah's son and successor, Muhammad Ali Shah (1907–1909), who despised the constitution and assembly. But when the shah tried to stage a coup by storming the assembly, 4,000 constitutionalists barricaded the building.[71] And the Society of Guilds staged a general strike that overwhelmed Nuri's demonstration. The shah aborted the coup when the top clerics of Shiism, based in the holy city of Najaf (Iraq), issued decrees supporting the constitution as a bulwark against tyranny.[72]

The shah staged a second coup in June 1908, when he sent troops to occupy Tehran. He ordered the assembly building bombed when deputies refused to grant him the powers of the German emperor, including full control over the military. More than 200 people were killed. The siege launched a civil war.

For the next year, the center of the revolution moved to the northern city of Tabriz. It survived in the provinces through its grassroots networks and committees. With support of Bakhtiari tribal leaders and radical fighters from Tabriz, the revolutionaries retook Tehran and restored constitutional government in July 1909. A revolutionary tribunal deposed Muhammad Ali Shah and replaced him with his twelve-year-old son, Ahmad. The tribunal also charged Nuri with the murder of four constitutionalists and ordered him hanged in a square opposite the assembly building.[73]

The execution of Nuri met wide approval, but it alarmed clerics, including Behbahani and Tabatabai. Sensing a threat to religious authority, Behbahani and Tabatabai broke with the civil war's heroes—the tribal and socialist radicals from Tabriz. Political views polarized and split the revolutionary coalition. It was at this juncture that the idea that Islam opposed democracy gained political traction.

The new Democrat Party, under the leadership of a merchant named Hasan Taqizadeh, abolished the assembly's clerical council, demanding the separation of religion and state. Taqizadeh also called for complete equality of Muslims and non-Muslims. Magazines like *Adalet* (the name means "justice") advocated a social revolution that openly threatened elites: "O you partisans of justice and equality, strive to educate the workers and to build a more just world, so that the rights of all classes . . . are preserved."[74]

Behbahani and Tabatabai joined the opposing Moderate Party, whose members included royalist landowners and tribal chiefs. They now adopted Nuri's methods: they attracted a wide following among artisans and merchants by accusing the Democrats of being atheists.[75] Behbahani even demanded Taqizadeh's expulsion from the assembly.

The shift in political balance is demonstrated by the changing views of Nazem al-Islam and the Secret Society. Nazem al-Islam had gone into hiding when Nuri took control of Tehran in July 1909. He was dismayed at the seeming defeat of the constitutional cause. He blamed the ignorance of the masses, blamed Behbahani for taking bribes and compromising principle, and blamed newspapers for intervening in Islamic affairs.

The Secret Society quietly dropped its earlier socialist and pluralist ideals.[76] It increasingly looked to the early Muslims of the Prophet's era for a model of constitutionalism. And Nazem al-Islam cautioned members that the term constitutionalism *(mashrutiyyat)* was dangerous. They must emphasize its meaning as being similar to *mashruiyyat,* a word that refers to the application of Islamic law and justice.[77] And when conservative clerics criticized the Secret Society's modern schools, it reassured them: "A constitutional government is one which governs according to the principles of the Shari'a (Islamic law)."[78]

Nazem al-Islam also sympathized with a fellow Secret Society member Arshad al-Dowleh, who switched allegiances to the shah because he feared chaos if Democrats overthrew the monarchy. The people no longer want the constitution, Nazem al-Islam wrote, "because of the corruption, chaos and war of factions." We need to educate the people first, he continued. "There is no point to having a constitution in a country full of ignorant people."[79] His reasoning echoed that of Muhammad Abduh, who turned against the Urabi revolution in Egypt.

On July 15, 1910, Behbahani was found murdered in his home. The city was shocked, and the bazaars closed. Democratic leader Taqizadeh fled to Istanbul amidst suspicion that he was linked to the crime. Government troops shot thirty Democrats who protested in defense of Taqizadeh.

Demoralization set the stage for Russia's intervention, which would virtually end the revolution in December 1911. The assembly had hired an American advisor, Morgan Shuster, to reorganize state finances and administration. Shuster cut the palace budget, eliminated the salt tax on the poor, and increased revenues from wealthier citizens. By the fall of 1911, the Democrats used the new revenues to implement compulsory free education and build a secular judiciary. Their ambitions were trimmed, however, when Shuster's tax collectors stepped on Russian prerogatives in northern Iran. With support from the American and British ambassadors, the Russians issued an ultimatum to the assembly: fire Shuster or Russian troops will invade.

In a December 1 vote, the assembly unanimously rejected the Russian ultimatum. Some 50,000 people protested in Tehran streets, proclaiming Iranian sovereignty and rights. In response, the Russian army occupied Tabriz, Rasht, and Khurasan. Constitutionalists stood their ground. A group of women even stormed the assembly building to forbid deputies from backing down.

On December 11, the top clerics of Najaf and Karbala issued a decree calling for holy war (jihad) to defend Muslim sovereignty. Like Winston Churchill, they reasoned that democracy was the least bad form of government. The alternative was the shah's tyranny, which they compared to the despotism of the evil Caliph Yezid, who had slain the Prophet Muhammad's grandson Husayn.[80]

But on December 24, as the Russians stood hours from Tehran, the conservative cabinet violated the constitution to fire Shuster and suspend the assembly. In Tabriz, hundreds of constitutionalists were arrested and killed by Russian troops. Conservative clerics chanted, "We don't want the constitution, we want religion!"[81] Shuster left Iran, and the constitutional revolution effectively ended. Revolutionary committees and newspapers were shut down around the country. Power returned to the palace, which ruled in neglect and violation of the 1906 constitution until the fall of the Qajar dynasty in 1925.

In his 1912 book, *The Strangling of Persia,* Shuster condemned foreign subversion of Iranian democracy:

> With a knowledge of the facts of Persia's downfall, the scales drop from the eyes of the most incredulous and it is clear that she was the helpless victim of the wretched game of cards which a few European powers, with the skill of centuries of practice, still play with weaker nations as the stake, and the lives, honor and progress of whole races as the forfeit.[82]

Shuster correctly predicted the enduring consequences for relations between peoples of the Middle East and of Europe and the United States. Distrust sown in 1911 would be inscribed in the political programs of Iranian constitutionalists for decades to come. As in Egypt, they learned the lesson that the struggle for democracy was a transnational process, determined in part by the actions of distant rulers.

The written constitutions adopted in Istanbul in 1876, Cairo in 1882, and in Tehran in 1906 broke with the old Circle of Justice. Their language of rights and implicit assertion of popular sovereignty refuted the patrimonialism of the sultan, the khedive and the shah.[83] No longer would citizens' welfare depend on the beneficence of the monarch. They claimed justice as a right.

A new model of justice, Islamic constitutionalism, crystallized in Iran in 1906–1907, observes sociologist Said Arjomand. Islamic law acted as a limit on government, but not as the basis of it. "Although it was arrived at in a long process of popular constitutional struggle," Arjomand concluded, the 1906 Iranian constitution "can be considered the most logical outcome of the pledge in the Ottoman Rose Garden Charter of 1839 that the Tanzimat laws would be in accordance with the *sharia.*"[84]

Constitutionalists mobilized popular support around two principles: sovereignty and equality. They promised to strengthen government and to bring all citizens under one law. In 1907 Iran, civil equality was won for non-Muslims in a bargain that gave clerics oversight of legislation. Egypt's revolutionary government at Cairo declared equality for Muslim and non-Muslim, Arab and Turk, in the summer of 1882. And in the Ottoman empire, the 1876 parliament had included a disproportionate number of non-Muslim deputies.

Constitutional government would finally realize the promise of equality made in the 1839 Gulhane decree, Midhat Pasha argued, by fusing the diverse peoples of the empire into one Ottoman citizenry. "Out of this fusion should spring the progressive development of the populations, to whatever nationality and whatever religion they may belong," he wrote in an 1878 article. "It is the only remedy for our ills and the sole means we have of struggling with advantage against enemies at home and abroad."[85]

Enemies at home and abroad, however, cut short the constitutional revolutions. Foreign powers took advantage of the revolutionary moment to invade, annex, and occupy territory in Iran, the Ottoman empire, and Egypt. In short, they punctured the hope that constitutions would strengthen sovereignty. The promise of rule of law was undermined when monarchs resumed power and persecuted constitutionalists. Nor was Gulhane's promise of equality realized. Sultan Abdulhamid reversed Midhat's multiculturalism and promoted the Ottoman empire as an Islamic power. In Egypt and Iran, too, internal enemies of constitutionalism fueled a backlash against non-Muslims. Not only were non-Muslims scolded to keep to their subordinate place, but they were also accused of being proxies of foreign powers and threats to Islam.

As sociologist Charles Kurzman observes, the Great Powers supported the global constitutional wave at the turn of the twentieth century only to the limits of their self-interest. As soon as their interests were placed at risk, they threw support to antidemocratic landowners, soldiers, and kings. Constitutional leaders in the Middle East reacted bitterly to Europe's false promise of universal justice.[86]

The trauma of World War I brought the era of popular constitutionalism to an end. Hopes of knitting together a multicultural Ottoman society through representative government dissolved disastrously into sectarian, ethnic, and nationalist violence in Turkey and Palestine. Britain and France's rejection of Arab constitutional appeals after the war gave rise to a new model of Islamic government that opposed liberalism as a European model of justice.

The sense of injustice, or justice betrayed, has poisoned political relations between Europe and the Middle East ever since. After the Paris peace talks of 1919–1922 authorized British and French occupation of Ottoman Arab lands, constitutionalism lost its hegemonic power. For decades, constitutionalism disappeared as the rallying cry of political coalitions—precisely because it had failed utterly to protect sovereignty.

But while constitutionalism was no longer popularly seen as the means toward justice, it would remain a goal. Constitutional principles had sunk deep roots in Middle Eastern politics. Constitutionalists had forged a vernacular language of rights and representation understood by common citizens. For the remainder of the twentieth century, constitutional principles of elections and representative government, of freedom and equality, would remain at the heart of politics.

II

MOVEMENTS FOR LOCAL AND COLLECTIVE MODELS OF JUSTICE, 1920–1965

4

HALIDE EDIB, TURKEY'S JOAN OF ARC

The Fate of Liberalism after World War I

On the afternoon of May 19, 1919, a small figure of a woman dressed in black climbed a podium in front of Istanbul's city hall. British warplanes buzzed the crowd from above; black draperies shrouded the stage. Halide Edib, age thirty-five, looked out at the 50,000 people before her. She saw black veils, white turbans, red fezzes, a few hats, and the flowered headscarves of ordinary women. With a deep breath, she began, "Brothers, sisters, countrymen, Moslems: When the night is darkest and seems eternal, the light of dawn is nearest."[1]

The Ottoman empire had surrendered to the Allies six months before, and its future was bleak. Just four days ago, the Greek army had landed at Izmir, the empire's second city. Meanwhile in Paris, the victorious Allies were meeting to divide the empire among themselves, as spoils of war and as punishment for the mass extermination of Armenians. The word "genocide" had not yet been coined, but the trials of Ottoman leaders for war crimes were under way.[2] Eager to save his throne, Sultan Vahideddin bartered away much of what remained of Ottoman sovereignty.

No one seemed to care that the vast majority of Ottoman Muslims were miserably poor, utterly exhausted, and near starvation. Edib cared. It felt like the French Revolution, she recalled as she went up to Yildiz Palace after her speech. The crowd had elected her to present their collective demand: the sultan must protect his people from the greedy contempt of Europeans. Royal officials greeted her coldly. "I found myself wondering if we were repugnant to them in the same way that the French crowd were to Louis XVI," Edib wrote. "Nothing is so likely to upset a royal palace, with strong hereditary and divine rights, as the assertion of the people's will in some outward demonstration." As she waited in an outer room, Edib thought of the irony of her petition: her own father had been a royal secretary and as a child she had run through these same halls, a pampered client of the monarchy. After a long wait, the sultan sent word: he was too ill to meet the people today.

Edib became the oracle of the coming Turkish revolution, where a nationalist war of independence would oust non-Muslims and enable establishment of a republic in 1923. It was one of many revolutions that followed the carnage of World War I, in which 10 million soldiers and untold millions of civilians died. In the spring of 1919, Germans at Weimar were replacing their monarchy with a republic, Egyptians rebelled against British rule, and Mahatma Gandhi was arrested in an anticolonial protest where British troops killed 379 Indians. On May 4, Chinese university students demonstrated in Tiananmen Square to protest against the imperialist policies of the Paris Peace Conference, which had approved Japan's occupation of China's Shandong province.

Edib's voice—like that of activists around the world—rallied popular masses to defend their rights against European occupation. Much has been written about the harsh terms imposed on Germany after World War I. The consequences of Great Power expansion into the Middle East were just as dire: it sealed the demise of liberal constitutionalism as a popular political movement.

Edib's greatest speech—one of the greatest orations in Middle Eastern history—came days later on May 23 at Sultanahmet, also known as the Blue Mosque. "It was the meeting of the revolution," she recalled. An unprecedented 200,000 people gathered in Istanbul's oldest precinct, filling the vast square between the magnificent seventeenth-century mosque and the sixth-century Hagia Sophia cathedral. Long black flags fluttered from the mosque's tall minarets. Religious men chanted lowly, "God is Great, God is Great. There is no God but God. . . ."

Soldiers with bayonets escorted Edib to the speakers' platform, now draped with a banner reading "Wilson's Twelfth Point." Edib had placed her faith in the American president's promises that every peace-loving nation "be assured justice and fair dealing" and that even small nations have the right to self-determination. Among Wilson's famous Fourteen Points, a list of war aims, the twelfth stated that "the Turkish portions of the present Ottoman Empire should be assured a secure sovereignty."[3]

But now, as British warplanes again swarmed overhead, Edib's internationalist faith wavered. Britain had authorized the Greek invasion at Izmir, even after agreeing to support Wilson's League of Nations. Edib feared that the Allies planned to erase her homeland from the world map. She also feared renewed bloodshed. In a world still riven by racial hatred and national rivalry, there was as yet no neutral world court of appeal.

Edib also feared the anger of her own people. Contrary to Wilson's Twelfth Point, the European Allies viewed Turks as savage and inhuman. Like their German allies, they were deemed unworthy of human rights, deserving only of punishment. The religious chants in the crowd inspired a solution: nationalism can be a moral force, not a destructive one. "Islam, which means peace and the brotherhood of men, is eternal," she recalled thinking as she neared the podium. "Turkey, my wronged and martyred nation, is also lasting. I must also interpret what is best and most vital in her, that which will connect her with what is best in the universal brotherhood of men."

Edib channeled both Wilson's ideals and the "just wrath" of her people into her unforgettable appeal. Her speech began:

> Brethren, sons, and countrymen!
>
> From the tops of the minarets nigh against the heaven, 700 years of glory are watching this new tragedy of Ottoman history. I invoke the souls of our great ancestors who had so often passed in procession through this very square. I raise my head before the just wrath of those invincible hearts. . . . The aggressive policy of the allied powers of Europe has been applied during the last generation in the land of Turkey always unjustly, sometimes even treacherously. . . . At last they have found a pretext, an opportunity to break to pieces the last empire ruled by the crescent [Islam]. And against this decision we have no European power to whom we may appeal.

The crowd fell silent as she spoke. Edib promised them that one day Wilson's League of Nations would provide an international court of justice to assure every nation its rights. But for now, Turks had only the sympathy of other peoples, and their own will to fight:

> Brethren, and sons, listen to me. You have two friends: the Moslems and those civilized peoples who will sooner or later raise their voices for your rights. The former are already with you, and the latter we will win over by the invincible justice of our cause. Governments are our enemies, peoples our friends, and the just revolt of our hearts, our strength.[4]

Edib's name became legend. "Governments are our enemies, peoples our friends" was repeated often in coming weeks and years, as Turks credited her speech with launching the war that saved their country.[5]

Edib's speech uncannily sketched the path of Middle Eastern politics after World War I. First, it signaled the rise of mass politics. After 1918, political power would flow not to dynasties but to activists who inspired the collective action of citizens. Second, the speech signaled the war's threat to liberal ideals. After the war's mass death, many in the Middle East came to believe that justice must be based first on collective security and a strong leader who would defend sovereignty. Constitutionalism, with its emphasis on individual rights, became a secondary goal. Third, Edib's speech encapsulated the growing tensions between piety and politics. She insisted upon a fusion of religious and liberal values. But the cracks in worldview between popular Islamists and secular nationalists would split into a wide gulf after the war.

Liberalism, religion, and nationalism coexisted more easily in theory than in practice. On that day at Sultanahmet, Edib spoke in Turkish to Muslim Turks. Yet almost half of the people in her city were neither Turkish nor Muslim. Even as Edib feared sectarian war, she embraced a world order based on nation-states. Her reasoning was defensive: Turks must protect their homeland from foreign occupation. Edib argued that nationalism be directed inward, to strengthen one's own society. A strong people, she reasoned, would be inclined toward peace, not war. Significantly, Edib made no mention of the non-Muslims in the homeland she now envisioned as Turkish.

Weeks after her Sultanahmet speech, Edib joined the underground nationalist movement to secure Turkish sovereignty over Anatolia. The Turkish War of Independence blocked the return of Armenians and ousted Greeks from Anatolia. In 1923 Turks established the Republic of Turkey, ending the nearly 600-year-old Ottoman dynasty and ending a millennium of Muslim-Christian coexistence.

In the Darwinian world of 1919, the liberal sense of self and tolerant Ottomanism had no place, Edib wrote. "I suddenly ceased to exist as an individual. I worked, wrote, and lived as a unit of that magnificent national madness."[6]

Edib's story, of transformation from liberal individual into a tool of collective survival, dramatizes the fate of liberalism throughout the Middle East after the Great War. Throughout the region, the war broke down the political coalitions that had supported liberal constitutionalism. Edib's later career also suggests why Turkey, uniquely, recouped liberalism as a model of justice later in the twentieth century. Within the cleansed world of the Republic of Turkey, Edib joined liberals to enact the Middle East's first transition to democracy, in 1950. The link between sovereignty and the survival of liberalism was clear.

Edib is unusual among the activists profiled in this book. Known at the time as "Mother of the Turks" and the "Turkish Joan of Arc," she was not in fact the leader of a political organization. She organized women's groups and nationalist clubs, led reforms in education for girls and the poor, volunteered as a war nurse, fought in battles of the Turkish War of Independence, and acted as press secretary for General Mustafa Kemal.

But the pen—not the sword or the podium—was her instrument of political action. She was the muse, the impresario who imagined for her collective readers, her nation, a better future. Her early novels inspired Turkish nationalists during the wars, and a later one about the late Ottoman era, *The Clown and His Daughter*, is still assigned in Turkish classrooms today.

Edib is especially valuable as a lens on the fate of liberalism because of her ambiguous place in Turkish politics. She had gained access to politics because of her elite social status but advanced a populist, democratic vision of Turkey. Her writings express a tortured effort to reconcile her precocious vision of human rights with her "plunge" into nationalism in the decade of 1913–1923. While she fought in the Turkish War of Independence, she chose exile rather than support the authoritarianism of Mustafa Kemal, Turkey's first president. But in exile she remained ambiguously silent about the violent exclusion of pious

Muslims, Christians, and Kurds from the new Turkish nation. Upon her return to Turkish politics in the 1940s, she advocated a more human and pious brand of liberalism, opposed to the state's elitist, secular republicanism. Although she won a parliamentary seat, she was no triumphalist. Her writings, and Turkey's politics today, remain haunted by the dark side of the republic's history: the Darwinian deal made to exclude, deport, and murder fellow citizens in the pursuit of national survival.

REVOLUTIONARY AWAKENING

Edib grew up in the 1890s with the first generation of Turkish girls to attend schools and read women's magazines.[7] Her mother died when she was young, and her father, Edib Bey, was a secretary in Sultan Abdulhamid II's palace. When writing her memoir forty years later, Edib marveled less at her aristocratic household than at the diversity of the cultures that shaped her childhood. The family physician was German, her music teacher was Italian, and her English governess taught her nursery rhymes, Shakespeare's plays, and the novels of George Eliot. Their neighbors were mostly Greek, and Edib's kindergarten teacher also spoke Greek.

In 1899, Edib Bey enrolled Halide as one of the first Turkish Muslims in the American College for Girls. Her first friend was an Armenian who, like Halide, struggled to master English. Halide's closest friend was Bulgarian. "She was to be a doctor and I a violinist, and we would study in Paris."[8] The college promoted Ottomanism as a kind of American melting pot, stressing mutual respect between Muslims and Christians.[9]

Edib devoted much of the first chapters of her 1925 memoir to describing her roots in Turkish, Islamic culture. She studied the Quran, Arabic, and Persian with tutors. From her grandmother, descended from a family of Sufi mystics, she absorbed a folk spirituality. Edib also enjoyed Turkish puppet shows and Islamic folktales. Her favorite figure was the Caliph Ali, the Prophet Muhammad's cousin and son-in-law, because he ruled the Muslim world with compassion and protected children by slaying dragons.

Some Muslim Turkish traditions were unjust, Edib noted. Her father's multiple marriages caused much tension in the home, and Edib condemned polygamy. She was also disturbed to learn that puppet shows portrayed Jews and African slaves as troublemakers and inferior to Turks. At the college she learned that her own skin was considered dark—and therefore inferior. She resented the lighter skinned, blue-eyed girls who were portrayed as heroes in storybooks. The villains shared her brown eyes.

Political dissidents who gathered at her house blamed injustice on Sultan Abdulhamid, who had ruled since 1876 as an absolute monarch, in violation of the constitution. In Edib's young mind, Abdulhamid violated Islamic ideals set by the virtuous Caliph Ali: "The wonderful Islamic democracy, based on the people's choice of great and idealistic leaders, full of humanity and common sense, became an Asiatic despotism of dynasties."[10]

In 1901, upon graduating from the American College for Girls, Edib married her tutor, Salih Zeki Bey, a famous mathematician. He was the one true love of her life. She gave birth to two boys and led the life of a devoted wife and mother. Domestic virtue, however, did not satisfy. Secluded at home on a beautiful island near Istanbul, she suffered bouts of depression.

At breakfast on a summer morning in 1908, Edib's world was turned upside down. Her husband walked in with the newspaper and read aloud a four-line item: the sultan had restored the 1876 constitution. "Consternation overcame us," Edib recalled. For decades, the word "constitution" had been banned from the dictionary. Now here it was, on the front page. Edib rushed to Istanbul to join the celebrations.

"There was a sea of men and women all cockaded in red and white," she wrote. "In three days the whole empire had caught the fever of ecstasy." From the Balkans to Jerusalem, citizens gathered to proclaim a new era of "equality, liberty, justice and fraternity." On Istanbul's streets Edib watched Christian and Muslim, rich and poor, male and female, greet each another in joy. "I was stirred to the depth of my being," she wrote. "It looked like the millennium."[11]

Unknown to Edib, on July 23 a secret revolutionary movement had issued an ultimatum to Abdulhamid. The movement, called the Committee of Union and Progress (CUP), was based in Monastir, home to the Third Army in Macedonia. Junior officers were frustrated that Istanbul refused to send troops to round up lawless bands of Bulgarians, Serbs, and Greeks. They feared that the Great Powers would use disorder in Macedonia as a pretext for invasion—much as Russia had done in 1877. Only representative government, the CUP believed, could preserve the state's sovereignty. In its ultimatum, the CUP declared the constitution restored and threatened to send the Third Army to march on Istanbul if the sultan did not comply.[12]

That fall, joyful crowds paraded election urns through the streets to city hall, where ballots were counted. The CUP won nearly all the seats in parliament. Half of the 288 seats went to Muslim Turks; Arabs took sixty seats; Albanians twenty-seven; Greeks twenty-six; Armenians fourteen; Slavs ten; and Jews four. Parliament opened on December 17, 1908, in the Justice building behind the great Hagia Sofia.[13]

"In the general enthusiasm and rebirth," Edib recalled, "I became a writer."[14] Activists founded hundreds of newspapers and magazines to promote democracy and equality among peoples. Newspapers virtually replaced the sultan's council as the forum to air complaints about injustice. They conducted opinion polls, published letters, and conducted debates on issues of the day. When peasants in Eastern

After the constitution was restored, crowds gathered on December 11, 1908 at the Istanbul post office to escort election urns full of ballots to be counted. (*L'Illustration*, December 19, 1908)

Anatolia complained that a local boss stole their land, for example, the *New Gazette* sent reporters out to investigate. Although they never got the land back, the peasants felt satisfied, the editor noted, because "the oppression of the boss had come before the public eye."[15]

Edib joined the staff of one of the most important papers, *Tanin* (the *Echo*), as a columnist on cultural and social issues. She received hundreds of letters from women. Some even paid her personal visits. They complained of poverty, lack of schools, and husbands who could not find work.

"It was through these visits that I first became aware of the some of the tragic problems of the old social order," she wrote. "The surface of the political revolution was of passing interest, but the undercurrents of life, which started in the social depths of Turkey, drew me irresistibly into its whirlpool."[16] She wrote many columns on the need to educate women, the poor, and the peasants. She also helped to found the Society for the Advancement of Women to train women to fight the old regime that had drafted, jailed, and murdered their men.[17] One of the society's featured speakers was Isabel Fry, a British Quaker, suffragette, and teacher who became Edib's close friend.

Like constitutionalists before her, Edib saw no conflict between her religion and her politics. She understood the Prophet's message of the equality of believers before God as applying to the world of public affairs too. She demonstrated her refusal to accept an opposition between religion and politics by remaining veiled and secluded from men: she never met the editors of *Tanin* in person, at the office.

And so it was a shock in January 1909 when she received a death threat in the mail, warning her to stop writing her *Tanin* column. Islamic activists had begun to campaign against the constitution, secularism, women in public, and equality for non-Muslims. "I did not capitulate before the physical terror," she wrote. "Those who sent me the note were fighting not only the Union and Progress but any form of new thought."[18]

Three months later, in April, assassins attempted to murder the editor of *Tanin*. They sparked a counterrevolution by clergy, religious students, bureaucrats, shopkeepers, and artisans who had had not prospered under the CUP. Much as Shaykh Nuri had done in Tehran, they called for Islamic law, not a secular constitution, as the basis of government.

Edib's name appeared on a hit list, and she fled to Egypt and then England. Meanwhile, the CUP's "Action Army" occupied Istanbul and imposed martial law. The parliament deposed Sultan Abdulhamid and amended the constitution to limit the powers of his successor, Mehmed V. Reshad. Many leaders were executed, and many more CUP opponents were purged from government and the military.[19]

The counterrevolution altered the course of the revolution—in favor of a centralized state and military control, against the grassroots social revolution that Edib favored. Edib blamed foreign powers for undermining the fragile constitutional democracy. Since July 1908 Greece had claimed Crete, Austria had annexed Bosnia, and Bulgaria had announced its independence. The military's hold on power only tightened more in 1910–1911, when Albanians rebelled and Italy invaded Tripoli (Libya). Within the CUP, antiliberal hard-liners took over.[20]

Edib turned to literature as an inspiration for battling injustice. She loved Emile Zola, who wrote about social oppression in France, for his passionate fight for truth.[21] Her stories featured romantic triangles set during the 1908 revolution. Like Zola, Edib envisioned social justice achieved through moral choices made by individual citizens. In her novels *Raik's Mother* and *Seviye Talib*, she imagined the modern Turkish family as a cornerstone of the nation. Loyalty and good parenting became acts of patriotism.[22] Her female protagonists broke through their traditional silence to join the revolution. Indeed, Edib's male characters fell in love with them precisely because they were progressive activists. As one scholar noted, Edib used the men's admiration as "patriarchal camouflage," to highlight women's significance in Ottoman society.[23]

Edib's novels were partly autobiographical. In 1910 her beloved husband Salih Zeki took a second wife. Appalled at the prospect of polygamy she convinced him to divorce her. Her novels were also popular, and read as political interventions. They challenged the CUP's secular elitism with a message that popular Islam (not clerical dogma) can be the fount of revolutionary ideals.[24]

War and Edib's Plunge into Nationalism

Edib took what she called her "plunge" into nationalism after Italy's invasion of Tripoli in September 1911. Istanbul exploded in patriotic anger. Heroic young men shipped to North Africa to defend the terri-tory. In October 1912, the Balkan War broke out. Bulgaria, Greece, Serbia, and Montenegro attacked the empire and won almost all of its European territory. The hometown of many CUP leaders, Salonika, was lost along with Monastir, the birthplace of the 1908 revolution.

In the grim climate of war, Edib wrote the novel that became the Turkish national manifesto. Published in 1912, *The New Turan* imag-ined a reawakening of Turks in a new Asian homeland called Turan, stretching from Istanbul to Mongolia. The story is set in the future 1929, after the CUP has fallen from power. The new Young Turan Party rejects the CUP's authoritarianism and the corruption of the old elite. The plot centers on Kaya (the name means "rock" in Turk-ish), who loves the Young Turan Party leader Oguz. To save Oguz from prison, Kaya marries Hamdi Pasha, the corrupt leader of the ruling Young Ottoman Party. In the end, Oguz is assassinated and Kaya leaves Hamdi to work for the revolution.

The revolutionaries in Edib's *The New Turan* appear more like New England Puritans than French sansculottes. Edib modeled her utopia partly on the Quaker family of her friend Isabel Fry, whom she visited in England. They were a hardworking, egalitarian family who led a simple life devoted to the public good.[25] Women in *The New Turan* have the right to vote and wear long, gray, practical robes. They mix with men at Turkish Hearth meetings to plan projects to improve society.[26]

The New Turan turned Edib into a household name. It was so pop-ular that several cafés adopted the name (*Yeni Turan*, in Turkish).[27] Nationalists proclaimed her the "Mother of the Turks."[28] *The New Turan* also marked Edib's shift away from Ottoman liberalism. The multicultural ideal of Ottomanism was absent from her utopia of *Turan*. Her nationalism emphasized solidarity over individual rights. Women should perform national service, not shriek like suffragettes, she wrote in her articles. Rather than battle men, women should work in solidar-ity with them toward national progress.[29]

Edib joined the Turkish Hearth, a network of nationalist clubs, as its first female member. She was inspired by lectures she heard there by Ziya Gokalp, who argued that Turks would become strong again only if they threw off their Persian and Arabic traditions and returned to the simple virtues of the Steppe. Edib also loved Gokalp's revival of a more muscular folk Turkish, which contrasted with flowery Ottoman Turkish.

Edib embraced nationalism when liberals' failure to build a viable popular party became dramatically clear. In 1912, Ottoman liberals looked as corrupt as the villain Hamdi Pasha in her novel. Edib had once shared the views of liberal leader Prince Sabahaddin, a great-grandson of the Tanzimat's father, Sultan Abdulmecid. Sabahaddin envisioned a federal empire on the model of the United States. He emphasized local autonomy and decentralized government, which appealed to many Armenians, Arabs, and other non-Turks in the empire.

But after the counterrevolution, Sabahaddin and the liberals were marginalized in the hard-line CUP. Sabahaddin allied instead with conservatives in the Liberal Entente Party, which came to power in the summer of 1912, when Edib began writing *The New Turan*. Dominated by palace officials and religious patriarchs, the Liberal Entente was no longer liberal in the democratic sense.[30] "It was a period of utter disillusion. They repeated every single misdeed of their political rivals," Edib recalled.[31]

In January 1913, the CUP staged a coup, effectively ending the constitutional revolution. A segment of the public welcomed the CUP's military dictatorship. Many were horrified that the Second Balkan War had brought enemies to Edirne, a former Ottoman capital just 150 miles away from Istanbul. A Turkish nationalist pamphlet alerted citizens to grim Darwinian truths: "Nature does not have a parliament meeting from time to time and does not adapt its laws according to our weaknesses and wishes. It is autocratic."[32]

Edib came to know the CUP's triumvirate of dictators fairly well. She had already met Jemal Pasha, military commander of Istanbul, who had introduced himself to her as a devoted "New Turanist." She met Talaat Pasha in 1913 and for two years they exchanged holiday visits. And she met Enver Pasha through her family doctor, Adnan Adivar.

In her memoir, Edib admitted that the CUP leaders were politically naïve, with a penchant for tyranny. But she chose to ally with them as a least-worst choice in a time of national collapse. Turks had little room for political maneuver in 1913, she wrote a decade later, still furious at the Bulgarians' massacre of Turks in the Balkan wars. Refugees had streamed into Istanbul, bringing cholera with them. Edib worked as a nurse in a military hospital during that winter of 1912–1913. "The resigned and pathetic patience and the dumb dignity of these men was past belief," she wrote. "I realized then the extent of my affection for my people and for my land."[33]

In the bellicose mood of revenge, and in fear of the empire's imminent demise, the CUP entered World War I the following summer—as an ally of Germany. Britain and France had shunned Ottoman overtures for an alliance, and Ottomans feared that Russia would occupy Istanbul. In the minds of Istanbul's elite, Germany appeared as the best promise for survival.[34]

It was a vain hope. World War I destroyed not only the imperial state, but also much of its population. Early victories at Gallipoli and in Iraq were matched by defeats on the Russian front and at Suez. Lacking industry, the Ottomans suffered severe shortages by 1917. They were forced to surrender in October 1918 when supply routes from Germany were cut and when British and Arab troops took Damascus.

Casualty rates matched those of the trenches in Europe. More than a quarter of the 2.8 million Ottoman conscripts and officers who served died—most from disease and hunger. To these more than 750,000 military dead were added another 750,000 wounded in action. Less than one in three men drafted into the army returned home after 1918. Overall, the war cut the empire in half: by 1918 it retained just 1.3 million square kilometers of territory with just 10 million people. Civilian deaths included about a million Armenians, massacred and starved to death during the expulsions of 1915, and a half-million Arabs, who died of famine and disease due to crop failure, Ottoman requisitions, and the Allies' blockade. Ottoman historians outside of Turkey generally agree that the Armenian deaths were intentional, and constituted genocide.[35]

In the face of the catastrophe, Edib backpedaled on her nationalism. In 1916, she spoke out against the Armenian deportations in a Turkish Hearth lecture. Many in the audience of 700 cheered her, but the CUP leaders were furious. She condemned fanatics for the "exterminations" and distanced herself from Gokalp, Talaat, and Enver. Edib did not, however, break completely with the CUP over the Armenian question. That December, she accepted Jemal Pasha's invitation to Beirut and Damascus, to organize girls' schools and an orphanage for Armenians, Kurds, and Turks.

"When the deportations became general, public opinion was sincerely against the government," she explained later. "[But] every Turk was deeply conscious of Turkey's danger." Edib's memoir reflects the strain of a conscience that is not fully willing to recognize the war crimes and human cost of saving the Turkish nation. Her prose oscillates between languages of national defense and of liberal universalism. Of her stay in Beirut, she writes about Arabs, Armenians, and Kurds as separate nations and lower races to the Turks. And yet she also writes with compassion for all suffering, especially of children.

In the memoir's most tortured passages, Edib appears to justify the Armenian catastrophe. Later, she wrote, she came to understand that her 1916 speech had been naïve and that, in fact, Armenians had rebelled against the Ottoman state. Omitting direct reference to Armenians' mass extermination, she writes of "mutual massacre" and recounts the suffering of Turkish widows, mothers, and soldiers. Edib wrote most bitterly about the Allies' complete disregard for the thousands of Turkish orphans who received no aid. She rejected accusations that she had forcibly converted Armenian orphans to Islam. The children were given Turkish and Muslim names, Edib explained, because the state had opened the orphanage for Muslims only. She and Jemal Pasha bent the rules out of humanitarian concern for the non-Muslim orphans. In a particularly bitter passage, Edib even accused Armenians of kidnapping Turkish children from Muslim homes.[36]

Unlike most Turkish nationalists, however, Edib did not completely erase or excuse the violence of the state toward its citizens: "I have lived in an age when the politicians played with these human hearts as ordinary gamblers with their cards," Edib wrote. "I who had dreamed of a nationalism which will create a happy land of beauty, understanding and love, I have seen nothing but mutual massacre and mutual hatred."[37]

The Ottoman Circle of Justice—already undermined by Tanzimat reforms and Ottomans' peripheralization in the world economy—had finally shattered. This mood led Edib to the podium in May 1919.

EDIB'S ROLE IN FOUNDING THE REPUBLIC

Edib returned to Istanbul before the armistice in October 1918. She rejoined her two sons, enrolled at Robert College, and her new husband, Dr. Adnan Adivar, head of the Red Crescent (a Muslim version of the Red Cross). The city was in turmoil, as Enver, Talaat, and Jemal fled the country and courts-martial against lesser CUP officials opened. Allied soldiers roamed the streets, and Greeks unfurled national flags of Greece. Under cover of the Allies, some Christians dared to taunt the Turks in public. Edib wrote painfully of humiliating episodes on trams and ferryboats.

Istanbul was an inferno, a world turned upside down, a nightmare of injustice. The sultan was a traitor, the Allies were greedy imperialists, and the miserable people were on the brink of revolt. Why should poor, ordinary Turks pay for the crimes of the CUP, Edib wondered. Most appalling to her was the absolute absence of a just and neutral arbiter.

This explains why Edib stood at the podium in May 1919 with a banner reading Wilson's Twelfth Point. The American president had called for a League of Nations that could be the just arbiter that common Turks needed. To Edib, the United States was the sole beacon of justice. "It is admirable that Europe and America sets a value to Christian blood but some first person or power must set a certain value to Turkish and Mohamedan blood as well," she wrote American philanthropist Charles Crane. "All we ask is a little impartiality and wisdom."[38]

She helped to found the Wilson Principles Society and applauded the words of Caleb Gates, president of the American Robert College, to the Paris Peace Conference: "To save the Armenians and Greeks you must save the Turks also."[39] As hope in Paris dimmed, Edib advocated an American mandate as a way to avoid war. But the Americans rejected her appeal.[40]

Justice would be achieved, she decided, only if Turks fight for full sovereignty. Her house soon became "a fountain of revolution." By night, Edib translated Turkish documents into English and sent them to diplomats. By day, she conducted a poster and speech campaign to pressure the sultan's government to hold elections. In September, she organized another mass protest against partition—100,000 attended. "Our effort for a foreign mandate is wrong. The Turks will be the sovereign of their own destiny, and none else," she told an activist after her speech.[41]

Exhausted by the Great War, Turks rallied themselves for another one. Saber-rattling pamphlets presented war as the sole choice. One

Halide Edib gave one of the greatest speeches in modern Middle Eastern history on May 23, 1919, at the first Sultanahmet Square protest against the Greek invasion of the Ottoman empire. She called on Turks to unite in a humane nationalism that respected the peoples of the world but resisted the aggression of governments. The banner below her podium reads "Wilson's Twelfth Point."
(Underwood & Underwood/From Halide Edib, *The Turkish Ordeal* [New York: Century, 1928])

pamphlet entitled "The Extermination of the Turks" predicted that all Turks would be killed if the Allies were permitted to partition Anatolia. Darwinian fear rendered "null and void any consideration of the suffering of the Armenians," according to one historian. By the summer of 1919 a grassroots nationalist movement claimed Anatolia's eastern provinces—emptied of Armenians during the 1915 deportations—as the Turkish homeland.[42]

Edib won some write-in votes in the fall 1919 election, but parliament soon became a sideshow. She joined the underground, called Karakol ("the Guard"), which smuggled weapons and fighters to Anatolia. As a way station, it used the same Sufi monastery in Uskudar (Asian Istanbul) where Edib had hidden in her flight to Egypt in 1909.[43]

In January 1920, Edib's husband Adnan Adivar joined the majority of deputies in parliament in ratifying the Anatolian movement's National Pact. It rejected partition, a mandate, or any accommodation of Christian (Armenian and Greek) claims. The pact vowed to defend the sovereignty of the Ottoman nation, now defined explicitly as Muslim. It was a virtual declaration of war on Ottoman Christians in Anatolia.[44]

Britain reacted by occupying Istanbul on March 15,1920, and arresting many members of parliament. Edib and her husband had escaped the previous night, by way of the Sufi monastery. The war of independence had begun, and it would not end until September 1922, when Turks expelled Greek troops and destroyed Izmir, the heavily Greek city known in ancient times as Smyrna.

Edib's flight to Anatolia was a second political awakening. For the first time in her thirty-six years, she wrote in her memoir, she joined the life of common Turks. She ate dry bread and slept on the filthy mattress of her peasant caretakers. Their simplicity and fortitude, she realized, was the backbone of the new nation. Edib turned her back on cosmopolitan Istanbul: her political mission now focused on the peasants.[45]

Edib arrived at Ankara a heroine. The press rushed to greet her as she stepped down from her train to shake the hand of the nationalist leader, Mustafa Kemal. She became Kemal's press secretary, directing propaganda to recruit peasants for the war.[46] One of her first tasks was to edit Kemal's inaugural speech to the Grand National Assembly in Ankara, on April 23, 1920. "I was beginning to feel that he was going to be our George Washington," she recalled.[47]

Edib was condemned to death as a traitor by the sultan's government in Istanbul. She blamed the British for turning her into a criminal, just because she opposed the partition of her country into pieces. British Prime Minister David Lloyd George was a moving force behind the draft Treaty of Sevres, which offered the Ottomans only a rump state of less than one-third of Anatolia, under heavy Allied oversight. The Americans refused to sign it.

"They [the British] cannot burn me like Jean [sic] d'Arc," Edib wrote defiantly to her American friend, Charles Crane. She asked Crane to take her boys to safety in the United States. "I think that the struggle in Anatolia will be long and terrible for the mere right of existence. The peace offered to us is a masterpiece of greed and civilized brigandage."[48]

Edib's second memoir, *The Turkish Ordeal,* portrayed the Turkish War of Independence as a popular democratic movement. It dramatized the contributions of many leaders and common people to the war. She praised General Kazim Karabekir for his "glorious" Eastern campaign in late 1920, which preempted the Treaty of Sevres' plan for an Armenian state in Eastern Anatolia. Her most passionate chapters describe how she joined the people in the fight. She worked as a battlefront nurse in 1921 and then volunteered as an ordinary soldier in the army. She was present at the crucial Battle of Sakarya, where the Turks defeated the Greek army and turned the tide of war in September 1921. Victory had come at a high and brutal cost and Edib was assigned to document war crimes committed by the retreating Greek army.[49]

The Turkish Ordeal ends with the Turkish army's march into Izmir, the last bastion of the Greeks. The army passed village after village, each one burned and looted. Kemal forced Edib to join the officers in the victory parade entering the city. She was sorry not to walk with the rank and file. "They were far greater and more significant than the passing celebrities in the decorated cars," Edib wrote.[50]

Edib portrayed Kemal as a dictator cut from the same tyrannical cloth as the CUP—a view echoed in a recent biography by a Princeton professor.[51] In an early clash between them, in August 1920, Kemal demanded unquestioning obedience from her. She replied, "I will obey you and do as you wish as long as I believe you are serving the cause." Edib claims that Kemal responded with a threat: "You shall obey me and do as I wish." Later, Kemal would deemphasize the war's popular base and promote himself as the sole savior of Turkey.[52]

Edib returned home to Istanbul in late 1922, by then famous as "Colonel Halide." The old imperial capital was a shadow of its former self. Bureaucrats had moved to Ankara, and, under Kemal's order, thousands of Greeks were expelled from the neighborhoods their families had lived in for centuries. By 1924, 1.2 million Christians from Turkey had been transferred to Greece, in exchange for 400,000 Greek Muslims.[53] Turkish leaders had indeed made their Muslim country from the cinders of the empire.

Edib's fame nearly matched Kemal's. Even the *New York Times* featured her as the Joan of Arc of Turkey.[54] And in April 1923, a movie based on her wartime novel, *The Shirt of Flame,* premiered at

Istanbul's Beyoglu Palace cinema. Lines stretched down the street for tickets. Even Mustafa Kemal attended.[55] *The Shirt of Flame* told the story of Turks' determination through the eyes of a war victim who lost his legs in the victorious Battle of Sakarya. He writes from his hospital bed about how Ayesha, a woman from Izmir, had inspired him to fight for Turkey. Like Edib, Ayesha serves in the war as a field nurse. She falls in love with the noble officer Ihsan. They both turn their backs on the luxuries of life in Istanbul to join the people in their democratic battle to "cleanse our country morally."[56]

But Edib was a heroine without a function. Kemal declined to appoint her as minister of education because he thought the public wouldn't accept it. Edib irritated him by calling for women's suffrage at a press conference in January 1923. She had until then remained distant from the vibrant women's movement, rooted in the late Ottoman era. She drew close for a time, as feminist leader Nezihe Muhittin founded the Women's People's Party that year. However, their petitions for suffrage fell on deaf ears in Ankara, where conservatives held a majority in the national assembly.[57] "Fraternity" in the Republic of Turkey, as in the French Republic, extended citizenship primarily to brothers in arms. This was not to be the utopia of *The New Turan*.

In October 1923, Kemal secured a near-monopoly of power when the national assembly declared the Republic of Turkey and elected him president. The sultanate had already been abolished, and in March 1924 the last Ottoman heir, Abdulmecid II, was stripped of his title as caliph and sent to exile.

Edib turned from feminism to a broad defense of liberalism. She helped to found the Progressive Republican Party (PRP), in opposition to Kemal's Republican People's Party (RPP).[58] The PRP manifesto emphasized civil liberties and state support for public health and education. The PRP argued that dictatorship was a betrayal of the revolution. It demanded separation of executive and legislative powers, the rule of law based on "the principles of justice," and freedom of religious belief.[59]

Kemal quickly crushed the PRP, using the pretext of a Kurdish revolt in Eastern Anatolia to expand martial law in March 1925. The Kurds and the PRP were both accused of mixing religion with politics, now a capital crime. The PRP was officially banned in June.[60] Trials and executions followed.

The liberal cause was dead in Turkey. Kemal deployed his power as a war hero to impose reform from above—much as Mahmud II and the CUP had done. In the next three years, he used one-party rule to remake Turkish society into the modern, educated, and secular nation that Young Turks had dreamt of.[61] Islamic law was banned outright and replaced by the Swiss Civil Code. Fezzes were out; hats were in. Kurdish language and Arabic script were outlawed, and a new Turkish in the Latin alphabet was taught in every school.

Edib, meanwhile, joined the ranks of the populist reformers like Katib Chelebi and Midhat Pasha who battled Turkish authoritarians, and lost.

FROM EXILE TO PARLIAMENT

In March 1925, Edib traveled to Vienna for medical treatment. When she and her husband Adnan Adivar learned that many of their friends had been arrested, they decided to remain in exile. Later that year, she began to write her memoirs in Oxford, England, where her friend Isabel Fry lived. She wrote them in English, to set the historical record straight for the world.[62] What anguish, to have fought so hard and then to lose her country.

In October 1927, President Kemal delivered a famous thirty-six-hour speech to the national assembly. He cast himself as the founder of the independence movement and the PRP as traitors.[63] He specifically condemned Edib for advocating an American mandate. She responded with her second memoir, *The Turkish Ordeal,* to correct Kemal's official history. Her epilogue summoned Turks to the next battle, the "Ordeal of Freedom."[64]

The ordeal of exile forced Edib to regroup. Unable to publish in Turkey, she could no longer play the literary activist. Turkish reviews of her memoirs were negative, dismissing her as a bitter loser. So Edib joined the ranks of the women globetrotters of her era: the aviators Amelia Earhart and Beryl Markham, *Life* photographer Margaret Bourke-White, the literary stars Virginia Woolf and Gertrude Stein. A *New York Times* article compared Edib to Gertrude Bell, the Englishwoman who helped to found the British mandate in Iraq.[65] In New York, Edib published her memoir with the Century Company, run by

Morgan Shuster, the American financier who had written *The Strangling of Persia*.

In 1928, Edib cut her hair in a fashionably short bob and gave the opening address at a prestigious conference on foreign affairs at Williams College in Massachusetts. The Republic of Turkey would educate Turks to assure their prosperity, she told her audience. And Turkey would remain capitalist, as Soviet influence was already on the wane.[66] In 1931 Edib taught a course on modern Turkey at Barnard College in New York and then she moved to Paris, where her husband accepted an academic post. In 1935, she traveled to India, where she met Mahatma Gandhi and gave a series of lectures on Islam, politics, and sectarian conflict.

In November 1938 Kemal died of natural causes. Four months later Edib and her husband returned to Istanbul, ending fourteen years of exile.[67] Edib was by then fifty-five years old, no longer the stylish figure she had once been. She accepted a post at Istanbul University as professor of English literature. Her popular classes on Shakespeare became forums for debate about liberalism and democracy.[68] And as World War II loomed, she wrote newspaper articles for *Aksham (Evening)* condemning fascism and racism.[69]

Edib regained her celebrity in Turkey in 1942, when her novel *The Clown and His Daughter* won the RPP's literary prize. The prize was controversial, because Edib did not follow Kemalist orthodoxy. Set in the era of Edib's childhood, the novel embraced mysticism and spirituality, and the justice of ordinary people in a popular neighborhood of Istanbul.[70] The protagonist is a bold and talented young woman who chants the Quran at mosques. She falls in love with an Italian musician and he converts to Islam in order to wed her. As Hulya Adak observes, the story is an allegory for the way Turks should absorb Western culture into their own—not by imitation but by assimilation. For Edib, the rhythm of true change beat far from the battlefield and the palace.[71]

As World War II ended, Edib returned to politics. Just before her return from exile, Kemal had granted women suffrage, and she intended to use the rights she had lacked in 1923. Her newspaper columns called for free speech and democracy in the universities, women's right to work, and a just peace in Europe and Japan. She also advocated a two-party system and joined leftists to produce a pro-democracy magazine, *Tan* (the *Dawn*).[72]

Retribution from the official RPP party was swift. In December 1945, the *Tan* printing house was attacked by nationalist students while police looked on. Edib was caught inside, as the vandals smashed the presses.[73]

But dissidents within the RPP heard the voice of protest. They called on President Ismet Inonu to cancel undemocratic laws. In the climate of the Cold War, Turkey could not afford to be seen as an antidemocratic country. Inonu hoped to attract some of the American aid that was flowing to Europe under the Marshall Plan. So in July 1947 he legalized the first opposition party in Turkey since the 1920s, the Democrat Party (DP).[74]

Edib continued to call for electoral reforms in her newspaper columns, as the DP slowly built a grassroots network across Anatolia. It appealed to peasants and to small businessmen who had benefited little from the RPP's urban and industrial policies. In February 1950, when the national assembly finally liberalized the electoral law, Edib praised it as a historic return to the democratic path set in 1876 and 1908.[75]

Edib decided to run for an assembly seat. In May 1950, she entered the election as an independent candidate in Izmir, on the DP list. She gave campaign speeches to crowds numbering in the thousands, reminding voters that democracy was the best defense against the spread of communist dictatorship. Newspaper photos show her wearing a headscarf, speaking to audiences that included many women.[76]

On May 14, 1950, Edib won a seat in a landslide victory for the DP. The upset stunned all of Turkey, as the DP claimed 408 seats in parliament, against the RPP's sixty-nine. To the world's further surprise, Inonu accepted the result and turned over power. Turkey was one of the first, and very few countries in the so-called Third World, to achieve such a peaceful democratic transfer of power. The 1950 election was remarkable, too, because it turned out of power a bureaucratic class that had dominated government since the nineteenth century.[77]

Thirty years after her flight from the British, Edib made her second historic trip to Ankara. This time she traveled the whole way in the comfort of a train. Her hair was now gray, gathered in a bun. She wore big owl-like glasses, in the style of Jean-Paul Sartre. Standing at the

The Democrat Party (DP) won an overwhelming majority in parliament in Turkey's 1950s elections, the first democratic transition in the modern Middle East. By rallying peasants and businessmen, the DP turned out of power the bureaucratic elite that had effectively ruled since the late nineteenth century. Pictured above is the DP prime minister, Adnan Menderes, at a 1957 rally in Samsun.
(AP Photo)

podium, Edib looked at her fellow deputies and proclaimed election day a national democratic holiday, like July 4 in the United States. "On May 14, the sun of faith and reason sent a light shaft of democracy into the minds of our noble nation," she said. She then proposed that Turkey liberalize its education system to promote democratic thinking. "Reactionaries, racists, communists are all the same. You can't pick one over the others—they are all viruses in the civilized world and the only vaccine against them is the democratic rule."[78]

Edib exercised her right to free speech to demand amnesty for her old communist friend Nazim Hikmet. She succeeded in gaining his release from prison. She also founded the first Turkish chapter of the international PEN club, to promote freedom for writers. But in 1951 the Democratic parliament passed a law to ban public criticism of Kemal.[79] Edib was forced to excise criticisms about him from the Turkish translation of her memoirs.[80]

Turks enjoyed four years of prosperity and stability after the 1950 election. Civil liberties expanded and rules on religion were relaxed, permitting the call to prayer in Arabic. The national assembly funneled aid to poor farmers. A Turkish scholar noted, "The Democratic Party is the first political party in Turkey which through its origin, activity, and spirit came close to the wishes of the people."[81]

In 1954, however, Edib formally broke with the DP and declined to seek reelection as a deputy. As she neared her seventieth birthday, perhaps she was tired. But she gave another reason in her column, "Farewell to Politics," in *Cumhuriyet* (the *Republic)* newspaper. She accused the Democrats of dictatorship and of betraying the democratic revolution of 1950 with the Ataturk protection law. Thanking the people of Izmir for the privilege of representing them, she concluded, "The voice of the people is the voice of justice."[82]

The farewell was a perfect end to Edib's public career. She had always insisted that she was a writer first, a politician only second. Whenever she entered into politics, her intellectualism confused fellow politicians and alienated citizens, observed her biographer, Ipek Calislar. But through literature, she inspired Turks with a vision of what justice could look like.

After Edib left parliament, the economy soured and the DP deepened its dictatorial methods. She lived to witness the 1960 coup that deposed the DP's president, Adnan Menderes. She opposed his death sentence.

In the early days of 1964, just before her eightieth birthday, Halide Edib Adivar died. Newspapers announced her passing on their front pages. There was no state ceremony, but a funeral service was held at Istanbul University. Ten years later, a women's group raised a bust of her in a park at Sultanahmet, where she had captured Turkish hearts in 1919.

A Turkish poll conducted in the 1940s ranked Edib eighth among the most famous Turks of the twentieth century. She is remembered today primarily as a novelist. Few recall her political career after her return from exile. Indeed, Edib's alternate vision of a fused Islamo-populist democracy was leached out of school lessons, while the state appropriated her stories as Kemalist propaganda. Only now are Turks unpacking Kemal's official history of the republic to discover the continuities between the DP, Edib's PRP of 1924, Midhat Pasha, and the populists of the Ottoman past.[83]

Viewed at full length from 1908 to 1954, however, Edib's career appears as an allegory for the political history of the twentieth-century Middle East. Turkey's 1950 election was a triumph of values first embraced in the 1908 constitutional revolution—and interrupted by World War I. World War I and European imperialism destroyed the political base for liberal constitutionalism. Edib's "plunge" into nationalism abandoned Ottoman pluralism for the solidarity of ethnicity and race, in the Turks' war for survival and sovereignty. Kemal had left in place a republican constitution, which his successor Inonu could revive. The DP mobilized to retake rights lost. Despite Ataturk's break with the Ottoman past, Democrats asserted an essential continuity. Victory in the Turkish War of Independence had assured Turkish sovereignty, and so continuity in the constitutional tradition. In a sense, Edib recouped her role as a liberal voice in Turkish politics in 1950 precisely because she had betrayed her liberalism in the nationalist war.

The cost paid for Turkish sovereignty had been heavy, not just in Turkish lives, but also in the eradication of non-Muslims and non-Turks in Anatolia. The sordid history of death and expulsion cast a shadow over Edib's conscience and it has haunted Middle Eastern politics since then. After 1918, nationalism spread beyond Anatolia in a popular, zero-sum contest for survival. Nationalists supported the expulsion of minorities in the belief that only social engineering could produce unity and stability. As in the nineteenth century, they targeted minorities as a fifth column, disloyal and subversive.

More than ever, sovereignty was viewed as the primary prerequisite for justice and rule of law. Turkey was unique in mustering the military power to push back European troops. Iran continued to live under the shadow of foreign spheres of influence, while the former Arab provinces of the Ottoman empire were largely occupied—under the fig leaf of "mandates" authorized by the League of Nations. The U.S. Senate rejected Wilson's plan, and the league became an instrument of European influence.

Turkey's success in independence made it a regional model. Iranian and Arab politicians admired Ataturk as a leader who built schools and modern factories for his people. By contrast, British and French mandates (in Iraq, Jordan, Palestine, Syria, and Lebanon) were run on a shoestring. Arabs and Iranians also attributed Turkey's success to Kemal's unchallenged leadership. After independence, nationalists in Syria, Iraq, and Egypt would build one-party states that imposed social reforms from above. Kemal's dictatorship became an ideal of antiliberalism in the Middle East.

Others saw Turkey's success in its populism and republicanism. They mobilized mass movements around promises of cultural revival. Attempts at a democratic transition like that of Turkey in 1950 were hampered, however, by the legacies of colonial rule. Whereas Turks had little or no aristocracy, the British and French ruled in the Arab mandates by expanding an elite of landowners, religious patriarchs, and tribal chiefs who profited from foreign rule—and who opposed democracy. It was this colonial difference, more than a difference in culture, that accounted for Arabs' inability to mimic Turkey's success in recouping the liberal constitutionalism that had incinerated in the Great War.

In the Arab Middle East, the decades between 1920 and 1960 were a dynamic time of political invention, organization, and rivalry. Popular parties emphasized collective models of justice, to the sacrifice of liberal rights, as the best path to sovereignty and justice. Most powerful were nationalist, Islamist, socialist, and communist movements, although each drew different strength in each country. More surprising than the demise of liberalism perhaps was the persistence of its memory and the endurance of constitutionalism as an ultimate ideal.

5

DAVID BEN-GURION AND MUSA KAZIM IN PALESTINE

Genocide and Justice for the Nation

On September 7, 1915, Ohannes Pasha Kouyoumdjian arrived by train at Aleppo, Syria, and checked into the famous Baron Hotel, a favorite lodging for travelers on the Orient Express. Except for his fez, he might have been taken for a European tourist: aged fifty-seven, he dressed in a fine, long frock coat, pince-nez glasses favored by Woodrow Wilson, and goatee. Fluent in French, Ohannes was governor of Mount Lebanon, and he had just won permission for an official leave from the commander of the Ottoman Fourth Army, Jemal Pasha.

Ohannes was not on vacation. He was in flight for his life. As an Armenian himself, he had grown alarmed at rumors about how Armenians in Eastern Anatolia were being disarmed, starved, forced into labor camps, and deported en masse. Now, the same pattern seemed to take hold in Mount Lebanon. Decrees from Istanbul ordered the disarmament of Christians. Committee of Union and Progress (CUP) officers arrived to accuse Christians of treason, simply for contact with the French before the war. And food became scarce.[1]

Like many Christians on Mount Lebanon, he feared the CUP regime had marked him for expulsion, or extermination. He knew that even some Muslims had begun to fear the same fate. In August, as Armenian refugees arrived with stories of massacres, Jemal hanged prominent Arab Muslim leaders for treason. Arabs began to refer to the CUP leader as "the Butcher."

Ohannes had taken the post of governor of Mount Lebanon in January 1913, the same month that the CUP staged its coup. He had been a true Ottomanist back then. His father was one of the first Armenian bureaucrats to rise in the post-Tanzimat Ottoman bureaucracy. Ohannes himself was elected deputy to the 1908 parliament, in the belief that constitutionalism could knit the empire's peoples together.

In 1913, Mount Lebanon was a promising laboratory of the Ottomanist ideal.[2] Since the 1860 massacres, it had remained fairly peaceful under a special regime where a Christian governor (now Ohannes) ruled in tandem with a democratically elected, intercommunal council, under the oversight of an international board.

In early 1915, however, a new CUP governor at Beirut began pressuring Ohannes to police Christians for subversion. That spring, the harvest failed and a wave of locusts attacked the remaining crop. The ports were blockaded by Britain and France, and the army had requisitioned all supplies for its soldiers at Damascus. Ohannes arranged to have mountain muleteers—descendants of Tanyus Shahin, the rebel leader of 1858—bring grain from Syria to hungry Lebanese villages. But Jemal, the CUP's military governor at Damascus, ordered his troops to fire upon mule trains.

When Jemal's men rigged elections to take control of Mount Lebanon's administrative council, Ohannes decided to resign. He felt physically threatened by Jemal's henchmen, he wrote in his memoir.[3]

Aboard the train to Aleppo, Ohannes and his wife saw tents of Armenian refugees pitched under the hot sun in an isolated valley. Long lines of refugees marched slowly on foot. The couple was relieved to check into their room at the Baron Hotel, a buzzing hive of wartime intrigue much like Rick's Cafe in the movie *Casablanca*. (A year later, Halide Edib would stay at the Baron Hotel on her way to organize orphanages for Jemal Pasha.) Turkish officials and German advisors mixed incongruously with foreigners and Arab Muslims who were being deported to Anatolia. The owners of the Baron Hotel were the Mazloumians, Armenians like Ohannes who had rallied in 1908 to the cause of Ottoman constitutionalism. They got on well with the local Ottoman officers, who often used the hotel for meetings.

Shortly after Ohannes's arrival, an Armenian couple rushed into the lobby, reporting that their relatives were trapped, with other deportees, on a train north of town. Baron Mazloumian ran to the police station and used his contacts to obtain safe-conduct passes. The couple returned an hour later with their relatives. All were in tears, and the wife fainted. "Imagine," she said when she revived, "that in the middle of the horrible, suffocating jumble of railcars, we recognized friends, neighbors whom we had to abandon to their fate."[4]

Quotes like this suggest that guests at the Baron Hotel had lost faith in Ottoman justice. Under the old Circle of Justice, the sultan had long held the sacred duty of protecting his citizens from famine and danger. Now, in the name of saving the state, the CUP killed them. As Ohannes put it: "Previously there had been in Turkey only one tyrant: Abdul-Hamid II. Now, there were three, each more cruel and unscrupulous than the Red Sultan."[5]

Ohannes vowed to travel to Istanbul immediately, where he still had political allies. He feared the British might win the battle at Gallipoli (Mustafa Ali's sixteenth-century hometown), and occupy the capital before he got there. After ten days in Aleppo, Ohannes found a good "old Turk," the inspector of the military depot. He possessed, in Ohannes's view, the Islamic morality that the CUP triumvirate lacked. The old Turk helped Ohannes and his wife find a place on a train. As they left Aleppo station, they saw more refugees marching toward death. "The locomotive sounded a strident cry and we pulled away from the horrible misery," he recalled. "I will always have in my eyes the tragic spectacle of an industrious and prosperous people reduced to the state of nomads, that hideous camp on bare rocks, and that swarm of human beings fighting over a few drops of water in the desert."[6]

Ohannes escaped to Rome and in 1920 penned his memoir as a plea for an Armenian state. The formerly liberal Ottomanist now scorned the entire regime in the same racialist terms that Turkish nationalists used. The Armenians, he concluded in his memoir, are a superior race to the Turks, more energetic, more industrious, and more civilized. The Turks were barbarians, collectively responsible for the crime against his people, planned in Istanbul but implemented by common Turks in the provinces. These facts, he argued, "condemn Turkey as a whole."[7] In outrage, Ohannes embraced nationalism as his new ideal of justice. Primal fear of an omnipotent state's machinery fed the belief that safety lies only in a homogenous state peopled only by one's own kind.

The word "genocide" did not yet exist, but Turks and Armenians of the time used the words "extermination" and "annihilation" to describe the mass deportation and murder of Armenians. Deportation to the Syrian desert was a death march. Those who were not killed or starved en route found themselves in camps deprived of sustenance. No one knew the magnitude of death then, but later evidence suggests that up to 1 million Armenians had died. Virtually no Armenians remained in Eastern Anatolia. Today the Turkish state officially rejects the term "genocide" for what happened to the Armenians. Historians outside of Turkey, however, point to evidence of CUP intent to destroy Armenians as a culture and an ethnic group in Anatolia. Such intent fits the United Nations' definition of genocide.[8]

As a state official, Ohannes likely knew that in late May 1915 the Ottoman cabinet had decreed a Temporary Law of Deportation on Armenians.[9] "Every time I recorded the secret orders given in cipher documents I trembled," recalled Naim Bey, an official at Aleppo, in memoirs delivered in 1918 to missionaries. "A great nation was sentenced to death with its women and babies." One of the messages Naim Bey received, in November 1915, from Talaat Pasha's Ministry of the Interior, made the goal of deportation abundantly clear: "The purpose of sending away Certain People [euphemism for Armenians] is to safeguard the welfare of our fatherland for the future, for wherever they may live they will never abandon their seditious ideas, so we must try to reduce their numbers as much as possible."[10]

What Ohannes could not know is the degree to which ordinary Turks complied with the order. Much historical study remains to be done, but it appears that a significant number of Turks resisted. Before issuing the deportation order, the CUP had been forced to dismiss the parliament in Istanbul, where deputies condemned the brutality and the official appropriation of Armenian property.[11] The CUP also dismissed governors for refusing to obey their orders. Aleppo's governor had even journeyed to Istanbul to petition personally for an end to the deportations. He was forced to resign.[12]

Ohannes was also unaware, in September 1915, that Aleppo had become a major way station for some 200,000 Armenian refugees. Many of the emaciated Armenians he saw on Aleppo's streets had fought their way into the city from camps out in the desert. By the end of 1915, 40,000 Armenian refugees were in the city.[13]

News of the Armenians spread through and beyond Aleppo. Remarkably, the Syrian press skirted censors to report on the deportations. "The newspapers expressed anxiety," writes historian Nora Arissian, that the policy would "transform into Turkish intolerance and fanaticism toward all other peoples of the empire regardless of religion." Public knowledge of the scale of death is suggested by a May 1918 article in a Damascus paper, which quoted a politician as saying the CUP intended "to inflict annihilation on the Armenian population."[14]

Many in the Arab provinces had reason to fear they were next on the list for annihilation. Like the Armenians, Assyrian Christians in Iraq had suffered deportation and roadside massacres. Lebanese were thrown into labor camps. They and Syrian Arabs believed that Jemal denied them food. More than 200,000 died of famine in 1915–1916 brought on by grain shortage, a harsh winter, drought, locusts, the Allied blockade, and Turkish mismanagement.[15] As far south as Jerusalem, officials learned of the massacres and marches by October 1915. Thousands of Armenian refugees soon straggled into the Old City, seeking the safety of relatives.[16]

Nationalism captured collective anxieties of peoples who had lost all sense of security in the rule of law. Once a cultural idea debated in elite salons, nationalism now inspired the first mass movements to enter the Middle Eastern political stage.

Nationalism was not just the lizard-brain reaction to the threat of mass death, but also a strategy. In his effort to gain justice from the Great Powers in Paris, Ohannes adopted the strict nationalist vocabulary of President Woodrow Wilson's principles, that every people, whether large or small, deserved self-determination. Wilson's speeches had been translated and printed in full in Arabic newspapers since 1917. Arabs, like Armenians, Kurds, Turks, Jews, and others, looked to Wilson's arrival at Paris in December 1918 as the promise of justice. Their leaders clamored for visas to attend the peace conference. Like Ohannes, they adopted Wilsonian language in their petitions for independent states.[17]

But the Wilsonian world order—where even small nations would have a state and where conflicts were to be decided without war and without prejudice by a League of Nations—did not yet exist. The years 1918–1922 were a gray zone, when global politics wavered between the black past of Great Power imperialism and the bright prospect of a Wilsonian world ordered by international law. Ohannes made his case to Paris both in the old spirit of minorities seeking Great Power protection and in the new spirit of demanding his nation's rights. Likewise, Maronite Christians in Lebanon petitioned France for a Christian enclave and Zionists won Britain's promise for a Jewish homeland in the 1917 Balfour Declaration. They would both seek to translate promises into international law after the war.

Every "small nation" in the Middle East knew that the competition for national salvation would be decided in London and Paris, where the old politics of Great Power privilege combined in a double helix with the new Wilsonian politics of national rights. The Great Powers announced the winners and the losers in the 1920 Treaty of San Remo, which awarded France a mandate in Syria and Lebanon and Britain mandates in Palestine and Iraq. San Remo fulfilled the wishes of Zionists and Maronites, but it sparked armed revolts in Syria, Lebanon, and Iraq where Faysal and other Arab Muslim leaders demanded the right of self-determination.

The worst losers were the Armenians and the Kurds, who received no state at all. The Kurds were split among emergent states of Turkey, Syria, Iraq, and Iran. Ohannes waited in vain for an answer to his plea. The Armenian state promised in the Treaty of Sevres disappeared as the Turks defeated the Greeks in the battle for Anatolia. Ohannes died, a refugee in Rome, in 1933.

The postwar tensions between right and protection, sovereignty and imperialism, and law and force ran deepest and longest in the British mandate of Palestine. The origins of the Jewish-Arab conflict are found in the political dilemmas bequeathed by World War I. Upon occupying Palestine in 1917, the British played the time-honored role of protective power, rescuing beleaguered and backward peoples from their local tyrants (this time, the Turks). But they also had to formulate policy, under the League of Nations mandate, in the language of national rights, sovereignty, and political participation. Jews and Arabs, too, played the double game of seeking protection and rights.

The "Wilsonian Moment" in Palestine was both the apex of collective existential fear and the nadir of expectations for justice dashed. In the fog of transition between international regimes based on force and on law, San Remo made one thing clear: the rights of Jews to a home in Palestine required the denial of Wilsonian rights of consent to Christian and Muslim Arabs. Conversely, the right of Arab majority rule would negate dreams of Jewish national justice. The conflict undermined liberal constitutionalism as the dominant model of justice in Palestine—and in much of the Arab world. It also plunged Palestine into a nightmare of violence that continues today.

DAVID BEN-GURION AND THE TRIUMPH OF ZIONISM

David Ben-Gurion (1886–1973) was an exile in New York City when, in early November 1917, he received two pieces of astounding news. First, the Bolshevik revolution overthrew the Russian tsarist regime that had oppressed Jews in his hometown of Plonsk (Poland) and throughout the mass ghetto known as the Pale of Settlement. Second, Great Britain declared its support for a Jewish homeland in Palestine, in anticipation of imminent conquest.[18]

These two events exhilarated the Russian-Jewish community in New York. But they split over two strategic choices: should they go home to join Lenin's revolution for a utopian workers' society, or go to Palestine to build a new Jewish society? Members of Poale Zion, the Workers of Zion Party, chose Russia. They invited Ben-Gurion to help establish the party back home.[19]

Ben-Gurion declined their invitation. The choice between socialist justice and national justice was clear to him. By age ten, in the squalor of Plonsk, he had harkened to the name of Theodor Herzl as a new messiah. Herzl's book *The Jewish State* argued that Jews would never see justice in Europe, that they would always be outsiders: marginalized, abused, and persecuted. Justice would come to Jews, Herzl argued, only in their own state where they were a majority. For Ben-Gurion, Eretz Israel (the Land of Israel) would be the only place where Jewish culture, ethics, and life could thrive. In 1901, at age fourteen, Ben-Gurion founded his first Zionist group, to teach Hebrew to Plonk's ghetto children.[20]

Ben-Gurion would become the founder of the state of Israel in 1948, but in 1917 he was a minor activist in a disorganized, scattered, and international Zionist movement. His letters, speeches, articles, and memoirs show how he was driven by a faith in the justice of a national state for Jews and how he unified Zionists around that goal.

Ben-Gurion's decision to emigrate from Poland came in the disappointing wake of the 1905 Russian Revolution. It had raised hopes at first, but ended in a new round of pogroms: state-sponsored mob violence against Jews. While the tsar scapegoated Jews for economic crisis (at the same time that Iran's shah scapegoated sugar merchants), the Russian parliament and press made constant, anti-Semitic attacks on Jews. The violence climaxed in late 1905, when 300 Jews were killed in Odessa by mobs as police stood by.[21]

In response, Ben-Gurion jumped aboard a ship sailing from Odessa to Palestine in 1906. Upon arriving in the port of Jaffa, he received a rude shock: the city was filled with Arabs, not Jews. He left Jaffa immediately for Petah Tikvah, a Jewish agricultural settlement a few miles away.

"Petah Tikvah—Gate of Hope!" he wrote in a 1917 memoir. "The howling of jackals in the vineyards; the braying of donkeys in the stables; the croaking of frogs in the ponds; the scent of blossoming acacia; the murmur of the distant sea . . . everything intoxicated me."[22] There were 1,500 pioneers living at Petah Tikvah in 1906. Suffering bouts of malaria, malnutrition, and backbreaking labor, they had built the farm with only rudimentary tools. Most of the 35,000 pioneers who arrived in Palestine in the second wave of immigration (1904–1914) gave up and left.[23] Ben-Gurion did not. By 1914 he was one of 80,000 Jews living in the Yishuv (Jewish community). Most lived in cities, but 12,000 worked on 650 square miles of farmland bought by Jewish benefactors in Europe.

From his first weeks in Palestine, Ben-Gurion promoted Jewish nationalism. He joined the local Workers of Zion Party and immediately took up battle against Marxists. He opposed party members who spoke in Russian or Yiddish; he permitted only Hebrew. Jewish pioneers, he argued, would ignite a Jewish cultural revival only if they cast off the foreign culture of exile.

In particular, Ben-Gurion battled against Marxist efforts to unite Jewish and Arab workers in class solidarity. He opposed mixing with the Arab population and especially pioneers' use of Arab workers and guards in their settlements. His faction rigged party elections to defeat the Marxists and issued a party manifesto to prepare the land for a Jewish state and a separate Jewish economy. Zionists who bought Arab farmland were now pressured to expel the Arab peasants working on it and to amend the deed so that the land could not be sold back to Arabs.[24]

The 1908 Ottoman Constitutional Revolution brought new challenges. Arab leaders organized efforts to retrieve the land that the Jews had bought. Ben-Gurion dismissed them as ignorant bandits. Zionists had bought the land legally. "This was the first winter after the promulgation of the new Turkish Constitution, and the simple peasants understood it in their own way: henceforth there was to be neither judge nor justice," he wrote.[25]

Ben-Gurion demanded segregation, but he also embraced the 1908 revolution's spirit of Ottoman coexistence. He intended to organize the Hebrew-speaking minority in Palestine as another of the many plural communities of the empire—not unlike the effort of the Maronite Church to make Mount Lebanon a Christian enclave. All Jews in Palestine, Ben-Gurion told workers in Jaffa, should become Ottoman subjects and petition parliament on Jewish interests, as Arabs in Palestine did.

Like Halide Edib, the 1908 revolution inspired Ben-Gurion to become a journalist. He moved to Jerusalem and became an editor of the party newspaper, *Ha-Achdut (Unity)*. His first editorial embraced the Liberal Party's platform against the CUP's centralism. Ben-Gurion argued that the Ottoman empire would be strengthened by uniting the Ottoman peoples into a decentralized federation. He took the pen name "Ben-Gurion" (his birth name was David Gruen), after a Roman-era mayor of Jerusalem who rallied the city during a revolt.

In 1911, Ben-Gurion decided to run for the Ottoman parliament in order to advance Zionism. He learned Turkish, read the CUP's party newspaper, *Tanin* (which Halide Edib wrote for) and enrolled in law school in Istanbul. He even wore a fez. As war loomed, he rallied Jews to support the empire: "Turkey has freed itself from the yoke of tyranny and the domestic enslavement of absolute monarchy, and now frees itself from the chains of exploitation by the Great Powers," he wrote in *Ha-Adchut*.[26] But his efforts largely failed: fewer than 100 Jews took Ottoman citizenship and only forty volunteered for a Jewish brigade.

In the meantime, Ottoman police discovered—from checks drawn on a bank in Tel Aviv (a Jewish twin city of Jaffa founded in 1909)—that Zionists intended to establish their own state within Ottoman territory. Jemal Pasha closed the bank, disarmed the Jews, and ordered all Jewish noncitizens deported on December 17, 1914. In January, Jemal shut down Ben-Gurion's newspaper and arrested him and his friend Yitzhak Ben-Zvi. In Ottoman eyes, Zionism was treason. Jemal ordered them both deported. When Ben-Zvi pleaded for amnesty, Jemal replied: "Poale Zion has no place in this country. You want to establish a Jewish state."[27]

Ben-Gurion's Ottomanism withered. In February 1915, he left the empire for New York with prospects for a Jewish state in Palestine dimmed to near black. Immigration ceased, and the Yishuv shrank from 85,000 Jews to 65,000. Many Jews left by choice, fearing the fate of the Armenians. In late 1915, Jews exiled in Egypt sent a report to New York: "In Van alone, 35,000 were slaughtered at one time. . . . And the piles of bodies are food for crows. In the air the question circulates among those who welcome it and those who fear it: when will our turn arrive?" Ben-Gurion wrote to his father: "Jemal Pasha planned from the outset to destroy the entire Hebrew settlement in Eretz Israel, exactly as they did the Armenians in Armenia."[28]

Undaunted, Ben-Gurion switched sides and toured the United States for recruits to a Jewish brigade in the British army. "A ray of light pierces through the abysmal darkness that shrouds our people at this critical hour," he told a New York audience in September 1915. "The urge for redemption is searing a path for itself in the heart of the nation."

The contradictions in Zionist ideology were revealed in that day's debate. Ben-Gurion reassured socialists in the audience that building a Jewish state in Palestine was an act of self-preservation, not imperialism: "We do not ask for the Land of Israel for the sake of ruling over its Arabs, nor seek a market to sell Jewish goods produced in the Diaspora. It is a Homeland that we seek, where we may cast off the curse of exile, attach ourselves to the soil." However, Ben-Gurion undercut his liberal egalitarianism with racialist condescension. Like the pioneers who settled America, he vowed, we will fight "wild nature and wilder redskins" in Palestine to bring the homeland back to life.[29]

After campaigning in dozens of American cities, Ben-Gurion found only 100 Jews willing to become pioneers. His hopes sank to their lowest in October 1917, when the first reports of the Bolshevik revolution inspired many Jewish activists to return home.

Unknown to Ben-Gurion, a group of Zionists in Britain pursued a higher road to a state. At its center was Chaim Weizmann, a chemist who met the future prime ministers David Lloyd George and Winston Churchill when he invented an acetone process to enable mass production of explosives for artillery shells.[30] "The fortunes of Zionism were transformed by World War I," writes historian David Vital.[31]

Weizmann had already met Arthur Balfour, a naval official and future foreign minister. After many meetings in 1916–1917, he and other Zionists convinced the Cabinet that a Zionist Palestine, detached from the Ottoman empire, would serve Britain well. They argued that Britain's promise of a Jewish home in Palestine would ease political tensions within Europe and aid an Allied war victory. Lloyd George, an evangelical Christian, embraced the religious implication of a Jewish return to the Holy Land. Last-minute objections that Palestine's Muslim population might oppose the idea were dismissed.[32]

On November 2, 1917, Lord Balfour declared Britain's support of Zionism in the form of a letter to the most prominent Jew in England, Lord Rothschild. It read:

> His Majesty's Government view with favour the establishment in Palestine of a national home for the Jewish people, and will use their best endeavours to facilitate the achievement of this object, it being clearly understood that nothing shall be done which may prejudice the civil and religious rights of existing non-Jewish communities in Palestine, or the rights and political status enjoyed by Jews in any other country.[33]

Weizmann called the Balfour Declaration a redemptive act of justice, the "Magna Carta of Jewish liberties."[34]

Overnight, Zionism's fortunes reversed. Jews around the world celebrated with parades and speeches. Many national leaders, including President Wilson, endorsed the declaration as a moral and humanitarian triumph. In New York, Ben-Gurion won notice in the newspapers with a Balfour Declaration celebration at Cooper Union Hall. He convinced the crowd of 2,000 to pledge they would devote their energy to building a national home in Eretz Israel. He launched another fundraising tour and found 1,500 volunteers to depart immediately for Palestine—a huge increase over the 100 pioneers he had recruited in the previous two years.[35]

But a declaration does not a nation make, as Ben-Gurion himself preached. He knew, as the majority of Russian Jews also knew, that nationalism was not a natural political opinion. Most people chose their immediate, personal welfare over building a collective haven of justice. And nationalists faced serious competition from socialists. Ben-Gurion's career from his return to Palestine in 1918 to his rise as leader of the Yishuv in 1934 is a story of intrigue, deception, brilliant opportunism, and commitment. He justly earned the admiration of many for his tireless organizing.

"Great changes are taking place now which will bring us together sooner than I had imagined until recently," he wrote to his wife Paula from Egypt in September 1918. They had met in New York two years earlier and were expecting their first baby when Ben-Gurion joined the Fortieth Batallion of Royal Fusiliers. "The birth of our child is taking place at a happy moment, when our land has been redeemed." They named their new daughter Geula, Hebrew for "redemption."[36]

Soon afterward, Ben-Gurion met the second-most important partner in his life, the labor organizer Berl Katznelson. Katznelson had emigrated in 1909 to Palestine from Belarus and had spent the war on a kibbutz (communal farm). One night in a tent, they drew up a plan to unify the Yishuv by building a common labor organization. It would offer a job to every able immigrant and provide schooling and health care to their families.[37] They also set up a provisional government. Elections were soon held for the future state's legislature.

In February 1919 Ben-Gurion and Katznelson held a landmark conference in Jaffa, where they convinced workers of other parties to join a common labor union called Achdut ha-Avodah (United Labor). Ben-Gurion was elected chairman. "The debate lasted two entire days, and I myself spoke for three hours," he wrote Paula.[38] The Achdut ha-Avodah attracted nearly 5,000 members in its first year. In 1921 it united with remaining independent unions to create a single labor union for all Jewish workers. The Histadrut (general labor federation) built farms, factories, and schools to help settle immigrants. It became the strongest and largest organization in the Yishuv, and Ben-Gurion rose to prominence as its leader. While he admired Lenin as a leader, he preferred a socialism built from the ground up to Soviet-style dictatorship.[39]

By 1932, Ben-Gurion had built the Histadrut as a political base and founded the Mapai (Palestine Workers') Party, which became the most powerful bloc in the Yishuv's elected assembly. "We are today met in a city where all labor, the heaviest as the lightest, is done by only Jewish hands," Ben-Gurion proclaimed to the assembly. "Tel Aviv is a household word not because of its Jewish shops or Jewish banks or Jewish mayor . . . but because, as no other city is, it is a metropolis of Jewish labor." The Histradut, he concluded, proved wrong those who had advocated working with Arabs in mixed labor unions.[40]

Tel Aviv had been built north of Arab Jaffa as a Jewish city after 1909. Its architecture was European and self-consciously modern. It dramatized the fact that Arabs and Zionist Jews lived in "two separate worlds."[41] Most Jewish immigrants settled in strictly Jewish neighborhoods, settlements, and cities, learned Hebrew, and remained ignorant

David Ben-Gurion speaks at the opening of the House of Labor in Jerusalem in 1924. In just five years he had risen to lead the largest Jewish labor federation in Palestine. He would use that power to obtain supreme political power in the Jewish community (Yishuv).
(Central Zionist Archives)

of Arabic and the Arabs who constituted 90 percent of Palestine's population.

Along the way, Ben-Gurion and Katznelson had to defeat important advocates of neighborly coexistence with Muslim and Christian Arabs. Many British officials in London and Palestine, for example, had advocated a mixed, binational society. One of them was Mark Sykes, a Foreign Ministry official involved in preparing the Balfour Declaration. "It was the destiny of the Jews to be closely connected with the Arab revival," Sykes declared in December 1917. "Cooperation and goodwill from the first were necessary or ultimate disaster would overtake both Jew and Arab."[42]

At a June 1919 meeting, Ben-Gurion defeated Zionists who proposed negotiating with Arabs. "We must not build our national home on the ruins of others," Haim Kalvaryski argued at the meeting of the Provincial Council of Palestinian Jews. "I am sure that the agreement with the Arabs could be carried out and that it would be a blessing for us all." Ben-Gurion argued that good relations with Arabs cannot be a precondition for Zionist settlement because the clash of interests could not be bridged: "The question is a national question: we want the land to be ours, and the Arabs want the land to be theirs, as a nation."[43]

At no time in the 1920s did Ben-Gurion seriously engage the Arab majority in Palestine. He advocated separate Jewish and Arab economies because he believed Jews must build their own society in order to revive their culture. He shunned talk of political cooperation because he believed that Jews as minorities would always suffer injustice. By 1925, most Zionist efforts at dialogue with Arabs subsided.

Soon, Palestine's Arab Jews also began socializing, working, and intermarrying with their European coreligionists. The mixed neighborhoods of Jaffa gave way to the separate neighborhoods of Tel Aviv.[44] In building a separate national community, Zionists eroded the Ottomanism that Sephardic Jews, long resident in Palestine, had embraced.[45]

Zionists also challenged the democratic principles that Wilson had proclaimed were the goals of the war. They argued that a higher moral principle was at stake: the restoration of a people threatened in their very survival, suffering the pains and humiliation of diaspora for centuries. The moral mission of Jews, as God's chosen people, would redeem their return and empower Jews to spread justice throughout the world.

Such a case could not be made forthrightly in the Wilsonian world, where every nation claimed equal rights. In Ben-Gurion's mind, more important than dialogue was an alliance with a Great Power that would enable Jews "to stand up to the Arabs."[46] Indirection and the quiet creation of *"faits accomplis"* (facts on the ground) was the necessary strategy, agreed William Ormsby-Gore, a British Zionist and future colonial secretary.[47]

And so Ben-Gurion did not rush to demand a Jewish state. Like Mustafa Kemal Ataturk in Turkey, he wagered that numbers, not law, would secure national sovereignty. He kept public silence about the Arab Question and focused on building a social infrastructure that could absorb as many Jewish immigrants as possible.

In 1933, Ben-Gurion clinched supreme power in the Yishuv, when the Mapai Party won a majority of seats in the Jewish Agency (formerly the Zionist Commission). By then, more than 100,000 Jews had immigrated since 1919, raising the Jewish proportion of Palestine's population from 11 to 17 percent. Ben-Gurion likely had little inkling that the Nazis' rise to power in Germany would double the Jewish population in the next five years. He knew well, however, that Jewish immigration vexed Palestinian Arabs more than any other issue.

The Arabs Respond to Balfour

On November 2, 1918, the Zionist Commission sponsored a parade in Jerusalem to celebrate the first anniversary of the Balfour Declaration. The Ottomans had just signed the armistice, and Britain extended its military rule over the remainder of Palestine and Syria. Jews marched through the streets of Jerusalem, celebrating Balfour's year-old promise. As British authorities feared, there was a scuffle when the parade reached the old city's Jaffa Gate.

The Arab residents of Jerusalem were shocked by the public proclamation of a Jewish state in Palestine. The British had not yet formally notified them of the Balfour Declaration. Military censors had blocked out news so well that the editor of a top Arab newspaper, *Filastin*, learned about the Balfour Declaration only after the Ottoman defeat in late October 1918.[48]

In protest, the city's Arab mayor led a delegation of more than 100 notables to the office of the British military governor, Ronald Storrs. The mayor was Musa Kazim Pasha al-Husayni (1853–1934). He had retired in 1914 from a distinguished career as governor in many Arab districts of the empire. Fluent in Turkish, Arabic, and English, Musa Kazim dressed as Ohannes did, in the trademark fez and long frock coat of the Ottoman ruling class. He was also a leader of one of Jerusalem's most prestigious families. The Husaynis routinely rotated the city's posts with their two rivals, the Khalidis and the Nashashibis.[49]

Despite his age, Musa Kazim became the leader of the Palestinian national movement in the 1920s. His career has been overshadowed in public memory by his nephew, al-Hajj Amin al-Husayni, who rose to power as mufti of Palestine in the late 1920s and 1930s. Musa Kazim's career, however, reveals that political choices made earlier— in the transition from Ottoman to British rule—were much more critical to the future of the Palestinian national movement. The British appointed Musa Kazim mayor shortly after their occupation of the city in December 1917. He helped found the city's first important nationalist group, the Muslim-Christian Association. From 1920–1928, he was the elected president of the Arab Executive and led several national delegations to London. Musa Kazim was, in effect, Ben-Gurion's Arab counterpart in the competition for Palestine.

On the eve of the Great War, Jerusalem was a dynamic and diverse city of about 80,000 people, roughly half Jewish, a quarter Christian, and a quarter Muslim. Half of the city's Jews were European immigrants, half local or Sephardic Jews who socialized within a dominant Arab culture. Jerusalem was the principal city of what the British called Palestine—a province of about 750,000 people living in 800 mountain villages and the booming coastal cities of Jaffa and Haifa. During the war, however, Jerusalem had suffered terribly from food shortages and its population shrank by a third. Most residents welcomed the British arrival with hope that their suffering would end.[50]

Storrs had named Musa Kazim mayor in March 1918, on condition that he not meddle in politics. So Musa Kazim knew he crossed a forbidden line when he entered Storrs's office that November 3, with a petition that expressed the injustice that the Arabs of Jerusalem felt. It began:

We have noticed yesterday a large crowd of Jews carrying banners and overrunning the streets shouting words which hurt the feelings and wound the soul. They pretend with open voice that Palestine, which is the Holy Land of our Fathers and the graveyard of our ancestors, which had been inhabited by the Arabs for long ages who loved it and died in defending it, is now a national home for them.[51]

The petition expressed the same Darwinian fear of collective annihilation that Edib, Ohannes, and Ben-Gurion felt. It also expressed fear that Arabs would be placed under Jewish rule:

We Arabs, Muslim and Christian, have always sympathised profoundly with the persecuted Jews and their misfortunes in other countries as much as we sympathised with the persecuted Armenians and other weaker nations. We hoped for their deliverance and prosperity. But there is a wide difference between this sympathy and the acceptance of such a nation in our country . . . ruling over us and disposing of our affairs.

The sting of injustice lay in the inversion of status, where a "weaker" nation might rule over Arabs. The petition proposed Ottoman pluralism as the proper model of justice, in the familiar post-Tanzimat language of fraternity and equality:

[We] expect that a Power like Great Britain well known for justice and progress will put a stop to the Zionists' cry. Furthermore, it will establish a just ruling for immigration to Palestine by Muslims, Christians and Jews equally, in order that the country may be saved from being lost and the inhabitants from being persecuted. In conclusion, we Muslims and Christians desire to live with our brothers the Jews of Palestine in peace and happiness and with equal rights. Our privileges are theirs, and their duties ours.

The petition was signed by Musa Kazim and more than 100 individuals, along with an array of organizations: the Muslim Benevolent Society, the Arab Club, the Greek Orthodox Benevolent Society, the Muslim Educational Society, the Society of Brotherhood and Chivalry, and the Greek Catholic Society.

The November 3 petition was an impromptu action, but it forecast the nature of Palestinians' response to Zionism and British rule for the next decade. Appeals to Wilsonian principles of national rights and to the Ottoman status quo ante would be repeated in many more petitions. And the list of individuals and groups who signed them would remain long, reflecting the fractured state of Palestinian politics.

Musa Kazim did not leave a memoir, but through his letters and speeches, and the memoirs of those around him, we can begin to understand the injustice he felt, and his decision to remedy it by plunging into four years of negotiation with the British. He acted as though he believed Wilsonian principles might hold. He rejected calls for armed revolt—like those in Turkey, Syria, and Iraq—and seemed to aim to retrieve the Ottoman world before 1914. In negotiations, he kept open the possibility that Jews might settle, as Armenians had, among the Arabs as equal citizens in a plural society that, in his view, was rightly governed by elites from the Arab Muslim majority. Musa Kazim energetically rejected Ben-Gurion's demographic plan to build a separate Jewish society. But he would fail to budge the British. After years of political limbo, in 1931 Musa Kazim finally joined a Gandhi-inspired youth party in boycotting British rule.

Arabs like Musa Kazim were aware of plans to establish a Jewish state long before the 1918 Balfour Day protest. Since 1910, newspapers like *Filastin (Palestine)* of Jaffa and *Al-Karmil* (named for Mount Carmel) of Haifa had alerted readers about land sales to Zionist settlements and the plight of dispossessed peasants. *Al-Karmil* had even published translated extracts of Herzl's book *The Jewish State.*[52]

Arabs in Palestine were not, by and large, nationalists in 1918. They had no nationalist parties. Indeed, after five years of martial law there were few political groups at all. The standard of justice that they evoked was rooted in their experience of the 1908 revolution. Many Arab leaders in Palestine, including the Husayni family, had rallied to the Ottomanist ideal of brotherhood and equality. When war broke out in 1914, Jews and Christians had joined Muslims in patriotic promises to defend the empire. And Christians, Jews, and Muslims sat on the board of the Red Crescent society. The absence of Jews named on the November 1918 petition, however, signaled that the bonds of Ottomanism were loosening.[53]

Arab leaders had also participated in parliamentary elections and embraced constitutionalism as their new norm of justice. Wilson's principle of government by consent was therefore received not as a foreign innovation, but rather as a familiar and accepted principle.

In the wake of the Balfour Day protests, on November 7, the British and French issued the Anglo-French Declaration. It was posted throughout the city of Jerusalem, in the press, and in other towns of Palestine. It began with what sounded like an endorsement of Wilson's call for government by consent:

> The goal envisaged by France and Great Britain . . . is the complete and final liberation of the peoples who have for so long been oppressed by the Turks, and the setting up of national governments and administrations that shall derive their authority from the free exercise of the initiative and choice of the indigenous populations.[54]

The declaration encouraged Palestinian Arabs to battle for Wilsonian rights to self-determination, although it did not promise Palestine independence.

Later in November 1918, Musa Kazim and other city notables established the Muslim-Christian Association (MCA) in Jerusalem. Members included twenty-eight Muslims and ten Christians, drawn from the city's educated elite. The group registered itself as nonpolitical, but in December the British forced Kazim to step down as its leader, because it violated the conditions of his office as mayor.[55] He continued, however, to play an informally active role in the association.

MCA members from fourteen Palestinian cities and towns met in Jerusalem for two weeks between January 27 and February 9, 1919, at the first annual Palestinian Arab Congress. They vowed to persuade the British that the majority rights of Muslim and Christian Arabs should prevail over those of the Jewish minority. They differed on means: younger politicians favored revolt; their elders like Musa Kazim preferred political maneuver. Views also split on whether to seek independence as part of Greater Syria, or separately. Finally, the 1919 Congress agreed on three main resolutions, demanding sovereignty, affirming Palestine's links with Syria, and rejecting the Balfour Declaration: "In accordance with the rule laid down by President Wilson, we consider invalid every promise or treaty made regarding our country."[56]

Perhaps unknown to those attending, Wilson had already endorsed the Jewish homeland in Palestine. Behind closed doors in Paris that same January, Wilson also endorsed mandates on former Arab provinces of the Ottoman empire.

The British consequently rejected the Palestinian Arab Congress's call to send a delegation to Paris. Prince Faysal was permitted to attend, but only as representative of the kingdom of Hedjaz in Arabia, not Syria. In his testimony on February 7, Faysal demanded that Britain and France fulfill their promise of November 1918 to liberate all Arabs. Weizmann presented the Zionist case for a future "commonwealth" for the stateless, Jewish people, once enough immigrants had arrived to attain a majority in Palestine.[57]

Contrary to Wilson's call to end secret treaties, the sessions of the Council of Ten were held largely in private. The fog of transition between the old international regime and the new grew thick. The Great Powers unilaterally decided the fate of nations even as an enthusiastic international public clamored for a new Wilsonian world order.

During the February 1919 hearings, Lord Balfour wrote an urgent note to British prime minister Lloyd George. He acknowledged that his promise of a Jewish homeland violated Wilson's principle of self-determination. And he admitted that the Arab majority in Palestine would reject the homeland, if they were consulted. But, he assured Lloyd George, "Our justification for our policy is that we regard Palestine as being absolutely exceptional, that we consider the question of the Jews outside Palestine as one of world importance, and that we conceive the Jews to have an historic claim to a home in their ancient land; provided that home can be given them without either dispossessing or oppressing the present inhabitants."[58]

Balfour's plea for an exception to emergent international norms was, in Arab eyes, a throwback to the old world order of nineteenth-century Great Power politics—and a betrayal of Wilson's principles. As we have seen earlier, however, the Great Powers had intervened on behalf of minorities in the Ottoman empire out of imperial interest, not humanitarianism. Wilson had aimed to end this Great Power game with the League of Nations. But he, too, viewed the cause of persecuted and stateless Jews in Europe as a sacred exception.

In keeping with the principle of self-determination, however, Wilson sent a fact-finding commission to poll Arabs' views on who should govern them. Forty members of the Jerusalem MCA met the King-Crane Commission in June 1919. They again demanded full independence and rejected Jewish immigration and a Jewish home. The MCA again argued that minority rights must not prevail over the majority.[59] In its final report of August 1919, the King-Crane Commission advised a reconsideration of the Balfour Declaration. Establishing a Jewish state cannot be accomplished "without the gravest trespass upon the civil and religious rights of existing non-Jewish communities in Palestine."[60] The report was shelved, however, by the British and French. The United States lost interest later that fall, when Congress voted to reject American membership in the League of Nations.

After a cold winter of discontent, violence flared in March 1920. The Syrian Congress declared Faysal king of the Syrian Arab Kingdom and unilaterally proclaimed independence. Demonstrations broke out around Palestine. Abandoning all civility, protesters shouted hateful slogans like "Palestine is our land and the Jews, our dogs." Zionists, meanwhile, mourned the death of Josef Trumpledour, a Jewish settler killed in a firefight with Arabs in northern Palestine. Songs and poems praised Jewish martyrs against unnamed and dehumanized Arab marauders.[61]

The next month, Musa Kazim lost his job after a holiday riot ended in the deaths of six Jews and the injury of 200 more. Tens of thousands of Muslims poured into Jerusalem for the religious feast of Nebi Musa (Prophet Moses) on April 4. As mayor, Musa Kazim was called upon to give a speech. From the balcony of city hall, he urged the crowd to fight against Zionism, while his young cousin, al-Hajj Amin al-Husayni (1897–1974) held a picture of Faysal and yelled "This is your king!" Fired up by the speeches, some pilgrims—especially from the southern city of Hebron—began throwing stones at Jewish pedestrians and shops. Violence continued for two more days. As the British declared martial law, the new Jewish defense militia, the Haganah, evacuated 300 Jews from the Old City.[62]

Storrs dismissed Musa Kazim and sent him, briefly, to Acre Prison. He appointed the leader of another leading family, Raghib al-Nashashibi, as mayor. The rivalry between the families deeply divided the Palestinian national movement.

On April 26, just three weeks after the riots, the Great Powers publicized the San Remo resolutions. They formally endorsed the Balfour Declaration and awarded the mandate of Palestine to Britain. France won the mandate for Syria, despite vigorous protest in Damascus. In July 1920 French troops invaded Syria and ousted King Faysal's constitutional monarchy. Palestinian Arabs had lost their chief ally.

San Remo's provisions were officially promulgated as part of the Treaty of Sevres in August 1920. Arabs regarded the treaty as every bit as unjust as Turks did. The mandates, and Balfour Declaration, had become international law in a process that granted them neither the right of representation nor the right of consent.

Musa Kazim still saw hope in Mustafa Kemal's war in Anatolia against the Allies. If the Turks defeated the Greeks, he reasoned, they would block the ratification of the Treaty of Sevres. He also received encouragement from local British officials in Palestine and politicians and journalists in London who opposed the mandate.

Musa Kazim rallied the MCA to the diplomatic fight. In the process, he became a Palestinian nationalist. "This was Musa Kazim's hour of greatness," writes historian Ilan Pappe. A week after Faysal's defeat, he addressed a meeting of activists: "Now, after the recent events in Damascus, we have to effect a complete change in our plans here. Southern Syria no longer exists. We must defend Palestine."

He waxed romantic in his vision of the Palestine nation at the third Palestinian Arab Congress, held in December 1920: "This is the story of Palestine, the land of miracles and the supernatural. . . . And this is the Congress born from the suffering of Palestine."[63] The Congress responded by condemning the Balfour Declaration as a "violation of all laws of God and man."

Musa Kazim decided to pursue negotiations with Britain to prevent the Balfour Declaration from being inserted into the final text of the mandate. Now out of office, he was free to take leadership of the Arab Executive, the governing board elected by the Palestinian Arab Congress.

But the odds were long and the obstacles high. The first high commissioner for Palestine was Herbert Samuel. He was Jewish and he stood by the Balfour Declaration, although he signaled an intention to rule evenhandedly. Less flexibility could be expected from the League of Nations: its first secretary-general was none other than Balfour's former secretary at the Paris Peace Conference, Sir Eric Drummond.

After forty-seven Jews and forty-eight Arabs were killed in May Day violence in Jaffa, the fourth Palestinian Arab Congress voted to send a delegation to London for talks. Musa Kazim spent much of the fall of 1921 and spring of 1922 waiting in painful loneliness in his room at the Cecil Hotel. In November, Weizmann agreed to meet him, under British pressure. Their encounter ended in anger. Meanwhile, Churchill refused to meet the Palestinians, preferring to negotiate through intermediaries and written messages. Musa Kazim demanded a democratic government based on proportional representation for Muslims, Christians, and Jews. Churchill refused, insisting that Jews and Arabs must have equal representation.[64]

Musa Kazim disputed points of policy in long memos that are painfully repetitious to read today. He addressed every issue: limits on Jewish immigration, unfair preferences for Jewish firms in the award of government contracts, the boundaries of Palestine, and the unjust proportion of Jewish representatives in a proposed legislature. He even disputed the need for the mandate, which was theoretically supposed to train Palestinians to rule themselves. The population of Palestine had long practiced local self-government, he argued, and had even sent representatives to parliament in Ottoman times.

On June 17, Musa Kazim closed his final memo to Churchill on a note of despair. Jewish immigrants from around the world, he wrote, "enter Palestine by the might of England against the will of the [Arab] people who are convinced that these have come to strangle them." He foresaw the coming cataclysm:

> Nature does not allow the creation of a spirit of co-operation between two peoples so different, and it is not to be expected that the Arabs would bow to such a great injustice, or that the Zionists would so easily succeed in realising their dreams. The fact is that His Majesty's Government has placed itself in the position of a partisan in Palestine of a certain policy which the Arab cannot accept because it means his extinction sooner or later.

In the end, Churchill issued a report to parliament on July 1, 1922, affirming that the British would uphold the Balfour Declaration and that a Jewish home would be founded in Palestine "as of right and not on sufferance."[65]

Musa Kazim's delegation left London in abject failure and met a storm of protest in Palestine. Against his counsel, the fifth Palestine Arab Congress voted to boycott Samuel's project for a constitutional government because it would give the Jewish minority the same number of legislative seats as the Arab majority. It insisted on proportional representation.[66] Likewise, Musa Kazim rejected Samuel's proposal

for an official Arab Agency: While the Zionist Agency enjoyed autonomy, the Arab Agency would be controlled by the mandate.

Many Palestinian Arabs took a lesson from Mustafa Kemal, that
the power of guns, not law, was the sole means of achieving justice.
After defeating the Greek army in 1922, Kemal forced the Great
Powers to abandon the Treaty of Sevres and recognize the Republic
of Turkey. However, the Treaty of Lausanne made no change in the
language about mandates in the Treaty of Sevres. In September 1923,
Britain finally put the Palestine mandate into force, thereby establishing the Balfour Declaration as international law.[67]

Meanwhile, as Ben-Gurion built the Histadrut, a militant competitor emerged in Ze'ev Jabotinsky's Revisionist Party, modeled in part
on Italian fascists. Jabotinsky did not ignore the Arab problem, but
rather prepared for the coming clash. "The tragedy lies in the fact that
there is a collision here between two truths," he said in 1926, "but our
justice is greater."[68]

Musa Kazim's political horizons dimmed further when Samuel appointed his young cousin, Hajj Amin al-Husayni, as grand mufti of
Palestine and head of the new Supreme Muslim Council. The Council
disbursed significant funds around Palestine for mosques, courts, and
schools. By the late 1920s it appeared to eclipse the influence of Musa
Kazim's Arab Executive. *Al-Karmil* also turned against Musa Kazim.
The net result of negotiation, rather than active revolt, wrote its editor, Najib Nasser, in 1927, had been the arrival of 100,000 Jewish
immigrants, the Jewish purchase of more than one million dunums of
land (about 250,000 acres), and Jewish dominance of commercial
resources.[69]

Musa Kazim quietly worked to mend fences. He achieved an important victory at the seventh Palestinian Arab Congress in June 1928,
when he secured an alliance with his erstwhile archrival Raghib al-
Nashashibi (who had accepted to replace Musa Kazim as mayor in
1920). They began negotiations as a united front with the new high
commissioner, Sir John Chancellor, in early 1929.

However, the young mufti's politicized alarms about the safety of
Islam's holy sites in Jerusalem precipitated a crisis that changed the
course of Palestinian history. On the Jewish fast day for the Temple,
August 15, a group of 300 militant Zionists staged a demonstration
at the ancient Temple's Western Wall, waving Jewish flags and singing

a national anthem.[70] In response, on August 16, the Prophet's Birthday, a crowd of 2,000 Muslims left Friday prayers at the al-Aqsa
mosque, marched to the Western Wall, and beat Jewish worshippers.
The following week, Arabs again marched into the city, this time attacking Jews and burning their shops. The violence spread to the town
of Hebron, south of Jerusalem, where an Arab mob brutally massacred sixty-seven Jews. In all, 133 Jews were killed, mainly by Arabs,
and 116 Arabs died, mainly at the hands of police.

The Western Wall riots put a river of blood between Arabs and Jews.
High Commissioner Chancellor recognized the political implications
of the violence. Calling the Balfour Declaration a "colossal blunder,"
he invited Musa Kazim, the mufti, Raghib al-Nashashibi, and Alfred

Musa Kazim Pasha al-Husayni stands at the far right with the 1930 delegation
to London. For more than a decade he had led negotiations with the British,
demanding Arab sovereignty in Palestine. With him are other prominent
Palestinian nationalist leaders. From left: Raghib al-Nashashibi, Alfred Roch,
and Hajj Amin al-Husayni, the mufti, next to him.
(Library of Congress)

Roch, a Catholic leader, to London in 1930 for a new round of talks about self-government. But the talks led nowhere, and a British proposal to limit Jewish immigration was withdrawn after Zionist complaints. The reversal, the Arab Executive declared, "has destroyed the last vestige of respect every Arab had cherished towards the British Government."[71]

In 1931, ten years after his first trip to London, Musa Kazim formally renounced cooperation with the British. He wrote a fifteen-page letter condemning the Zionist economic policies that Ben-Gurion celebrated in Tel Aviv for creating a separate Jewish society. Zionists caused profound distress to Arab peasants, Mula Kazim wrote, by banning the sale of Jewish land to non-Jews and prohibiting Arab labor on Jewish land. These bans violated Zionists' promise to "develop the homeland common to both into a prosperous community." The Zionists' separate economy, he concluded, is "a policy of injustices, the like of which is not seen in history."[72]

Mula Kazim could also blame the British for the rise of the mufti as an Islamic hero, which undermined Arab unity by alienating Arab Christians. The mufti also opposed Musa Kazim's reconciliation with the Nashashibis. The British had played the families against one another, preempting the growth of a unified political movement.

Musa Kazim drew closer to the new Istiqlal (Independence) Party. In a defiant break with the older generation, the Istiqlal Party demanded immediate independence and Arab unity beyond the borders of Palestine. Taking a cue from Gandhi, it threatened noncooperation with the mandate government unless demands were met. Without the cooperation of Palestinian elites, the party reasoned, British rule in Palestine would collapse.[73]

One of the party's cofounders was Akram Zuayter, a recent graduate of the Najah School of Nablus, famous for its nationalist teaching. As editor of a Jerusalem newspaper, *Mir'at al-Sharq (Mirror of the East)*, Zuayter wrote in the language not just of rights and promises, but also of "brother citizens" and their patriotic duty to their nation, the honorable sacrifices of martyrs, the will of the people, and of revolution *(thawra)*.[74] In 1930, Zuayter attempted to mimic Gandhi's famous Salt March by planning a march across Palestine to discourage land sales to Jews. But the British preempted the plan by arresting him. Zuayter then published three articles advocating a Gandhian program of civil disobedience in Palestine. He later returned to the Najah School to teach students methods of civil disobedience.[75]

In October 1933, the Istiqlal Party and other groups organized demonstrations against the spike in Jewish immigration following Adolf Hitler's rise to power in Germany.[76] In Jaffa and in Haifa, Nablus, Jerusalem, and elsewhere, workers, peasants, even members of Bedouin tribes marched against the eviction of peasants from Jewish land and against high prices and taxes.[77] The demonstrations marked a new phase in Palestinian Arab politics—as the power of a mass movement gathered around a new goal—complete rejection of British colonial rule.

Musa Kazim was by then eighty years old. But on October 27, he accepted the invitation to lead the demonstration in Jaffa. The high commissioner had personally warned Musa Kazim not to march, but the youthful activists were thrilled at his presence. Musa Kazim led the 7,000 demonstrators—including women, workers, and peasants from nearby villages—out of a mosque and through Jaffa's streets toward the government building, where he intended to file a petition. Police blocked the demonstration from crossing the main square, and violence erupted as protestors threw stones. Police fired into the crowd and killed twenty-two demonstrators and bystanders.

Musa Kazim also fell victim: he was brutally beaten to the ground by the sticks of British police. He never fully recovered from his injuries and died in March 1934. He was buried at the al-Aqsa mosque in the Haram al-Sharif, the holiest site in Islam outside of Arabia. With him died the Arab Executive.[78]

Musa Kazim left behind little in political legacy. He had obtained virtually no concessions from the British, nor had he built a strong national movement. He was an antihero, in the eyes of historian Rashid Khalidi, the exemplar of a "failure of leadership." He upheld Palestinian claims with the dignity of a gentleman, Khalidi concedes, but he failed utterly to build a movement that could match Ben-Gurion's Histadrut.[79]

Khalidi and other historians criticize the enduring hold of the "politics of notables" in Palestine during the crucial decade after World War I. Some suggest that if Palestinians had staged an armed revolt in 1921–1922, rather than wait for Musa Kazim's delegation in London, they might have forced Britain to change its policy. The notables dominated politics by virtue of family prestige, not because of their organizing skills. Some had even sold their lands to Jews. Inexplicably, Musa Kazim himself sold land near Jericho to Jews who built a kibbutz.[80]

But the stubborn persistence of Musa Kazim in these years gives pause. He was not a man without principle. He was not simply a Don Quixote, tilting at the windmills of British justice and Wilsonian rights. The problem lay less in personal flaws of old-fashioned nobility than in social conditions. Zionism was rooted in the vigorous political life in Russia in the era of the 1905 Revolution. Zionist leaders were also well schooled in the politics of Whitehall in London and the Quai d'Orsay in Paris. Palestinian Arabs, by contrast, had had little prior freedom to build political movements—just four years between 1908 and 1912. They lived under martial law from 1914 to 1920 and then confronted a civilian high commissioner who would grant little autonomy and little representation and who split the movement with the Supreme Muslim Council.

Prospects for building a mass political movement were also limited because Palestine's Arab society was dominated by illiterate peasants. While the members of the MCA, the Istiqlal Party, and labor unions began organizing urban workers, the gulf in education and class made it difficult to unite city and village. It is questionable that such a society could have produced a viable competitor to the Histadrut by 1934. It is also questionable that armed revolt would have wrought liberation. Postwar revolts around the colonial world failed to do so.

The timing of the conflict also appears to be critical. Zionists challenged Palestinian Arabs at their weakest moment, when they were still traumatized by war and lacked a government of their own. Zionists used the absence of a robust political movement to set the terms of international debate. The effendis or urban notables, they claimed, were recklessly stirring up a controversy. The Arabs, they insisted, benefited from Zionist economic development. The Zionist argument was disproved in 1936–1939, when the Istiqlal Party's general strike sparked the largest peasant revolt in modern Middle Eastern history.

THE POWER OF APOCALYPTIC NATIONALISM

By the time of Musa Kazim's death, the power of apocalyptic nationalism was ascendant. Zero-sum political views had moved from secret memos and boardrooms into the streets. In 1928 the mufti had launched an international campaign to save Muslim holy places in Jerusalem, marking the territory in exclusive religious terms. He did so in response to Zionist propaganda that circulated pictures of the Dome of the Rock with a Star of David hovering over it. Militants on both sides played out the rhetoric in street violence.[81] This was a far cry from the language of coexistence and equality used to protest the Balfour Day demonstration in November 1918.

Polarization was not inevitable, but rather a product of political choices made on all sides, Arab, Jewish, and British. The narrowing of choices was manifest in the ostracism of Judah Magnes, president of Hebrew University in Jerusalem. After the 1929 riots, Magnes revived the idea of Jewish-Arab coexistence in a shared state. In a talk to university students, he called for an "organic law based on justice" that would unite the two communities democratically in a binational state:

> I think we have all of us not been nearly diligent enough in finding ways of living and of working together . . . if we cannot find ways of peace and understanding, if the only way of establishing the Jewish National Home is upon the bayonets of some Empire, our whole enterprise is not worth while.[82]

The university community exploded in protest. Ben-Gurion responded at a labor meeting by publicly condemning the binational idea.[83]

In 1934, Magnes reestablished contact with Ben-Gurion and arranged a disastrous meeting with Awni Abd al-Hadi, cofounder of the Istiqlal Party. Abd al-Hadi argued that Jewish immigration violated the economic rights of Arabs. Ben-Gurion responded that Jews had no choice but to settle without Arab consent, now that the Nazis were in power. Jews might help Arabs achieve a unified state somewhere else in the Arab world, he proposed, if Arabs accepted a Jewish state in both Palestine and Transjordan.[84] Later, Zionists and the British would discuss transferring the Arab population, following the example of the 1923 Greek-Turkish population exchange.[85]

Momentum toward general revolt quickened in 1935. In November, Zuayter organized a one-day national strike against British rule. Roads emptied and shops shut. The silence, Zuayter wrote, was the "screaming voice of the nation" calling on the British to evacuate.[86]

Meanwhile in Haifa, an Azhar-educated preacher named Izz al-Din al-Qassam became a popular leader, calling for justice for the poor.

He organized a guerrilla force, and days after Zuayter's general strike, led it into the hills near Jenin. His goal was to spark a military revolt against British rule. But when a guerrilla shot a Jewish guard, British police flooded the hillside, found Qassam, and killed him.

Qassam's death stunned Palestinian Arabs, who proclaimed him a martyr—much as Trumpledour had become a symbol for Zionist militants. Zuayter condemned calls for armed revolt and joined Istiqlal leaders in channeling anger into a funeral procession and a series of memorials. In January, Abd al-Hadi told an audience of 3,000 in Haifa: "We buried Qassam and, with him, we buried British justice!"[87]

In April 1936, Zuayter and Abd al-Hadi launched a general strike that united merchants, Muslim youth groups, scout troops, and labor unions to protest British rule and to put "an end to Jewish immigration, whose continuation puts in danger the existence of every Arab in the country."[88] For six months, Arab public life in Palestine shut down. Zuayter's delegates toured Palestine, Gandhi-style, to teach methods of civil disobedience.[89] Even the mufti agreed to join the strike's leadership, the Arab Higher Committee. The strike was the most dramatic anticolonial revolt to date. News of it spread to Arabs in colonial North Africa and as far as India.

But events flew out of Zuayter's control. The British responded to violence in Jaffa by demolishing a large section of the old city and arresting dozens of activists. Zuayter spent a year in a prison camp before escaping to exile.[90] When the leaders called off the strike in September, the revolt flared in the countryside.

By 1937 Palestine was engulfed in a full-scale insurgency led by peasants who targeted the British as the primary source of their economic distress. Some attacked Jewish settlements, too. Peasants also displayed resentment of the urban landowning class. In a role reversal, they called on urban Palestinians to doff their fezzes and don the rural headscarf, the black-and-white checked *kufiyyeh*.[91] Musa Kazim's son, Abd al-Qadir al-Husayni, led a guerrilla band and by 1938 commanded the region from Jerusalem south to Hebron. By year's end, however, British troops crushed the revolt. The mufti escaped to exile, others were arrested, and many executed.

The Palestinian Arab revolt came at a high cost. Arabs lost an entire generation of political leadership. Zionists, meanwhile, prospered. As the arrival of German Jews doubled the Jewish population,

Ben-Gurion built the Haganah into a virtual army that aided the British in fighting what Zionists viewed as Arab pogroms. A new ethos of the Jewish fighter now vied with the old model of worker-nationalist. In 1939, Ben-Gurion openly embraced the militants' goal: the violent conquest of Palestine for a Jewish state.[92]

These conditions laid the groundwork for a new round of battles after World War II. In 1945, Zionist militants launched their own revolt against Britain. The British finally decided to withdraw from Palestine in 1947. They turned the mandate over to the new United Nations, which voted to partition Palestine into two states. This set off a civil war between Arabs and Jews. The mufti, crazed by hatred and racism in exile, sowed discord and poisoned world opinion against the cause. By May 1948, the Jews gained an upper hand, with superior weapons and organization. Without a government of their own, hundreds of thousands of Arabs fled from Jaffa, Haffa, and the Jerusalem area.

Ben-Gurion declared independence on May 14, 1948, while standing under a portrait of Theodor Herzl. However, Israel was born in the midst of war, not as the utopian refuge envisioned by Herzl fifty years before. One day later, Arab countries invaded on behalf of the stateless Palestinians. The war lasted until winter. The United Nations did little more than house the more than 700,000 Arab refugees who had emptied the cities of Haifa and Jaffa and 400 villages. Zionists would call their victory in 1948 a miracle. Arabs viewed 1948 as a catastrophe and an injustice.

World War I was the crucible of the enduring Palestine-Israel conflict. Now approaching its 100th year, it is rooted in an injustice, not merely a misfortune. Arab-Jewish relations did not degenerate in a Hobbesian vacuum. They were explicitly arranged under international law by the League of Nations. In its oversight of the Palestine mandate, the league did not act as the transparent and impartial forum for resolving conflict that Wilson had intended it to be.

Britain could not, and did not, keep both halves of Balfour's promise, to establish a homeland *and* to protect civil and religious interests of Arabs. In theory, such a failure may be a mistake; but in the history told here, it was an injustice. Britain and France occupied the Middle East after World War I for imperial goals, in disregard for the welfare of the people. Not only did they refuse to consult Arabs on their preferences for a mandate, they assumed the trust of mandates without the means to govern them. Having depleted their resources in the trenches of the Western Front, Britain and France administered their mandates on a shoestring. The British did not tutor the Palestinian Arabs in self-government; nor did they leave behind a functioning state. Jews fared better than Arabs in Palestine because they could depend on investment and aid from abroad. Their skepticism about Britain's pledge of security revived when Britain closed Palestine's borders just as World War II broke out.

Nor was the problem with the mandates a belated discovery. It was apparent at the outset. Mandates were criticized as fig leafs for war spoils as early as November 1919 by American senators and officials who refused to collaborate with "Old World" imperial aggression.[93] That same year, Judah Magnes and the German-Jewish philosopher Martin Buber condemned the Balfour Declaration. Zionists must shun "imperialism masquerading as humanitarianism," Buber wrote. "Can Jewry be truly liberated so long as Judaism's unswerving demand for justice and truth for *all* nations is shouldered out of the way?"[94]

Britain's failure to uphold the trust of the mandate may have been due to unforeseen consequences. But its pursuit of imperial claims in the face of evidence (as when Churchill refused to meet Musa Kazim's delegation) nonetheless constituted a passive form of injustice. Judith Shklar argues in *The Faces of Injustice* that passive injustice is of graver consequence than an ordinary crime, because it involves the systemic failure "to see that the rules of justice are maintained."[95]

The political effect of Britain's policy tainted at birth the project of establishing universal norms of justice in the Middle East. The effect was worse because the League of Nations had raised expectations of impartial justice, only to thwart them. The United Nations' assumption of the trust of mandate, and imposition of unenforced international law, further compounded the damage.

Historians have long explored the link between the draconian punishment imposed on Germany in 1919 and the later rise of Nazism. They now appreciate that the peace of World War I altered the course of politics in the Middle East as well. The Treaty of Sevres, which partitioned Anatolia, encouraged the revival of the violent exclusionary nationalism of the CUP in Mustafa Kemal's War of Turkish Independence. Likewise in Palestine, the mandate encouraged a brutal nationalism that silenced liberal humanism on both sides.

Nationalism, as a new model of justice, sought redemption for "righteous victims" whose moral duty was simply self-survival. In the game rules set by Balfour, Jews were encouraged to pursue a politics of exceptionalism and separatism. Arabs had no role but to resist. Mandate politics privileged the insular views of the Eastern European Zionists who led the Yishuv. They had little experience in plural societies and little reason to trust the binational vision of Buber and Magnes.[96] To share sovereignty in a diverse society was simply anathema.[97] Arabs, denied equal rights as a nation, were reluctant to opt back into Europe's universalizing project after the war. While liberal Arabs condemned Nazism and the Holocaust, they viewed Jewish suffering not as a crime against humanity, but as a European sin to be atoned for in Europe.[98]

The conflict in Palestine came to epitomize the injustice of European rule over all Arabs. This experience, more than any predisposition of Islamic culture, explains why the cause of liberal constitutionalism stalled in the region after World War I. As we shall see, the destruction of constitutional movements in Syria and Egypt in 1919–1920 led directly to a reformulation of Islamic justice on an explicitly anti-Christian, anti-Jewish, and anti-European basis.

6

HASAN AL-BANNA OF EGYPT
The Muslim Brotherhood's Pursuit of Islamic Justice

On February 12, 1949, a taxi waited on a quiet boulevard in central Cairo, outside of the Young Men's Muslim Association building. Shortly after eight o'clock, a bearded man of medium build, wearing a fez and overcoat, walked down the building's ornate stone staircase. Just as he stepped into the cab, a black car pulled up. Two gunmen jumped out and shot him. The victim was Hasan al-Banna, the forty-two-year-old leader of the largest political movement in Egypt, the Muslim Brotherhood (MB). Banna was rushed to a hospital, where he died that night. The Egyptian government declared a state of emergency and banned all public mourning. Only Banna's immediate family was permitted to walk in the funeral procession, guarded by armored cars and tanks. Privately, across all of Egypt, more than a half-million members of the MB mourned him.

To his followers, Banna was a saintly martyr and Egypt's greatest political leader. The MB had grown, in just twenty years, into a major rival of Egypt's top party, the Wafd Party. Its campaign for Islamic justice had mobilized poor and middle-class Egyptians who lived far from the elites in parliament, from King Farouk's palace, and from the British, who still ruled from their embassy and bases on the Suez Canal. These Egyptians sought access to the political arena that excluded them. They viewed Banna as an honest everyman who battled the corrupt world of Egyptian politics.

Not only the poor and Muslim venerated Banna. One of his greatest public supporters was a Christian politician, Makram Ubayd Pasha, who resented Britain's increased political role in Egypt since World War II. Ubayd Pasha jumped the police line around Banna's home to join his funeral procession. Another supporter was Judge Ahmad Kamil Bey, who in 1951 would dismiss charges of sedition against the MB and then declare that he so admired the organization that he would join it. A third prominent supporter was Anwar Sadat, the future president of Egypt who helped mount the 1952 Revolution that toppled King Farouk and who would sign a peace treaty with Israel twenty-seven years later. "He had a surprising, intuitive grasp of the problems facing Egypt," Sadat wrote of Banna in 1954. "The welfare of Egypt was the thing he cared more about than anything else in the mortal world."[1]

To King Farouk and the British, Banna was a traitor and a terrorist. He had refused the king's invitation to join his party and had mobilized the MB against the British in Palestine. After the Arab defeat in the 1948 war, militants in the MB assassinated Egypt's prime minister in December 1948. To many in the ruling elite, the murder of Banna two months later appeared as just retribution. Even the political opposition—both nationalists and socialists—viewed Banna's murder with a bit of relief. To them, he was a demagogue who deluded the masses with a simplistic vision of Islam. Contrary to the court's judgment, they blamed Banna for the rise in political violence after World War II.

Americans diplomats followed the British and regarded Banna as a dangerous eccentric.[2] The *New York Times* described the MB as an "extremist" political movement with "mystic and fascist overtones" and possible communist support. The *Los Angeles Times* called Banna "an ardent foe of the Jews" who "proposed an Arab government in the Holy Land."[3]

Was justice done on February 12, 1949, or was justice denied? The memory of Banna and his murder remains highly politicized and fiercely debated. Historians in Egypt and beyond have not come to agreement on how much Banna knew about the violent plots of the MB's militant wing. Nor do they agree on Banna's political vision. Some point to his message of equality, freedom, hard work, and aid to the poor as consonant with liberal values. Other scholars read Banna's speeches and pamphlets in an opposing light, as a demagogic program to construct an Islamic state, impose conformity on the people, and wage perpetual war against non-Muslims. One reason for disagreement is political bias; another, however, is the complexity and ambiguity of Banna's own words. As his brother Gamal al-Banna said, "Hasan al-Banna was a genius in organization, but when it came to theory, he was nothing."[4]

Banna must not, and cannot, be judged by searching his writings for his true intentions or for a coherent philosophy of Islamic justice. His memoirs, speeches, and pamphlets reveal a man devoted more to action than to thought. His vision of justice must be understood in the specific contexts in which he wrote and spoke. His views and methods of activism evolved rapidly. In the early 1930s he was a quiet, earnest teacher who took weekend hikes to proselytize in the poorest villages of Egypt. By 1939, he was a national politician with personal ties to the palace and leaders of parliament. In the 1940s, he commanded a greater political following than the Wafd Party, the nationalist opposition party founded by Saad Zaghlul.

Like Halide Edib and other nationalists, Banna turned his back on liberalism as a European model of justice with false claims to universality. He advocated Islam as a distinct and superior model of justice. His Islam was modernist, following Muhammad Abduh and the first generation of Islamic reformers who aided the 1882 Urabi revolution. Like them, Banna regarded Islam as a holistic vision of heavenly and earthly justice, with specific standards of government and social relations. Like them, he argued that the vitality and flexibility of Islamic law would provide the basis for modern, constitutional government.

Banna's career suggests one way that popular movements redefined justice in the wake of liberalism's decline after World War I. The MB was the first and the largest mass Islamic movement in the region. Its history challenges common assumptions about the relationship of Islam to democracy and about the predilection of Islamists for violence. Banna founded the movement with nationalist aims to roll back British imperialism. In the 1930s, he recruited Egypt's modest classes whose suffering during the world depression was ignored by the political elite. He empowered them with a message of cultural pride and spiritual uplift, against an elite that justified its hold on power by its claim to superior knowledge of Europe. Banna did not oppose democracy, but rather, like Zaghlul, opposed the factionalism that paralyzed policymaking in parliament. He accepted Egypt's 1923 constitution, with some revisions.

The MB's political trajectory was defined by the revolutionary violence that spread in Egypt in the 1940s. Banna turned against Zaghlul's Wafd Party because it was corrupt and it collaborated with the British during World War II. King Farouk wanted to harness the MB's popularity for his own benefit, but Banna kept a distance. When Banna tried to run for a parliament seat in the early 1940s, these rivals struck back, with Britain's blessings. They forcefully excluded the MB from the political arena. It was then that the organization aligned with other opposition movements in what became a general revolt against the regime in the late 1940s. While Banna had once restrained militant members who preached revolution, he now permitted militants to join other political groups in a wave of assassinations that crested with the 1948 Palestine war and led to the 1952 revolution by Gamal Abdel Nasser and the Free Officers.

Banna left a powerful dual legacy. By building the first truly mass movement in the Arab world, he profoundly altered the rules of politics. The MB shook the foundations of the elite system built by the British since 1882, demonstrating people power to other opposition groups. And by recasting political and social justice in explicitly Islamic terms, Banna fundamentally altered Egypt's political culture. The elites' liberal model of justice—based on the nineteenth-century belief in Islam's essential agreement with other world civilizations—gave way to views that divided Eastern justice from that of the capitalist and imperialist West. Banna captured the moral outrage of ordinary Egyptians who—decades after Ahmed Urabi—still resented European support of Egypt's landowning elite. The consequences of the political realignment, however, were dire for Egyptian Christians and Jews. Modern Islamism "solved" the problem of equality raised in the Tanzimat era by marginalizing minorities.

FROM DREAMS TO ORGANIZATION

Like Urabi, Banna (1906–1949) grew up in the Nile Delta north of Cairo. His village, Mahmudiya, is perched on a riverbank near the

Mediterranean coast. Sailboat manufacturing was a major industry. Banna's father, the village imam, had studied at al-Azhar with Muhammad Abduh. He also owned a watch repair shop where Banna, as the eldest of seven children, worked every day after school. In that shop, friends said, Banna learned the habits of patience and precision that would enable him to build the MB, step by careful step.[5]

Banna was just twelve in March 1919, when Egypt exploded into the largest protests since the 1882 Urabi revolution. Nationalist leader Zaghlul organized a delegation, or *wafd,* to attend the Paris Peace Conference and demand independence. But the British refused to let Zaghlul attend, just as they had denied Palestinian Arabs. Egyptians waged massive protests when the British arrested Zaghlul and exiled him to Malta. Peasants and workers, Christians and Muslims, even women joined demonstrations for his release. Peasants, impoverished during the war, cut railroad lines to Cairo, isolating the capital for weeks. The British freed Zaghlul in April, only after securing Great Power support for a continued British protectorate over Egypt. More than 800 Egyptians were killed, along with thirty-one Europeans and twenty-nine British soldiers, in protests that lasted through the summer.[6]

The 1919 revolution was a formative moment for Banna. "I still remember the scenes of the demonstrations, strikes and processions," he wrote in his memoirs. Even as British soldiers chased citizens and beat them, nationalists led the crowds in patriotic songs with words like "Love for the homeland is a duty of our faith. It is the call of the Angel of Allah! If we fail to gather in Independence, then we shall surely meet in Paradise!"[7]

Banna wrote his memoirs in the 1940s, so they cannot be read like a diary, reflecting his actual feelings as a boy.[8] But because the memoirs were serialized in the MB press to provide a model for followers, they offer insight into how Banna translated his experience into a message for recruits. His recollection of 1919 showed how the MB integrated national patriotism with love for Islam and the Muslim community *(umma).*

Banna opened his memoirs by describing his first teacher, Shaykh Muhammad Zahran, as a model for the kind of leader that Banna wanted to be. "He kept a very strict watch on his students without making them feel that they were being watched. He always extended his moral support to their good deeds. He rewarded them for their good actions and punished them for their wrong acts."[9] Banna also introduced to readers his Sufi shaykh as a model teacher. As a boy, he perched alongside grown men at the feet of the holy shaykh who taught them physical and spiritual discipline. He enjoyed the camaraderie of other boys and the gentle mentorship of elders as they gathered on the carpets of the small mosque in Mahmudiya. They spent hours in silent prayer, study and discussion. Banna was known for his love of reading and his prodigious memory. By age thirteen, he had memorized the Quran.

Banna had an activist vision of his religious mission. Like Edib, as a child he loved stories of Islamic heroes. He organized games with playmates reenacting battles of Saladin against tyrants who had usurped the rights of believers. The 1919 revolution was just such a battle, against British usurpers. "It was my belief that this was *jihad* [holy war] and that there was no exception for a Muslim," he wrote. "I was obliged to take a leading part in the National Movement."[10]

In April 1923, Banna took an oath of allegiance to the Hasafi Sufi order, a local spiritual group founded upon the strictly orthodox teachings of Hasanayn al-Hasafi. With his best boyhood friend, Ahmad Sukkari, he founded the Hasafi Charitable Society. It aimed to "build the moral character of the people and to eradicate social evil," he recalled, and especially to "check the growing activities of the Christian Biblical Mission."

Banna portrayed his utopian village community, a haven of peace, happiness, and brotherhood, as threatened by the invasion of American missionaries. They had settled in the Nile Delta after World War I, and Banna feared their girls' school and orphanage would disrupt the harmony of his village. "They were preaching Christianity in the guise of teaching embroidery work and providing asylum to the orphan children," wrote Banna. "The Hasafi Welfare Society encountered the activities of this mission with full force and earned laurels from the people. Later on, this struggle was taken over by the Muslim Brothers."[11]

Banna believed that only Muslims who were ignorant of their religion were vulnerable to missionary influence. So he conceived his life mission to educate Muslims and so defend Islam. To that end, in 1923 he moved to Cairo to enroll at the Dar al-Ulum teachers' college. He loved the college, and classmates remembered him as a gregarious and kind fellow, not as a harsh ideologue.

But outside of college, Banna's social anxiety grew. Cairo was not only a huge city—home to a million inhabitants—but it also seemed to be a foreign city. Ordinary Egyptians and elites lived in worlds apart. Most Cairenes lived in poverty. But a half mile from the sacred al-Azhar university (which many Egyptians remembered was desecrated by Napoleon Bonaparte's troops in 1798), Cairo's booming theater district attracted wealthy Cairenes in European fashions to Gilbert and Sullivan operettas and nightclubs.

"Just after the First World War, a wave of atheism and lewdness engulfed Egypt," Banna wrote in his memoir.

> I felt that my cherished Egyptian nation was torn asunder between the two conflicting ideologies. On the one hand there was their revered faith, Islam. . . . It had brought glories in the past and was still capable of lending dignity and honor to its followers. And on the other hand there was the fierce attack of Western thought and culture to destroy the old values. It was armed with wealth and the outward temptations of life.[12]

In Banna's eyes, liberals were not tolerant universalists, as Edib had viewed them in Turkey. Egypt's liberals were landowners who ruled in cooperation with the British. They laid claim to European modernity as a marker of social superiority. When Lutfi al-Sayyid, an elite nationalist of the older generation, reformed the Egyptian University, he made it an inhospitable place for ordinary Egyptians. "By now a novel concept of research and university life had emerged," Banna recalled. "A university could not become a secular university until it waged a crusade against religion and its social traditions."[13]

It was an issue not just of class oppression, but also of sovereignty. Like many Egyptians, Banna felt the British had usurped the nation's sovereignty after 1919. They had imposed a constitution in 1922, when Zaghlul was still in exile. While the constitution formally ended the protectorate, it did not grant full independence: it preserved British control of military and foreign affairs and granted the king preponderant power over a weak parliament. When Zaghlul returned to Egypt, he and the Wafd Party easily won election to parliamentary seats. But Zaghlul soon discovered that he wielded little power as prime minister against the interests of the king, the British, and their crony landholding elite.

For Banna, the problem of sovereignty grew acute when Turkey abolished the caliphate in 1924. Banna spent sleepless nights worrying about the fate of the *umma*. The caliph had been the last independent Muslim ruler in the world, a beacon for Sunni Muslims who lived largely under colonial rule. Worse, Turkey abolished the caliphate as part of its turn toward European secularism. Mustafa Kemal seemed to adopt—as did Egyptian elites—the European view that Muslims must disavow Islam in order to become modern.[14]

Banna found support among religious conservatives in Cairo. They organized a protest in 1925 against a book that argued the Quran did not in fact require a caliph or an Islamic state. The government banned the book and al-Azhar fired the book's author. The protestors also called for the restoration of Islamic law and Islamic government. At their head was Shaykh Rashid Rida.

Rida was an important influence on Banna and on the rise of Islamic politics across the region. A native of Tripoli in Lebanon, Rida had been Muhammad Abduh's protégé. He now edited the prestigious Islamic journal, *al-Manar* (*The Lighthouse*), which was read widely across the Arab world.[15] Rida was also a political activist. In 1920, he returned to his native land to become president of the Syrian Arab constitutional congress in Damascus. Rida supported constitutional monarchy—as clerics in Iran and the Ottoman empire had in 1906 and 1908—because it fulfilled the principles of Islamic governance, that a ruler must consult with his people and must uphold Islamic law. In 1920, Rida still held the views of his mentor, that Islam shared basic values of liberal justice with Christianity and other world civilizations.

Rida's views changed dramatically when French troops invaded Syria, forcing him to flee back to Cairo. He turned his back on liberal constitutionalism as a universal model of justice. Like Musa Kazim Pasha al-Husayni in Palestine, he scorned the hypocrisy of Woodrow Wilson's League of Nations, which had authorized the French to destroy a sovereign democracy. In 1923, Rida developed a theory of Islamic government and campaigned to preserve the caliphate, which he considered the cornerstone of justice, truth, and freedom from tyranny for Muslims. Without an Islamic state to enforce Islamic law, he argued, there could not be an Islamic *umma*.[16]

Banna visited Rida several times to discuss the future of Islam. He shared Rida's view that Islam represents a way of life and a model of justice quite distinct from liberalism. Rida was an old man by then, and he would never organize a mass movement. He inspired Banna to take up the mantle. Banna joined with Islamic reformers in Cairo to found the Young Men's Muslim Association, modeled in part on the Young Men's Christian Association's program of combined physical and spiritual strength. They promoted a modern form of Islam as an alternative to secularism and raised funds for charities.

Banna grew impatient with elitist and apolitical approaches, however. One night in 1927, he scolded his fellow reformers for conceding victory to Egyptian secularists. "What are you afraid of?" Banna asked. "In fact, the people are with you. You face them. They are the Muslim nation. I have seen the Muslim nation in the coffeehouses, in the mosques, on roads and footpaths; everywhere I found the hearts of this nation throbbing with the love of Faith [Islam]."[17]

The manifesto for Banna's career as an Islamic activist was the senior essay he wrote at the teachers' college. He vowed to bring Egyptians back to true Islam, not as a religious scholar, but as a schoolteacher. "I believe that the best people are those who achieve their happiness by making others happy and counseling them," he wrote. Banna would teach that Islam—not European fashion—was the true source of happiness. "I wish to impart education to the children in the daytime during the major part of the year and preach to their parents at night," he wrote.[18] That is exactly what he did for the next decade.

On the morning of September 19, 1927, Banna set out by train eastward from Cairo, to the Suez port city of Ismailia, where the government had appointed him to his first teaching post. He would teach Arabic in a primary school. Three weeks earlier, the great nationalist leader Zaghlul had died. The long funeral procession wound through the streets as "an appalled silence spread over all the city."[19] Zaghlul had built Egypt's first political party, the Wafd, and had inspired patriotism in Egyptians who lived in villages far from Cairo.[20] Banna decided he would build a new kind of movement, from the ground up, not top down. It would inspire common Egyptians with Rida's ideas of restoring the vitality of Islamic society.[21]

"Ismailia created very strange feelings in my heart," Banna wrote in his memoir. "The British cantonment on its west side cast its influence over the city, filling every respectable and dignified Muslim with sadness."[22] The city was named for Ismail Pasha, who had opened the Suez Canal in 1869. The Suez Canal Company now loomed over the city as a gleaming symbol of European imperialism. European workers settled in the city on streets with names that were not even written in Arabic. Banna's Islamic revival became an anticolonial mission.

Banna took his message to the coffeehouses, as Sayyid Jamal-al-Din al-Afghani had done before the 1882 revolution and as he saw Christian missionaries do. Each evening he visited three cafés where ordinary workers gathered and twice a week he preached short, fifteen-minute sermons in them. At first astonished, his audiences soon listened. "I restricted myself to the presentation of those facts which could create a feeling of awe and hope in them. I did not go into the details of the problems. As a result of this, people started taking interest in Islam because now they had clear ideas about it," he recalled.[23] Banna answered their questions about the nature of God, the Day of Judgment, and a Muslim's basic duty to pursue goodness and avoid evil. He soon found himself training eager adults in the proper rituals of prayer.

One day in March 1928, Banna wrote in his memoir, six Suez Canal Company workers came to see him. "We are weary of this life of humiliation and imprisonment," they told Banna. "Arabs and Muslims have no respectable place in this country. They are just the hired hands of foreigners." They asked him to lead them in action against the injustice toward Muslims. That day, they took an oath to work as brothers for the glory of Islam and to save the *umma*: "We are united to serve the cause of Islam, and therefore, we are brothers and shall be known as the Muslim Brothers."[24]

The MB opened a night school in Ismailia to teach proper recitation of the Quran, Islamic history, correct rituals, and the lives of saintly shaykhs. Seventy students enrolled. Banna's memoir describes it as a utopia of brotherly love, like his childhood village Mahmudiya, and clearly intended as a model for all Egyptian society in the 1940s. Members helped their brothers who lost their jobs and charged each other only the cost, with no profit, for goods and services. They practiced absolute honesty with one another and publicly condemned the dishonesty of Europeans. In 1929, they raised money to build a mosque, because Ismailia had very few. "We bought two truckloads of stones," Banna recalled. "It was a great day in the life of the Brothers."[25]

Hasan al-Banna (1906–1949), founder of the Muslim Brotherhood, gives a weekly Tuesday sermon in this undated newspaper photo, likely from the late 1930s or early 1940s. Each branch of the Muslim Brotherhood held Tuesday meetings, devoted not only to prayer but also to lectures on contemporary topics and practical training.
(Muslim Brotherhood/Ikhwanweb)

Meanwhile, Banna's closest friend Ahmad Sukkari established an MB branch in Mahmudiya. In 1929 they published their first pamphlet together, calling for more religious education in government schools.[26] By 1932, the majority of Muslims in Ismailia had joined the MB, and branches had opened in towns across the eastern Delta and Suez region. Success drew critics, who accused Banna of being, variously, a fascist, a communist, and a Muslim fanatic. Banna responded that he lived peacefully with Jewish and Christian neighbors. The MB aims not to divide Egypt, he wrote, but rather to unify it against colonial rule and to restore justice.[27]

The year 1932 was a turning point. Banna got married (he did not mention his wife's name in the memoir, out of modesty) and moved back to Cairo to establish the MB's national headquarters. He and Sukkari trained cadres of missionaries to proselytize in Egypt's towns and villages. The branches also provided social support to peoples impoverished by the depression and neglected by the government. With donations from wealthy patrons, they taught the illiterate to read and brought medicines to the ill.

The MB promised dignity. In 1933, Banna founded a weekly newspaper that championed the ordinary Egyptian as an agent of modern progress. Under a masthead that translates as "Voice of the Message of Truth, Strength, and Freedom," the paper's news stories showed Egyptians actively improving their society, alongside opinion columns on social reform and proper religion. In response to Europe's theft of Egyptian sovereignty, the MB showed Egyptians how to retrieve their culture and their historical agency.

Banna also inspired Muslim reformers with his stamina and charisma. He toured villages in the hot summer sun and never fell sick from bad water.[28] Weekdays, he woke early to work at the MB's headquarters before heading to school to teach. Weeknights, he returned to headquarters for meetings and lectures. He wore a neat black beard and stylish imported suits. Photographs show a sparkle in his dark eyes, and a sincere, open smile. As Ihsan Abd al-Qaddus, later a famous writer, recalled: "He would always greet you with a big smile and a verse from the Qur'an, then a line or two from a poem, and finally, a laugh full of life and energy."[29]

Banna's voice was his most powerful gift. He delighted audiences with his ability to recall anecdotes from Islamic literature and facts about contemporary events. His Tuesday night lecture series became popular in the neighborhood and throughout Cairo. "When he speaks," wrote one admirer, "the old and the young, the highly cultured, the illiterate, and the ignorant understand him. . . . In his voice there is a deep resonance and from his tongue comes magic."[30]

Banna was also an organizational genius. As the movement grew, he switched recruitment from coffeehouses to mosques, respectable spaces that were sheltered from police. The bottom tier of the MB's three-tiered, federated organization allowed local branches to tailor activities and message to local tastes. To build community support, branch directors focused activity on a common social project, like building a mosque, opening a school or clinic, or supporting local industries. The projects demonstrated tangible, immediate benefits to recruits. Only on the upper tiers of the MB were members disciplined and trained to adhere to its official doctrine. The tier system made it easy for large numbers to join. It also sheltered local branches from government repression, which began in the 1930s and intensified in the 1940s.[31]

Banna could be compared to his American contemporary Dale Carnegie (who wrote *How to Win Friends and Influence People* in 1936) in his mastery of new methods of motivation and publicity. In 1935, two years after opening the newspaper, Banna organized the Rovers, a youth scouting organization. In public parades, the Rovers sang the MB's new anthem, "Ya Rasul Allah" ("Praise to God's Prophet"). Slogans like "God is Great and Glory to Islam!" became so popular that other parties adopted them. The MB also devised a six-point credo, which members chanted at Tuesday night meetings. The credo mainly called the faithful to praise God, but it also expressed a new militant spirit: "God is our goal. The Prophet is our leader. The Qur'an is our constitution. Struggle is our way. Death in God's service is the loftiest of our wishes. God is great, God is great."[32]

Banna's strategy succeeded beyond expectation. By 1936, the MB had quietly opened 100 branches across Egypt.[33] Few outsiders had yet heard of it. Many mistook it for a typical Islamic charity. Banna continued to cultivate his image as a humble servant of God, who set out every weekend to walk quietly from village to village, bringing a message of moral uplift and self-help to common Egyptians.

But change was in the air. In the early months of 1936, Egyptians and other Arabs raised protests for independence. As a national organization, the MB shared in the spirit of change. When a new king took the throne, Banna decided to address him in an open letter.

Entering the Political Arena

Banna's 1936 letter to the sixteen-year-old King Farouk became a political manifesto, republished for decades under the title "Toward the Light" *(Nahwa al-Nur)*. Like the Ottoman bureaucrat Mustafa Ali in 1599, Banna addressed the king as God's regent and guarantor of justice. "Your Majesty, God has delegated rule of this nation to you, and has made its interests, its affairs, its present and its future, your trust and charge," Banna began. But unlike Mustafa Ali, Banna urged the king to modernize Islam, not return to tradition. Like Colonel Urabi in 1881, he warned the king that sovereignty is the prerequisite to restoring justice. Reviving the nation requires two stages: "First the liberation of the nation from its political chains to regain its liberty and retrieve the independence and sovereignty it has lost," he wrote. "Second, building it anew to take its place among other nations and compete with them in social progress."[34]

Banna also urged the king to embrace an Eastern model of progress and justice. The letter is a striking rejection of European modernity and liberalism. While Urabi and Musa Kazim in Palestine had scolded the British for betraying universal principles of justice, Banna voiced no expectation of justice from Europeans. His dim view reflected the deplorable state of Europe in the 1930s: "[The West's] political foundations are being razed by dictatorships, its economic foundations battered by crises," he wrote. "Humanity is in dire need of the purifying waters of True Islam." Islam condemns the brute militarism of Benito Mussolini, Adolf Hitler, and Joseph Stalin and their "armies of injustice," Banna wrote. Muslims are taught to use violence only as a last resort, if their homes are invaded. And Islam's "police of justice" respect the law and refrain from killing children, women, and the elderly.[35]

Banna blamed capitalism as the root of European materialism, aggression, and greed. Islamic principles of private property, thrift, and equity offer the world a more humane path to prosperity. "The pursuit of comfort and worldly goods has shaken the foundations of Europe," he counseled the king. "Be the first to offer, in the name of God's Prophet (May God bless and save him!), the Qur'an's medicine to save this sick and tormented world."[36]

In essence, Banna proposed that King Farouk become the anti-Ataturk, a Muslim ruler who refuses to cede all historical agency to Europe. He reproduced the letter in his memoir with another one he wrote in June 1936, scolding Prime Minister Mustafa Nahhas for praising Turkey as a model modern state for the East. Ataturk built a European state, Banna wrote. The East needs a state suited to the values of Muslims.[37] The Muslim world must follow its own path to wealth and power, Banna further reasoned. Revival would spring from the East's deep spiritual strength, not from the West's scientific materialism.

Banna did not advocate revival of the caliphate or a theocracy; rather, he called for government based on Islamic principles. This is an important distinction that would be lost later in the twentieth century.[38] The context of 1936 is important to understanding Banna's intent. The king was negotiating an independence treaty that would once again limit Egypt's sovereignty. Britain would continue to station troops at the Suez Canal zone and control Egypt's defense. And the "oriental secretary" at the British embassy would continue to influence internal Egyptian politics while politicians would continue to fawn over him. Banna rejected the deference to Britain. He represented a new wave of nationalists who recognized that imitating Europe would never bring sovereignty to colonies. In a sense, Banna's letter to Farouk anticipated Frantz Fanon, who wrote a quarter century later in *The Wretched of the Earth* that colonized peoples must "vomit up" Western values in order to become masters of their own future.[39]

Banna assured the king that an Islamic government would not be backward. God commands Muslims to seek knowledge and honor his creation; the king must therefore support the study of biology, physics, and geology. Islamic government would also be just. God intended that there be diversity among humankind, and the Quran counseled Muslims to treat minorities with goodwill and justice, Banna said, citing another verse: "O mankind, We have created you male and female and have made you nations and tribes that you may know one another." The Quran advises Muslims, he added, to keep peace with Christians and Jews, who "are no other than brothers."[40]

Banna closed his letter to King Farouk with fifty practical steps toward reform. Political reforms should promote unity, strong military defense, laws that accord with Islam, and a culture of merit, not corruption. Social reforms should establish a welfare state, where the Islamic tithe *(zakat)* would provide care for the poor, aged, and orphaned. The state should also provide jobs for the unemployed and protect employees from the "oppression of monopolistic companies," a direct reference to the Suez Canal Company. And it should expand public education; ban alcohol, gambling, and ostentatious dress; and solve the "woman problem" through Islamic teaching, not "deviant notions."

Banna's model of justice in "Toward the Light" was not a reactionary throwback to the village world he had left in Mahmudiya. There, the state had been absent, the wealthy had neglected the poor, and the

A Cairo street, south of Al-Azhar University, in 1934. Neighborhoods like this, where ordinary Egyptians were gaining an education and jobs in commerce and the civil service, were recruiting grounds for the early Muslim Brotherhood. (Library of Congress)

people were defenseless against laws and missionaries who undermined their values. Banna's vision of the modern Islamic state, not unlike Mustafa Ali's, would not neglect the poor. Women would also play an active role in the modern Muslim community; while in Mahmudiya (at least according to Banna's reconstruction of it), they had been absent. Islamic feminists supported Banna's message and established an independent organization, the Muslim Sisters.[41]

Palestine became a second political issue for the MB in 1936. Ties to Palestinian activists went back to the early 1930s, when Izz al-Din al-Qassam formed a branch of the Young Men's Muslim Association in Haifa. In May 1936, Banna met the mufti of Palestine to arrange support for the Palestine Arabs' general strike. The MB's national network collected pennies and supplies of wheat by staging "Palestine Days" in villages and towns across Egypt.

In the summer of 1938 the MB published an explosive political pamphlet, "Fire and Destruction in Palestine," with descriptions and pictures of British atrocities against Palestinian Arabs. The British confiscated it. Police violently repressed pro-Palestinian demonstrations and raided the MB's offices in Ismailia. Banna was arrested and jailed for four days.[42] Protest continued with a boycott of British and Jewish goods and vicious propaganda about Jews as the enemies of Islam. The campaign against Egyptian Jews was new, and it contradicted Banna's assurances about tolerance in his letter to the king.

The MB emerged as the foremost political opponent of British influence in Egypt. As he sat in his jail cell, Banna became, in the eyes of many, heir to the mantle of Zaghlul and Urabi. Membership in the MB tripled between 1936 and 1938 to 300 branches. With an estimated 100,000 members, it rivaled Egypt's largest opposition party, the Wafd. While the Palestine issue inspired many urban students to join, the MB's base remained in villages and towns across Egypt where a newly educated middle class joined for fellowship, mutual aid, and spiritual uplift. Membership mirrored the full spectrum of middling classes in Egyptian society: semiliterate peasants and urban workers, civil servants and students.[43]

Young militants pressured Banna to sever relations with the palace and launch a revolution. Banna rejected their call: "The nature of our Islamic mission is building, not destruction! The Brothers prefer peace and love to confrontation and war." In a May 1938 editorial, however, Banna announced that the MB was ready for its second phase, moving from propaganda to action. Action must begin with engagement, Banna told the militants. Only if the government refuses to cooperate with our agenda, "then we are at war with every leader, every party, and every organization that does not work for the victory of Islam!"[44]

Banna's threat may have alarmed government officials, but militants were not appeased. Against Banna's orders, they provoked violence in the summer 1938 demonstrations and planned to send soldiers to Palestine. After Banna expelled their leaders, the militants seceded from the MB. In late 1938 they founded a new group, Muhammad's Youth, and issued a manifesto preaching revolution, against Banna's participation in the political system: "The Islamic mission can only be successfully accomplished through the spontaneous power of the people and sincere Islamic guidance of public opinion, without being dependent on the rulers."[45]

In January 1939, the MB convened in Cairo for their Fifth Congress, which stands at a historical crossroads for the movement. In his memoir, Banna recalled it as a huge success. "The Congress was, in fact, a marvelously powerful call to expand the mission," he wrote. The congress adopted reforms that allowed the MB to double in size to more than 1,000 branches by 1942. The reforms also ensured that the MB controlled its message more closely, by appointing branch directors centrally from Cairo. And they set a standardized weekly schedule of branch activities, with visits to saints' tombs, lectures, study and prayer nights, and military drills. Finally, Banna wrote, the Fifth Congress established three important committees: to recommend revisions in the 1923 constitution to weed out violations of Islamic principles, to write a handbook of the MB's philosophy for new members, and to design a new headquarters building in Cairo.[46]

In his keynote address at the Fifth Congress, Banna publicly announced the movement's new political mission. The MB would no longer merely advise politicians; rather they would exert active pressure on them to follow the Islamic path. Banna assured his audience the Islamic path was wide. Islam is not, as some believe, simply a set of rituals, or a spiritual escape, or outdated dogma, he said. If Muslims looked at their faith, they would find it provides "a complete tonic to the human soul." Islam is not a fixed code of law. When Islamic principles guide the impartial judge, he implements the law justly. If a fanatical judge interprets the letter of the law, he judges in error.[47]

Banna's own errors of judgment, however, proved most pivotal. Decisions taken at the 1939 Cairo congress opened the way to the MB's violent showdown with the government nearly a decade later. At issue was not simply the stubbornness of hotheaded youth in the ranks. While Banna had always advocated peaceful avenues of reform, his speeches routinely used military metaphors about battling colonialism and corruption. Now he turned rhetoric into action.

Rather than quashing all talk of violence, Banna appeased his critics at the 1939 meeting with a promise to organize official armed battalions. The battalions must obey his orders, he warned, and wait for the right moment to act. "Those among you who want to pick the fruit before it's ripe, or pick the flower before it blooms, well, I don't agree with them. It is better for them to leave this mission and go to another."[48] Before considering military action, he said, the MB needed to train 300 battalions, or 12,000 troops. Only a select few would ever be qualified to perform such a true jihad, or holy struggle. When the elite battalions are ready, he promised, "I will conquer the skies for you and I will lead the attack with you against every stubborn tyrant."[49]

A hint of what sort of battle Banna envisioned came in the form of a veiled ultimatum to the king. If government corruption continues, he warned, the MB will be forced to act:

> Accordingly, the Muslim Brothers don't demand rule for themselves. But if we don't find anyone to rule according to that [Islamic] program, then we will take steps against any government that does not implement the will of God. In this case, the Muslim Brothers reason that it must take on the important task of government for itself.[50]

Banna qualified his call to battle by stressing that before waging jihad, Muslims had to judge the effects of the use of force and to resort to it only when they see no alternative to uphold the faith.

Banna closed his 1939 keynote speech by condemning political parties and calling for national unity against European colonialism. The MB was to rise above partisan politics. "It is our duty to explain all this to the people, and to teach them that Islam wants nothing less for its sons than the freedom and independence needed for their sovereignty. . . . For death is better than this life, a life of slavery and oppression!"[51]

POLITICAL EXCLUSION & DESCENT INTO VIOLENCE

After the January 1939 congress, Banna made good on his promise to lead the MB directly into the political arena. In June, he and Sukkari held a reception for parliamentary deputies, thanking them for supporting religious education in public schools. In August, on the eve of World War II, Banna began a tour of southern Egypt to publicize the MB's new political mission. In October, he wrote a letter to Prime Minister Ali Mahir, the MB's most prominent ally. He urged Mahir to resist Britain's demand for war support beyond levels required by the 1936 treaty. Mahir should use the war as a time for reforms, especially to permit loyal dissent and to stamp out nepotism.[52]

Banna's relations with the government plummeted during the war, and especially after Mahir was forced to step down in June 1940, for refusing to declare war. The MB's police contacts still provided protection, so its press openly called on Egyptians to use the war as an opportunity to oust the British. The government shut down the MB's press and banned political activity by religious organizations. In February 1941, the government sent Banna to internal exile for four months in the southern town of Qena. Banna and Sukkari were arrested again in October 1941 for anti-British activity. Hundreds of petitions with 11,000 signatures won their release a month later.[53]

It was the most perilous moment of the war, as German troops in Libya approached Egypt's border. Many Egyptians resented the appearance of British soldiers on Cairo's streets and blamed the British for the scarcity of food. Fearing a popular revolt, the British staged a virtual coup in February 1942, forcing the king to appoint the Wafd Party's Nahhas as prime minister. For its collaboration, the Wafd Party suffered a near-fatal blow to its reputation.[54]

Perhaps sensing a political opening, Banna announced his candidacy in the parliamentary election in March 1942. But Nahhas forced him to drop out of the race. Banna made a second run for a parliamentary seat in 1945. The government permitted him and other Muslim Brothers to campaign but rigged the election outcome. Banna was defeated in his oldest stronghold, Ismailia.[55] It was a severe setback. Banna had publicly promised that he would take the MB's agenda into parliament and the palace. Now it was clear that entry into the formal institutions of Egyptian politics was closed.

The MB met greater success in grassroots organization. To recruit workers in the booming wartime industries, it presented itself as a nonsocialist alternative to communist-led trade unions. The MB also built its own factories to employ workers and offered an extensive public health program and Islamic finance system. Meanwhile, branches opened more than 100 social welfare offices to distribute food and other aid to the poor, while their clinics treated 21,000 patients. Because of this aid, wrote a scholar in 1952, "the movement enjoyed a great success among the majority."[56]

Meanwhile, Banna used his serialized memoir to stoke revolutionary fervor. He picked up his pen at war's end, when Egyptians mounted massive demonstrations demanding a full evacuation of British troops. The MB was born, he emphasized, in response to colonial injustice of Ismailia, where foreigners' villas contrasted with "the

Hasan al-Banna spent more time in suits than in religious robes. The Muslim Brotherhood aimed to integrate Islamic spirituality, ethics, and law into modern life, and so Banna decided to run for parliament in the early 1940s.
(Muslim Brotherhood/Ikhwanweb)

narrow and dark hutments of the Arab laborers." Banna raised the call to nationalize the Suez Canal Company a full decade before Nasser did so in 1956.[57]

Riots broke out later in 1946, when Britain denied Egypt's appeal for full independence. Banna issued an ultimatum to the prime minister calling for noncooperation with the British. In response, the prime minister shut down the MB's newspapers and schools and arrested its leaders, including Sukkari. Banna was on pilgrimage in Mecca at the time.

The consequences of Banna's vacillations in his 1939 address now played out. Barred from formal politics, the MB regrouped its battalions into what became known as the Special Section.[58] As early as 1942, Banna was involved in gun smuggling, according to Anwar Sadat. Sadat's secret group of officers was planning an armed revolution, and they needed the MB's popular base. Banna appeared interested.[59] By 1948, the MB's military corps grew to 1,000 members. Few rank-and-file Muslim Brothers likely knew of their existence.

Opinion is divided about the MB's military wing. Gamal al-Banna argues that the rapid growth of the MB fundamentally altered his older brother's politics: "Hasan's style of leadership changed, he could no longer know everyone personally. He became revolutionary." Gamal actually refused to join the MB, he said, because it had become as dogmatic as the communists. "In 1946, my brother sent a message to me," he recalled. "'Why have you never come to us?' . . . I told him I wanted to be a scholar, to write books."[60]

Historian Richard Mitchell, on the other hand, argues that "militancy and martyrdom had been elevated to central virtues in the Society's ethos." The MB's September 1946 newsletter was typical, Mitchell remarked, in addressing its branches as "battalions of salvation for this country afflicted by calamity."[61]

By 1947 Banna was close enough to militants in the Special Section that they convinced him to expel his oldest friend from the organization. Sukkari, they claimed, was too cozy with the Wafd Party; Banna agreed.[62] But the episode may have been a personal crisis for Banna. His memoir, written in that era, contained a tender description of how Sukkari followed him to Cairo in the early 1920s. Banna even quoted his 1927 senior essay: "The center of my love is that friend who lives in me like a soul, and I have dedicated my love to him [Sukkari] who is the axis of my friendship."[63]

It may be impossible to unravel the ties between Banna's roles as battalion leader, politician, and humanitarian. Between 1946 and 1948, Banna renewed relations with the king and organized an independence campaign, even as the Special Section contributed to the riots and assassinations that rocked Egypt. At the same time, the MB expanded the number of its welfare offices from 100 to 500.[64]

It was in this atmosphere that Banna sat down to lunch in August 1947 with Philip W. Ireland, the first secretary at the American embassy in Cairo. The Americans were supporting the British position at the United Nations (UN), and so the lunch got off to a rocky start. Ireland described Banna in terms far different from his admirers:

> I found him a man of less than middle height with a sallow face, slightly pockmarked and topped by curly receding hair and surrounded by a scanty frizzled beard. From his nervous and impulsive actions and his mobile face one might suspect that he was inclined to nervous disorders.

Or he was just nervous about meeting an American. Ireland did note that Banna was "quick in speech and agile in debate."

As they began lunch, Banna asked Ireland why America allied with Britain. Britain's condition for withdrawal, a military alliance, was unacceptable. If Britain didn't negotiate, Banna warned Ireland, he would have to "demand that Egypt notify the world that the 1936 treaty was null and void." When Ireland asked Banna if he was preparing a jihad, he smiled and said such reports were exaggerated. Banna then reminded him that Egypt and America shared experience as British colonies. Why did the United States now back its former colonizer? America should join Egypt in pursuing common interests, like fighting communism.[65]

The luncheon is striking in two respects. First, Banna showed remarkable openness to working with the United States. The American had expected him to be hostile. Second, he revealed a basic continuity in his political vision: focus on retrieving Egypt's sovereignty—the goal that drew him to the 1919 revolution and inspired him to found the MB. In August 1947, Banna's MB was part of a wave of mass movements that aimed to turn the Allies' victory in World War II into liberation from colonial rule: the Baath Party in Syria, the Congress Party in India, communists in Indochina and China, and the National Liberation Front (FLN) in Algeria.

A month later, however, the UN formally denied Egypt's appeal for independence. Socialists staged a ceremony at Urabi's grave, reviving memory of the forgotten leader who had defied the British in 1882. Prime Minister Mahmud Nuqrashi wept as he descended from his plane from New York. Britain "has no place in our midst henceforward," he declared. The MB issued its own declaration: "Oh noble-hearted people, unsubmissive people, only one way is left to you: to fight!"

Four days later, a cholera epidemic broke out. "The epidemic confirmed a sense of injustice suffered," wrote Jacques Berque, a French historian who lived in Egypt at the time. "Justice, and Egypt's hopes, were flouted when she failed to gain admittance to the international debate" at the UN. A leftist, Berque respected Banna as a basically honest man. Even the most critical of political magazines, *Rose al-Yusuf,* praised him because he "seeks to teach the people their religion afresh, which is not a bad thing to do, after all."[66]

However, events soon swallowed Banna's political mission into the vortex of violence that would lead to his death. In November

1947, the UN voted to partition Palestine into Jewish and Arab states. "The Arabs felt that they were the victims of a *zulm,* an injustice, or rather a denial of justice," Berque wrote.[67] Banna mobilized the battalions for jihad. Palestine beckoned again as a battlefield to fight British imperialism.

In May 1948, the MB began sending volunteers to fight in Palestine. Banna also led a committee to declare "*jihad* against the Jews" in Egypt. He demanded that the government recognize Islam as Egypt's official religion.[68] Police suspected the MB in the bombing of Jewish homes in Cairo.

Meanwhile, the MB won popular praise for its valor in Palestine and humiliated the king by rescuing defeated Egyptian soldiers. The government struck back. In November, police discovered a cache of weapons in a jeep in Ismailia. Then Cairo's police chief was murdered.

On December 8, 1948, Prime Minister Nuqrashi took to the radio waves to outlaw the MB as a terrorist organization. Police surrounded its headquarters. Thousands were rounded up in concentration camps. At this point, Mitchell and others believe, Banna lost contact with the remaining cells of the Special Section. He likely had no foreknowledge when, on December 28, a young Muslim Brother shot Nuqrashi dead.

All that Banna had built in twenty years was crushed, as the government seized the MB's funds and closed down its various businesses, publications, and social welfare networks. The government unleashed a campaign of torture and terror and decreed the death penalty for anyone in possession of explosives.

Banna condemned Nuqrashi's murder. Visibly shaken, he admitted the MB's errors and even agreed that it should be dissolved. But another cell of the Special Section bombed the Cairo courthouse, and the government cut off negotiations with him. In his last pamphlet, written in early February, Banna denied the terrorism charges and condemned the government's brutal persecution. His own murder followed a few days later.[69]

Banna's murder left behind a controversial legacy. Scholars and politicians in Egypt and beyond still debate whether Banna was responsible for the violence and assassinations of the Special Section. The evidence assembled here suggests that he had long fought against random violence but had laid plans for armed battle, either in defense or for revolution. Banna's actual turn to violence was clearly a reaction to changing circumstances. He made fatal strategic errors amidst the wave of political violence that carried Egypt toward revolution in 1952.

Was justice done that day in February 1949? The Egyptian courts ruled no. Two years later, they would exonerate the MB of charges of sedition and intent to overthrow the government. Many others—in Egypt and outside—answered yes, because they regarded the MB as fascist.[70] The movement's record, however, fits poorly with scholarly measures of fascism. Like European fascists, the Muslim Brothers saw themselves as victims of decadent, cosmopolitan liberalism. They also carried on a vicious campaign against Zionists and, later, all Egyptian Jews. But unlike European fascists, they did not act on ideas of racial purity, nor did they demand the total submission of the individual conscience to group goals. And though they flirted with the palace at times, they made no alliance with conservative elites against the left.[71]

The fascist label was tossed around freely in the 1940s. From the outset of World War II, the British branded all opponents of their rule fascist. The aim was to discredit them, especially in the eyes of American diplomats who might sympathize with an anticolonial movement.[72] Philip Ireland may have been surprised when Banna extended a hand of friendship because the American embassy worked closely with the British—and supported Britain's claim to maintain troops in Egypt. Weeks after their lunch, however, Americans pressured the British to accommodate Egyptian nationalism into their policy.[73]

Fascist or not, Banna's murder held profound implications for the rule of law and the future of democracy in Egypt. The regime had murdered the leader of the largest political movement in the country. The stakes of mounting opposition rose mortally high in 1949, as Egyptians' anger at their regime crested. The MB's only serious rival, the Wafd Party, was in steep decline. The political arena was left to smaller parties and to a growing but yet unorganized labor movement. Into this vacuum would step Sadat and his fellow Free Officers, who preempted popular revolt with a military coup in 1952. The Free Officers abolished the 1923 constitution and established a one-party dictatorship that would repress its opposition—communists, liberals, and the MB—with even greater force.

The MB did not die with Banna on February 13, 1949. A Syrian Muslim Brotherhood had been founded in 1945, and soon branches opened in Jerusalem, Lebanon, Transjordan, Iraq, North Africa, and Sudan. In Egypt, the MB regrouped but was unable to find a strong leader to replace Banna. It played a relatively minor role in events leading to the 1952 revolution. It was in the revolutionary prisons that a new leader, more rigid in his views, emerged. Sayyid Qutb would inspire a rebirth of the MB and revolution against the revolution's Ataturk-style secular state in the 1970s.

More generally, Banna inaugurated two long-lasting shifts in Arab politics. First, he transformed the terms of political debate, to revolve around a dichotomy between the East and the West. While Europeans had used that dichotomy to justify the modern West's colonial rule over the East, Banna inverted the formula to promote Islam as more modern and more just than Christianity. To British claims that Islam was despotic, Banna declared that Islam supported a constitutionalism based on its own Eastern heritage. European tutelage was not only unnecessary to Egypt's development, it was also detrimental to it. An important consequence of Banna's rhetorical strategy was the rejection of a single, universal model of justice.

The consequences of this shift are demonstrated by popular reactions to the UN in the Arab world. The UN Universal Declaration of Human Rights, issued on December 8, 1948, was not welcomed by Arabs as Wilson's Fourteen Points had been. The MB and a new generation of anticolonial activists had driven a deep wedge between Arabs' sense of justice and the West's. The UN had lost prestige in Egyptian eyes by supporting Britain's continued military presence in Suez and by partitioning Palestine without sending support to establish a Palestinian Arab state. In Egyptian eyes, this did not accord with the declaration's pledge to uphold "the inherent dignity and of the equal and inalienable rights of all members of the human family."

By recasting justice in Islamic terms, however, Banna was dividing his own nation. It was not clear how Egyptian Christians and Jews would enjoy equality in an Islamic Egypt: the MB expressed varying views on tolerance and coexistence. Despite Ubayd Pasha's public support for Banna, some Muslim Brothers vilified non-Muslims as collaborators with foreigners. Worse, the MB's anti-Semitic rhetoric and attacks on Jews amplified intolerance in Egyptian politics. More than 20,000 Jews fled Egypt in 1948–1951, and within two decades most of those remaining also left.[74] Coptic Christians, who claimed to be descendants of the original Egyptians, also faced prejudice and marginalization as Islamism spread. As we will see, these fears crested in the 2012 presidential election that brought a Muslim Brother to power as president.

Banna's second effect on Arab politics was to demonstrate the power of the people. The MB was the first major mass movement to appear in the Arab Middle East. By 1948 an estimated 600,000 Egyptians had joined more than 2,000 branches. The MB claimed to represent a million Egyptians, including unofficial sympathizers.[75] Banna adopted local organizational techniques, like those of the Hasafi Sufi order, and mobilized large numbers with a new symbolic repertoire of Islamic nationalism.

It was not long before the precocious MB encountered rivals. In every country where the MB opened branches, they competed with young nationalists, liberals, socialists, and communists who were also building mass parties. But they never seriously rivaled the MB's popular power in Egypt. Banna had made it easy to join the MB. He also made the MB's structure more flexible—so that it survived state repression better than the communists and other groups.[76]

Elsewhere, however, other mass parties prevailed over the MB with rival models of popular justice. In Iraq, communists built the region's second great mass movement. A key factor was the talent of another organizational genius, Yusuf Salman Yusuf.

7

COMRADE FAHD

The Mass Appeal of Communism in Iraq

It was called "Al-Wathbah" by the thousands who witnessed it. The word is inadequately translated into English as "the Leap," as in the leap of the Iraqi people into history. In 1948, ordinary citizens rudely interrupted their prime minister's plan to prolong Britain's presence in their country.[1] At news of the secret Portsmouth Treaty, they flooded the streets of Baghdad. Through the month of January, crowds of 100,000 repeatedly gathered. As historian Hanna Batatu observed:

> It was the social subsoil of Baghdad in revolt against hunger and unequal burdens. It was the students and the Schalchiyyah [railway] workers braving machine guns on the Ma'mun Bridge and dying for their ideas— or, as cynics would have it, for vain illusions. It was the political representatives of the various layers of the middle class—the National Democrats, the Liberals, the Independence party—resentful of constraints or plotting for political gain.[2]

And behind the scenes were the communists. Though illegal, the Iraqi Communist Party (ICP) was the largest grassroots organization in the country. Communists mobilized their networks to augment student demonstrations against the Portsmouth Treaty, which aimed to extend British use of air bases—and British political influence—for an extra fifteen years. Hundreds of people were shot and killed by police aiming at demonstrators from rooftops and even from minarets of mosques.

The Wathbah marked a line in the sand between the Iraqi people and the monarchy that Britain had created in 1921. By 1948, Iraq was already known as the most tyrannical state in the Middle East. Power was concentrated in the palace and particularly in the hands of Nuri al-Said, a minister infamous for throwing opponents into concentration camps and executing them. The political elite—which excluded nearly all but Sunni Arabs in a country of great ethnic diversity—monopolized Iraq's wealth. Just 1 percent of landowners owned 55 percent of farmland, a far higher concentration of land wealth than in Turkey, Syria, or Egypt.

To repress dissent against such inequality, Iraqi political police worked closely with intelligence agents in the British embassy. Laborers on strike were routinely shot and killed. In 1948, protests by workers, students, communists, and middle-class nationalists continued through the spring. But in May, as Iraq sent 15,000 troops to Palestine, the government declared martial law. In December, as defeat in Palestine undermined the state's prestige, Nuri rounded up hundreds of communists and ordered the execution of the party's leaders. The Abu Ghraib prison was already notorious for torture.[3]

The defeat of the Wathbah and the communists in 1948 only delayed the revolution for a decade. The party went deep underground and nurtured a new revolutionary generation. On July 14, 1958, sympathetic army officers overthrew the monarchy and proclaimed a republic. On the radio, they played "La Marseillaise," the French song of revolution that Turks had sung in 1908. The streets filled with jubilant Iraqis. Communists rallied tens of thousands of new members in support of the new republic.

Nine months later, on April 17, 1959, the communists gathered a million citizens and marched again in Baghdad. (The capital had a population of just 795,000 residents out of 6.6 million Iraqis total.) Thousands from the countryside arrived the night before and slept in al-Kilani Square downtown. The next day, they marched peacefully through Baghdad for twelve hours, carrying pictures of their beloved leader, General Abd al-Karim Qasim (1914–1963), and placards that denounced "war mongers" and "imperialism."

Ten years before Woodstock, the communist event was a virtual love-in. Marchers called for peace and for the army to hand power over to civilians. Religious leaders carried signs urging believers "to enter into peace." Others sang folk songs to the tune of musical bands. Girls dressed in white like doves passed by on floats. A local paper reported:

> All categories of people: the soldier, worker, peasant, wage-earner, intellectual, student, civil servant, merchants . . . Arabs, Kurds, Assyrians, Armenians and others, who flocked from every corner of Iraq. . . . The procession was rained with flowers, sweets and bouquets from balconies along both sides of the streets.[4]

That utopian day is an almost surreal memory to Baghdadis today. Their city has been nearly destroyed by decades of war, dictatorship, and sectarian conflict.

Fatefully, Qasim did not invite the communists into government. He consequently lacked a popular base, and so was overthrown in 1963 by the Baath Party, which eventually established the dictatorial regime of Saddam Hussein. Dominated by Sunni Arabs, the Baathists overturned Qasim's inclusive republic. The multicultural, cross-class unity of Iraqis that the communists had fostered disappeared. The ICP was the only truly national party Iraq has ever had.[5]

Through the mists of memory, the image of one man in particular has endured: Comrade Fahd (1901–1949). He transformed the ICP from an intellectual club into a mass political party. From the deep obscurity of his headquarters, he led the illegal ICP in a campaign to establish a constitutional monarchy. Teachers, students and industrial workers were the party's forward troops. Their marching orders were to oust the British, alleviate poverty, and advance democratic reforms. "[Fahd] made communism attractive to a lot of people," recalled a party leader. "He was able to dispel the image of communism as atheistic."[6]

Fahd was also a martyr: he was hanged in 1949, two days after Hasan al-Banna was shot in Cairo. His story, retold in pamphlets and magazines, exemplified communists' reputation in Iraq for patriotism, honesty, and justice in the struggle against poverty and tyranny. "We used to idolize Fahd as if he was a god or a prophet," recalled the party's leader in the early 1950s.[7]

The party's failure to gain power under Qasim has agonized its followers ever since. Some blame a split among party leaders for not launching a worker's revolution when Qasim refused to let the party

Comrade Fahd (born Yusuf Salman Yusuf) built the Iraqi Communist Party into a popular, nationwide organization in the 1940s, before he was executed in 1949. The party still honors him annually on February 14, the date of his death, and with paintings like this one, from 2004.
(Iraqi Communist Party)

in government. Others blame the conditions of the Cold War. They believe that Qasim refused communist support because he feared the United States. Although the ICP had virtually no ties to the Soviet Union, Americans were not inclined to take chances in a region at the heart of world oil supplies.[8]

From a longer perspective, we can see that the rise and fall of Iraqi communism was yet another response to the collapse of Ottoman justice after World War I. The thousands of workers who followed the ICP were part of a wave of movements for social justice—like the Muslim Brotherhood—that arose amid the privations of World War II to challenge the undemocratic regimes that Europeans had imposed after World War I.

But the ICP's tolerant pluralism contrasted sharply with the projects of homogeneity pursued by Mustafa Kemal Ataturk in Turkey, Banna in Egypt, and its opponents in Iraq, the Baath Party. Iraqi communists created a brief but important opening for a popular culture of democracy. They achieved this in part through the support of what

Antonio Gramsci might have called organic intellectuals. Fahd's underground network of worker-teachers spread a new moral economy among Iraq's poor. Like the peasants in 1858 Lebanon, they coupled their demands for bread with demands for rights.

THE ROOTS OF THE ICP

Iraqi communism had multiple roots, but its origin as a mass movement lay in the revolutionary spirit and bleak poverty of the southern provinces. To understand how a secular ideology imported from the Soviet Union captured the hearts of Iraqi Muslims, Christians, and Jews, we must begin in the humid marshlands and palm groves around the ancient city of Basra.

Comrade Fahd was born Yusuf Salman Yusuf in 1901, in Baghdad. His parents were Christian Arabs from the north, and his father sold pastries from a street cart. For unknown reasons, he moved the family 300 miles south to Basra in 1908. The city of 40,000 was the region's gateway to the Persian Gulf. To the north lay vast salt marshes, where rice was grown. To the south, hot, flat desert stretched into the Arabian Peninsula. Basrawis were not yet Iraqis. They had more ties with neighboring tribal families in Kuwait and with merchants who sailed to India than with Baghdad. Most Arabs in the region were Shii Muslims. Their religious sympathies extended to the holy cities of Najaf and Karbala and to Persians across the Shatt al-Arab waterway.

Yusuf's family presumably lived in the small Christian enclave of the city. He attended the Syrian Church school and, at age thirteen, the American mission school. Two years later, his father fell ill and he was forced to quit. Yusuf left behind a classmate, a wealthy boy named Bahjat Atiyyah, who snubbed him as low class. They would meet again thirty years later when Atiyyah, as chief of the political police, arrested Yusuf (by then Comrade Fahd) and sent him to death row.

At age fifteen the young Yusuf was not yet a revolutionary. Family photos show him as a handsome young man with dark penetrating eyes and a strong chin. His brothers and sisters gathered around him, dressed in suits and flouncy country dresses. The Salman family was poor, but not desperately so.[9] Yusuf worked in a small ice factory and then at the port, where he viewed the changes in Basra since the British occupation.

The British first came to Basra in the late nineteenth century, using the city as a link in steamship routes between the Suez Canal and India. Dates were a major export, representing 85 percent of dates on the world market. To meet demand, African slaves were imported and poor village women migrated to Basra every September to process and package the date harvest. While Basra's merchants and landowners prospered, workers earned low wages. And weavers lost their livelihoods to imports of British cloth.[10]

In 1914, British troops occupied Basra as a wartime stronghold. The British navy depended on the Iranian oil fields at Abadan, thirty miles south of the city. When the British ousted the Ottomans from Baghdad in March 1917, General Stanley Maude famously proclaimed that they came as liberators, not conquerors. At war's end, the British broke that promise, united the three provinces along the Tigris and Euphrates Rivers, and ruled them as the mandate of Iraq.

Iraq's three million inhabitants lived in what had been three neglected provinces of the Ottoman empire: Mosul, Baghdad, and Basra. The Ottomans had delegated power to local notables and expended few Tanzimat resources on improving roads, railways, or schools. The population was more sparsely distributed and poorer than in Syria, Egypt, or Palestine. In contrast to Egypt, it was quite diverse, with concentrations of Kurds in the northeast; Sunni Arabs north and west of Baghdad; and Shii Arabs in the south. The southern tribal chiefs were infamous for their resistance to any direct Ottoman intervention. Those who profited from British trade accepted the mandate, those north of Basra did not.[11]

The Iraqi Revolution of 1920, as it was later called, started when a leading cleric (ayatollah) issued a fatwa declaring the mandate illegal. Shii tribal leaders took up arms against British imperial troops.[12] Rebellion soon spread to the Kurdish north, engulfing much of the country. After four months and 6,000 Iraqi deaths, the British put down the revolt.[13]

Yusuf claimed the 1920 revolution inspired his first feelings of Iraqi patriotism. He watched the revolution from Nasiriya, a center of revolt in the south. He and his brother had moved there to run a grain mill. Tribal leaders chased the British out of the province (called Muntafiq) for several months.

After the revolt, the British built a regime of loyal elites to control the population. They chose Faysal ibn Husayn, recently ousted from Syria, as king. Faysal brought with him Iraqi soldiers, called Sharifians, who had fought against the Ottomans and helped rule in Damascus. Among them was Nuri al-Said, a former Ottoman officer who became a loyal friend to the British. He parceled out land, tax breaks, and later oil revenues to the tribal oligarchy that kept Iraq's poor out of politics. Nuri and the British also excluded from the regime most Shii tribal shaykhs and Kurdish leaders as punishment for the 1920 revolution. They ensured that loyal Sunni shaykhs gained political power in Baghdad by rigging elections to parliament.

Yusuf witnessed the consequences of British rule in the southern countryside, as he shuttled between jobs in Nasiriya and Basra in the early 1920s. Poor farmers became sharecroppers for a new class of tribal landlords. Most were chained by debt and by new feudal laws. They lived in a world apart from the elites of Basra, who traded at the port and worked for the British colonial officials. The loyalty of Basra's Shii elites to the Sunni rulers in Baghdad had limits, however. In 1927, they formed a political party opposed to military conscription.[14]

By then Yusuf had become immersed in radical politics. Communist ideas arrived in Basra on British steamers from India, in books and magazines, and in the mouths of Indian soldiers, servants, and employees of British firms. British police later claimed Yusuf learned his communism from a Russian agent, but that is disputed.[15] In either case, Yusuf came to view the Iraqi state as an instrument of imperial exploitation. It was structured to serve the interests of Britain and its loyal oligarchy, not of common Iraqis. He also concluded that the neo-feudal basis of Iraq's economy was an obstacle to economic development. Prosperity, in other words, would never trickle down.[16]

Socialist ideas had floated around the Arab world since the turn of the century, when Abdul Rahman al-Kawakibi, a native of Aleppo, published his book *The Attributes of Tyranny*. "Human beings share the hardships of life in an unjust way," he wrote. One percent of the population, he estimated, enjoys half of society's wealth. "Justice requires other than that inequality," Kawakibi argued. "The elevated should take the lowly by his hand and bring him close to his rank and mode of life."[17]

Kawakibi and other Arabs saw communism as an Islam for the twentieth century. In the Prophet Muhammad's ideal city of Medina, Kawakibi wrote, Muslims lived under the same "conditions of a Communist existence" that contemporary socialists envisioned. "I am a Communist," declared the Iraqi poet Ma'ruf al-Rasafi in 1937 to parliament. "But my communism is Islamic for it is written in the Sacred Book: 'And in their wealth there is a right for the beggar and the deprived.' . . . And it was the Prophet that said: 'Take it from their wealthy and return it to their poor.' Was this not communism?"[18]

Rasafi's views were likely shaped by Husain al-Rahhal, leader of a Baghdad Marxist circle in the 1920s. Rahhal and others learned of communism from copies of the Anglo-Indian communist journal, *The Labour Monthly,* sold at the city's famous Mackenzie's Bookshop. Rahhal was a strict secularist, but most Iraqi communists likely shared Rasafi's view of it as an expression of Islamic social justice.

Back in Nasiriya, Yusuf established a communist circle in late 1927. His communism was born not of intellectual debate, but of his life of labor. "Nothing made him happier than being called a 'worker,'" the historian Batatu remarked. Yusuf's communism was also inspired by his work with the Iraqi National Party. "Before Fahd was a communist, he was a nationalist who struggled against imperialism," wrote Zaki Khairi, a fellow communist.

In the early 1930s, Yusuf's communist circle grew to sixty members. They were a mixture of manual laborers and the educated lower middle class. The leader in Basra, Ghali Zuwayyid, had been born a slave. He spoke easily with the sharecroppers in the palm groves. Membership rose as the world depression caused the price of Basra's dates to slump. Civil servants lost their jobs, and port workers and rail workers saw their wages slashed.

In December 1932, Yusuf printed the first communist proclamation in Iraq to be adorned with a hammer and sickle. He posted it in eighteen places in Nasiriya: "Workers of the World Unite! Long Live the Union of Workers' and Peasants' Republics of the Arab Countries!" it began. "The unemployed fill the streets. . . . Their women and children have nothing to eat. Has the government contemplated helping them in this cold weather? Nothing of the kind has happened. . . . Workers! The people have rights which they can only secure by force."[19]

When Arabic translations of the communist manifesto started circulating in Nasiriya, the police arrested Yusuf. He made no apologies. According to the police report, "he admitted he is a communist, and gave a tirade about the capitalists and the toiling masses."[20]

Meanwhile in Baghdad, Faysal obtained Iraqi independence in 1932, shortly before his death from heart failure. But all was not well. The young King Ghazi, Faysal's son, encouraged the palace elite's conspicuous consumption, even as shantytowns of peasant migrants sprouted at the city's edge.

British writer and photographer Freya Stark captured Baghdad's social contradictions in the early 1930s: "In early spring, before the first buds show on peach trees, a sort of luminous transparency envelops the distant city of Baghdad and its gardens," she wrote. "The blue domes melt into heaven of their own colour . . . and everywhere there is the voice of doves." But as the traveler enters the city, she remarked, a "sordid" poverty appears in the streets, where "the crowd looks unhealthy and sallow, the children are pitiful."[21]

Stark was shocked by the contempt of the British colony for the city's poor. British women told her proudly that "wogs" never crossed their doorstep. They expected Iraqis to be humbly grateful for the gifts of civilization that Britain gave them: bridges, police training, and education.[22]

Iraqis were less and less grateful. Newspapers in Arabic wrote "rude things about the English," Stark noted. In 1931, Baghdad's first labor union called a general strike against an increase in taxes on artisans. For two weeks shops remained closed, buses stopped, streets filled with demonstrators and speakers. The strike spread to the southern cities of Kufa and Diwaniya, and Basra.[23]

In 1934, the scattered cells of Iraqi communists gathered in the capital. Yusuf attended as a representative of Nasiriya. They formed the Committee against Imperialism and Exploitation and issued a manifesto proclaiming workers (not the monarchy) as the true basis of the nation. Their demands: cancellation of foreign debt and nationalization of oil, railways, and banks.

In 1935 the group became the ICP and published its first newspaper. A hammer and sickle with the slogan "Workers of the World Unite" adorned the masthead. The ICP joined the wave of unrest that swept across the Middle East in 1936. Kurds and Shiites staged tax revolts. The ICP joined an Iraqi front to demand democratic freedoms, reduction of poverty, and equality.[24] But by year's end, the state suppressed their activity.

From 1936 to 1941, nationalist army officers staged a series of coups to challenge the power of the palace. Ubiquitous British advisors protected the king and defeated the officers. They tended to blame poverty on deficiencies in Iraqi culture, not on their own policies.[25] The ICP criticized the British view, arguing that Iraq's economic underdevelopment and poverty were products of British policy and the political regime they had built.

Out of shared feelings of humiliation, the political right and left united temporarily against imperialism. The ICP initially supported the coups, but eventually it condemned military rule. The officers tended to be Sunni Muslims who excluded non-Muslims and non-Arabs from their view of the nation.

Yusuf was largely absent from Iraq in these years. In 1935, the party had sent him on scholarship to Moscow, where he attended the Communist University of Toilers of the East (KUTV). The university trained promising leaders from the colonial world in Marxist-Leninist theory and in practical skills of underground organizing, espionage, and guerrilla warfare.[26] We have little information on Yusuf's experience at KUTV, except that he married a Russian woman named Irina Georgivna. They had met in the summer of 1935 and had a baby daughter named Susan. At graduation, however, students were told to write farewell letters releasing their wives from their wedding vows. They pledged to devote themselves to "selfless service of the Revolution."[27]

Yusuf broke that pledge to write a letter to Irina in November 1937 from Paris, where he had gone for further training. Written in Russian and English, it is one of the only personal documents we have from him. As a glimpse into the human side of the activist, it is worth quoting at length:

Paris 26/11/37

Irina Darling,

I hope you are in the best of health and happiness. I am very sorry that I could not write to you earlier. I congratulate you on your birthday. I bought something as a birthday present. I hope you will accept this humble present. I sent it to your address. You will find the receipt enclosed and I hope that you will receive them. I am very anxious to know about your health and how you managed after I left you.

I trust you will forgive me. Write to tell me everything, and quickly.

I hope that Mamenska and Raphael and the rest are O.K. My salute and best wishes to them. I wish you were in Paris to see the exhibition. It was a grand thing. . . . [28]

Two months after mailing the letter, Yusuf arrived back in Baghdad. He took on his new name and identity as Comrade Fahd. The lessons he had learned in Moscow and Paris equipped him to build Iraq's first—and only—truly mass party.

COMRADE FAHD ESTABLISHES A MARXIST-LENINIST PARTY

Having left his family in Moscow, Comrade Fahd was believed to shun all relationships with women, outside of a few rare accounts of flirtation. He now found companionship in party comrades. Closest to him was Zaki Basim, codenamed "Comrade Hazim." He would room with Fahd through much of the 1940s and accompany him to the gallows. A Sunni Arab, Hazim was twelve years younger than Fahd. He worked as an apprentice tanner and a clerk in the water department while earning a high school degree at night school. When he met Fahd in 1942, he instantly became his most loyal follower. "I found him a patriot who worked in the public interest with unwavering fidelity and conviction," Hazim later told police. "He opened his heart to me and asked me to join him in the struggle."[29]

Fahd's other close ally was Husain Muhammad al-Shabibi, codenamed "Comrade Sarim." Sarim was a Shii schoolteacher from Najaf who shared Fahd's view that the ICP must be founded on the recruitment of workers, not the bourgeois intellectuals in Baghdad. "The Iraqi working class is the basic pillar of building the party and its struggle," Sarim wrote.[30]

War conditions gave Fahd and the new ICP an opening for wider recruitment. Since the Soviet Union joined the Allies in 1941, police had eased up on repression of communists. Fahd would gain even more freedom in 1943, when the Soviets dissolved the Comintern, which had imposed Moscow's policy on local parties. The ICP would be free to determine its own political strategy. It would become not just a worker's party, but an Iraqi party.

Fahd's battle with old-guard communists in Baghdad began in November 1941 at an ICP central committee meeting. The party's secretary general had just been arrested and Fahd claimed leadership for himself. A member demanded to know if he had a mandate from the Comintern in Moscow. Fahd responded that he did. The meeting voted to confirm him, but with lingering doubt. "I had at that time some misgivings about a Christian leading the organization," wrote another member at the meeting, himself a Christian.[31] Fahd's challenger, a Sunni Arab teacher and novelist, recruited other intellectuals in a revolt against his leadership. In the summer of 1942, Fahd expelled them from the party.

By early 1944, Fahd was strong enough to eliminate the remaining rebels in the party. They opposed Fahd's "dictatorship" and demanded a democratically elected leadership. Fahd's response to the bourgeois intellectuals, as he called them, was entitled "A Communist Party, Not Democratic Socialism." His most-quoted and most-reproduced essay, it became a manifesto for the transition of the ICP into an underground workers' party. Fahd argued that an illegal party cannot hold open elections because secrecy is the key to survival. Police would easily discover any system of publicizing candidates and any general meeting at which a vote would be held. Quoting Vladimir Ilyich Lenin, Fahd also attacked the intellectuals' dilettantism. He posed as the communist professional, trained in Moscow. Revolutionary theory is not just intellectual amusement, he said. Nor is it a dogma. It must be adapted to the real world of working people. "Marxism is a recipe to give everyone food for all situations," he wrote. But elite Marxists are like "a young bride who opens her cookbook to read recipes for kibbeh and beans with oil," he wrote. She follows the recipe literally, but with no experience or training in method. "The result, her husband finds at the dinner table, is an inedible disaster."[32]

The essay signaled clearly that Fahd intended to build a movement tailored to the needs of Iraqis, not an arm of Moscow. Nor did Fahd appear to impose a vanguard leadership upon the Iraqi membership. While he positioned himself as the expert and as the sole leader of the party, he also envisioned a party organically nurtured from the ground up.

In March 1944, Fahd convened the ICP's first national conference. It was held, secretly, at the Baghdad home of Ali Shukur, a locomotive driver. Four central committee members met with fourteen representatives of provincial branches. The meeting consolidated the party under his undisputed leadership. Fahd's "charisma and political commitment were increasingly unassailable," wrote one observer. "However," noted a member, "he was vainglorious."[33]

In his notorious monotone, Fahd reported on the growth of British influence and tyranny in Iraq. Hazim reported on workers, and Sarim reported on the party's education program. Without debate, the fourteen representatives approved the party program. Called the "National Charter," the program called for independence, constitutional democracy, economic development, lower taxes and more land for the poor, and rights for women and Kurds. The first step would be to recruit oil, port, and railroad workers. The meeting ended by adopting the party's slogan, "A Free Homeland and a Happy People."[34]

The central committee that convened the ICP's 1945 congress demonstrated its new social base. They met at the home of Yahuda Siddiq, a Jewish schoolteacher who would also join Fahd on the gallows in 1949. In addition to Fahd, Hazim, and Sarim, the committee included Fahd's brother Daud, an electrician; an ex-railway worker; a "coffee man"; a shoemaker; a musician; five schoolteachers; and an employee of the irrigation ministry. Most were born outside of Baghdad, and most had joined the party after 1941. Five were Christians, two Jews, three Shiis, four Sunni Arabs, and one Sunni Kurd. They claimed to represent the working people of Iraq, who were 90 percent illiterate and mostly peasants. Iraqis' average income was much lower than in Syria or Lebanon.[35]

The meeting affirmed the ICP as a "working class" party united by "iron discipline" against the state's "arbitrary and Nazi laws." For security reasons, members swore to avoid contact with police and foreigners and agreed to meet only rarely. Fahd and Hazim would direct the party on a day-to-day basis.[36]

The committee also agreed on a two-stage plan for revolution, which was announced in an April 1945 booklet entitled "A Free Homeland and a Happy People." The first stage would establish a democratic regime in Iraq, which would restore political rights and permit the party to organize publicly. The second stage would establish a "dictatorship of the proletariat."

Most of the booklet detailed plans to promote democracy. It reproduced the party's National Charter as a list of twelve immediate goals: 1) sovereignty; 2) democratic government; 3) end to food shortages; 4) economic expansion; 5) end to seizures of peasants' lands; 6) unions and health insurance for peasants; 7) lower taxes for people of small incomes; 8) expansion of education; 9) equal political, social, and economic rights for women; 10) equal rights for Kurds; 11) humane treatment of prisoners and soldiers; 12) diplomatic ties with the Soviet Union.

The booklet also reproduced Fahd's speech to the 1945 party congress, calling for a democratic fight against fascism and imperialism:

> Comrades! Remember always that we live in an age and at a time when a handful of financial businesses houses in the colonized countries wish to impose their open class dictatorship. This barbarous gang which is impersonated in Nazi-Fascism, probed for a gap and launched its offensive against the weak and the disintegrated forces of democracy.[37]

Fahd noted that Iraq's government had dissolved ten political parties since achieving independence. Like others in the Middle East, he argued that justice would not prevail without sovereignty.

The biggest obstacle to democracy and prosperity was British imperialism, Fahd claimed. The British directly advised Iraq's Ministry of the Interior on methods of repressing political opposition, he said. Worse than British agents were the Iraqi elites who cooperated with them: "Every minister in this Cabinet knows that he is serving the British rather than Iraqi interests." Such collaboration is a crime, he continued. Prime Minister Nuri violated constitutional guarantees of sovereignty when he granted sugar and date monopolies to British companies, hired British officers into the Iraqi government, and permitted British spies to travel inside the country.

Fahd became a marked man after publishing that attack. Political police, led by their British advisors, launched a search for him and his printing press. British intelligence quickly led police to the printer who had reproduced copies of the National Charter. They soon arrested six men caught distributing it to Iraqi soldiers: under a 1937 law, communist recruitment in the army was a capital crime.[38]

But the ICP's propaganda machine kept running. Sami Michael, a Jewish party member, translated communist materials from English into Arabic. He and his team distributed their translations in handwritten pamphlets and gave lectures to neighbors in Baghdad. "The Iraqi people would come and listen to us with great respect," Michael said. "We were their heroes who fought colonial rule. We were Iraqis, communists and patriots. Patriotism was very important for us."[39]

Inspired by the Atlantic Charter to wage a war for democratic ideas, the ICP opened a printing house in September 1945. Dar al-Hikma (the House of Wisdom) published books and pamphlets on politics, the economy, arts, and even science.[40] The party's newspaper, *Al-Qaeda* (the *Base*), reached a daily circulation of 3,000 by 1947. It was distributed most widely in Baghdad, the Kurdish north, and the Shii south.

Financing was local. Contrary to the accusations of government officials and the British, the ICP received little support from the Soviets. The party raised 6,000 dinars to open the House of Wisdom. Daily expenses were funded primarily by members' dues. Fahd and the others lived on pay from day jobs.[41]

The party also established the League against Zionism. Led by young Baghdadi Jews like Michael, it opposed Zionists who tried to convince Jews to emigrate to Palestine. The Jewish community of Baghdad, numbering more than 110,000, had roots in Iraq going back more than 2,500 years. While Jews favored the intercommunal life of Baghdad, they worried that Arab nationalism threatened their future. In 1941 riots had broken out when the British defeated leaders of a pro-German military coup. During a brief interregnum, a mob hit the streets and looted Jewish homes and shops. An estimated 200 Jews were killed. A few mob leaders were fired by anti-Zionist ideology, but most were apparently poor people seeking instant gain.[42]

The ICP's League against Zionism addressed Jews' fears of nationalism by promoting its vision of plural and democratic justice. "Minorities cannot have peace of mind until the Iraqi working class comes to power," claimed a 1946 handbill of the Free Jewish Youth. The league's newspaper published articles blaming British and American imperialism for the growth of nationalism and sectarian violence. The paper reportedly reached an impressive circulation of 6,000 copies daily.[43]

Meanwhile, Fahd's right-hand man Sarim founded the National Liberation Party (NLP). It promoted the "principles of rights and justice," with emphasis on Kurdish rights, protection for children, and an end to hunger. The NLP and the league attracted thousands of students and teachers, turning the colleges of Baghdad into "revolutionary beehives."[44]

The ICP built its strongest popular base among urban workers.[45] Communists headed fourteen of sixteen labor unions, including those at Baghdad's railroad yard, Kirkuk's oil fields, and Basra's port. Ali Shukur, the locomotive driver, headed the railway union and in April 1945 led its 1,700 members on a successful strike for pay raises.

In all, the unions gave the ICP the muscle of nearly 10,000 workers in addition to perhaps 10,000 students and civil servants who supported the party or its affiliates. The first peasants to join the ICP were migrants living in reed huts outside of Baghdad, mostly Shiis from the south. Full members of the party still numbered under 3,000, because Fahd remained strict about proper training. For security, members were organized in small cells of three to seven members each and linked to Baghdad through three regional committees: in the south, the north, and the central region around the capital.

The ICP was small compared to Banna's half-million members of the Muslim Brotherhood in Egypt. But its growth was impressive, given the constraints of being an illegal, underground movement. Banna had run a public party and was a well-known charismatic figure. "Fahd was unknown, not a Che [Guevara]," recalls a former party member.[46] "He was more like Ho Chi Minh," a strict and inspirational organizer known mainly to activists through his pamphlets and his underground newspaper. Only after his first trial in 1947 did Fahd become publicly known.[47]

STAGE ONE OF THE REVOLUTION

In 1946, no other political organization in Iraq came close to the popular influence and power of the ICP. Its core idea—that tyranny was not natural or divinely sanctioned—was a revelation. Like Banna's Muslim Brotherhood in Egypt, the ICP convinced thousands of Iraqis that they could act collectively to establish justice in their lifetime.

Under continued economic stress, workers felt freer to rebel against their bosses. Also like the Muslim Brotherhood, the ICP was the sole party to address the immediate needs of common people, by staging protests against inflation and food shortages. The ICP promised to restore justice to the social order; Iraq's elite liberal parties merely called for honest elections.

Tribal shaykhs felt threatened enough to form an anticommunist bloc in parliament. By early 1946, urban elites felt anxiety too. "A creeping fear of Communism is spreading steadily among Iraq's princes of privilege and economic royalists," reported an American diplomat. "The forceful and persistent propaganda which the Communist party is spreading among Iraqi workers is having effect." Rumors flew in Baghdad about the "fabulous Fahd" who signed the "scurrilous" leaflets attacking imperialists, reactionaries, and thieving politicians.[48]

The state initially responded with a concession, legalizing five elite parties (not the ICP) and proposing electoral reform. The ICP used the political opening to ally with liberals against the Sunni Arab ruling elite and to stage worker strikes. Fahd issued a flurry of leaflets and articles demanding Britain's evacuation as a first step toward economic reform. Most influential was his article "Necessities of Our National Struggle," which called on politicians to end useless negotiations for independence. They should instead inspire courage among Iraqi citizens, for only mass mobilization will force the British to evacuate.[49] Fahd wrote the article in June 1946, when Egyptians and Zionists also staged mass protests against British rule.

The great battles of the summer of 1946 were set when massive student protests to free Palestine brought down the liberal government in May. The parliament's anticommunist bloc maneuvered to install a hard-liner, Arshad al-Umari, as prime minister. Umari's violent response to protests that summer only heightened the ICP's prestige.

The first battle came on June 28, 1946, when communists organized 3,000 workers and students to march through Baghdad to protest British injustice in Palestine and call for Britain's evacuation from Iraq. "We wanted to escalate the situation," recalled Michael. Police opened fire and killed a communist student named Shaul Tuwayyiq. His body fell on top of Michael, who jumped up, covered in blood, and began screaming at the policeman. Out of nowhere, a black wall rose up. "Women dressed in their traditional black threw themselves between us, to keep him from shooting me," Michael recalled. "And they beat him [the policeman] up severely."[50]

The second battle came on July 3, 1946, in Kirkuk, north of Baghdad. ICP member Hanna Ilyas led his union of 500 oil workers on a strike for higher pay. For ten days they held rallies in a park, reciting poems and giving speeches. Police then charged their horses into the crowd, killing ten workers. The union refused to call off the strike until it won a raise six days later.[51]

The ICP accused the state of terrorism and of protecting British oil interests to the detriment of its own citizens' rights. In league with liberal parties, they staged protests that brought Umari down in November. To their dismay, however, the dreaded Nuri replaced Umari. He ordered Fahd's childhood nemesis, Attiyah, now head of the political police, to find him.[52]

Fahd was on the run, never sleeping in the same place twice. He and Hazim (Zaki Basim) were finally arrested on January 18, 1947, at the Baghdad home of a Jewish pharmacist, Ibrahim Naji Shumayyil. All three were taken to the Investigation Department in central Baghdad, shackled, and "flung like dogs into a latrine overflowing with filth," Hazim later reported. After repeated beatings, an interrogator informed Fahd that spreading communist ideas was illegal. The law, Fahd replied, "is out of accord with the Iraqi constitution, which has conceded the freedom of belief to every Iraqi citizen."[53]

Fahd and Hazim were transferred to the infamous Abu Ghraib military prison in the desert west of Baghdad and confined to narrow, damp, airless cells. On June 13, 1947, they launched an eight-day hunger strike, until prison authorities finally brought them to Iraq's High Criminal Court. They faced charges of treasonous ties to a foreign government (the Soviet Union) and to communists in Iran and Syria; of plotting armed insurrection; and of propagating communism in the military.[54]

Fahd used his trial to speak in public for the first time—in defense of democracy. He denied all charges and insisted that communists should not be prosecuted simply for their beliefs:

> We stand before your respected court and we do not ask for mercy, because mercy is for the guilty. We don't want to protect ourselves for the

sake of our own interest. We want justice, because we want to protect the reputation of Iraqi law. . . . A democracy that cannot tolerate activities of its most ardent and persistent activists, who understand the ways of the imperialists, cannot be a democracy in the eyes of liberal world public opinion.[55]

On June 23, 1947, the court condemned Fahd, Hazim, and the pharmacist Shumayyil to death by hanging for proselytizing in the military.

The death sentences caused an uproar. At this point, historian Tareq Ismael recalls, Fahd became a household name. Iraqis protested to foreign embassies and to the United Nations, forcing the Iraqi appeals court to reject the verdict.[56] The government commuted their sentences to penal servitude at Kut prison, 100 miles south of Baghdad.

Fahd turned the prison into a school for communism. Prisoners due for early release were trained in better methods of underground organizing and taught to avoid mistakes that risked arrest. Fahd maintained links with the party leadership on the outside by writing notes of advice in invisible onion juice. Party networks were soon restored, and the party newspaper again published 3,000 copies a day.[57]

In November 1947, Fahd sent a secret order to ICP cadres to restore the coalition with liberals: "Lead it and expand its activities, focusing on the issues of bread and democratic freedoms."[58]

Stage one of Iraq's revolution, as in so many others, began at a time of economic crisis. "The issue of bread, especially in big cities, was devastating and it really worried the people," recalled Aziz Sbahi, a teacher and party member. "There were long lines of women, men and children gathering in front of the bakeries in Baghdad beginning at four in the morning and even before four o'clock, they waited to get a few cold unappetizing loaves."[59]

As in Iran in 1906, the state showed little concern. It adhered to a balanced-budget policy and spent little on social welfare. Its total budget for 1947, corrected for inflation, was actually lower than its 1938 budget had been. State neglect and violence turned a student protest into the Wathbah.[60]

The Wathbah started when news of the Portsmouth Treaty leaked to the public in late December 1947. College and high school students responded with a march on January 5, protesting the treaty's extension of Britain's military presence in Iraq. Mounted police beat the demonstrators with clubs and shot into the crowd. To protest the violence, the law school shut down and students announced a general strike. While only six of the thirty-nine students arrested were communist, legend has it that a letter arrived from Fahd ordering the ICP to send all of its forces into the street. He appointed Kamil Qazanchi, a lawyer and great orator, to lead the demonstrations.

On January 16, the government sparked a new round of protests when it publicized the terms of the Portsmouth Treaty. Students marched again, now to demand the prime minister's resignation. On the fourth day of protests, January 20, communist railroad workers joined the student march down Baghdad's main avenue, Rashid Street. Police again fired into the crowd, killing several people. They fired again the next day, upon students carrying coffins to the Royal Hospital. Two more fell dead. This outrage provoked the middle class to join the protests.

"Crowds, thick with Communists and armed with huge canes, clashed with the police, who became much like flotsam in a wrathful sea. An atmosphere redolent of social revolution enveloped Baghdad," Batatu wrote.[61] The regent, Prince Abd al-Ilah, called an emergency meeting of the cabinet and parliament—and renounced the Portsmouth Treaty that night.

The Wathbah defeated the treaty, but it did not end there. Demonstrations spread to Basra, Mosul, and other cities. On January 23, the Prophet's birthday, huge crowds flooded Baghdad's main avenues shouting "Long Live the Unity of the Workers and Students!" and "Give Bread to the People!" They carried Kamil Qazanchi on their shoulders. He jumped atop the Wadi coffeehouse and shouted: "Let us declare it a great people's revolution!" The crowd marched on, yelling, "Release the Leader Fahd!" and "Long Live the Republic!"[62]

The Wathbah came to a climax on the night of January 26, when Prime Minister Salih Jabr made a radio broadcast that urged calm, in threatening language. Baghdadis poured from their homes in defiance. Police machinegun fire echoed in the midnight streets. The next morning, protesters flowed across the Mamun Bridge into the city center.

"On the 27th of January, the capital became a battlefield," wrote historian Abd al-Razzak al-Husni. "The police blocked the side streets and armored cars moved into the main city squares and placed the machine guns on top of the high buildings and on top of the minarets of mosques." When a group of demonstrators tried to cross the Tigris River, the police "started to shoot at them from the two minarets on top of the mosques at both sides of the bridge entrance." Many were killed, but the people prevailed. The police retreated and the people crossed the bridge.

Party member Aziz al-Hajj joined another march to the royal palace. "The demonstration rushed from the medical college to face a stream of bullets," he recalled. "The police met us with machine guns. I took refuge with others in a municipal grocery store." The crowd then headed to the palace, where they protested to a spokesman. New waves of gunfire killed four.

Jabr made more threats, and protests surged again in Baghdad, Mosul, Kirkuk, and Basra. "This was like pouring oil on fire," Husni recalled. "The people rushed to burn the British *Iraq Times* newspaper building and everything to do with the English. Orders were given to shoot at the chest [to kill] and they cut the people as a scythe cuts wheat, until the policemen were shivering from fear and anxiety themselves."[63]

Demonstrators claimed victory that day. They had shamed the government by forcing it to shoot its own citizens. Two cabinet ministers, the president of parliament, and twenty deputies resigned. At eight o'clock that evening, Prime Minister Jabr resigned as well. Along with Nuri, he fled Baghdad.[64]

They left bloodstains and bodies spattered across what became known as Martyrs' Bridge. Government estimates put the number of dead at around 100, but police and communist files suggest that more than 300 may have been killed.[65] The brother of one of the eighteen ICP members killed on January 27 composed a poem entitled "My Brother Jaafar," which he recited to Sunnis, Shiis, and Jews gathered at the Haydarkhana mosque. The verse "Do you know or do you not know/ That the wounds of victims are a mouth?" became one of the most famous in modern Iraqi Arabic poetry.[66]

The communist imprint on the Wathbah was everywhere. The nationalist parties had tried to call off the protest after January 20, when the treaty was withdrawn. "Many youth demonstrated against their [nationalist party] leaders' orders," Sbahi wrote. "It was also remarkable that officers and enlisted soldiers joined with the demonstrating masses in their uniforms, and heard speeches about democratic power."[67]

Protests continued through the spring, with forty-day memorials for victims and strikes by municipal, textile, oil, railway, and port workers.[68] In May, oil workers organized "The March," in homage to Mao Tse-tung's Long March in China. Some 2,000 started walking from Haditha to Baghdad, 145 miles away. Police trapped them at Falluja, thirty-five miles short of Baghdad, and arrested fifteen leaders for threatening state security.[69]

Iraq was "on the verge of revolution," warned local newspapers and British observers.[70] On May 15, the day after the Haditha workers' arrest, the government declared martial law and shut down the ICP's newspaper and unions, on the pretext that communists were supporting Israel in the Palestine war. The Soviets' recognition of Israel—and the Arabs' defeat in Palestine—deeply compromised the ICP and led indirectly to Fahd's death.

In December 1948, police captured the holy grail, the small ICP printing press hidden in a member's home that had printed the pamphlets of "fabulous Fahd" three years before.[71] They also caught the party's interim leader, Malik Saif, who revealed that Fahd had directed the Wathbah from his cell in Kut prison. Fahd and his two closest comrades, Hazim and Sarim, were dragged to a military court at Abu Ghraib prison.

In the same atmosphere of anger and panic that led the Egyptian state to murder Banna, the Iraqi regime used this evidence to retry Fahd on capital charges. Nuri, again prime minister, blamed Jews and communists for the Arabs' defeat in the Palestine war and vowed to "settle accounts with the communists." He ordered a secret trial for Fahd and his comrades, which quickly issued a sentence of death.[72]

Fahd was hanged secretly, and the circumstances remain obscure. According to one account, he was hanged in al-Karkh, on the west bank of the Tigris, at dawn on February 14, 1949. His body was left for hours in an open square, with a placard listing his crimes. Comrade Sarim was said to be hanged the same morning across the river at Mu'atham Gate, the gathering place for the Wathbah demonstrations. Comrade Hazim, Fahd's beloved aide, and Yahuda Siddiq, briefly party leader after Fahd's arrest, were hanged the following morning.[73]

"The importance of the Iraqi communists is not in any proportion to the power they attained for themselves. It lies, instead, in the agenda they set for others to follow, for they were frequently the only voice that spoke for the masses, the majority of the people," wrote historian Tareq Ismael.[74] As a boy, he saw the bodies of communists hanging on a sunny February morning in 1949 as he walked to school.

While Banna was carried solemnly in public procession to his grave, Fahd's body was never returned to his family. A month later, in face of protest, the Iraqi police justified Fahd's execution by falsely linking the ICP to Zionism.[75] The people were not convinced. They would avenge the state's act of terror in the summer of 1958.

"Fahd dead proved more potent than Fahd living," wrote the historian Batatu in 1978. "Far from dying out, communism became in the fifties a more powerful passion." Communists became national martyrs, known for their willingness to stand up to injustice. They also inspired new artistic movements that expressed an Iraqi brand of modernity. Marxism became so dominant that even Jabr (the prime minister forced to resign by the Wathbah) named his new party the "Socialist Party of the Nation."[76]

The 1950s were also a grim era of grinding poverty and dictatorship. Oil revenues soared, noted historian Walter Laqueur in 1956. "Yet there is no prospect in the near future of an increase in the standard of living of either the peasants or the majority of the urban population." He compared conditions in Iraq to Russia in 1917, when Bolsheviks rose against the tsar. Even the British diplomats began to worry about the "slums of mud huts" circling Baghdad and the "hideous squalor and poverty" in the southern provinces. Peasants were starving.[77]

Communist writers drew dark portraits of state terror in their country. Novelist Gha'ib Farman, exiled in Egypt, wrote in *The Black Regime in Iraq* that "every Iraqi family has a *shahid* [martyr], prisoner, or deportee."[78]

Despite repression, the ICP revived under the leadership of Kurds. Iraq's Kurdish northeast was as underprivileged as the Shii south. Power shifted from students to workers and from revolutionaries to moderates. Although we have no data on total membership, the ICP appears to have remained strongest in Baghdad and the south. Perhaps one-fifth of party members were still drawn from the army's rank and file. After a period of factionalism, a unified command emerged in 1956 that included a Kurd, a Sunni, and a Shii. The last was Hussein al-Radi, a quiet former schoolteacher who became Fahd's successor as the ICP's secretary-general. He took the codename Salaam Adil (A Just Peace). The trio agreed on a program of gradual change and in early 1957 entered a national front in opposition to Nuri's regime—which grew more authoritarian as new oil fields funneled new profits into state coffers.

Not all Iraqis were so patient. On July 14, 1958, a dissident group of military officers engineered a coup against the monarchy. They proclaimed Iraq a republic:

> Noble People of Iraq,
> Trusting in God and with the aid of the loyal sons of the people and the national armed forces, we have undertaken to liberate the beloved homeland from the corrupt crew that imperialism installed. . . . Power shall be entrusted to a government emanating from you and inspired by you . . . realized by the creation of a people's republic. . . .
> (Signed) The Commander-in-Chief of the National Armed Forces[79]

The Free Officers' proclamation echoed the language of Fahd and the ICP, with its appeal to anti-imperialism, popular sovereignty, and democracy. Their leader, General Abd al-Karim Qasim, became prime minister.

While many Iraqis danced in the street, others took revenge. According to a soldier's memoir, the young King Faysal II and Crown Prince Abd al-Ilah were gunned down senselessly in their palace courtyard, after having surrendered. A mob mutilated the body of Abd al-Ilah and dumped it into the Tigris River.[80] Nuri's body, too, was dismembered and dragged in the street.[81] These vicious acts echoed the brutal killings of the Wathbah, the terror and torture of Nuri's prisons, and the dishonor done to Fahd's body. Revenge haunted the days of revolutionary joy in July 1958.

Freedom soon became the byword of the revolution. Prisoners were freed, exiles returned, the arts flourished anew. The King Faysal Bridge that the army crossed to reach the royal palace on the morning

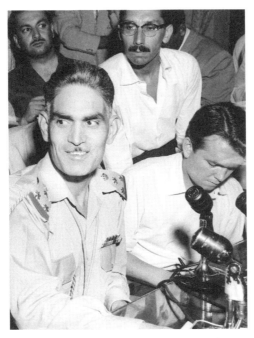

Brigadier General Abd al-Karim Qasim holds a press conference in Baghdad on July 27, 1958, thirteen days after leading a coup to overthrow the Iraqi monarchy and establish a republic. He was not a communist, but the Iraqi Communist Party's popular support turned the coup into a revolution. (AP Photo)

of July 14 was renamed Jisr al-Ahrar (The Bridge of the Free).[82] Crowds pulled down the statues of General Maude and King Faysal I. Qasim commissioned a Freedom Monument to replace them.

The Freedom Monument, a 150-meter limestone wall symbolizing a banner carried in a demonstration, still stands in Baghdad's Tahrir (Liberation) Square. Its fourteen bronze, bas-relief panels tell the story of the 1958 revolution in modernist style, combining Picasso's cubism with ancient Assyrian and Sumerian motifs. The story begins on the right with a powerful horse, symbolizing the vitality of the people, then moves to a mother weeping for her martyred son and an intellectual sitting in a prison cell. A soldier liberates them, in the central panel of the frieze. The figure of freedom follows, depicted as a woman holding a torch, and on the left end, final panels show Kurdish and Arab peasant women carrying palm fronds, an unborn child, and a spade; a freed bull; and a worker.[83]

July 14, 1958, Batatu argued, was "the climax of the struggle of a whole generation." While the ICP had not directly organized the coup, the party had done much to educate and encourage the 100,000 people who poured into the streets and turned the coup into a revolution. The ICP's leader Hussein al-Radi embraced the revolution as the first, democratic step in the two-stage revolution.[84] He and other communists organized a "monster" demonstration in August to show support. In coming weeks, tens of thousands of Iraqis joined communist organizations like popular militias, the Peace Partisans, the Women's League, labor unions, and peasant unions.

The relationship between the ICP and Qasim was so close that most Iraqis believed Qasim was a communist. He was not. Qasim supported the liberal National Democratic Party, but he encouraged ICP support because he believed that 70 percent of Iraqis sympathized with the communists. Qasim also defined the revolution's primary mission as the restoration of social justice. He redistributed the land of royalist elites to 35,000 families, raised taxes on the landed rich, reduced housing rents and bread prices, issued labor regulations to improve workers' conditions, and built homes and schools for 10,000 families living in the slums around Baghdad.[85]

The ICP's ideological hegemony did not, however, lead to political hegemony.[86] Although the communists became the popular vanguard of the 1958 revolution, they never captured the government. Three factors—the military, oil revenues, and the Cold War—tilted politics in the new republic against the left and toward dictatorship. The Free Officers were weakened by a split in leadership. While Qasim favored the secular, Iraq-centered, National Democratic Party, his partner, Abd al-Salam Arif, leaned toward Islam and the pan-Arabist Baath Party. While Qasim rallied communist crowds to the regime, Arif organized an armed revolt. In March 1959, Baathists ambushed communists on the streets of Mosul after a Peace Partisans rally, killing hundreds. Qasim's troops and communist militias fought back, and after much bloodshed, prevailed. Arif's supporters were purged from government and several were executed, including Fahd's nemesis, Attiyah.

Success at Mosul inspired the ICP to demand that Qasim appoint communists to his cabinet. That was the reason for the million-strong peace march in April 1959 and for another monster march on May Day. Qasim, however, rejected the communists' bid to share political power. In late 1959, he openly turned against the ICP. He ordered the arrest of hundreds of communists, shut down their public branches, demobilized their popular militias, and removed communists from control of the peasant unions and the press.[87]

ICP leaders convened an emergency meeting in late May 1959 to consider their options. Rival factions argued whether to overthrow the government in favor of the workers' revolution or to adhere to their two-stage plan and so cooperate with Qasim first to establish a democracy. The faction advocating the latter won the fight. They published a pledge of loyalty to Qasim, admitting error in pushing too hard for government posts and praising his promise to legalize political parties and hold parliamentary elections. But the damage was done. Public support for the communists ebbed as Qasim pursued a campaign to discredit them as violent anarchists.[88]

Why had the communists so sheepishly submitted to Qasim's dictatorship, when the party enjoyed a preponderance of public support? Historians have debated this question for decades. Many agree that Qasim was so personally popular that it would have been political suicide for the party to defy him. Some argue that the decision to cooperate with Qasim reflected the party's true, constitutional nature. Tens of thousands of Iraqis who joined the party after July 1958 viewed it as a democratic organization. They had little training or indoctrination in revolutionary ideology.[89]

"The ICP now found itself hoist on the petard of its own moderation," wrote historians Marion Farouk-Sluglett and Peter Sluglett. In the absence of a true democratic system, they argued, the ICP should not have tried to behave like a political party. If the ICP had mobilized workers and peasants, the poor majority of Iraq, it might have succeeded, agreed historian Samira Haj.[90]

Aziz al-Hajj, one of ICP's leaders who had signed the loyalty pledge in the summer of 1959, argued that revolution was simply not an option—because of the international situation. Qasim faced threats from both pan-Arab Baathists and Nasserists who wanted to dissolve Iraq into the United Arab Republic. "In such circumstances, the launching of an armed movement would have played into the hands of the enemies of our independence," al-Hajj argued.[91]

Qasim also faced threats from the United States, some argue. Although the ICP had no substantive links to Moscow (the Soviets were more interested in Egypt's Gamal Abdel Nasser), the American Central

Intelligence Agency (CIA) was in a frenzy over the apparent spread of communism to Iraq. The 1957 Eisenhower Doctrine promised aid to anti-Soviet forces in the Middle East. In April 1959, at the time of the million-strong peace march, American newspapers quoted CIA director Allen Dulles as saying the situation in Iraq was "the most dangerous in the world today."[92]

Dulles—and the British before him—ignored the indigenous and democratic quality of Iraqi communism. The ICP's membership was inspired by the same political values as other Arab liberation movements: national sovereignty, constitutionalism, and social egalitarianism. Only a defeated minority advocated an immediate workers' revolution. Dulles also neglected State Department reports on the local social conditions that had made the ICP popular: the domination of a landowning class, the flight of sharecroppers to the city, and the denial of freedoms by the British-backed monarchy.[93]

The Qasim dream ended quickly. The Iraqi Baath Party rebuilt itself in exile, infiltrated the Iraqi army, and prepared a better plot than it had in March 1959. In February 1963, key targets around Baghdad were relatively undefended while the Iraqi army battled a revolt in the Kurdish north. On the morning of February 8, the Baathists bombed the airport, took the radio station, and broadcast another revolutionary call on the radio, echoing that of July 14, 1958.

But this time, demonstrations broke out to defend the regime from the coup. Communists and workers poured into Rashid Street and surrounded the Defense Ministry, calling "There is no leader but Karim [Qasim]!" Shortly after ten o'clock, communist placards appeared on city walls: "To Arms! Crush the Reactionary Imperialist Conspiracy!" Thousands flooded the central city, fighting Baathist tanks with sticks and pistols. Qasim, however, refused to release weapons to the communist-led crowds. He remained besieged in the Defense Ministry, where he was killed.[94]

The communists' turn came next. Their former strength within the military had weakened and they were left virtually defenseless. Hundreds of communists were killed in fighting between February 8 and 10. The poorest districts of Baghdad, dominated by Shiis, held out the longest, as did communists in Basra. Claiming revenge, Baathist leaders then waged a campaign to annihilate the ICP that surpassed in terror and brutality that of Nuri. They conducted door-to-door searches and threw thousands of communists into sports stadiums as makeshift prisons. By November, 7,000 communists were in prison and at least 150 had been executed.[95]

The ICP was crushed in 1963 as it had been in 1949; this time, however, it would not regain the mass power it had previously wielded. The failure of communism in Iraq cannot be blamed solely on the errors of poor leadership. External factors played an important role. The Baath Party had found an important ally in Nasser. These regional forces, in turn, were stoked by the Cold War rivalry of the Americans and the Soviets.

The destruction of the ICP marked the end of an era in the Middle East. Since 1900 labor unions and communist parties had organized new urban working classes throughout the region. Labor movements had played pivotal roles in Egypt's 1919 and 1952 revolutions and in winning important social protections in Syria and Lebanon. Most of all, they had provided the muscle in popular challenges to dictatorship.

In the Middle East, the world wars played a role opposite to the one they played in Western Europe. Historian Geoff Eley has argued that the wars created "transnational conjunctions" in Western Europe that broke down obstacles to democracy.[96] Paradoxically, it had been Europe's socialists who played the democratic vanguard. In the Middle East, by contrast, the world wars had only raised false expectations of a Wilsonian Moment or the Atlantic Charter. World War I ushered in an expansion of European colonial rule, which in turn enriched and empowered a new landowning elite in Iraq, Egypt, and Syria. After World War II, the new colonial elites blocked democratization with the aid of rival superpowers in the Cold War.

Britain's dogged support of Nuri and the Eisenhower administration's fear of communism combined to defeat popular democratic forces. The Baath Party established a dictatorship that made use of the same Abu Ghraib prison and even more terrifying methods of repression. Arab socialist regimes—Baathist and Nasserist—took their cues from Turkey's Kemal, not Fahd. They transmuted the socialism of grassroots movements into a state machinery of reform from above.[97]

The Cold War's unliberating effect on poor people's movements for justice was dramatized in finer detail in the story of a peasant movement in Syria, Iraq's neighbor to the west. In contrast to the ICP, that movement's leader, Akram al-Hourani, actually gained access to high office in government, following the democratic measures that Iraqi communists advocated. Hourani faced similar pressures as the Cold War heated up on the 1950s. In response, he made fateful strategic alliances with the military and the Baath Party that triggered a coup in Syria at precisely the same moment as in Iraq, in February 1963.

8

AKRAM AL-HOURANI AND
THE BAATH PARTY IN SYRIA
Bringing Peasants into Politics

On a September evening in 1951 a small, wiry man stood before more than 10,000 cheering peasants in the northern Syrian city of Aleppo. Akram al-Hourani, leader of the Arab Socialist Party (ASP), looked out at the banners praising him and declared:

> My friends! We are weak when we are alone, but stronger than iron and fire when united! With the blood of our ancestors flowing through our hearts, we can rebel against tyranny and injustice![1]

The 1951 Syrian peasant congress "opened a new chapter in the life of the country and its future," according to a local paper. The congress brazenly called on the poorest of citizens to challenge wealthy land-owners' control of Syrian politics. Hourani demanded full inclusion of all citizens in the political arena, on the basis of equal rights. He grounded his vision of justice in the belief that Arab society had been strongest when it was egalitarian. Colonial rule had deepened class divisions and weakened Arabs. Peasants, Hourani preached, would rescue the nation from colonial corruption.

The congress was unprecedented in the Arab world. Since the 1858 Lebanese peasant republic, Middle Eastern peasants had not mounted a sustained political movement. Iran saw a wave of peasant and tribal revolts in 1929, followed by Palestinian peasants' armed revolt in

1936–1939.[2] A new wave of unrest rolled across the region's farm-lands after World War II. Even as Hourani spoke, Egyptian peasants were staging revolts against the country's largest landowners. And as we saw earlier, Iraqi communists had begun recruiting rural migrants in Baghdad who had fled the poorest provinces in the south.

Hourani's peasant congress reflected not just peasant discontent, but also the growing interest of political leaders in rural conditions. Since the turn of the century, Arabic novels and movies had featured romanticized portraits of the peasant as the bedrock of the nation, unmoved and uncorrupted by foreign rule. In the 1940s, the new Arab middle class began to take notice of peasants' actual condition. In Egypt, 60 percent of rural families were landless. In Syria, few vil-lages had electricity, water, schools, or clinics. Politicians like Hourani awoke to the reality that the future prosperity of their nation hinged on improving conditions for the majority of citizens who still lived in the countryside. In contrast to the urban-based politics of the early twentieth century, the new political movements built a following by proposing to redistribute land from large estates to the rural poor. Peasants would become the moral—and economic—backbone of a new, just society.[3]

In Turkey, just a year before the Aleppo congress, the Democrat Party had won elections by recruiting peasants who had been left out of Mustafa Kemal Ataturk's economic plans. Turkey's 1950 election was the first democratic turnover of power to an opposition party in the Middle East. Like Hourani, President Adnan Menderes and Ha-lide Edib believed that enfranchising peasants would make politics more democratic and unleash forces of progress and prosperity.

Unlike Turkish Democrats, however, Hourani's party faced a hos-tile and powerful landed elite in parliament. He therefore turned to socialist ideas to justify more forceful means of bringing pressure on the landlords. His ASP united urban workers with rural peasants in northern Syria. Increasingly, the party allied with the Damascus-based Baath Party to become the dominant force in Syrian politics. How-ever, throughout the Arab world, landowning elites empowered un-der colonial rule had so far succeeded in defeating rural challenges.

In another time and place, Hourani's effort might have produced a Scandinavian-style social welfare state. But conditions inside and out-side of 1950s Syria did not favor such a democratic transition. While

Turkish Democrats received agricultural aid from the United States in the 1950s, Hourani and Syrian socialists earned American suspicion and hostility. Hourani was (wrongly) labeled a communist and his opponents sought political leverage against him from the Americans and their allies in the region. Foreign intervention in Syria further undermined democratic politics.

Even without the pressures of the Cold War, Hourani would have had a very hard row to hoe. Had he been able to read the histories of democratic movements that we have today, notes political scientist David Waldner, Hourani might not have been so optimistic. Landowning classes in countries around the world have blocked transitions to democracy and harnessed the state and urban businessmen to protect their interests. Rarely have peasants succeeded in undermining landlords' power through parliamentary means. This has been especially true among developing countries emerging from colonial rule.[4]

From today's perspective, it is not surprising that Hourani fought a losing battle—to the point that he betrayed his own principles. From at least 1949, he cultivated a loyal faction of left-leaning officers in the army in order to shield his movement from landowners. In late 1957, his leftist-front government faced a coup organized by landowners with American help. As North Atlantic Treaty Organization (NATO) troops gathered on the Syria's Turkish border, Hourani betrayed his communist allies. He canceled elections when he feared a communist victory would trigger a NATO invasion. The Syrian political arena collapsed and the military took the reins of power. Circumventing Hourani and the parliament, the military elite merged Syria with Egypt to create the United Arab Republic. Under Egyptian president Gamal Abdel Nasser's dictatorship, democracy died in Syria.

Hourani's peasants never entered a democratically elected parliament. Instead, they would be recruited into a new, military-based Baath Party that took power by coup in 1963 and that still rules Syria today. Hourani fell from the pinnacle of Syrian politics into prison. In a final twist of fate, the very same peasants he had inspired to join the Baath Party sent him into permanent exile in 1965.

Hourani is an example of how Arab social democrats paradoxically laid the foundations of the military dictatorships that have dominated the Arab world since the 1960s. His story is unknown even to many Syrians, because the military's neo-Baath Party erased him from history and never allowed him to return. In the late 1980s, Hourani gave up on efforts to reenter Syrian politics. He sat in an apartment outside of Paris, with a shotgun by the door, and instead wrote himself back into history.[5] Thanks to his 3,500-page memoir, we can gain insight into how the 1951 peasant congress's demands for justice were denied.

A SWASHBUCKLER AND A POET

Hasan Akram Rashid al-Hourani opened his memoir with his birth on a snowy day in November 1911. His family lived in Hama, seventy-five miles south of Aleppo. It was an ancient city nestled against a rocky bluff along the Orontes River. Giant medieval water-wheels still lifted water from the river into aqueducts that served many of Hama's 50,000 inhabitants. Rashid al-Hourani, Akram's fa-ther, was a textile weaver by trade and a shaykh of the Rifa'i Sufi or-der. The Houranis had introduced the order to Hama in the sixteenth century when they migrated from the Hawran, in southern Syria.[6] The religious fraternity taught members to care for the poor and at-tracted a large peasant following.

By the time of Akram's birth, Rashid al-Hourani had assembled a modest landed estate and entered city politics. He became a census taker and a member of the Hama city council, which included repre-sentatives of the city's wealthiest families: the Barazis, the Azms, the Kaylanis. These landowners controlled the city's mosques and schools and owned 100 villages outright. Their arrogance was brutal. Accord-ing to family legend, a particularly snobbish council member loudly remarked one day that the chamber's drapes appeared to come from Hourani looms. (This was an insult, because aristocrats did not work with their hands.) Quick with his wit, Rashid al-Hourani retorted that the only reason the councilman recognized their provenance was that the drapes were so exquisitely well made.

The Azms, Kaylanis, and Barazis owned the best lands along the river, where a literate elite of peasants tended fragrant gardens of fruit trees and vegetables. Peasant sharecroppers tended grain fields and sheep pastures in hundreds of nearby villages. Not unlike 1858 Leba-non, the feudal landlords lived in city villas and sent brutal henchmen to keep order on their estates.[7]

Rashid al-Hourani resented the feudal lords because they overtaxed the poor. The Azm family earned £6,000 per year from its villages, while a typical sharecropper annually earned just £10.[8] Hourani's father also resented the Ottomans. Sultan Abdulhamid supported Hama's elites despite their injustice, and even appointed one as shaykh of the Rifa'i order. After the 1908 Revolution, Rashid al-Hourani joined an opposition party that favored autonomy for Arab provinces against the Young Turks' centralization. But he did not live to see the Arab revolt or the establishment of Faysal's Arab kingdom in Damascus. He died of cholera early in the war, in 1915.

Akram al-Hourani came of age in the post-Ottoman world, under the French mandate in Syria. He was just nine years old in 1920, when French troops marched into Damascus and crushed Faysal's Syrian Arab Kingdom. Hourani and his brothers attended the Arab school that King Faysal had built in Hama. Teachers encouraged him to write patriotic Arabic poetry, read newspapers, and listen to political speeches. Hourani did not learn Turkish as his father had, but he followed events in the new Republic of Turkey with interest. Later in life, when his democratic struggle stalled, Hourani despairingly considered the "the Ataturk option" of dictatorial, top-down reform. As one historian put it, "Like Huey Long of Louisiana, Hourani can be described as a populist."[9]

Hourani's Arab nationalism also sprang from his idealism. "Hourani was a romantic, attracted to poetry and novels," wrote Sami al-Jundi, a future Baath Party comrade from Hama. Like Hasan al-Banna, Hourani loved stories of ancient Arab heroes. In 1925, when Hourani was fourteen years old, Syrians mounted a national revolt against the French. He kept a scrapbook of articles about the battles and called the failed revolt "the most beautiful memory" of his life.[10] Hourani attended Syria's finest Arab high school, the Maktab Anbar in Damascus, and then the Syrian University law school. In 1935, he organized the one-thousandth anniversary celebration for the classical Arab poet al-Mutanabbi.

After earning his law degree in 1936 Hourani returned to Hama and joined a branch of the Syrian Social National Party (SSNP). The SSNP opposed foreign rule with a program to unify Greater Syria, now split into the mandates of Lebanon, Syria, Palestine, and Transjordan. The SSNP's militant tactics likely appealed to Hourani's combative nature. The party's platform certainly matched his political goals: 1) full national sovereignty, 2) abolition of feudalism, and 3) unity and tolerance among Muslims and Christians under a secular state.

These goals inspired Hourani's career for the next thirty years. But Hourani grew impatient with the SSNP's methods. Party members were afraid of common people and so remained an elitist faction. An effective political movement cannot rely solely on high school and college students, he realized. He aimed to build a mass, popular movement.[11]

Economic injustice, more than colonialism, motivated Hourani. In 1938 he and his cousin Uthman al-Hourani organized the Youth Party of Hama to build an urban-rural coalition strong enough to challenge Hama's feudal establishment. Hourani quickly attracted a mixed following of young men from popular quarters. He was street-smart, full of bravado, and willing to take on gang leaders and imitate neighborhood strongmen. He used the tough methods of traditional city leaders *(zuama)* in order to beat them at their own game.

The Youth Party also succeeded because Hourani liked people. His greatest pleasure, he recalled in his memoir, was to sit with farmers and discuss the year's crop. He also owed success to his silver tongue. His swashbuckling image masked an acute political intelligence. In simple language he conveyed basic political principles. With a "call for equality and justice" he urged neighborhoods and villages to form "a popular mass against the large landowners' oppression."[12]

People began to hang pictures of Hourani in their houses. They wore badges with his picture and the slogan "There Is No More Fear," recalled Izz al-Din Diyab, a schoolboy in Hama at the time. "I knew him from stories that were told about him, like legends about heroes and knights," Diyab said. "The peasants felt there was someone standing beside them if someone attacked them."[13]

HOURANI'S DEMOCRATIC CAMPAIGN IN PARLIAMENT

It was an outrageous act of murder in late 1942 that brought Hourani into national politics. The victim was the daughter of Tawfik al-Barazi, who lived across the street from the Hourani home in Hama. "Her cousin, Salih bin Khalid al-Darwish al-Barazi, surprised her. He shot her and let her drop dead," Hourani recalled. "When I returned home, I found my mother weeping."

The girl belonged to a lesser branch of the prominent Barazi family, which tried to cover up the murder as an honor crime. They claimed the girl was having an illicit affair and was punished for dishonoring the family. Their ruse was discredited, however, when an autopsy showed that she was a virgin. Hourani discovered the real motive: inheritance. If Tawfik al-Barazi died without an heir, Salih would inherit his land. One branch of the family was murdering the other branch for its land.

"The crime of Salih al-Barazi was just one of a chain of crimes that represented the cruelty that targeted women and girls on the pretense of defending their honor," Hourani wrote.

Hourani was appointed to represent the girl's father. The case was politically explosive because it exposed to the public the hidden crimes of the feudal elite. "It motivated the people of Hama to act against them."[14] The local court, however, found Salih innocent: in Hama, law was subordinate to feudal privilege.

Hourani's co-counsel, Raif al-Mulqi, was the local leader for the Damascus-based National Party. Mulqi recruited Hourani to run for parliament in 1943. As middle-class professionals, party leaders hoped that Hourani might break the feudal elite's monopoly on the city's seven parliamentary seats.

"The Hama campaign was one of the most violent in Syrian elections," Hourani wrote. He ran as a youth candidate against the "feudal old men." He also appealed to workers who had lost their industrial jobs during the Great Depression. As he told his first campaign rally: "This World War has opened great opportunities for our people to realize our national goals. So we must choose qualified, trustworthy men, lest we lose this opportunity."[15]

Hourani's campaign slogan was coined at the last nightly rally, held in a tent, west of the city. People played drums and sang songs and then, after his speech, began to chant: "Fetch the Basket and the Shovel to Bury the Agha and the Bey!" (Agha was a title like "Lord" used by the Barazis; Bey was the title used by the Azms.)

The slogan "spread like fire in straw," Hourani recalled. And it shocked Hama's elite. Rarely did people dare to voice such anger in public. Hourani's campaign had emboldened people who normally kept their resentments hidden. Riots broke out in the city, damaging the Azm family's houses.

National Party leaders panicked and apologized to the Azms. But Hourani refused their plea to withdraw from the race. Finally, the National Party leader in Damascus, Shukri al-Quwwatli, conceded and let Hourani run.

On July 26, 1943, Hourani won a parliamentary seat. He had cracked the feudal monopoly by drawing new voters to the polls: turnout in Hama was double that of other cities. Shop owners, artisans, and literate peasants had cast their first ballots ever, and they had chosen Hourani.

For Hourani, the campaign was also a personal turning point:

> The campaign rallies were an astonishing discovery—like a hurricane— that would affect my conduct in national service for the rest of my life. . . . I discovered the great misery of these good citizens at the rallies. I saw the lame, the paralyzed, people with faces pale from anemia, people wearing tattered rags, and people of terrifying thinness and weakness. People who could buy a kilo of rice for their family only once a year, to celebrate Eid al-Fitr.[16]

He took his shock and anger with him to Damascus, 100 miles to the south.

As Hourani entered parliament on opening day in late 1943, he must have felt as out of place as his father had on Hama's city council. At age thirty-one, he was the youngest deputy and the only one from a modest background. Most deputies wore fezzes, Ottoman-style morning coats, or the black robes of tribal chiefs. The victors of the National Party, led by the new president, Quwwatli, staged their challenge to the old guard by wearing expensive white suits. Hourani became the butt of jokes: "Journalists wrote articles about me that I was 'The Za'im [political leader] who Entered Parliament in Short Pants.'"[17]

Hourani learned his lessons for two years, and then made his move in 1946 with an attack on tribal shaykhs' privileges. As the last French troops departed from Syria, he proposed to strip tribal shaykhs of the subsidies France gave them for their loyalty. Neither should tribes live under a separate set of laws, he declared. The constitution declared all citizens equal under the law. Political equality was just one of

Alawite women and children gleaning, northern Syria, 1938. The poverty of peasants like these inspired Akram al-Hourani's Arab socialist movement. (Library of Congress)

Hourani's goals: he also aimed to weaken tribal chiefs' support for landowners in parliament.

"No sooner had Hourani made these points than Sheikh Trad and other tribal representatives leaped to their feet, pulled out pistols, and began shouting raiding cries," notes historian Jonathan Owen. "Most people in the Chamber, including the Speaker and the Government, had hurried to the exits upon seeing the extent of the Bedouins' firepower." But Hourani stood his ground. Parliament abolished the Tribal Authority shortly thereafter.[18]

Hourani's victory was the first step on the road to breaking the feudal hold in Hama, which he now understood ran through Damascus. He soon built alliances with like-minded opposition leaders, including Khalid Bakdash of the Syrian communist party, Mustafa al-Sibai of the Syrian Muslim Brotherhood, and especially the leaders of the Baath (Renaissance) Party, Michel Aflaq and Salah Bitar.

Baathists recruited students in Damascus with a vision of a new Arab golden age, which would come if Arabs renounced colonial-era boundaries and united into a single nation. Soon after the party held its first formal congress—at a Damascus café in April 1947—hundreds of followers rallied to its slogan, "Unity, Liberty, Socialism."[19]

Baathists' call for an Arab renaissance was another jeremiad, a call to restore ancient glory much like the calls of Mustafa Ali and Rashid Pasha to revive Suleyman the Magnificent's glory to justify Ottoman reform, or Banna's call to revive the ideals of the Prophet's Medina. Baathism was a secular mirror to Banna's belief that spiritual revival would lead to political justice.

The Baath Party's vision was more inclusive. It aimed to unite all Arabic speakers as equal members of the Arab nation: the majority Sunni Muslim Arabs, Greek Orthodox Christians, Alawis, Druze, and Kurds. In a controversial speech at Syrian University, Aflaq (a Christian) declared Islam the sublime expression of Arab culture. Arab Christians, he said, therefore share in the cultural heritage of Islam. "The power of Islam," he said, "has revived to appear in our days under a new form, Arab nationalism."[20]

In 1947 Hourani and the Baath Party allied to gain parliament's approval for single-stage, direct elections. As they staged street demonstrations, Hourani publicized the issue in his newspaper, *The Awakening (Al-Yaqitha)*. The old voting system, where voters chose deputies through a two-stage nomination system, he wrote, was notoriously open to corruption, favoring wealthy incumbents. The paper's circulation reached 8,000 copies daily.[21]

The impact of electoral reform was immediate. Hourani ran as an independent candidate in the 1947 election on a program to reclaim farmland from the Ghab marsh near Hama and to distribute the land to poor peasants. He won easily. Across Syria, opposition parties won a total of thirty-three new seats, giving them command of fifty-three seats in parliament against the National Party's twenty-four. Landowners managed to maintain their dominance, however, by violating electoral laws, falsifying the ballots of illiterate voters, and confiscating peasants' identity cards.[22]

The lingering corruption in the 1947 elections triggered a political crisis. Quwwatli's National Party, once a force of change, now cultivated the support of reactionary landowners and tribal leaders. Quwwatli "sat on top of an edifice of nepotism and mismanagement eroded at the base by price inflation, by crop failures due to drought, and by rumblings of discontent from the emerging labor unions."[23]

When Quwwatli forced through parliament a constitutional amendment allowing him to run for—and eventually win—a second term as president in 1948, a new opposition front formed. The People's Party, founded by businessmen in Aleppo, joined Hourani's Youth Party, the Baath Party, and the communists in protests. Michel Aflaq was arrested for circulating a leaflet that called Quwwatli a feudalist who enslaved the people.

Hourani took the parliament floor to defend Aflaq and the constitution. Now that Syria is independent, he declared, it must be free: "Newspapers must enjoy full freedom, and especially under government officials who had tasted repression under the French and the Turks."[24] When a Quwwatli supporter tried to steal the microphone, a fistfight broke out. "Chairs flew in the air, as did insults and curses."[25]

Aflaq was released a few days later, but Hourani's fears for the republic did not subside. Even as he joined the leftist front, Hourani maintained contact with an old friend from Hama, Colonel Adib al-Shishakli. Their friendship grew warmer as they fought together in Palestine in the winter of 1947–1948. They bonded around Hourani's old flame, Arab nationalism. Hourani also began to see the army as the "Ataturk option" in his back pocket. He encouraged Youth Party recruits to attend the new national military academy. If peasants replaced the elitist officers of the French era, Hourani reasoned, the army could become an instrument of social change.[26]

HOURANI AND THE MILITARY COUPS OF 1949

In November 1948, Quwwatli's regime teetered on collapse when demonstrations by Baathist students, Hourani's party, and the Muslim Brotherhood blamed him for defeat in Palestine. Quwwatli declared martial law and called in the army to enforce a curfew. This was the first explicit use of the army in politics since the French withdrew in 1946.[27] Syrians had much to fear from those troops on the streets. Regimes in Egypt and Iraq responded to defeat in Palestine by destroying Banna's Muslim Brotherhood and Comrade Fahd's communists, respectively.

That winter, Colonel Husni al-Zaim, the army chief, planned a coup with advice from the American Central Intelligence Agency (CIA). The CIA encouraged the coup because it feared instability would open the gates to Soviet influence in Syria.[28] Following the American script, Zaim ordered Colonel Shishakli to march on the capital in the early hours of March 30, 1949. While the leftist opposition welcomed Quwwatli's demise, the elderly Speaker of parliament, Faris al-Khuri, called Zaim's coup the worst disaster since the Young Turk dictatorship of World War I. By summer Za'im alienated all of his supporters and Colonel Sami Hinnawi deposed him. Four months later, Hourani's friend Shishakli staged the third coup of 1949. His military dictatorship would last four years.[29]

The coups reflected the deep split between old landed elites and a new middle class of technocrats, both civilian and military. Many Syrians, however, blamed Hourani personally for bringing the military into politics. His memoir devotes many pages to denying the accusations. Scholars agree he didn't plan the coups. However, Hourani admitted that he cooperated with military rulers because they promised to return to constitutional government—and because they supported land reform. Hourani was typical of many 1950s politicians—in the Middle East and the United States—who believed a short period of revolutionary dictatorship could sweep away obstacles to democracy and economic development.[30]

Hourani used the first three years of military rule to advance agricultural reform free of interference from the landowner-dominated parliament. "My passion for the issues of planting, forestry, and the protection of woodlands was one of the reasons I accepted the post of Minister of Agriculture after the coup by Sami al-Hinnawi," he explained. "I could not let an exceptional opportunity pass."[31]

He was virtually the only government official who understood the problem and importance of agriculture. He knew, as most elites did not in 1949, that Alawi peasants living near Homs and Hama barely grew enough to eat. They lived in hopeless villages handicapped by high rates of illiteracy and infant mortality. The reason for such poverty, in Hourani's view, was the unjust distribution of land: About 97 percent of Syrian farmers owned small plots of less than twenty-five acres, while an elite of 8,000 landowners owned 37 percent of the farmland. Only one in five villages had a tractor; some didn't even have a single truck.[32]

From a dusty drawer, Hourani retrieved an economic development report that he had commissioned in 1946. Quwwatli had ignored it.

He ordered agriculture ministry staff to draft economic development plans based on it. He also started a program to send Syrian students to agricultural institutes abroad. The program's graduates returned to start agricultural schools in Syria that significantly boosted Syria's farm yields. Hourani also launched a pilot land reform plan: in a chosen village, forced labor and sharecropping were abolished and state lands were redistributed to poor peasants.[33]

Landlords fought back in the November 1949 parliamentary election, which Colonel Hinnawi conducted as promised. Hourani carried land reform to the people with a pamphlet titled "Feudalism in Hama Must Be Attacked." Landlords terrorized villages and sent their henchmen to block Hourani's entry. In a show of force, Hourani drove straight into a village where a death warrant was issued on him. "I couldn't back off from this threat," he wrote later. When he arrived, just one family dared to greet him. "The main goal," Hourani wrote, "was to encourage the peasants and free them from the nightmare of fear."

Landlords also mobilized religious leaders to condemn Hourani as an atheist. He reminded voters of his ancestors' tolerant Sufi traditions against the Sunni sectarianism of Hama's religious elite. "We serve religion but we don't serve the oppressive feudalists," he said.[34]

Once again, however, the landowners trumped the elections. Hourani was one of only two socialists to win a seat in the 1949 parliament. Corruption under Hinnawi had been as bad as it had been under Quwwatli. In protest, Hourani resigned as agriculture minister.

Hope for a return to parliamentary government disappeared completely the next month, when the People's Party proposed that Syria merge with Iraq. While the party claimed to act in the spirit of Arab unity, it also acted in the interest of Aleppo businessmen with interests in the city of Mosul and in a British petroleum company that wanted to build a pipeline from Iraq to the Mediterranean.

Conservative landowners also saw little problem in uniting with a monarchy (this was before Iraq's 1958 revolution). Hourani and his opposition bloc saw a threat to the republic. Even the head of the Syrian Muslim Brotherhood joined Hourani.[35] "Colleagues!" Hourani addressed the Chamber, "I absolutely believe that preserving the republican system is as urgent as preserving the independence and full sovereignty of the country."[36]

It was army officers, not fellow deputies, who answered his call. On the morning of December 19, Colonel Shishakli arrested Hinnawi and promised the Syrian people by radio that the army would assure "the continued existence of the country and its republican system." Whether or not Hourani collaborated with Shishakli, he once again chose to cooperate with a military regime. He accepted the post of defense minister, because the rising cohort of graduates would accept no one else.

Amidst the political whirlwind, Hourani met his future wife, Naziha al-Homsi, a twenty-four-year-old graduate of Syrian University and a social science teacher. A former member of the Syrian communist party, Homsi had first heard of Hourani when his electoral reform committee awarded women the right to vote. They became a celebrity couple, with their engagement announced on the front page of newspapers.[37]

By April 1950, Hourani had grown disenchanted with Shishakli's regime. He resigned as defense minister amid protests against a proposal to make Islam the state religion. In his memoir, Hourani described his horror when Shishakli told him, over dinner, that an army officer would succeed him as defense minister: "This sin opened the door to the army, which began to covet power in government."[38]

Hourani refrained from public criticism of Shishakli, however, because he needed the dictator's good will to support agricultural reform. In order to pressure Shishakli, Hourani devoted the next eighteen months to building the peasant movement.

THE PEASANT REVOLT OF 1950

Hourani established the ASP as the nationwide successor to his Youth Party of Hama. The party called for land reform, agricultural development, republican government, religious tolerance, and women's rights. In the spring of 1950, it launched a campaign to recruit peasants to its vision of justice.[39]

"From the first day, the ASP went into the countryside and distributed membership cards," recalled Izz al-Din Diyab, who joined the ASP in his village outside Hama. ASP recruiters sat down with peasants and talked about how their landlords should have built schools, roads, and clinics for them. They gained the peasants' trust by then helping them build a road, clinic, or school. Then they explained how landlords became wealthy by exploiting peasant labor.

"When we told the people 'This land can be yours,' there was a kind of explosion," recalled Dr. Aziz al-Saqr, an Alawi peasant who joined the party.[40]

The ASP opened its Hama headquarters with a big party. "Delegations came from all parts of the city, by foot, by car, by bus. When Akram al-Hourani gave his speech, the crowd chanted his name and women whistled. He got the greatest applause of his life," recalled Diyab.[41] Literate peasant-gardeners rubbed shoulders with wage workers, soldiers, civil servants, shop owners, students, and professionals. A crew of *qabadayat* (neighborhood strongmen) stood on call at a coffeehouse nearby. At the first report of abuse in a village, they would rush out to defend the peasants.

In June 1950, the ASP began organizing peasant revolts. Hourani toured villages near Hama, where even women and children came to cheer him and beat drums. Peasants staged rent strikes, refusing to pay their landlords. In some villages, peasants scared landowner families off the land. Henchmen arrived and violence broke out. Several peasants were killed.[42]

A hostile newspaper scolded Hourani: "Ever since your youth, you have been feeding on spite, malice and dissension. You love to play with fire, even at the risk of burning yourself, your people, and your country." Some newspapers hinted at the need to assassinate Hourani.[43]

Hourani was careful to couch the revolt in religious terms, in order to fend off criticism from elite clerics. He enjoyed a unique appeal among peasants because of his association with the Rifa'i Sufi order.[44] Among urban followers, he rooted the revolts in the Islamic reformism of Sayyid Jamal al-Din al-Afghani and Muhammad Abduh and in the example of Abu Zarr, who had called for social revolution in the time of the Prophet.[45]

Slowly, a powerful peasant leadership emerged northwest of Hama, altering the balance of power in the city's rural hinterland. Christians, Alawis, Druze, and Sunni Muslims joined the movement. No other party in Syria could claim such a grassroots following; no other single personality wielded more power in politics.[46]

Hourani used the momentum of the peasant revolts to achieve a second victory: a new constitution. Syria's September 1950 constitution stands as one of the most democratic ever adopted in the Arab world. It included a twenty-eight-article bill of rights that guaranteed freedoms of speech and assembly as well as economic and social rights. Articles promised to distribute state land to poor farmers, limit the size of landholdings, and establish a code of regulations on landlord-peasant relations.

The 1950 constitution represented a political pact between socialists and progressive business, against the old economic order. Even businessmen of the People's Party, who had opposed Hourani over the proposed Iraq merger, supported it. They shared Hourani's belief that state investment and regulation would promote economic development.[47] Despite its support for constitutionalism, the People's Party was not willing to give up the power it had won in parliament in the corrupt elections of 1949. When the party refused to hold new elections, Hourani briefly resigned his parliamentary seat in protest.

Hourani's intense frustration with parliament was evident in the ASP manifesto he issued in October 1950. It bluntly proclaimed revolution: "I am sure there is no life for the Arab people except through the destruction of feudal conditions in Arab countries and the building of a just socialist system on the basis of cooperation, love, and harmony among members of society."[48]

He launched the "The Land Belongs to the Peasant" campaign the following spring. The ASP hailed workers as the source of national sovereignty and wealth and pledged to defend peasants from exploitation.[49] Hourani held parliamentary hearings on peasant demands for legal protection from expulsion, a fair share of profits, and a just distribution of land. And ASP-Baath Party demonstrations forced the government to nationalize the French tobacco company which virtually owned many poor villages in northern Syria.

By the summer of 1951, nearly 10,000 peasants, workers, and small shopkeepers had joined the movement. "It was like a flood tide coming in and we never had the time to keep count," Hourani wrote. Northern Syria exploded in another round of peasant revolt, partly because worms had decimated the cotton harvest. Peasants attacked a Barazi family estate, refused to give landowners shares of their crops, and drove their agents from their fields. When landlords tried to occupy land newly reclaimed from the Ghab marsh, peasants drove them out.[50]

Large landowners grew so concerned that in August 1951 they convened an emergency meeting in Aleppo. They sent a telegram to Shishakli's government in Damascus, condemning efforts to limit the size of their estates, calling Hourani a communist, and accusing the ASP of "sowing dissension among landlords and peasants."[51]

In fear and exuberance, ASP leaders responded with a vote to hold a peasant congress in Aleppo—right in the feudalists' lion's den. They scheduled it on the fourth day of the biggest holiday of the year, Eid al-Adha, when peasants would have the day off.

At daybreak on September 15, convoys of cars, buses, and trains rolled out of Syria's villages and towns toward Aleppo. Hourani's car headed north from Damascus, packed with activists and journalists. "Party members stopped us in every village and asked: 'When will the Chief arrive?'" Few yet recognized their leader's face. Thousands waited to greet Hourani in Hama. "I never heard voices yell so loud," he recalled.

The peasant convoy stretched ten kilometers long when it finally pulled into Aleppo. "How many of them had not eaten that day, so they could afford to rent a car?" asked Hussein Shabani, editor of an Aleppo newspaper. "How many left their villages under the wings of darkness, knowing that they would return to meet the whip of the landowner?"[52]

Spectators jammed streets and balconies as the peasants paraded through the city into a public park. The crowd—estimated between 10,000 and 40,000—overflowed into the streets.[53] People carried Hourani on their shoulders to a speaker's platform draped with banners declaring "Long Live the Father of Arab Socialism, Akram al-Hourani!" "The People Are the Source of All Power!" "Ownership Is a Social Duty!" and "No Sectarianism, No Racism, No Classism in Our Socialist System!"

After speeches by workers, poets and lawyers, Hourani finally spoke:

Arab Socialists! Comrades in the struggle! We have waged many years of mortal battle on many fronts: against foreigners, against feudal lords, against imperialism, against capitalism. There were times when I sat by myself and worried about our ability to achieve what is the best for our people. But whenever I find myself among you, I feel a great power, an awesome power, that makes all obstacles small and all difficulties simple. This is the power of the Arab people![54]

The speech crystallized a political vision long in the making. In his 1943 campaign, Hourani had believed civic virtue sprang simply from youth; now, he believed it flowed from labor. Hourani was no Comrade Fahd. His socialism was rooted not in Marxist theory but rather in personal experience, Arab culture, and Islamic morals. His ideas about feudalism were distilled from the brief lessons he had learned in the SSNP: feudalism was foreign, a product of colonial rule; it caused a moral inversion in Arab society; and it doomed Arabs to poverty and parochialism.

To restore justice, Hourani told the crowd, we must begin by "placing our economic system on the basis of cooperation and justice." Capitalism and colonialism had created a false and tyrannical elite that rules. Only by destroying the economic base of their tyranny will Arabs regain their freedom and resume their historical, humane mission as a people. In other words, Hourani argued, land reform was the first priority.

He then warned the peasants of the danger they faced:

Those who exploit the people and whip them, they are now organizing themselves and they are using every means possible—sometimes power, sometimes manipulation and immorality—to keep their privileges. They depend on foreign apparatus to support them.

He reassured his audience that they acted in the right. The ASP is not an anarchic movement, he said. It upholds rule of law and the constitution. It is the landowners who resort to violence and illegal land seizure. In conclusion, Hourani thundered:

Isn't the worker a human being? Isn't the peasant a human being? We are the builders and they are the attackers. We are ready to judge them before the laws of heaven and earth!

The congress ended in a spirit of victory. Hourani had done the unthinkable. He had publicly accused Syria's wealthiest elite of being criminals.

And he was able to do it only because his hometown friend, Shishakli, ruled as a dictator.

Hourani also crafted his message, as reformers since the nineteenth century had, in familiar language of honor and restoration. He preached in the form of jeremiad just as Reshid Pasha had done in 1839, and as Banna did in his pamphlets. Like them, he combined a new language of rights with a vision of justice as a return to forgotten values, to the indigenous virtue of Arabs that had been stolen by colonial powers.

The congress was so powerful that four months later, in January 1952, Shishakli issued Decree No. 96 on land reform. It canceled feudal lords' claims to unregistered state lands and set a ceiling on the size of their estates. Land exceeding the limit was to be distributed to "needy peasants."[55]

Akram al-Hourani debating in Syrian parliament, 1956. Hourani had by then merged his Arab Socialist Party with the Baath Party. They formed a leftist reform front with communists and independents to assert brief control in Syrian politics in the mid-1950s.

(Syrianhistory.com)

Shortly after issuing the decree, however, Shishakli turned against the peasant movement, calling it a threat to order. His reversal echoed a similar move by Kemal (whom he also admired). In the 1930s the Turkish dictator had granted women suffrage and then outlawed the Turkish women's movement on the pretext that its work was done. Within months, Shishakli outlawed parties and shut down newspapers and eventually took full control of the state away from civilians.

In January 1953, Hourani and the Baathists escaped to exile over the snowy mountains of Lebanon. He wrote a letter to his wife from Beirut in which he compared himself to another martyr for constitutional justice. The thought had come to him that morning, upon waking from a nightmare. "I turned on the radio and listened to the Holy Qur'an," he wrote. The verse calmed his fears: Allah "urged the faithful to be patient, and vowed that tyrants will come to a bad end," he wrote. "I will keep my promise to myself, whatever comes my way, just as the hero Ahmad Urabi did in his exile."[56]

FROM PARLIAMENTARY RESTORATION TO THE UNITED ARAB REPUBLIC

Like a political phoenix, Hourani returned to Syria under an amnesty in late 1953. In his last months before exile, Hourani had united the ASP with the Baath Party in their common battle against Shishakli's dictatorship. It was the military, however, that finally ousted Shishakli in a February 1954 coup. The coalition triumphed in the elections that followed.

Between 1954 and 1958 Syria returned to civilian rule, what later generations would call a golden era. Hourani rose to become Speaker of parliament in this period, when he worked closely with other leftist parties in a national front. Newspapers flourished and labor unions organized to claim right for workers. The moment seemed auspicious for Hourani's revolution.

His peasant movement would never, however, launch the grassroots revolution he envisioned. Landowners proved too powerful and Hourani was unable to extend the movement into Syria's south and east, where conditions were quite different. Two other factors also interfered with Hourani's plan: the military's meddling in politics and foreign intervention. They gained influence because Shishakli had left political society so weak: in less than five years of rule he had thoroughly subverted civilian government, decimated civil society, and gutted instruments of republican politics.[57]

In late 1957 these factors drove Hourani to make the greatest mistake of his career. He canceled municipal elections and jump-started negotiations to merge Syria and Egypt into the United Arab Republic. Hourani effectively ended his political career and his lifelong dream of constitutional reform. Nasser dissolved the Baath Party and imposed a dictatorship harsher than Shishakli's. A neo-Baath Party arose within the military, unbeknownst to Hourani, and helped to end the United Arab Republic. In a 1963 coup it established its own military dictatorship. After years of house arrest, Hourani was forced again into exile in 1965—this time never to return.

Hourani's rise and fall in the 1950s is an astonishing story. How could a savvy political player, at the top of his game in 1951, make mistakes so huge? Examining the choices he made during this crucial decade reveals how difficult it was for democratic socialists to conduct politics openly in so stressed a political atmosphere. It offers insight into how Arab socialists not only failed to install democratic regimes but also spawned military dictatorships across the Arab world.

Hourani's first strategic choice was to join forces with his longtime allies, Bitar and Aflaq. Their Baath Party offered a wider base in cities beyond Hama. The merged party, called the Arab Socialist Baath Party (ASBP), united Baathist strength among students, especially in Damascus, with the ASP's rural base in northern Syria. By late 1953 it claimed 6,000 registered members and the sympathy of tens of thousands more.[58]

Like the Iraqi Communist Party, the ASBP was an integrative movement. It united Druze, Alawi, Ismaili, and Christian minorities under a common Arab national identity. Sons of peasants from these minority groups joined the ASBP as a means of entering a political system long dominated by the Sunni Muslim elite.[59] To them, the ASBP offered an egalitarian model of justice that Ottomanism never had, by building using Arab nationalism as a bridge between the dominant urban elite of Sunni Muslims and non-Sunni peasants.

The new party also emphasized democracy as the best guarantee of national security.[60] Hourani's first party publication, written from exile in May 1953, argued against the military's claim that its control of politics was necessary for defense against communist, Zionist, or American threats: "It is up to you, activists, to liberate yourselves from fear . . . to welcome the leadership of the popular masses as the best defense and a challenge to military conditions, dictatorship, and reactionary politics." At parliament's first meeting on March 7, 1954, he repeated that argument, in calling for the full enfranchisement of peasants and workers: "We think that if free and neutral elections are not guaranteed, the country could become a stage for foreign conspiracy."[61]

After a summer of demonstrations by women, peasants, workers, and students, an interim government organized Syria's freest elections to date. For the first time, secret ballots were used. And to discourage corruption, local election officials were transferred to different districts.[62]

The ASBP rallied workers and peasants by organizing unions, hiring lawyers to prosecute abusive landowners, and sending campaign trucks into villages. Landowners and Islamists fought back, with violence. In Hama, landowners' henchmen beat up any suspected Baath Party supporter. Bombs exploded on the streets, at times near Hourani's home.[63]

Hourani compared the 1954 election to Egypt's 1882 constitutional revolution, when the "Arab hero Ahmad Urabi battled the British occupation of Egypt." It appears that he had read the biographies of Urabi published on the eve of Egypt's 1952 revolution. He reminded voters that British-backed clerics had issued a fatwa accusing Urabi of apostasy, to delegitimize the constitutional movement. Syria's elite was using the same tactic today. "If they accuse the Baath [of atheism], then they are condemning tens of thousands of citizens for apostasy," he declared. "Islam is a message of love and tolerance and peace. It was spread on Earth because it carried a message of justice and freedom and equality."[64]

The September 1954 election was a landmark. The socialists won a landslide victory in Hama: Hourani's list swept five seats, winning more than 90,000 votes in the district, compared to landowners' 50,000 total. Across Syria, socialists defeated the People's Party in numerous districts, winning twenty-two seats against the People's Party's thirty. Khalid Bakdash became the first communist elected to parliament.[65]

And yet, reformers still held only a minority of seats in parliament (at most fifty-five of 142). Hourani battled against a conservative bloc of deputies from the National and People's parties. These latter wielded enough influence among independents to block reform bills and the incorporation of peasants and workers into politics.[66]

Hourani's grandstanding in parliament popularized the ASBP as the champion of the poor. When conservatives defeated his land reform proposal, for example, the sixteen Baathist deputies threatened to resign and return to the ranks of the people. Hourani then accused dissenting deputies of accepting bribes. Hourani's attacks were, according to historian Nabil Kaylani, "largely opportunistic, occasionally demagogic, but always characterized by deftness and acumen."[67]

The ASBP suffered another blow in August 1955, when its favored candidate for president, Khalid al-Azm, lost to its nemesis, Quwwatli. Historians support Hourani's contention Quwwatli owed his victory to Saudi money, which swayed many votes—especially from the People's Party.[68]

"Does anyone not know that our society is moving toward your justice?" Hourani asked defiantly, at a second peasant congress in the city of Homs. "The socialist mission has entered citizens' souls and empowered the Syrian countryside."[69]

Cold War politics, however, deepened the rift in Syrian politics. In early 1955, Iraq, Turkey, and Pakistan signed the Baghdad Pact with Britain. The Syrian government rejected the anti-Soviet pact in favor of neutralism. In April, Azm, the foreign minister, attended the legendary Bandung Conference of newly independent Asian and African nations, held in Indonesia. Nehru of India, Tito of Yugoslavia, and Nasser of Egypt also attended and condemned the Cold War alliances as a new form of imperialism. But neutralism was difficult to maintain, especially after Azm made a deal to buy weapons from the Soviets.[70]

The People's Party exploited Azm's deal to cultivate support from Iraq and the United States. In mid-1956, the Iraqi monarchy approached Shishakli to plan a coup. They intended to assassinate Hourani, Bakdash, and the chief of military intelligence, Colonel Abd al-Hamid Sarraj. Sarraj exposed the plot, however, in October 1956.

The highly publicized trial of forty-seven conspirators tilted the balance of power in Syria farther to the Left. Hourani, Azm, and Bakdash gained parliament's approval for a new National Front Charter. It committed Syria to fight against imperialism and atheism, defend Arab national movements, and pass laws to protect workers and peasants.[71] The year 1956 ended with Hourani's parliamentary bloc in the driver's seat of Syrian politics.

At the same time, however, the Suez War made Nasser, Egypt's revolutionary president, the most popular leader in the Arab world. Washington looked on with concern. And while external threats mounted, internal divisions deepened. Disagreements about priorities—Arab unity or socialism—threatened to split apart the National Front.

It is not clear when Hourani realized that his movement was on a collision course with the United States. His memoir makes little reference to American involvement in Syria before 1957. Yet, even as he staged the ASP's peasant congress in 1951, the Korean War intensified, Senator Joseph McCarthy's anti-communist campaign peaked, and Iran's prime minister, Mohammed Mosaddeq, expelled the British in a dispute over oil rights.

As 1957 opened, Americans sounded alarm bells about Syria. The *New York Times* reported that "the extreme Left in Syria had alarming strength" and warned that the Syrian "vacuum" might be filled by the Soviet Union.[72] In March, the United States issued the Eisenhower Doctrine, promising aid to any political group that battled communism. In April, Syrian socialists watched nervously as King Hussein of Jordan staged a coup against a left-leaning cabinet elected six months earlier. As the king violently purged communists and Baathists, American warships stood guard in the Mediterranean while Iraqi and Saudi troops stood ready at the border.[73]

Hourani's fears of American intervention were well founded. In the summer of 1957, the CIA hatched another plan for a coup in Syria. Sarraj, the Baathist chief of military intelligence, nipped it in the bud and expelled three Americans. In September, Turkish NATO troops appeared on Syria's northern border. The public panicked. Women joined men in forming self-defense militias. Hourani welcomed 3,000 Egyptian troops who landed at the northern port city of Latakia. Fearing assassination by American agents, Hourani cancelled his appearance at a third peasant congress. Then American envoy Loy Henderson appeared in the region. Henderson was widely known to have planned Mossadeq's overthrow in Iran in 1953.[74]

As tension mounted, Hourani reached the pinnacle of his parliamentary career. In October 1957 he narrowly defeated a conservative opponent to become Speaker of parliament. He made plans for

Syria's first-ever municipal elections. But in November, he canceled them, claiming that the siege atmosphere undermined democratic process. His true motive was more complex. The ASBP had not prepared well for the election, and it feared that the communists would win. A communist victory might trigger a NATO-led invasion from Turkey.

By canceling the elections, Hourani betrayed his May 1953 message from exile, that democratic politics is the best guarantee of sovereignty. Worse, he again chose alliance with a dictator. Two days after the elections were to have been held, Hourani staged a joint session of parliament with an Egyptian delegation headed by Anwar Sadat. Sadat hailed Syrians as "brothers in arms" in the defense of the Arab world from imperialist aggression. They convinced the joint parliament to vote for "a federal union" between Syria and Egypt. Hourani later boasted that the session had successfully marginalized Syrian communists.[75]

But he quickly recognized his miscalculation. As mass demonstrations broke out cheering for Nasser, he lost the reins of political authority. Angry communists in the military used public zeal to plot their revenge. In January, without consulting Hourani or any other civilian leaders, the communist-leaning army chief, General Afif Bizri, flew to Cairo to propose an immediate and full union to Nasser. Hourani was furious.

Hourani and the other ASBP leaders had no choice but to accept a fait accompli. Syrians danced in the streets for several days in February, when voters in both countries formally approved the establishment of the United Arab Republic.[76] It was Hourani's nemesis, President Quwwatli, who signed the union agreement in Cairo.

Publicly, Hourani played the union with Egypt as a victory. "The union of Syria and Egypt is a turning point of history and one of the greatest victories of this age," Hourani told the crowd gathered on February 2, 1958. "It is the road leading to a comprehensive Arab unity and the liberation of Palestine and Algeria and all Arab lands from the claws of Western imperialism."[77]

Behind the scenes, however, there was doubt and dissent. The ASBP had long recognized Nasser as a dictator. They had hoped to preserve Syria's parliamentary system by negotiating a federal system of government within the union. But the rush to union had left no room for negotiating conditions.

Nasser regarded Hourani as the single most powerful politician in Syria and so appointed him vice-president for the Syrian sector of the United Arab Republic. But Nasser's real intent was to isolate Syria's left and destroy it. In January he demanded the dissolution of all parties, except his own. Nasser then ordered Hourani to Cairo, where he was cut off from his political base. After the Nasser regime destroyed the Syrian communist party (Bakdash fled to exile), it rigged elections to assure defeat of candidates who had formerly belonged to the ASBP. Then Nasser posted his right-hand man, Abdel Hakim Amer, as a virtual dictator in Syria.[78]

In December 1959, Hourani openly broke with Nasser over the president's refusal to protest at the United Nations against Israeli plans to divert water from the Jordan River. That effectively ended his political career. He lived under house arrest until September 1961, when an army coup brought the United Arab Republic to an end. Aflaq and the Baath Party leaders then expelled Hourani from the party. They still dreamed of Arab unity and of restoring the United Arab Republic. Hourani staunchly opposed any return to union with Egypt.[79]

Hourani devoted his last months of freedom in Syria to reviving civilian government.[80] He revived his old ASP, which still commanded tremendous loyalty among peasants. And in 1962 he partnered with his old rival, Azm, to expand land reform and restore the 1950 constitution.

But on March 8, 1963, a secret military wing of the Baath Party overthrew the government. It had been formed by disenchanted officers during the United Arab Republic. Hourani was arrested "for socialist activities" in October 1965 and sent to the Mezza prison outside of Damascus. When he fell ill with stomach cancer, friends won his release on condition that he seek treatment in exile.

Hourani flew to Paris on a rainy day in December 1965. After his recovery, he lived for years in Lebanon and Iraq, organizing opposition movements that failed to depose the Baathist regime in Damascus. In the 1980s, he fell ill again and returned to France. That was where he wrote his memoir. It is said that in 1996, at age 85, Hourani requested permission to die in his homeland. Permission never came. He died in Jordan on February 24, 1996. One of his obituaries invoked this verse (33:23) from the Quran: "Among the believers are men true to what they promised Allah. Among them is he who has fulfilled his vow [to the death], and among them is he who awaits [his chance]. And they did not alter [the terms of their commitment] by any alteration. . ."[81]

Hourani was thrown out of Syria by the very peasants he had brought into politics. Among them was Hafiz al-Asad, ruler of Syria from 1970 to 2000. As a high school student in Latakia, not far from Hama, Asad had admired Hourani for his defense of peasant dignity and rights. He also followed Hourani's advice to poor peasant boys to attend the free Homs Military Academy.

Hourani's dream of democracy was denied, but not his dream of redemption for the poor: when Asad became president, he was hailed as the first peasant ruler of Syria and he enacted many of the agricultural reforms that Hourani had fought for. "Hourani was the agent of change, a midwife of the new Syria over which Asad was to preside," wrote Patrick Seale. "He roused the peasants, politicized the army, and gave the theorists of the Baath a cutting edge."[82]

To the end of the twentieth century, "Houranist" peasants preserved his memory and proudly displayed their crumpled ASP membership cards.[83] And Syrian landowners continued to demonize him for destroying the idyllic Old Syria of their memories and for masterminding a vengeful peasant dictatorship. "If he could have drunk our blood and eaten our flesh he would have done so," said a prominent landowner.[84] While living in Beirut in the 1970s, Hourani still believed that landowners plotted to murder him. The shotgun at his door in Paris bespeaks his continued fear.

Hourani blamed the failure of his movement and the triumph of military dictatorship on the Syrian public's foolish embrace of Nasser and on the landlords of the People's Party, who destroyed popular faith in democracy.

Posthumously, his memoirs were criticized for downplaying his own important role in politicizing the military.[85] The memoirs may self-aggrandize in their effort to correct the historical record, but they also leave the impression that Hourani was naïve about the wolf he had let in the door. It is difficult to understand how Hourani thought he would restore civilian politics in 1962. The military had plunged Syria into the United Arab Republic, pulled it out again, and plotted to rule Syria directly.

Critics also argue that Hourani had never been a true democrat or that he was simply a power-hungry "opportunist." The latter label, used by American diplomats, was taken up by Aflaq and other bitter rivals.[86] It is difficult to believe that Hourani was so cynical, given the copious evidence he presented in the memoir of his efforts to build and defend a constitutional republic. One critic called Hourani the Lenin of Baathism: he transformed ideals into political action and in the process destroyed the ideals.[87] That charge may, sadly, be more on the mark.

Hourani's is a story not of Arabs' weak democratic values, nor of ancient "Eastern" preferences for dictatorship, but of a struggle for social democracy against long odds—against the legacy of colonial rule that left a powerful landed oligarchy and against the interventions of Cold War superpowers and their satellites in the region. Hourani drew on a deep and rich reservoir of constitutional politics in Syria, dating to the 1908 Ottoman revolution and Faysal's Syrian Congress of 1920. He was a lawyer, not a soldier, and generally reluctant to sacrifice rule of law in his pursuit of social justice. Hourani was also a homegrown pioneer of Arab socialism, rooted in his lived experience in Hama.

Hourani's story also illustrates how peasant mobilization and populist politics produced military dictatorship. The military dictatorships of late twentieth-century Syria, Egypt, and Iraq must be understood as the product of social factors and political contingencies. As Comrade Fahd understood in Iraq, the neofeudal landowning elites would not willingly give up the political control that colonial powers had granted them. The growth of the rural population, migration to cities, and greater education enabled peasants and workers to mount their first collective challenges to feudal power—as in Syria in 1951 and Iraq in 1958. However, the conditions of the Cold War bolstered the power of conservative elites. The United States and Britain did just that in Iraq, Jordan, Lebanon, and Syria.

It was in this perilous climate of embattled sovereignty that Syria's country boys commandeered Arab socialist ideas and the military to build what some call the first true peasant state. Like Fidel Castro's rule in Cuba, Syrian Baathists suppressed civil liberties but raised the standard of living of peasants. As in Iraq and Egypt, Arab socialists destroyed constitutional government that had been planted in the late Ottoman era in order to defeat landed elites. They also built a wall of military rule against outside intervention, which seemed always to favor elites.

By the mid-1960s, they helped to end the era of mass mobilization that had begun after World War I. It passed into history under new technologies of military power and the external pressure of the Cold War. In the political vacuum of dictatorship, the moral high ground and the organizational space to resist dictatorship and foreign influence would be found in mosques and religious communities. It would also be found in the camps of refugees, like those of Palestinians exiled after 1948.

III

STRUGGLES FOR JUSTICE IN THE
ABSENCE OF A POLITICAL ARENA,
SINCE 1965

9

ABU IYAD

The Palestine Liberation Organization and the Turn to Political Violence

On November 13, 1974, Yasser Arafat stepped to the podium of the General Assembly at the United Nations (UN) in New York City. As leader of the Palestine Liberation Organization (PLO), he appealed for recognition of a Palestinian nation, as a step toward statehood. He ended his speech with a dare: "Today I have come bearing an olive branch and a freedom-fighter's gun. Do not let the olive branch fall from my hand."

The speech was Arafat's "apotheosis," according to British journalist David Hirst. It transformed him from a renegade guerrilla into a national leader.[1] Arafat won the hearts of Third World delegates who held a majority in the General Assembly. They sympathized with his complaint of colonialism's injustice and his demand for self-determination. By the end of the week, Palestinians won official observer status at the UN.

But Arafat did not win the support of states most crucial to his cause: the United States and Israel. The American delegates had refused to join the standing ovation that welcomed Arafat; the Israelis' seats were empty. In a rebuttal the next day, Israeli delegate Yosef Tekoah denounced the PLO as a "murder organization." He began: "I rise to speak in the name of a people, which having at long last regained its freedom and sovereignty in its national homeland, remains embattled." He reminded the assembly that "one third of the entire

Jewish people was annihilated in the Second World War." Arafat's true aim was not peaceful coexistence, he averred, but "the annulment of the Jewish people."

The exchange between Arafat and Tekoah at the UN reprised two irreconcilable motives that had dominated Middle Eastern politics since the fall of the Ottoman empire: the fear of annihilation (and the demand for sovereignty as protection) and the rejection of privilege and exclusion based on racial, ethnic, and religious identity (and the demand for equality and minority rights). Back in 1919 Turkish leaders had chosen to abandon pluralism and democracy, to establish a republic based on the exclusion of other national and religious groups. As seen in Chapter 5, Zionists had followed the same exclusionary protective principle, that only if Jews dominated the state could they guarantee their collective security.

They achieved that goal with the establishment of the Israeli state in 1948, at the cost of denying reentry to more than 700,000 Palestinian refugees. In the 1920s, Palestinian leaders had at first promoted a plural democracy in which Jews, Muslims, and Christians would enjoy equal rights and representation in proportion to their share of population. In the wake of violence, however, new leaders adopted an exclusive nationalism to mirror the Zionists'.

Arafat's speech followed a long tradition in denouncing Israel for excluding Arabs. But it also marked a fundamental shift in policy. Arafat had built Fatah into Palestinians' largest grassroots movement with the promise of reconquering all of Palestine. (Fatah literally means "conquest" or "opening" in Arabic; it is also an acronym, in reverse order, for "Palestinian liberation movement.") On that day in 1974, however, he proposed a Palestinian "mini-state" to exist alongside Israel. Essentially, he asked Israel to return the West Bank and Gaza, territory it had occupied in the June 1967 war.

Arafat now asked Palestinians to accept two major concessions: a smaller state and an end to their armed struggle. Since 1964, the PLO had vowed that only through force could justice be done. Palestinian exiles—many born in the camps set up after 1948—distrusted diplomacy. It had failed them in the past, as they watched the armed struggles of Mao Tse-tung in China, Ho Chi Minh in Vietnam, the National Liberation Front (FLN) in Algeria, and Fidel Castro and Che Guevara in Cuba succeed. To reassure his base that he was not surrendering, Arafat wore battle fatigues to the UN—and a holster rumored not to be empty. He also wore a *kuffiyeh*, the black-and-white headscarf that had become a symbol in the 1936–1939 Palestine revolt.

But Arafat's contradictory message—of olive branch and revolver, of negotiated peace in a mini-state and dream of fighting for all Palestine—weakened his appeal. Americans responded negatively to Arafat's threatening image on television. And his warning of violence handed Israelis a political opening to raise the specter of a new Holocaust. Tekoah warned:

> Arafat, today, prefers the Nazi method. The Nazis killed millions of Jews in death camps, the gates of which bore the sign "Work brings freedom." Arafat kills Jewish children . . . under the slogan of creating a "democratic Palestine."[2]

This, he concluded, "is what justice means to the PLO. This is what the PLO's olive branch is." Outside the UN building, Jewish demonstrators vowed to murder Arafat. His security team whisked him out of New York that night. No peace and no state would follow.

The failure of Arafat's speech was not the result merely of a wardrobe error, or of Israel's accusations. The muddied message was the product of the structural weakness of the Palestinian movement itself. November 1974 was a unique moment of unity in the movement's history, achieved only through athletic efforts to defang the beast of violent revenge let loose from the impoverished refugee camps. Without a state, Palestinians had neither legal recourse in international law nor standing at the UN to advance the cause of more than a million refugees. By the 1960s, Palestine had disappeared from the UN's agenda. Palestinians discovered that violence made the world take notice.

Casting a shadow over Arafat's day of "apotheosis" was another day, September 5, 1972. In front of 800 million television viewers, a Palestinian group called Black September took eleven Israeli athletes hostage in the Olympic village in Munich. Israel refused their demand to exchange the hostages for the release of Palestinian prisoners. Pictures of the hooded figure of a Palestinian, standing guard on a balcony with an AK-47, became the iconic image of terrorism. The day ended in a firefight between German police and the Palestinians. All eleven Israeli hostages, five Palestinians, and a policeman were dead.

After the Munich massacre, a leading Israeli newspaper condemned the PLO as a "murderous organization," prefiguring Tekoah's UN speech. Israel's deputy prime minister called the PLO a "a bestial clique whose sole object is genocide." A *New York Times* editorial linked the Jewish murders at Munich to the memory of Hitler's Berlin Olympics in 1936.[3]

The wages of violent terror were paid at the General Assembly in November 1974. While Arafat appealed to the militant sentiments of the recently decolonized Third World, Israel's Tekoah appealed to the guilty conscience of Europe, thirty years after the Holocaust. The fact that the PLO had killed Jews in Germany resonated strongly, especially among Europeans in the assembly.

These two days, two years apart, were entwined in a double helix of political aspiration and violent negation. The question of violence lies at the center of any historical investigation into the failure of peace: Why was it impossible to put the genie of violence back in the bottle after the 1948 war? Much has been written about why the Israeli state became a military powerhouse. Less has been written about why stateless Palestinians, emerging from the refugee camps, embraced violence at such disadvantageous odds.

Arafat remained, until his death in 2004, silent on the subject of Munich. Over time, he became the fatherly face of the Palestinian revolution, projecting an image that rose above the nitty-gritty of struggle. Arafat has been the subject of several biographies, but he never wrote a memoir. He would be a natural choice for this study of the Palestinian movement, but for the lack of sources.

However, Arafat ruled Fatah in the 1970s with the help of two other men who did write memoirs. Abu Jihad (Khalil al-Wazir) was the movement's military chief, who in the 1980s built its network inside the West Bank and Gaza. Abu Iyad (Salah Khalaf) was Fatah's political philosopher and intelligence chief, whose verbal skills rallied refugees in Lebanese camps and built diplomatic bridges with Europeans and Americans.

Abu Iyad's 1978 memoir, *My Home, My Land,* is especially useful as a window on how Fatah turned Palestinian feelings of injustice into a movement and how it first adopted and then changed its vision of justice. Abu Iyad was known as the "godfather" of the Black September operation at Munich. His text directly confronts the decision to wage the Palestinian struggle through violence. The memoir is both a justification of Fatah strategy and a cry for help at a moment of crisis: in 1978 the PLO's key ally, Egypt, was negotiating a separate peace with Israel, while its base in Lebanon eroded amid civil war.

Like several activists featured in this book, Abu Iyad directed his memoir to a foreign audience. It was written first in French with the collaboration of a prominent journalist for *Le Monde,* Eric Rouleau. Rouleau's reputation for integrity and his avowal that Abu Iyad largely told the truth support use of the book as a source on the PLO's true motives.[4]

Used in conjunction with other sources, Abu Iyad's memoir reveals how his effort to make the PLO a democratic political arena backfired terribly when Fatah leaders tried to rally support from the rank and file for peace negotiations. From 1974 onward, militant factions easily undermined Fatah's peace initiatives through assassinations and well-timed terror acts. One such faction finally murdered Abu Iyad in 1991.

Fatah was the most extreme case of a general trend in the Middle East after 1965: the pursuit of politics in absence of a political arena. As we have seen, the dynamic world of Arab mass politics in the 1940s and 1950s disappeared under the pressure of dictatorship and monarchy. Without space to organize, mass movements collapsed—or were crushed. Palestinians had no state, much less a parliamentary building or executive mansion. There was, literally, no space for politics to occur. After the 1967 war, half of the 2.7-million-Palestinian population living in the West Bank and Gaza fell under Israeli military occupation. They enjoyed few political or civil rights. The other half of the population were refugees living in camps, mostly in Jordan, Lebanon, and Syria.[5] Only in Jordan were Palestinians considered citizens of a state.

It was in these circumstances that Fatah attempted to reconstitute the PLO as a virtual political arena. At mobile congresses held in various Arab capitals, the PLO offered space to all Palestinian factions to debate and make collective decisions. Differences were tolerated beneath the common commitment to achieve sovereignty. Only with sovereignty—they understood as predecessors since Ahmad Urabi did—would they ensure their survival and social justice. It is therefore not in defects of personality but in the structural constraints of statelessness and political repression that we might best understand the causes of the PLO's failure and of the region-wide turn to political violence in the late twentieth century.

Origins of the Fatah Guerrilla Movement

Abu Iyad's opening lines introduced his memoir as an essay on violence: "May 13, 1948, is a day that will remain forever engraved in my memory. That day, less than 24 hours before the proclamation of the Israeli state, my family fled Jaffa for refuge in Gaza."[6]

He was a boy fourteen years of age, known by his birth name, Salah Khalaf. With his parents and four siblings, he followed thousands of Palestinian Arabs carrying suitcases to Jaffa harbor. They boarded a rickety boat, but shortly after the anchor lifted, a woman shrieked that her child was missing. "Caught under the heavy fire of the Jewish guns, we couldn't turn back," Abu Iyad recalled. The woman threw herself into the sea, and her husband followed. Neither could swim. "The angry waves finally swallowed them up under our very eyes."[7]

Accounts of children and infants left behind are common in Palestinians' memories of their flight in the 1948 war.[8] They left jewelry, photographs, and other valuables behind along with their clothing, bedding, dishes, and other everyday items. Abu Iyad's father carried the house keys in his pocket, assuring his children they would return soon.[9]

Fear made them run. Abu Iyad's family was among 100,000 Arabs who emptied Jaffa under artillery fire from Menachem Begin's Irgun. More than the shells, they feared a massacre like the one that Irgun reportedly committed on April 9 at Deir Yassin, a village near Jerusalem. "The news of the genocide spread like wildfire," Abu Iyad wrote. Fear of rape, also reported at Deir Yassin, also motivated them. Fathers evacuated families to protect their wives and daughters.[10] Concern for family honor destroyed the nation, in Abu Iyad's view. He would condemn such traditional values as a weakness when he became an activist in the 1950s.

The memoir also condemns European Zionists for destroying the tolerant coexistence of Arab Muslims, Jews, and Christians in Palestine. Abu Iyad was born in 1934 in northern Jaffa, which bordered the new European Jewish city of Tel Aviv. His father spoke Hebrew and ran a grocery store in the mixed quarter of Carmel. Half of his customers were Jewish, and they exchanged visits on holidays. As a child, Abu Iyad learned Hebrew and made Jewish friends. But in the 1930s the Sephardic Jews of Jaffa began to socialize primarily with European Jews.[11]

Abu Iyad titled his first chapter "Seeds of Hatred" and wrote it just after Begin was elected prime minister of Israel in 1977. Through anecdotes, he linked his own turn to political violence with Jewish violence. One day in 1945, he wrote, he rode his new bike to visit relatives on the other side of Tel Aviv. Jewish boys attacked him, chanting "Arab! Arab!" in Hebrew. They broke his bike to pieces. When he returned home by bus, he faced a new set of accusations. Jewish friends had falsely reported that he stabbed a Jew in a Jaffa riot. Impossible, Abu Iyad wrote. The riot occurred while he was being beaten up in Tel Aviv! Nonetheless, British police appeared that night at his home and dragged the eleven-year-old to a police station, where he was beaten.

> For the first time in my life I felt frustration and hatred—hatred for the English who oppressed my people, hatred for those of my compatriots who served them, hatred for Zionism that drove a wedge between Arabs and Jews.[12]

The boy was sentenced to a year of house arrest.

"The sense of despair I felt at the injustice was nonetheless compensated by the prestige I enjoyed by my peers," he recalled. When he returned to school, his principal publicly praised him. With such encouragement, he joined the nascent Arab militia, the Najjada, which taught him the history of the Balfour Declaration and the 1936 Palestinian Arab Revolt. It also taught him to uphold liberal values against racial bias: "The Najjada bans regional bigotry and provincial loyalty, as well as religious, tribal, and ideological zealotry."[13] As a PLO leader in the late 1960s, Abu Iyad advanced a similar democratic vision.

Najjada also taught him to meet violence with violence. After the Irgun bombed the British headquarters in the King David Hotel in

Jerusalem, Abu Iyad's father bought a gun: "My father, the mildest and most peaceful of men, meticulously cleaning and oiling a lethal weapon, caressing it affectionately! Abdallah and I were thrilled."[14] In the summer of 1947 Najjada staged its first attack, on a Jewish café in Tel Aviv, killing four Jews and an Arab.[15]

But Palestinian Arabs were leaderless, disorganized, and poorly equipped when Britain announced its intent to withdraw from Palestine that year. Arab rulers from outside of Palestine carried on the diplomatic fight at the UN, while British repression hindered organization within Palestine. After the UN voted to partition Palestine into independent Arab and Jewish states, a motley array of popular militias launched a civil war against Jews in Palestine.

Arabs scored some early victories, but the arrival of Czech arms turned the tide toward the Zionists. In April, with gunfire and terror tactics, they expelled Arabs from the major coastal cities of Haifa and Jaffa and emptied hundreds of villages. Some 300,000 had fled by the time David Ben-Gurion proclaimed the state of Israel on May 14, 1948. Hours later, the British mandate expired. Arab states immediately declared war but won back no territory. Israel kept the territory it had conquered beyond the UN boundaries and refused the return of Palestinians to their homes.

Palestinian leaders had unwittingly encouraged people to flee because they believed Arab states' promises to rescue them. "They should have stood their ground, whatever the cost," Abu Iyad wrote. "The Zionists could never have exterminated them [Arabs] to the last man. Besides, for many, exile has been worse than death."[16]

Abu Iyad's memoir invoked the same fear of collective annihilation expressed by Turks, Armenians, and Arabs after World War I. It also reflected contemporary Jewish fears. During the 1936–1939 revolt, Zionists raised alarms about the "rape of Palestine" and accused the British of failing to provide a haven for the Jewish people, who were "ostracized from the community of men."[17] Begin's 1948 memoir *The Revolt* justified Irgun's violence against the British, because "We were convinced that our people truly had nothing to lose except the prospect of extermination."[18]

Significantly, as will be seen, Abu Iyad did not address Jewish fears or the Holocaust directly in his memoir. This lacuna may reflect the disjuncture of his life experience from that of Israelis, or it may reflect the rhetorical war of annihilations that raged at the time he was writing the memoir.

Well before Arafat's UN speech, however, Zionists had turned nihilistic rhetoric on the Arabs who competed for a haven in Palestine. "There were no such thing as Palestinians," Prime Minister Golda Meir declared in a famous 1969 interview. "It was not as though there was a Palestinian people in Palestine and we came and threw them out."[19] Palestinian poet Mahmoud Darwish responded, in despair, that the world regarded Palestinians' claim to exist as a threat: "International security becomes conditional upon my absence from Palestine, and from humanity."[20]

The contradiction between international norms and Palestinians' permanent exile fed Palestinians' sense of injustice. In December 1948, as more than 700,000 Palestinian refugees settled into makeshift winter camps, the UN issued the Universal Declaration of Human Rights. It promised the right to leave, and return to, one's country. That same month, the UN also issued Resolution 194, which explicitly called for Palestinian refugees' return to their homes. No world power enforced these decrees.

The feeling of injustice festered in the refugee camps, where stories of the 1948 "catastrophe" were told and retold. Ten years later, Abu Iyad became a high school teacher in a camp and told his students stories of the bicycle attack, police brutality, and drowning parents.[21] The stories' lesson—that force must be met by force—became the DNA of Fatah ideology. That justice could be restored only by conquering Israel—and reestablishing Palestine as a unitary, democratic state—became the second strand of Fatah's DNA.

REVOLUTION AND THE RISE OF FATAH

"The years we spent in Gaza were among the saddest of my life," Abu Iyad wrote.[22] All seven family members lived in a single room of his uncle's house. When his father's savings ran out, he refused to let Abu Iyad take a job in a café because he thought it was shameful. After a fight, Abu Iyad turned his back on his father's traditional morality. He became a social rebel and a moral pragmatist.

Because Gaza was administered by Egypt, Abu Iyad was able to go to Cairo for higher education. He attended the Dar al-Ulum, the same college that Hasan al-Banna had attended. He also joined the Palestinian Student Union (PSU), which organized a sit-in at the Arab League building to protest cuts in scholarships. When the students refused to move, police arrested them. It was the first of many arrests for Abu Iyad.

Abu Iyad met Arafat, then an engineering student, in the fall of 1951. The odd pair forged a lifelong partnership. Abu Iyad was a large, hulking man of stubborn deliberation; Arafat was five feet four inches tall, light on his feet and always on the move. Arafat became a leader, Abu Iyad remembered, because his honest and affectionate manner won the hearts of students. In 1952, they elected Arafat PSU president and Abu Iyad his vice president.[23] Although Palestinian students were inspired by Algerians' war for independence, they could not found their own nationalist movement under Egyptian president Gamal Abdel Nasser's watchful and controlling eye. So Arafat took an engineering job in Kuwait, the one Arab country that permitted Palestinians to organize politically.

Upon graduation in 1957, Abu Iyad chose to return to Gaza to teach high school in the Bureij refugee camp. He wrote and staged a student play, *Days of Glory*, about his 1948 exile. He also taught students the philosophy of revolution, as he "devoured" the works of Karl Marx, Vladimir Ilyich Lenin, Mao Tse-tung, and Frantz Fanon. "I read *The Wretched of the Earth* countless times," he wrote. Students started a support group for the Algerian FLN. "He sowed seeds of revolution in the hearts of Palestinian youth," recalled one of them.[24]

In 1959, Arafat summoned Abu Iyad to Kuwait to help build a Palestinian national movement. Abu Iyad married his cousin (the daughter of the uncle he had tried to visit on his bike in 1945) and said good-bye to his students. Fatah was founded that October by a conference of 500 delegates from twenty Palestinian groups. The founders set two primary goals: 1) to establish a sovereign state; and 2) to regain their homeland by means of armed struggle.

The decision to wage his battle from outside of Palestinian territory was pivotal. In exile, Fatah enjoyed more freedom and resources than groups in the West Bank or Gaza. And so refugees would dominate Palestinian nationalism for the next thirty years. Not until the Intifada broke out in 1987 would initiative shift to Palestinians in the occupied territories.

Launching a revolution from exile was a long shot. Their models—Mao, Ho Chi Minh, Castro—all fought for liberation from within their territory. Fatah was in Kuwait, 775 miles from Jerusalem, with no military force. And yet they challenged not only the Israel Defense Forces (IDF), but also Jordan's King Hussein who controlled the West Bank and who claimed to represent Palestinians diplomatically. But Fatah appeared to have no other choice. Mayors on the West Bank remained loyal to King Hussein and imposed a quietism among the population. By contrast, exiled refugees were eager to fight.

Fatah began recruiting refugees with an underground newsletter, *Our Palestine,* edited by Arafat's second partner, Abu Jihad.[25] It argued that Palestinians could not trust Arab states to wage their fight for them. And it portrayed the Palestinian revolution as kin to other anticolonial movements, invoking Mao's lesson that power comes only through the barrel of a gun and Fanon's teaching that violence is cathartic and that war will make the people strong. Fatah vowed, "With revolution we announce our will, and with revolution we put an end to this bitter surrender, this terrifying reality that the children of the Catastrophe experience everywhere."[26]

Like past Middle Eastern movements, Fatah's goal was to restore Palestinians' sovereignty. "The ideological lodestone of the movement from its inception had been the simple but powerful concept of 'the Return,'" remarked Helena Cobban, a journalist with close ties to the PLO.[27] As Abu Iyad put it, refugees had no hope for justice: "A stateless people are a people without recourse, without defense."[28]

Abu Iyad began recruiting for Fatah in Gaza. During summer trips, he met former students at a café and in his home. His recruits formed Gaza's first Fatah cell in 1963. They later became the backbone of Abu Iyad's intelligence network.[29] Meanwhile, Abu Jihad set up an office in Algeria, where former FLN leaders trained Fatah's first guerrillas *(fedayeen).*

The goal of guerrilla operations was to win popular support. Fatah had no illusions about defeating the IDF, Abu Iyad wrote. "We believed that [armed struggle] was the only way to impose the Palestinian cause on world opinion, and especially the only way to rally our masses to the people's movement we were trying to create."[30]

But practice did not follow theory. Rival guerrilla factions clashed in their philosophies of violence. Abu Iyad's narrative of Fatah's ascent reveals the fundamental contradictions that both propelled the movement forward and stymied it. Fatah may have staged guerrilla operations for publicity, but their recruits and rivals took the battles seriously. Their cross-purposes eventually ignited a civil war in Jordan.

Fatah launched its first guerrilla operation in January 1965, with a failed effort to demolish an Israeli water pumping station on the Jordan River. Arafat and Abu Jihad had hastily staged the raid to compete with Nasser's new PLO.[31] The Arab League had created the PLO the previous year as a means of containing Palestinians, not mobilizing them.

The guerrillas made more than 100 minor raids on Israel in the next two years, contributing to the tensions that caused the June 1967 war. When Israel defeated Egypt and occupied the West Bank and Gaza in six days, Palestinians lost any lingering hope that Nasser would liberate their homeland.

Fatah seized Nasser's 1967 defeat as an opportunity. They decided to ignite a "people's liberation war" in the occupied territories before Israel established full control. On August 28, 1967, Arafat led guerrillas into the West Bank, moving "like fish in water" as Mao advised. But West Bank Palestinians did not rise up. Fatah had few contacts there and the Israelis easily defeated its inexperienced guerrillas. In early 1968 Fatah pulled its remaining guerrillas out.[32]

It was a moment of reckoning. Fatah would remain a militant refugee movement fueled by the pain of exile. And it would have to renounce its principle of independence, because it needed bases, arms, and financing from the Arab states.[33] They chose Jordan first—or it chose them.

Then came Fatah's moment of redemption. In March 1968, Fatah staged a heroic stand against Israeli troops at the Karameh camp, on the east bank of the Jordan River. While 15,000 Israeli troops flattened nearly every building in the camp, they did not scare the 300 guerrillas away. Nearly thirty Israeli soldiers died in the raid; about 100 Palestinians also died.[34]

Thousands of Palestinians came to pay their respects to the martyrs and to Fatah. Abu Iyad mesmerized the crowd with stories of the battle. Fatah paraded down Amman's streets, showing off abandoned Israeli war materiel; even King Hussein proclaimed, "We shall all be fedayeen."[35] In the following weeks, 5,000 young Palestinians—mostly from refugee camps—volunteered for Fatah, which accepted 900 for guerrilla training.

This was the "heyday of the guerrillas." The underground movement went public: Arafat's photograph landed on the cover of popular Arabic magazines—and *Time* magazine, too. Revolutionary culture spread to civilians, as Palestinians revived use of the *kuffiyeh*, symbol of the 1936 revolt, and of traditional embroidery on women's clothes. Che Guevara, recently slain, became a popular icon. Fatah radio played songs with lines like "O [Moshe] Dayan, drinking blood is the custom of our men," while armed guerrillas swaggered in the streets of Amman.[36]

Abu Iyad had quit his teaching job in Kuwait to become a full-time revolutionary. While Arafat and Abu Jihad tended to military matters, he became Fatah's principal ideologue and spokesman. He managed

Abu Iyad (Salah Khalaf), seated at center, was a leader of Fatah and a primary advisor to Yasser Arafat. He acted as the group's spokesman, as at this press conference held in Tripoli, Libya, on December 4, 1977. He announced a resistance front to oppose Anwar Sadat's bilateral peace initiative with Israel, along with George Habash of the Popular Front for the Liberation of Palestine (on Abu Iyad's right) and Nayef Hawatmeh, of the Democratic Front for the Liberation of Palestine (on Abu Iyad's left).

(© Alain Nogues/Sygma/Corbis)

press conferences with wit and aplomb and soon coordinated Fatah networks across multiple state boundaries. He lived in small, spartan apartments, changing his address frequently for security. A student who tracked him down in Amman—with great difficulty—found Abu Iyad and his roommate, Abu Lutf (Farouq Qaddumi), eating plates of hummus and beans for breakfast. They sat on simple iron beds, still in pajamas.[37]

Abu Iyad sported none of the guerrilla chic of Che Guevara. He wore what he called "Chinese suits": poorly tailored, beige civil servants' uniforms. But with a twinkle in his eye and a prodigious gift for storytelling, he inspired audiences. As Rouleau observed, "His mere appearance on stage was enough to unleash the enthusiasm of the crowds."[38]

After Karameh, Abu Iyad toured Arab capitals, seeking support. Nasser, chastened by defeat, promised a shipment of weapons.[39] The Saudi king gave them $30,000. Syria and Jordan had permitted Fatah to open training bases.

Karameh catapulted Fatah to leadership of the entire Palestinian movement. Its main rival was the Beirut-based Popular Front for the Liberation of Palestine (PFLP) led by George Habash. He recruited university students with a Marxist message of international revolution. The PFLP called for total revolution across the Arab world, beginning with the overthrow of monarchs like King Hussein, as a first step toward the liberation of Palestine.

Fatah, in contrast, grew from the ranks of common refugees, who were less educated, and from shop-owning families with links to the Muslim Brotherhood. Fatah's recruits were fired up by armed action but were less interested in theories of revolution. They simply wanted to go back to their home village—even if it was a razed mound inside the state of Israel. Fatah therefore honed to simple and concrete goals, to liberate the homeland and build a state there. Ideological dogma like the PFLP's had been the undoing of Palestinians in 1948, Abu Iyad believed.

The rivals clashed at a critical PLO meeting in February 1968. Abu Iyad urged all factions to unite behind Fatah. The PFLP refused. "If the bullet isn't loaded with clear philosophy," a PFLP representative argued, "then it will be useless." Abu Iyad retorted: "Wouldn't you consider the liberation of Palestine from rapacious occupation a clear idea? Is it really necessary to have slippery slogans like unity and nationalism and socialism that fragment Palestine and tear apart the ranks of activists?"[40]

Abu Iyad made a critical—and fateful—decision at this juncture. Rather than expel or defeat the PFLP, he insisted on the democratic inclusion of all Palestinian factions. He intended the PLO to be a prototype for the democratic state of Palestine, where all indigenous Arabs and Jews would be equal citizens. "Abu Iyad was Fatah's fighter in the democratic battlefield of Palestine," wrote an admiring student, Hasan Khalil Husayn.[41]

Five months later, in July 1968, the PFLP staged the first Palestinian plane hijacking, by diverting an Israeli El Al flight from Rome to Algiers. One motive was surely to upstage Fatah with a spectacular act. Habash proclaimed hijacking in more sublime terms, as a message to "a world that has not heard, for over half a century, the appeals of justice and international law."[42]

In February 1969, Fatah took full control of the PLO and enshrined Abu Iyad's democratic manifesto in the PLO charter. Arafat wept with emotion when the Palestinian National Council (PNC) elected him as president of the PLO. Fatah and the PNC amended the PLO charter to stipulate that "armed struggle is the sole way to liberate Palestine."[43]

Abu Iyad hoped that Fatah's control over the PLO would bring discipline. In an 1969 interview he defended Fatah's dominance as a practical necessity. "The PLO should have a backbone, or what in other fronts is termed as the leading force," he said.[44] Fatah tried to reincarnate in the PLO the open political arena that it had enjoyed in Kuwait. The PNC, its legislative arm, was to be a mobile public sphere that convened public meetings in different Arab capitals, but most often in Cairo. Guerrilla groups were allocated roughly one-third of the seats; the others went to civilian representatives of students, workers, women's organizations, and independents.[45]

But the PLO had grown too fast since 1967, without time to establish lines of authority. Arab states used their financial leverage to interfere with PLO governance, while dissident factions easily spoiled leaders' initiatives with unauthorized violence.[46] Most serious was the PFLP's refusal to defer to Fatah. Their continued hijackings and skirmishes on Amman's streets alarmed the Jordanian government.

Other factions, too, engaged in reckless violence. In 1969–1970, Palestinian guerrillas launched an average of 200 raids a month on Israel. Discipline disappeared, and even Fatah broke its ban on civilian targets, killing noncombatant citizens in Israel. Most ominously, guerrillas alienated Jordanian officials, who regarded them as a "hooligan fringe." The "Arab Hanoi" in Amman threatened the movement's social base.[47]

In response, some Fatah leaders demanded to eliminate the renegades—just as the Algerian FLN had murdered its rivals in order to enforce unity. But Abu Iyad and Arafat feared that bloodshed would ignite the kind of infighting that had weakened Palestinian resistance in the 1930s and 1940s. At a critical midnight meeting, Arafat flatly rejected the FLN option. "By God there will be no less than 100 lives sacrificed!" he warned. "Is Palestinian blood that cheap to you?"[48]

In July 1970, the conflict came to a head. After three years of low-level border fighting, Nasser and King Hussein appeared ready to accept an American peace initiative, the Rogers Plan. In exchange for peace, the plan offered Palestinians only a portion of historical Palestine. The PFLP condemned the Rogers Plan as an unjust capitulation to partition. Rumors flew of a plot to kill King Hussein.

Abu Iyad was visiting Castro in Cuba at the time. He rushed to catch a plane for an emergency meeting in Amman, where he convinced a majority of PLO leaders to oppose a coup against King Hussein. But then the king and Nasser publicly announced their support for the Rogers Plan. Fatah had no power to restrain the PFLP's reaction.

DESCENT INTO TERROR

On September 6, 1970, the PFLP hijacked three airliners and exploded them on an airstrip in Jordan. Arafat's first reaction was damage control. He expelled the PFLP from the PLO's central committee. But when Jordanians began shelling PLO locations in Amman, Fatah reversed itself and voted to join the PFLP revolt.

It was an error of near-fatal proportions: King Hussein's well-trained military routed the PLO in just ten days. "We were totally unprepared for the ordeal," Abu Iyad admitted. On September 20,

Abu Iyad was captured in Amman. Jordanian intelligence interrogated him and forced him to broadcast on radio a humiliating peace proposal. Nasser intervened to gain Abu Iyad's release and arrange a cease-fire on September 27.[49]

The next day, Nasser died of a heart attack. The Arab world stopped to mourn. The PLO licked its wounds. The war, later called Black September, had killed 3,000 to 5,000 people, mostly civilians. No Arab country had offered military support to the Palestinians. Worse, the PLO lost the sympathy of many Palestinians and government officials in Jordan. After his radio broadcast, Abu Iyad was nearly expelled from the leading ranks of Fatah. He worked furiously to save the PLO's remaining two bases in Jordan: Jerash and Ajlun. In May 1971 he made a famous speech to 10,000 refugees, mostly women and children, as Jordanian soldiers pointed guns from nearby rooftops. "This may be the last time you see me among you," he cried. "Be strong! The future is yours!" The crowd went wild.[50]

Two months later the Jordanian army destroyed the bases. In what Abu Iyad called a "massacre," hundreds died.[51] At a stormy Fatah meeting in September, Abu Iyad was again blamed. Arafat stripped him of his post as intelligence chief. He was a scapegoat, he wrote bitterly. Instead of making necessary organizational changes, his oldest friend began to centralize power in his own hands.[52] The meeting throws light on Abu Iyad's next, fateful move.

That same month Abu Iyad began organizing a group to exact revenge on King Hussein, called the Black September Organization (BSO). It assassinated Jordanian Prime Minister Wasfi al-Tal on the staircase of Cairo's Sheraton Hotel two months later. "Black September was never a terrorist organization," he wrote in his memoir. "It acted as an auxiliary of the Resistance." The operation was hardly the cool calculation of policy that Abu Iyad claimed, however. Writing seven years later, he still angrily described al-Tal as "one of the butchers of the Palestinian people."[53]

Abu Iyad also wrote in anger about the BSO's most notorious crime, the murder of eleven Israeli athletes at the 1972 Olympic Games in Munich. He claimed that the operation was a strategic response to the International Olympic Committee's refusal to permit Palestinians to compete. "This affront, coming scarcely six months after the annihilation of the last fedayeen in Jerash and Ajlun, gave rise to indignation and rage among our young fighters. The Black September leaders decided to take the matter in hand," he wrote.[54]

The operation leaders, he explained, were both refugees who had fought in Jordan. One, codenamed Mussalha, had earned a geology degree in Germany; the other, codenamed Che, was a lawyer. They set three clear goals: 1) to "affirm the existence of the Palestinian people"; 2) to profit from the Olympics' worldwide media coverage; and 3) to gain the release of Palestinian prisoners in Israeli jails.

Abu Iyad deemed Munich a partial success. While Palestinian prisoners were not released, "world opinion was forced to take note of the Palestinian drama." The murder of the Israelis, he insisted, had never been part of the plan. The first two Israeli deaths, at the Olympic village, were accidental and in self-defense. The murders at the airport were forced upon the Palestinians. When German snipers shot Mussalha and Che, he theorized, the other guerrillas "resigned themselves to killing the hostages and themselves when it was clear there was no hope left."

Abu Iyad's contention that the Munich attack was a means of reaching world opinion, scholars have argued, falls squarely into a long history of terrorism deployed as a form of communication. Terror has been a favored tool of parties who have been excluded from formal political arenas. Years later, one of the surviving terrorists, Jamal al-Gashey, spoke proudly of succeeding in this goal: "With the Munich operation, the world began to learn about the tragedy of the Palestinian people."[55]

Other scholars contend that political violence often erupts from structural causes. They argue that the spectacle of Munich was intended to earn prestige not so much in the world, but among Palestinian recruits. By 1972, they reason, the PLO verged on collapse from its internal contradictions. There were calls for Arafat to step down, as disillusioned cadres turned away. In desperation, Fatah turned to the same PFLP tactics that it had condemned, "international operations."[56]

The memoirs of Abu Daoud Odeh support the thesis that Munich arose out of organizational crisis. Abu Daoud was the Munich operation's on-site leader and a close friend of Abu Iyad in Fatah intelligence. While Abu Iyad denied any direct role in the BSO or Munich, Abu Daoud suggests otherwise. He argues that Abu Iyad deviated

Abu Iyad was the mastermind behind the terrorist attack at the Munich Olympic Games on September 5, 1972. In this photograph, a Palestinian kidnapper stands guard on a balcony of an apartment where Israeli athletes were held captive. All eleven Israeli captives and five of the terrorists were killed in a botched rescue effort by German police. This image became an icon, testifying to the success of one aspect of the operation, to create a spectacle before worldwide television cameras.

(© Kurt Strumpf/AP/Corbis)

radically from his usual moderate role in Fatah, where he had always been a strong voice for coexistence with Jews.[57]

In Abu Daoud's telling, the plans for Munich were drawn up hastily at a café in Rome just one month before the Olympics. He and Abu Iyad were angry about Israel's recent murder of a Palestinian writer and PFLP spokesman, Ghassan Kanafani. They feared that rank-and-file cadres would leave Fatah for more militant groups: "If we don't respond to their demand for vengeance, then we in Fatah will be finished as a movement." Only later did they notice a newspaper article about Palestinians' exclusion from the Olympic Games. That became the pretext for the operation.[58]

Abu Iyad personally chose the guerrillas, drafted communiqués, and smuggled six Kalashnikovs from Algiers to Frankfurt airport, Abu Daoud affirmed. The guerrillas hid the guns in sports bags and slipped into the Olympic Village in the early morning of September 5. They opened the door to an apartment where seven Israeli coaches and trainers slept, and the twenty-one-hour siege began.[59]

Abu Iyad's behavior after the operation also suggests that he intended it to rally potential recruits to Fatah—in competition with the PFLP and other more violent factions. He eulogized the guerrillas killed in Munich at a public funeral in Libya. Abu Iyad gained a reputation as the most radical of the three Fatah leaders.

But if communication to the world had been a goal, as Abu Iyad claimed, then success was far less evident. Major English-language papers reported Munich as terrorism, not a revolutionary act. They made direct links between the deaths of Israelis in Munich and the Holocaust thirty years before. "Belsen Survivor Describes Attack" headlined the September 6 front page of *The Times* of London, featuring the interview of an Israeli athlete who had been imprisoned in the concentration camp. If Palestinians had felt marginalized from humanity before 1972, the newspapers excluded them completely. "The Arab terrorists made it plain that their real target was civilized conduct among nations, not merely Israel," a *New York Times* editorial declared. Israeli prime minister Meir was quoted as calling the assailants "lunatics." The *Jerusalem Post* called for "War Against Terrorists."[60]

Palestinian newspapers reacted with dismay. *Al-Quds (Jerusalem),* scolded the BSO in a September 6 editorial: "It would have been so beautiful to see the Palestinian flag wave among the flags of other peoples raised at the Olympic Games in Munich. . . . But what happened at Munich wasn't beautiful at all, it distressed the whole world."[61] An Arabic paper in Haifa complained "the victims of this crazy crime are not just the innocent Israeli athletes, but also the reputation of the just cause of the Palestinian Arab people."[62]

Other Arab papers expressed mixed reactions. *Al-Ahram,* the official Cairo daily, ran sympathetic front-page stories about the Israeli victims and blamed Arab states for neglecting Palestinians' wretched condition. Lebanon's *al-Nahar* printed the BSO's press release, which explained that Munich was a result of the PLO's expulsion from Jordan. But another column called Munich unethical: the BSO aimed to exact revenge, not to seek justice.[63]

Within Fatah, mention of Munich soon became taboo. Arafat refused to discuss it and never took public credit for it. Abu Daoud concluded that it was a terrible mistake. "For a long time—perhaps too long—we believed that the recourse to violence, which had succeeded so well for Zionists, would succeed for us."[64]

Israel responded by bombing Palestinian bases in Lebanon, killing more than 200 civilians. Meir authorized an assassination campaign to avenge Munich. Abu Iyad was at the top of the hit list; he narrowly escaped assassination twice in 1973, in Beirut and Cairo.[65]

The ultimate effect of Munich may have been the election of Begin as prime minister of Israel in 1977. His Likud Party was established the year after Munich, and its aggressive policies would nearly destroy the PLO. Begin was Abu Iyad's nemesis. *My Home, My Land* opened with Begin's Irgun and ended with a complaint of Begin's current colonization of the West Bank.

In a dark irony, Begin had described the Irgun in his memoir, *The Revolt*, in terms that could have been Abu Iyad's: "Our purpose, in fact, was precisely the reverse of terrorism. The whole essence of our struggle was the determination to free our people of its chief affliction—fear," he wrote. "The essential thing was that there should be a State, that we should be a nation, a free nation in our own country . . . that we should not be downtrodden and humiliated by alien rule." Begin explained that the Irgun's terror was intended to undermine the British public's support for the Palestine mandate. Likewise, Abu Iyad had counted on Munich to raise international pressure on Israel to withdraw from Palestine.[66]

But as we have seen, no such international pressure materialized. Curiously, the media's link between Munich and the Holocaust did not appear in the memoirs of Abu Iyad, Abu Daoud, or the surviving Munich commando, Jamal al-Gashey. Neither Abu Iyad nor Abu Daoud mentioned any discussion in that Roman café about the insidious implication of killing Jews in Germany.

The reality of the Israelis' collective, existential fear did not appear to penetrate PLO consciousness. Palestinians like Abu Iyad apparently assumed that they could force Israelis to withdraw just as Zionists had forced the British out of Palestine. But the British had merely regarded Palestine as a costly colonial possession. Israelis, on the other hand, regarded it as their homeland, the only place on Earth where they were secure.

One solution to the puzzle is to recall that Palestinians of Abu Iyad's generation, thrown into exile, had little direct experience with

Zionism after World War II. Had Abu Iyad had any inkling of how prominent the Holocaust was in Israeli political discourse, he may have foreseen how disastrous a public-relations error Munich would be. Hawks pushed for war in 1967 by invoking the disastrous appeasement of Nazis by the British at Munich in 1938. They called Nasser a Hitler who planned to annihilate Israel. These warnings stirred mass hysteria in Israel.[67] After the 1967 war, Yad Vashem, the Holocaust museum in Jerusalem, prominently displayed a photograph of the mufti, al-Hajj Amin al-Husayni, meeting Adolf Hitler. Begin routinely compared Arafat to Hitler and called him "a two-legged beast."[68]

Abu Iyad, like many Palestinian leftists, condemned the mufti's wartime alliance with the Nazis and complained that it unfairly cast a shadow on their efforts to seek justice for refugees. But they did not believe that ordinary Jews were Zionists. In a 1969 interview, Abu Iyad suggested that Israelis might be deprogrammed from their Zionist brainwashing, once the Israeli state was removed. Zionism, he thought, was the ideology of an elite political clique that manipulated the Nazi past to create a "persecution complex" among Jews.[69]

This disconnect with Zionism helps to explain how the PNC in 1971 could pass a resolution to integrate Jews into the Arab nation: "the future state in Palestine liberated from Zionist colonialism will be the democratic Palestinian state, where those wishing to live peacefully in it would enjoy equal rights and obligations within the framework of the aspirations of the Arab nation." Zionists responded to the resolution with alarm, as a blueprint for the "liquidation" of Israel. For Arabs, an Israeli wrote in 1972, "justice is the denial of Israel's existence."[70]

Only later did a Fatah leader admit that "We were politically naive at the time."[71] The profound ignorance of Palestinians like Abu Iyad was a necessary, but not sufficient, cause for the Munich catastrophe. As we have seen, it was also rooted in the internal conflicts within the PLO, as more militant factions poached Fatah's followers. This rivalry, in turn, was fed by Abu Iyad's own insistence on democratic inclusiveness within the organization. The third cause of Munich derived from the second: Abu Iyad gave into his rage at having been the scapegoat for the expulsion from Jordan precipitated by the PFLP's hijackings.

The Gun and the Olive Branch

Just seventeen months after Munich, Abu Iyad stood in the auditorium of the Arab University of Beirut, shouting down a raucous student rally. Amid chants of "No compromise!" and "No peace!," he announced that Fatah now stood for peace negotiations. Armed struggle was no longer the only—and not even the primary—means toward justice, he declared.

The game changer was the October 1973 war, which Egypt and Syria launched in order to pressure Israel to return the Sinai Peninsula and Golan Heights (occupied in 1967). The Saudis supported them with an oil embargo that caused long lines at gas stations around the world. The United States responded with a cease-fire plan.

In his memoir, Abu Iyad explained his appearance on that Beirut stage as a defensive strategy. He feared the Americans would reintroduce the Rogers Plan, which had excluded the PLO from the peace talks. Far better to demand participation in negotiations than to be left out, he argued to the students on February 10, 1974. "I'm afraid I'm going to disappoint you," he told them. "The October War created a new situation in the Middle East, which calls for new and original decisions." Palestinians must face reality:

> The question we must ask ourselves today is whether, by our refusal to accept anything less than the full liberation of all Palestine, we are prepared to abandon a portion of our patrimony to a third party. Is it possible to let King Hussein, the butcher of our people, negotiate in the name of the Palestinians?[72]

The idea of a mini-state on just the West Bank and Gaza was anathema to most refugees in Lebanon. They wanted to go home, and they feared that in a mini-state there would be no room for all the refugees. The Lebanese camps rejected the land-for-peace swap and the diplomatic realities that Arafat and Abu Iyad perceived.[73]

Abu Iyad played a key role in Fatah's about-face. He and Arafat were removing a pillar of the Fatah movement—full return to a united Palestine—that had stood since 1959.[74] In speeches at Palestinian schools and camps, Abu Iyad dropped his usual verbal pyrotechnics to promote moderation and pragmatism.[75] Ben-Gurion had accepted partition in 1947, he argued, in order to build a stronger future for his people. So too, had Ho Chi Minh agreed to a temporary division of Vietnam. Palestinians must therefore reconsider the merits of accepting a mini-state.

"There is absolutely no doubt that none of these solutions corresponded to any criteria of justice or to the legitimate aspirations of our people," Abu Iyad admitted to the students. "But the mistake the leaders made was to accept nothing if they couldn't get everything."[76]

In a game to outwit militants, Abu Iyad also took the "Machiavellian" role and played devil's advocate for the PFLP, seeking public assurances from Arafat that the mini-state would be a temporary stepping-stone to full liberation of Palestine.[77]

In June 1974, he and Arafat claimed their first victory: they convinced the PNC to adopt the goal of establishing a "national authority" in any portion of Palestine liberated—meaning the West Bank and Gaza. The vote was a historic shift in PLO goals, toward eventual acceptance of Israel. It also marked a shift in methods, from armed struggle to diplomacy. Four months later, in October 1974, the Arab League formally recognized the PLO as the sole representative of the Palestinian people. The PLO became a government-in-waiting for a state. It was in this spirit that Arafat gave his speech to the UN General Assembly on November 13.

From this historical perspective, the contradictions in Arafat's UN speech clearly resulted from Fatah's struggles for compromise within the PLO. His reference to Israel only as the "Zionist entity" sounded hostile, but it was a necessary gesture to PLO hard-liners. They were already pulling out of the June 1974 PNC consensus and forming the "Rejection Front." The speech, written by a committee in Beirut, included other rhetorical gestures toward hard-liners, like calling Zionism an "imperialist plan" and an invitation to Jews to reject their "racist state." Arafat also retained mention in the speech of the mini-state as an interim step toward "one democratic state where Christian, Jew and Muslim live in justice, equality, fraternity."[78]

The rhetorical strategy appeared to succeed, at first. After the speech, militant factions of the PLO crowed that "Palestine has re-entered history." Palestinians inside the territories of West Bank and Gaza also celebrated the speech, with the first mass demonstrations since 1967. But euphoria died quickly.

Palestine Liberation Organization chairman Yasser Arafat addressed the United Nations General Assembly on November 13, 1974, and won observer status for the Palestinians. His offer of an olive branch and call for a Palestinian state in the occupied territories failed, however.
(Bernard Gotfryd)

The Geneva peace talks were never held, due in part to a spike in spoiler acts of terror by the Rejection Front.[79] A second reason was the shuttle diplomacy of U.S. envoy Henry Kissinger. He undermined plans for a multilateral peace conference by seeking individual bilateral treaties. In 1975, Kissinger negotiated a separate truce between Egypt and Israel, which Abu Iyad begged Egyptian president Anwar Sadat not to sign. After the Likud Party won the Israeli elections in June 1977, Sadat made his historic trip to Jerusalem. It led to a bilateral agreement, the Camp David Accords, which left out the PLO.

For Fatah leaders, the Camp David Accords were a resounding defeat, a return to their status before 1967, when Palestinians were just a problem, not a nation. Worse, even before the accords were signed, Israel had used the truce with Egypt to shift its military power to the north. In March 1978, Israel had invaded Lebanon, threatening the PLO's base. The invasion only added to the resentments Lebanese felt toward the Palestinians.

Israeli prime minister Menachem Begin spoke at Temple Emmanuel in New York City during a 1979 Holocaust memorial. New York became a primary arena in the conflict between Begin's Likud Party government and the bid of the Palestine Liberation Organization (PLO) to establish a state. Begin and the Israeli delegate to the United Nations linked PLO terror to Nazism. Paradoxically, Abu Iyad viewed Begin's own terror group, Irgun, as a model for the Palestinian liberation struggle.
(Bernard Gotfryd)

Abu Iyad published his memoir that same year, when all that had been gained seemed ready to unravel. Under Fatah, the PLO had defied tremendous odds to build a mass movement. Nearly every adult male Palestinian in Lebanon under the age of forty had served in the resistance. Refugees scattered in camps in Lebanon, as in Syria, Jordan, and the West Bank and Gaza, had found a sense of unity. And the PLO was, in spite of corruption and Arafat's autocratic tendencies, one of the more democratic regimes in the Arab world.[80] It had also built a state-within-a-state in Lebanon, with an army, schools, and a health-care system.

"The hour of reckoning has come," Abu Iyad wrote in his memoir's epilogue. "It is with profound bitterness that I must admit that our situation today is much worse than it was in 1958 when we were led to found our movement. I greatly fear that all must be started from scratch." He clearly saw the problem: "We are leading a movement which by its very nature cannot benefit from a coherent base." Governing Palestinians dispersed across several countries had proven impossible.[81]

In 1982, Israel invaded again, this time with the goal to oust the PLO from Lebanon altogether.[82] The war was as deadly as in 1948. More than 17,000 people, mostly civilians, had been killed by the time guns fell silent in September.[83] Observers compared the two-month siege of Beirut to Hiroshima and Berlin in 1945. It peaked in early August with twelve days of saturation bombing, which was said to kill more than 200 people a day.

At the end of August, PLO leaders decided to evacuate, because the Lebanese had become hostile and because no Arab state had come to their defense.[84] Arafat negotiated their departure on condition that the safety of Palestinians be guarded by international peacekeepers. After twelve years in Lebanon, more than 10,000 PLO personnel evacuated. On August 30, Abu Iyad and Abu Jihad joined a convoy to Damascus.[85] Arafat sailed to Athens.

Two weeks later, the Maronite president-elect was killed (not by a Palestinian) and Lebanese Maronite militias entered the Palestinian refugee camps of Sabra and Shatila. Under Israeli guard, they tortured, dismembered, and slaughtered hundreds of Palestinians—some say as many as 3,000—in their homes.[86]

The Struggle for Peace Negotiations

Abu Iyad reemerged in public five months later at the PNC meeting in Algiers. He appeared well composed, in a pressed safari suit scented with a whiff of cologne, recalled Patrick Seale, a British journalist. Abu Iyad impressed him as more informed and more worldly wise than the other PLO leaders present: Habash, Abu Jihad, even Arafat. "Calm, soft-spoken, and very steady, he was the sort of man to whom authority came naturally," Seale reported. "[He] had a sharp political brain and a fluent, seductive manner." And he still chain-smoked Rothmans cigarettes.[87]

The February 1983 PNC meeting was a stormy one. Delegates challenged PLO leaders as never before. Leaders strained to maintain unity in an organization broken at Beirut. They confronted the reality that Arab states had not aided Palestinians because they feared retribution from the United States. Eight years after Arafat's UN speech, noted PNC member Ibrahim Abu-Lughod, "Brutal power still inheres in the camp of opposition represented by Israel and the U.S., despite the abundant moral and political support for the Palestinians in the international community."[88] The meeting ended with an uneasy consensus of support for the "Fez peace plan," to pursue negotiations for a Palestinian state by means of both recognizing Israel and military pressure.

The fragile consensus shattered almost immediately. When Arafat initiated diplomacy, Fatah officers remaining in Lebanon rebelled. The split nearly destroyed the PLO as a common political forum. Meanwhile, Abu Nidal, a renegade expelled from the PLO, launched an assassination campaign against Fatah moderates. In these years, tens of thousands of Israelis settled the West Bank and Gaza, while the Reagan administration continued to refuse all contact with the PLO.

Fatah confronted these challenges from its new headquarters outside of Tunis, twice as far from Palestine as Kuwait had been, a quarter century before. From his office there, Abu Iyad headed an intelligence network that tracked terrorists who threatened to subvert peace negotiations. He was the "bedrock" of Fatah who kept things together, a journalist observed. While he remained loyal to Arafat, he also sympathized with rebels' criticism of Arafat's cronyism.[89]

Their first success was to convince the PNC to endorse talks with Jordan and Egypt, based on a revised understanding of Resolution 242. Adopted by the UN Security Council after the 1967 war, Resolution 242 blurred the line that defined the Palestinians' plight as an injustice rather than a misfortune. It called on Israel to withdraw to pre-1967 borders and Arab states to recognize Israel as a basis for peace. However, it made no reference to Palestinians as a nation with sovereign rights, only as a "refugee problem." In the PLO's eyes, Resolution 242 erased their nation and their claim to sovereignty. It cast them as nameless victims, mere collateral damage in a war between Arab states and Israel.

Arafat persuaded Abu Iyad to rethink that view and consider the resolution as the basis of a land-for-peace deal. Abu Iyad's skills of persuasion were crucial to Arafat's victory, according to a Palestinian student leader: "Many in the West who analyse Palestinian politics have yet to understand [Abu Iyad's] achievement of getting a Palestinian majority in the PNC to approve legislation that deprives 60 percent of the Palestinian people [refugees] from ever returning to their original homes in Palestine as it was before 1948."[90]

Acceptance of Resolution 242 signified a radical shift in Fatah's political strategy, from a base among exiled refugees to Palestinians inside the West Bank and Gaza. While the PFLP stoked the wrath in the camps, most Palestinians in the occupied territories supported Arafat's diplomatic campaign for a mini-state.[91] From 1982, Abu Jihad built networks of Fatah support by distributing PLO aid to students, farmers, and shop owners.

At the end of the decade, Fatah's seeds sprouted with the Intifada, a grassroots revolt in the West Bank and Gaza. Tensions had long been rising as Israeli settlers provoked anxiety and inconvenience, as Palestinian day laborers in Israel suffered hardship and insult, and as a young generation grew up with few prospects in life.

Revolt ignited first in Gaza's largest refugee camp, Jabaliya, on December 8, 1987, when an Israeli truck struck a car, killing four Palestinian workers. Rumors spread that the accident was a deliberate act of murder. Riots broke out, and when Israeli troops shot and killed a seventeen-year-old boy, they spread to other parts of Gaza and the West Bank.[92] As in the 1936 general strike, coordinating committees formed to organize months of demonstrations, boycotts, and shop closures. Communists and Islamists joined Fatah and student groups; grandparents and teenagers, peasants and city folk participated. The committees linked events in different towns and imposed a strict code of nonviolence.

The Intifada was the popular revolt that Arafat had hoped to ignite in the West Bank in 1967. While PLO leaders did not spark the Intifada, they rightly took credit for building the national solidarity that proved crucial to expanding the Intifada beyond Gaza. Abu Jihad nimbly stepped in after the December 8 riots to unite Fatah networks with local committees in the Unified National Command. Birzeit University professor Sari Nusseibeh, a leader of the Command, claims he converted Abu Jihad to the methods of nonviolence. Shortly afterward, in April 1988, Israeli agents murdered Abu Jihad in his Tunis home. A half-million refugees joined his funeral procession in Damascus, while Palestinians in the territories rioted in protest.[93]

If the image of a hooded terrorist at Munich defined Palestinians to the world in 1972, in 1988 the icon of the Intifada was a teenager throwing a stone. Yitzhak Shamir's government ordered soldiers to stop those stones with bullets. By mid-1990, the IDF had killed 609 Palestinians, wounded 12,000, and imprisoned 10,000. Israeli dead totaled eighteen, with 3,400 soldiers injured.[94]

The Intifada brought Abu Iyad's career full circle: its principal organizers included the communist, Islamic, and student networks he had left behind when he left Gaza for Kuwait in 1959. Since then, Gaza's economy had only declined and 67,000 Jewish settlers moved in.[95] Perhaps it was hope of returning home that turned Abu Iyad into an internationally prominent press advocate in 1989.

After laying Abu Jihad to rest, Arafat and Abu Iyad decided to declare a Palestinian state. "The uprising requires from us a political decision which shortens the distance to victory and to the Palestinian state," Abu Iyad told audiences on Voice of Palestine radio in October 1988. Fatah's urgency increased when Shamir and his hardline Likud Party were reelected in November.[96]

They called a PNC meeting in Algiers. Darwish, the poet, edited a draft of the declaration of independence. Arafat handed a copy to Edward Said, a Columbia University professor and PNC member who had condemned his 1974 UN speech. Said described how Abu Iyad won him over. He was at first persuaded by Habash's speech against a state, he wrote, because it would sacrifice the PLO's two bargaining chips: recognition of Israel and acceptance of borders.

> To which, in a meandering and yet always fascinating speech, Abu Iyad responded by saying that decisions had to be made now, not only in face of the discouraging realities of the Israeli elections, but because our people needed an immediate, concrete statement of our goals. What clinched it for me as I listened to Abu Iyad was the logic of his thesis that decisive clarity was needed from us principally for ourselves and our friends, not because our enemies kept hectoring us to make more concessions.[97]

Said was not the only delegate persuaded. After midnight on November 15, the PNC voted 253 for declaring a state, 46 against, 10 abstaining.

The 1988 PNC vote overturned the 1964 PLO charter. It declared a sovereign Palestinian state in the West Bank and Gaza, recognized Israel, and renounced terror. The stock phrases of "armed struggle" and

"Zionist entity" did not even appear in its resolutions. The historic meeting, Said remarked, freed Palestinians from the fatal trap of fear.[98]

The vote also broke the logjam in negotiations with the United States. In December 1988, Arafat renounced terrorism and the United States immediately authorized contact with PLO leaders—breaking the ban since 1974.[99] The following June, Abu Iyad met American ambassador Robert Pelletreau in Tunis. The meetings were held secretly because Israeli prime minister Shamir objected to them. He and Pelletreau talked about holding free and fair elections in the occupied territories. And Abu Iyad asked the United States to pressure Israel to accept Resolution 242's land-for-peace swap.[100]

Meanwhile, Abu Iyad embarked on an eighteen-month campaign to bring the Israelis to the negotiating table. In February 1989, he addressed a peace conference in Jerusalem, by way of a videotape. Seated next to a Palestinian flag, he looked into the camera and spoke directly to Israeli citizens.

"In the past we believed that this land is ours alone, and we did not believe in the idea of co-existence between two states, although we used to believe in the idea of co-existence as religions," he said. But now Palestinians have reversed that view. "These resolutions were not passed just by leadership: they proceeded from a legislative council which represents the Palestinian people in its entirety." He urged Israeli leaders to defy their violent extremists, as he and Fatah had done. "The realistic solution," he concluded, "is that we live side by side, and that we walk the path of peace."[101] The speech was later featured in the *New York Times*.[102]

In the spring of 1990 Abu Iyad published his most cited article in English in *Foreign Policy,* a prestigious journal published in Washington, DC. Titled "Lowering the Sword," it announced that Palestinians embraced the revolutionary spirit that ended the Cold War: "The PLO believes its initiative has breached the Berlin Wall that previously stood as insurmountable."[103] He offered Israel an olive branch—this time without also brandishing a gun.

But the stars were not aligned for peace in the summer of 1990. Shamir insisted that the PLO still intended to drive the Jews into the sea. Palestinian militants staged a raid on Tel Aviv's beach that shut down the PLO's talks with the United States. And Abu Nidal's group sparked a "battle of the camps" against Abu Iyad's forces in Lebanon.

Abu Iyad had come to realize the cost of democratic inclusion was too high for the PLO. He confessed to the journalist Seale: "I was responsible for not facing up sooner to the threat from Abu Nidal. I should have killed him fifteen years ago."[104]

It was Iraq's invasion of Kuwait in August of 1990 that brought the peace effort to a full halt. Iraq had become the PLO's primary financial backer, as funding from other states dwindled in the fractious 1980s. Abu Iyad and Arafat fought bitterly. Arafat needed the cash and believed Iraqi pressure would finally force the Likud Party to negotiate. Abu Iyad argued that the PLO could not turn its back on the United States and Kuwait, the cradle of their movement, and the thousands of Palestinians who lived there.

"The PLO will never condone the occupation of any country by force when we ourselves are victims of such policies," Abu Iyad told the Associated Press.[105] Abu Iyad's back-channel efforts to maintain contact with the Bush administration failed. The Americans cut off negotiations.[106] Rumor had it that Abu Iyad confronted Saddam Hussein in Baghdad and was kicked out of Iraq. By January 14, 1991, Abu Iyad was very nervous. That evening he drove by armored car from his office in downtown Tunis to the home of his old friend Abul Hol, Fatah's security chief, who lived in the suburb of Carthage. They needed to discuss contingency plans for the outbreak of war.

That same night, Israelis were also in a panic. Arafat's linkage of the Palestine issue to Iraq's war made them fear attacks on their soil. They scrambled for gas masks to protect them from chemical weapons. Newspapers, television, and political leaders compared Saddam Hussein to Hitler.[107]

Just twenty-five hours before the UN deadline expired, a Palestinian guard entered Abul Hol's living room in Carthage and shot Abu Iyad, point-blank, in the head. He died instantly. Abul Hol and a third PLO official were also killed. "There is no doubt that Abu Nidal killed Abu Iyad," concluded Seale. The assassin, Hamza Abu Zaid, confessed his links to Abu Iyad's longtime foe. Most Palestinians immediately suspected that Abu Nidal's organization was linked to Israel, but the Israelis denied involvement in Abu Iyad's murder. Abu Nidal's ties were mainly to Iraq. Experts still debate Abu Nidal's motive: personal revenge, because Abu Iyad had undermined his terrorist organization? Or as an agent of Saddam's revenge, for Abu Iyad's opposition to the PLO's alliance?[108]

Obituaries in the Israeli, British, and American press remembered Abu Iyad as a terrorist, despite his later peace efforts.[109] Palestinian reactions were muted at first by the war. Arafat flew immediately to Tunis to attend Abu Iyad's funeral. A photograph shows him standing at the grave next to Abu Iyad's wife Umm Iyad, hugging Abu Iyad's three daughters.[110] Meanwhile, Palestinians in the occupied territories mounted protests.

"So fell the brave knight of Fatah," wrote his student Hasan Khalil Husayn in a memorial book published months later. "The fiery tongue has gone silent."[111]

Abu Iyad's burial was grim, not only because of the cold winter rain that fell. In death he remained an exile along with the 2.7 million Palestinian refugees living mostly in Lebanon, Syria, and Jordan. Two million more Palestinians lived in their homeland of the West Bank and Gaza under Israeli occupation.[112]

Palestinians had not suffered genocide like the Armenians and Jews, but their mass deportation approached the scale of those of the Armenians, Greeks, and Turks in the early twentieth century. Their camps are a reminder of the crimes of World War I and the injustice of the Paris Peace Conference. They suffered most from the colonial aggression that all Arabs experienced and the Palestinian Question still rouses public ire across the region.

Fatah has floundered since Abu Iyad's death in 1991. At the one-year memorial service, Arafat lamented, "I have become a veritable orphan after his murder. He was the last one I could ask, in times of crisis, 'What should we do now?'"[113] Many Palestinians wondered the same thing. Alone at the helm of Fatah and the PLO, Arafat made decisions that his companion would have opposed.

In 1993 Arafat signed the Oslo Accords with Prime Minister Yitzhak Rabin of Israel's Labor Party. Israel finally recognized the PLO as the representative of the Palestinian people. In exchange, the PLO formally recognized Israel. Rabin promised to transfer governance to a new Palestinian Authority (PA) but not an independent state. Israel also retained control of security. Key questions regarding the return of refugees, borders, and status of Jerusalem were left unanswered. Arafat staged a victorious return to Palestinian territory in 1996, the first time in thirty years. Elected president of the PA, he set up government in Ramallah, on the West Bank.

The victory appeared hollow to many Palestinians, who thought Arafat had given much for little guaranteed return. Farouq Qaddumi, Abu Iyad's former roommate, refused to return to the West Bank. Darwish resigned from the PLO executive committee in protest. Said publicly condemned Oslo as "the instrument of Palestinian surrender, the Palestinian Versailles," referring to the peace conference that had divided Arab states under British and French rule.[114]

The Israeli right viewed Oslo as a betrayal, too. In 1995 Rabin had been assassinated by a Jewish activist who accused him of surrendering sacred land given to Jews by God. Even as Arafat took office in Ramallah, Israelis elected a Likud Party government that expanded settlements and, in essence, reneged on Oslo by stalling talks on the outstanding issues of Palestinian borders and refugee return.[115]

Four years later the second Intifada broke out. Gone was the hopefulness of nonviolence. This Intifada was violent from the first, with the ascendancy of Hamas and the advent of suicide bombings.[116] Arafat died after a sudden illness in November 2004, and two years later Fatah lost the legislative elections to the religious party, Hamas. Voters were disgusted by Fatah's rampant corruption, chauvinism, and disorder.

It is easy to dismiss Fatah as a failed movement. But the details of Abu Iyad's story resist simple judgment. Fatah had done the impossible by organizing youth across camps in different states. Between 1974 and 1977, redemption and sovereignty seemed to be within their reach. But success required that Fatah renounce the goal (reconquest of all Palestine) and the methods (guerrilla warfare) that had made it the strongest Palestinian movement. Fatah was not strong enough to impose those requirements—precisely because Abu Iyad and his allies had also insisted that Fatah would be a democratic and inclusive movement. By refusing to murder opponents, Arafat and Abu Iyad doomed their efforts to negotiate peace.

Success had also required international support from the Americans and Israelis, who were fatefully not won over by Arafat's talk at the UN in 1974. Instead, Likud Party governments from 1977 onward blocked diplomacy, expelled the PLO from Lebanon, and orchestrated Jewish settlement of the Palestinian territories. The PNC recognized that American military support had enabled Israel to expel the PLO from Beirut and that American diplomats had frightened Arab states into not aiding them in the 1982 siege.[117]

From all angles, Fatah had little chance of victory. Without sovereignty, without the ability to enforce laws and prosecute criminals, and without standing in international law, the Palestinians were doomed to annihilation as a political nation, just as Kurds and Armenians were, except for that short window of opportunity in the mid-1970s. We cannot know whether or when Abu Iyad came to regret the long shadow of Munich over Fatah's fate. On Arafat's 1974 UN speech, he wrote in his 1978 memoir, "That day, we felt that in the eyes of world opinion we were no longer merely a people of refugees and destitute beggars." He added hopefully, "We were no longer outlaws, 'bands of terrorists,' murderers."[118]

Abu Iyad's story has elements of tragedy in the classical sense. He had noble qualities. He held fast to his ideal of justice by organizing the PLO democratically, and at the end of his life he showed that he had learned from his errors. But he did not understand Israelis until it was too late. And despite his talents as a philosopher and diplomat, he gave in to his rage. It was an all too human flaw, but a fatal one for Fatah and the revolutionary generation that built the movement in the 1960s.

Fatah's most admirable legacy is perhaps its model of participatory, democratic mobilization. Much to Abu Iyad's credit, Fatah governed on principles of elected and consensual leadership. He remarked that the PLO was a beacon of democracy, and that more than Israel, it threatened the Arab dictators most of all.

As sociologist Michael Mann observed, liberalism—as a belief in universal human rights and the fundamental equality of individuals—makes almost impossible demands upon participants in a conflict. Ethnic cleansing, he argues, is the dark side of modern democracy, wherein the drive for majority power contains the potential for violence. The "people" as the masses slides into the "people" as the nation, exclusive of others—especially when relations between ethnic groups grow unequal.[119] Liberalism demands a mutual recognition of common human suffering, and Abu Iyad's memoir, like Halide Edib's, strained to achieve such a perspective.

Finally, Fatah's embrace of violence mirrored global trends in the age of Third World revolution. Without a state, Palestinians experienced an extreme version of the political vacuum that most Arabs, Iranians, Kurds, and at times even Turks confronted in the decades of the Cold War era. Military dictators and monarchs made political expression and negotiation impossible. At the same time, Abu Iyad, Arafat, and Abu Jihad truly believed, with Fanon, that violence could be cathartic and constructive, laying the foundation of a better world. Their violence was also an adaptation to the absence of a political arena.

The Palestinian precedent shaped the next movement to dominate Middle Eastern politics: Islamism. Islamists' violence in the late twentieth century was not grounded in religious tradition so much as in the political conditions that they shared with Palestinian guerrillas.

10

SAYYID QUTB AND ALI SHARIATI
The Idea of Islamic Revolution in Egypt and Iran

In December 1968, when *Time* magazine's cover featured Yasser Arafat as the face of Middle Eastern revolution, two manifestos were quietly circulating for the next revolution: Islam. Sayyid Qutb published *Milestones* in 1964 from an Egyptian prison cell. It called for revolt against the tyranny of Gamal Abdel Nasser's Arab socialism and the establishment of an Islamic state. In Iran, Ali Shariati galvanized Mashhad University with lectures on Islam as a permanent revolution. In the capital Tehran, many read his 1968 book *Islamology* as a challenge to Mohammad Reza Shah's monarchy.

These two manifestos sparked the Middle East's Islamic revival in the late twentieth century. Both texts hailed Islam as the fount of cultural sovereignty. Both expressed deep love for the Quran and its vision of justice. And both proposed a society-centered revolution in values against the state's domination of society. In a sense, they prefigured the antigovernment spirit of the Margaret Thatcher-Ronald Reagan era in the 1980s. Islamism, however, was neither neocapitalist nor neoliberal. It was to be the new "Third Way" between American and Soviet models. *Milestones* and *Islamology* combined influences of the Islamic reformism that had emerged at the time of the Ahmad Urabi and Iranian constitutional revolutions with long-deferred hopes for individual freedom and Third Worldist demands for social justice.

Qutb and Shariati inspired mass movements that carried Islamism beyond Hasan al-Banna's charismatic crusade. A single chapter cannot tell the full story of the Islamic revolution in the Middle East. But a comparison of texts and outcomes suggests the varied ways in which Islamism came to dominate Middle Eastern politics between 1975 and 2000. Four observations emerge from the comparison.

First, while Qutb and Shariati are often called Islamic utopians, their visions were only partly Islamic and not utopian at all. They called for revolutionary change to be implemented, not merely theorized. And they grounded their visions in ideas drawn from the spectrum of political ideas that emerged after World War I— not just Islam. Islamism has borrowed ideas from all major political movements active in the mid-twentieth-century Middle East. While Qutb's Islamism appealed to conservatives, Shariati's inspired Leftists.

Second, the texts did not determine events. Shariati's ideology inspired many to join the 1979 Iranian Revolution, but the victors of the revolution deviated from his vision to install government by clerics. In Egypt, Qutb's *Milestones* inspired both militant Islamists to assassinate Anwar Sadat and nonmilitant Islamists to enact a broader, quieter, and more successful revolution in society.

Third, Islamism supplanted Iran's monarchy and Egypt's Arab socialism as models of justice because it adapted well to the limits of politics under dictatorship. Like Fatah, Islamism emerged in the late Cold War era, when rulers severely constricted political arenas. Also like Fatah—which operated in liminal spaces within host countries— Islamist movements took shape in a gray and narrow zone of legality. Under constant surveillance of security apparatuses, they operated in mosques, charities, and university campuses. Islamists capitalized on the failure of top-down state reforms to guarantee justice or deliver prosperity. Between 1950 and 1990 poor peasants migrated en masse to Middle Eastern cities, leaving less than half the labor force working on farms.[1] Islamists built movements by providing services to citizens neglected by their states.

As for the fourth observation: Islamic revolutionaries turned to violence not because of the nature of Islam but because of circumstances— namely, the collision of social stress with brutal state repression. As in previous periods of political unrest, threatened regimes leaned on support from foreign powers. With American aid, the shah had built the fifth-largest army in the world. With Soviet aid, Egypt had become what one disenchanted revolutionary called a "Military Society."[2]

With little space for legal political protest, the opposition's radical fringe resorted to riots and assassinations. They gained popular sympathy and more recruits when the state overreacted. Islamists debated the merits of violence much as Palestine Liberation Organization (PLO) factions did, and militants have won the upper hand only in specific circumstances.

The stories of Qutb's and Shariati's manifestos show that Islamism was never a set of divine imperatives. It has never been a return to the past. Islamists used the rhetoric of jeremiad just as Mustafa Ali had: as a call to return to a golden age in order to justify reforms for a better future. They succeeded by adapting preexisting political repertoires to the nearly impossible task of challenging dictators backed by the superpowers. A major source of Islamism's appeal was that it gave agency back to ordinary people.

Both Qutb and Shariati came from provincial families of middling means. Qutb was a generation older, a child prodigy who traveled from an isolated village to the national capital, Cairo, for his higher education. Shariati came, by contrast, from a family of reformist religious scholars in an important shrine city. He arrived in Tehran after obtaining a higher degree in Europe.

Both men rejected what they found in their national capitals: a stodgy elite culture built on the belief that modernity and virtue resided in imitating Western intellectualism. They promoted an indigenous form of knowledge that would liberate their societies' minds from enslavement to Europe. And they invented a local model of revolutionary justice by reinterpreting Islam. Their manifestos, *Milestones* and *Islamology*, caught fire first among students and then among wider circles of activists who sought to break the power of authoritarian rule.

QUTB AND *MILESTONES*

Qutb penned his manifesto in a prison infirmary in 1963. His health suffered after eight years of abuse behind bars. Friends smuggled the text out and published it in 1964. With these opening lines, it caused an immediate sensation:

> Mankind today is on the brink of a precipice, not because of the danger of complete annihilation—this being just a symptom and not the real disease—but because humanity is devoid of those vital values which are

necessary not only for its healthy development but also for its real progress.[3]

The "annihilation" of mankind referred to the prospect of nuclear war. Qutb was confined to a prison cell, but he was not isolated from world events. He followed the news, and he likely referred to fears of nuclear war that crested in the 1962 Cuban missile crisis. His tone bears an uncanny resemblance to the famous opening lines of the American student manifesto, "The Port Huron Statement," issued in June 1962:

> We are people of this generation, bred in at least modest comfort, housed now in universities, looking uncomfortably to the world we inherit. . . . The enclosing fact of the Cold War, symbolized by the presence of the Bomb, brought awareness that we ourselves, and our friends, and millions of abstract "others" we knew more directly because of our common peril, might die at any time.[4]

Qutb, like the Students for a Democratic Society (SDS), viewed the Cold War as a symptom of a world gone morally wrong. But while SDS wanted to reform the system, Qutb proposed its replacement. While SDS offered a humanist and democratic vision, Qutb offered Islam as the solution.

Qutb's search for an egalitarian utopia of virtuous Muslims, freed of state tyranny, resembled Halide Edib's search in *The New Turan,* her 1912 novel that envisioned a republic of pious, community-minded Turks. Like Edib, Sayyid Jamal al-Din al-Afghani, and other Islamic modernists, Qutb saw Islam as an ideal union of Eastern spirituality and Western science. For example, Qutb wrote:

> It is necessary for the new leadership to preserve and develop the material fruits of the creative genius of Europe, and also to provide mankind with such high ideals and values as have so far remained undiscovered.[5]

The era of science is over, and likewise nationalism has lost its vitality, Qutb maintained. "At this crucial and bewildering juncture, the turn of Islam and the Muslim community has arrived."

Other sections of *Milestones,* however, earned its reputation as a terrorists' handbook. Qutb condemned not only capitalism and socialism but also all existing states in the Muslim world as un-Islamic and worthy of destruction. The short text (only 160 pages in its English translation) is more complex than either Qutb's admirers or enemies pretend.

It is therefore necessary to consider the text as it was written, in the context of Qutb's life and thought, before recounting how militants later interpreted it. Qutb's reputation as both a man of the people and an intellectual lent *Milestones* authority. He wrote not as a religious scholar (he had no degree from al-Azhar), but as an Egyptian citizen. He had devoted most of his life to a career in Egypt's education ministry and to literary scholarship. Qutb also wrote as a Muslim, deeply disappointed in the 1952 revolution. Nasser's Free Officers had turned against their supporters in the Muslim Brotherhood (MB) and instead built a secular, military regime. Civilians' sole weapon against such a regime was moral force, Qutb reasoned. Faith in Islam and the struggle for Islamic justice would liberate Egyptians from the grip of materialism, greed, and totalitarian rule.

Qutb's turn to Islamism came quite late in his life. He was forty-seven years old when he joined the MB in 1953. His life story elucidates the diverse influences on his vision in *Milestones*.

Qutb was born in 1906, into the same generation as Akram al-Hourani in Syria, Comrade Fahd in Iraq, and his compatriot Banna. His home village, 200 miles south of Cairo, had just one government school. Following Banna's footsteps a few years later, he moved to Cairo in the 1920s to attend the Dar al-Ulum (Abu Iyad would attend in 1950). Upon graduation in 1933, Qutb made a living first as an elementary schoolteacher, and then as an inspector for the Ministry of Education. He knew Taha Hussein, the minister of education and eminent writer who stirred controversy with books about pre-Islamic poetry and Egypt's essential links with Mediterranean (European) culture. Qutb became well known in literary circles for advocating modern poetry. And he joined the Wafd Party, which opposed the MB. Unusually for an Egyptian, he never married.

Qutb's 1946 autobiography gives a clue to the roots of his turn to Islamism in that decade. *A Child from the Village* is a realistic portrait of village life aimed at Cairene elites who romanticized peasants. Peasants were not a national symbol or national burden, Qutb seemed to say, in a plea for their humanity. He wrote passionately about his love for the government school but also about villagers' fear of the government. Officials terrorized villagers in heavy-handed campaigns to fight disease and confiscate illegal guns. The book was not a screed against government, but rather an argument to make it more locally controlled and more compassionate. Qutb also described his own moral awakening, when migrant workers came to tend his family's fields. He wrote letters home for them and alerted his father that the workers were hungry. He felt both shame and contempt for a society that endured such injustice.[6]

In the mid-1940s, Qutb became disenchanted with the secular elites who ruled Egypt. He came to regard their policies as the source of injustice. In *A Child from the Village* he rooted hope for justice in common people: not in their superstitions and ignorance, but in the moral community of the village.

A year later, in October 1947, Qutb founded a magazine, *New Thought*, with Naguib Mahfouz, the future Nobel Prize-winning novelist. They were not close friends, but Qutb had reviewed Mahfouz's novels about ordinary urban folk positively. The mission of *New Thought* was to raise consciousness about poverty in Egypt. Qutb's opening editorial echoed Hourani, his Syrian contemporary, in calling for the redistribution of farmland to the poor:

> We are still in the stage of feudalism and serfdom! We today only ask to elevate ten millions of this deprived people to the rank of the animal and the beast. The beast finds sufficient food and water, but these people do not.[7]

Unlike Hourani, Qutb rejected socialism as the solution. *New Thought* advocated a modernized Islam against communism, which was rising in popularity in Egypt. The magazine aimed to "bring back God's religion," and to translate Islam into laws and structures "so that we can bring social justice to the highest level."[8]

Qutb wrote his first Islamic book in 1948. *Social Justice in Islam* expanded his call for justice for the oppressed with a vision of a social order based on the Quran. The first chapter echoed Banna's warning that foreign models of justice were bankrupt: "It is apparent that our social conditions have no possible relation to justice; and so we turn our eyes to Europe, America, or Russia, and we expect to import from there solutions to our problems."[9] Islam is far superior to Christianity's otherworldly justice, Qutb argued, because it weds spirit and matter, values and practice, and so offers a holistic formula for social good in this world.

Qutb's Islam in *Social Justice* was liberal: it promised freedom under an elected ruler and legislature. It also assured security and equality, by cleansing the human heart of greed: "In the Islamic view, life consists of mercy, love, help and a mutual responsibility among Muslims in particular and among all human beings in general."[10]

Qutb envisioned a self-regulating society under minimal government. Muslims would live freely under only the sovereignty of God, without fear of the tyrant. There would be no priestly elite ordering society or imposing a moral code, either. The power of the Quran's poetry would inspire justice in believers' hearts:

> When the establishment of equality is rooted in the conscience, when it is safeguarded by religious law, and when it is guaranteed by a sufficiency of provision, the poor and the humble will not be the only persons to desire it. Even the rich and the powerful will support it.[11]

In other words, once Islam freed people from the dictates of capitalist greed, they would become virtuous citizens. Without the coercion of a socialist state, they would practice the Islamic principle of mutual social responsibility. Government would be limited to upholding Islamic law and collecting the *zakat* (Islamic alms tax) as a means of redistributing wealth.

The Egyptian monarchy, unsurprisingly, regarded Qutb's ideas as dangerous. Upon completing *Social Justice* in the summer of 1948, Qutb was promptly chosen for a two-year study trip in the United States. His visit only deepened his dim view of Western materialism and injustice. While studying in Greeley, Colorado, he was humiliated by Jim Crow laws at a movie theater, where he was directed to the "colored" entrance. In letters home, he complained that Americans talked only about movie stars and new car models and that they displayed shocking sexuality in advertising and the streets.[12]

Upon his return to Egypt in 1950, Qutb was greeted by enthusiastic fans. *Social Justice* was a popular hit that went immediately into multiple printings. He moved right into revolutionary circles and began contributing articles to a MB magazine. In 1951, he joined protests to demand Britain's evacuation of the Suez Canal Zone. In

January 1952, the British killed fifty police officers in the MB's home-town of Ismailia. Cairo burst into flames. Protesters—among them Muslim Brothers—burned symbols of Western culture: movie theaters, the opera, department stores. Six months later, in July 1952, Nasser's Free Officers deposed the king.

Qutb was regarded as "one of the intellectuals of the Revolution."[13] He had hosted Free Officers meetings at his home in the weeks before the coup. The MB endorsed the deposition of King Farouk as a "blessed movement." A few weeks later, revolutionary leaders invited Qutb to address the Officers' Club. He spoke to a packed auditorium about the need to bring Egypt to Islam. Officers embraced him and Nasser himself greeted Qutb afterward. Through the fall of 1952, Qutb worked long hours as the revolutionary council's cultural advisor, seeking to unite the military and Islamic wings of the revolution. In January 1953, Nasser named him to head the new official party, the Liberation Rally.[14]

But Islamists soon soured on the revolution. The officers refused to establish an Islamic government. In February, Qutb resigned from the Liberation Rally to formally join the MB as director of propaganda. He condemned all compromise with the Free Officers and published strident attacks against immoral art, women who sang in public, and cinema.[15]

Tensions boiled over in October 1954, when a Muslim Brother attempted to assassinate Nasser. Nasser reacted with fury, as the monarchy had done in 1948. Hundreds of Muslim Brothers were arrested, and their headquarters was burned down. Qutb was arrested, too, and sentenced to fifteen years in prison for "anti-government agitation." During his trial, Qutb lifted his shirt to display torture scars, remarking acidly, "Abdel Nasser has applied to us in jail the principles of the revolution."[16]

Shortly before his fiftieth birthday, Qutb walked through the gates of Tura prison and into the most revolutionary era of his life. His moral outlook became rigidly black-and-white as he wrote a personal commentary on the Quran. He renounced all of his previous writing as a waste of forty years of his life, because they placed human ideas above God's. And he revised new editions of *Social Justice* to excise its liberal elements.[17] He no longer believed in popular sovereignty or the republic. And he no longer viewed Islam as simply superior to other civilizations; it was the only civilization.

Qutb's new views crystallized in *Milestones,* written as a direct assault on Nasser's secular dictatorship. Qutb proclaimed, "the whole world is steeped in *Jahiliyyah,*" the moral darkness of the era before the Prophet received God's word. "*Jahiliyyah,*" he wrote, "is based on rebellion against God's sovereignty on earth." It was therefore the duty of all Egyptians, all Muslims, to shun idols—including un-Islamic rulers—and obey only God. By doing so, they would find equality and freedom. "Only in the Islamic way of life do all men become free from the servitude of some men to others and devote themselves to worship of God alone."[18]

New too was Qutb's embrace of a vanguard to lead the revival. Because most Muslims were now blind, they could not perform their duty to forbid evil and command the good. *Social Justice*'s vision of spontaneous, leaderless change was unrealistic.[19] Justice lay in the hands of the enlightened few. It was for such a vanguard that Qutb wrote *Milestones* as a handbook.

The tone of *Milestones* is postapocalyptic, in almost cinematic style: the vanguard are alone and few on a hostile planet, charged with reviving the pure spirit of another, ancient generation that had lived in the time of the Prophet. Like that first generation, they should read the Quran not as scholars do but "as a soldier on the battlefield reads 'Today's Bulletin,' so that he may know what is to be done."[20] They should also cut themselves off completely from the ways of ignorance. Prison cells became havens from contagion, like the caves of ancient monks—or like bunkers that blocked radiation in nuclear war.

Qutb's vanguard would not follow a leader. He rejected the top-down revolutionary model exalted by Nasser, Mao Tse-tung, Fidel Castro, or Ho Chi Minh—all such leaders were idols, inherently tyrannical. Islamism would instead be a diffuse movement, a mass conversion nurtured over years of quiet persuasion, as it was in seventh-century Arabia. "When, after hard work, belief became firm . . . then God, through this faith and through the believers, provided everything which was needed," he wrote. "The society was freed from all oppression, and the Islamic system was established in which justice was God's justice."[21]

Qutb's plan for quiet persuasion was, however, contradicted by other chapters in *Milestones* that justified violence toward any obstacle to Muslim proselytism. "No political system or material power should put hindrances in the way of preaching Islam," he wrote. "If someone does this, then it is the duty of Islam to fight him until either he is killed or until he declares his submission." Muslims enjoy an absolute right to preach, he wrote, because "this religion is really a universal declaration of the freedom of man."[22]

In effect, Qutb posed Islam as a challenge to another universal declaration, the 1948 United Nations (UN) Universal Declaration of the Rights of Man. Man-made law cannot assure global harmony the way Islam can, he argued.[23] And Islamic justice cannot coexist with other systems of belief. *Milestones* codified the disenchantment with international law that had spread in the Middle East since the 1919 peace settlement and the 1947 UN partition of Palestine.

Qutb also challenged establishment Islam, which viewed jihad as primarily defensive and which preached tolerance toward Jews, Christians, and other "peoples of the book." *Milestones* in effect reversed the historical trend toward equality among Muslim and non-Muslim citizens. It essentially restored the hierarchy of the premodern Ottoman era. Freedom of religious thought is possible only under the hegemony of Islamic law, Qutb wrote. Only then would the Islamic state respect individuals' rights of conscience.[24]

By 1964, when *Milestones* was published, Qutb had become the chief ideologue of the MB. *Milestones* was first read outside of prison by a small study group that had reformed after Nasser's repression. When Qutb was released from prison that year, due to a heart condition, the study group invited him to act as their advisor. Called the New Brotherhood, the group developed a plan to preach to Egyptians for thirteen years and then poll them. If 75 percent supported the idea of an Islamic state, they would enact a revolution.[25] Qutb reportedly endorsed this education plan and discouraged members who proposed plans to take immediate revenge on Nasser.[26]

Qutb was arrested again in August 1965, along with thousands of other Muslim Brothers. Nasser's regime accused him of collaborating in a violent assassination plot. Prosecutors offered *Milestones* as key evidence of Qutb's sedition. At his April 1966 trial, Qutb denied the charges. He insisted that he engaged only in education and that the struggle to end the *jahili* system was a long-term goal, not a call to war.[27]

Qutb was hanged swiftly after his conviction, in the early hours of August 29, 1966, at a police station in Cairo. Nasser rushed the exe-

Sayyid Qutb and forty-two other Muslim Brothers were tried in 1966 on charges of subversion with intent to commit terrorism and encourage sedition. The prosecution drew heavily on Qutb's book *Milestones* to support its case that they intended to overthrow the state. Qutb claimed that he planned only to educate citizens about true Islamic government. He is shown here, at bottom right, in a courtroom holding cell.
(Muslim Brotherhood/Ikhwanweb)

cutions despite protests from Amnesty International and other foreign observers. Like Comrade Fahd seventeen years before in Baghdad, Qutb was buried in an unmarked grave.

The shock of the sudden executions turned Qutb into a martyr. His memory would inspire the rise of a more powerful movement a decade later. The movement would be divided, however, by conflicting interpretations of *Milestones'* ambiguous message.

SHARIATI AND *ISLAMOLOGY*

Shariati wrote his handbook for Islamic revolution two years after Qutb's death. *Islamology* was not influenced directly by Qutb, but it bore the influence of Arab and Sunni reformers. As a young student, Shariati had translated an Arabic biography of Abu Zarr, a seventh-century follower of the Prophet who preached revolution and who also inspired Hourani in Syria. Shariati had read the works of Afghani and Muhammad Abduh at the Sorbonne, where he also translated Frantz Fanon's *The Wretched of the Earth* into Persian. These influences came together in his lectures on the history of religion at the University of Mashhad, the basis of *Islamology.*

Shariati was a generation younger than Qutb, born in 1933, the same year as Abu Iyad. His father, Muhammad Taqi Shariati, was a prominent and unorthodox religious scholar. He practiced a liberal, modern Islam and so removed his turban and taught in state schools. Like Qutb, Shariati's father promoted Islam against communism. His group, the God-Worshipping Socialists, embraced constitutionalism and actively supported Mohammed Mossadeq, Iran's reformist prime minister.[28] In 1951, Mossadeq nationalized the Anglo-Iranian oil company in order to devote its profits to public health and education. In retaliation, British and American spies helped conservative Iranian generals to overthrow Mossadeq in 1953.

To Shariati and many Iranians, the coup was a betrayal of democracy. At just twenty years old, he was leader of the pro-Mosaddeq student group at Mashhad's teachers' college. His speeches called for a republic and drew hundreds of students. In 1954, Shariati was arrested for the first time, for painting anti-shah graffiti on public walls.[29]

The Mosaddeq coup convinced Shariati that only revolution could establish justice in Iran. It inspired him to write his biography of Abu Zarr as a model for modern Muslims. Abu Zarr led a revolt against Uthman, the third caliph (successor to the Prophet). With his ornate palaces, Uthman had turned the holy caliphate into a worldly monarchy. "The humiliated working masses and the helpless were suppressed under the heels of usurers, slave merchants, the wealthy, and aristocrats," Shariati wrote, in indirect criticism of Iran's shah. Abu Zarr accused Uthman of violating the egalitarian principles of Islamic justice: "This capital, wealth, gold and silver which you have hoarded must be equally divided among all Muslims. In Islam's economic and ethical system, everyone must share in the others' benefits, and in all blessings of life."[30]

Modern Muslims must resume Abu Zarr's revolution to "save the authentic Islam of the poor," Shariati wrote. Like Qutb, Shariati turned away from foreign and secular models of justice to embrace Islam as a populist force for change.

While Qutb used a literary scholar's skill to evoke the power of the Quran's text, Shariati brought the mind of a sociologist to the holy book's message. He was less interested in the letter of the law than in the spirit of Islam's principles. And while Qutb recognized the power of the Quran to inspire the individual conscience, Shariati focused on the collective power of early Muslims to bring justice to their society. And while Qutb was a social conservative, Shariati was not bound by tradition. He rejected the marriage to his cousin arranged by his family and instead married a fellow university student. Neighbors in the conservative city of Mashhad expressed disapproval that his new wife was unveiled.[31] In 1959, he caused further scandal by accepting a scholarship to the Sorbonne.

Cosmopolitan Paris was a culture shock, however, and Shariati sought refuge in Iranian student circles. It was the era of revolution in both Algeria and Cuba, and Iranians in Paris became highly politicized. Shariati's translations of Che Guevara and Fanon aimed to show Iranians that tyranny and inequality were injustices common to much of the Third World. Like Fanon, Shariati scorned elites who slavishly imitated European ideas. Their intellectual stagnation perpetuated the colonial class system. Even though Iran was not occupied by Europe, its economy and culture had been colonized. Shariati literally embraced Fanon's advice to "vomit up" Western civilization in order to taste true freedom.

Shariati differed from Fanon on one crucial point: while Fanon insisted that revolutionaries must cast aside tradition, Shariati believed that local culture was a crucial revolutionary tool. Islam could inspire the masses and empower them to build a new, just society. With that goal in mind, Shariati studied Muslim reformers like Afghani and Abduh for ideas of how to modernize Islam.

Shariati returned to Mashhad in 1965 and became a professor of religious history at the city's university. His lectures became so popular that students passed around notes and tape recordings of them. Shariati's students even performed a play about Abu Zarr that compared him to Che Guevara. Clerics condemned the play as socialist, because it proclaimed that all property belongs to all of God's subjects. Conservatives also condemned Shariati for drawing inspiration from Sunni Muslim reformers.[32]

Islamology, based on Shariati's popular lectures, advanced an "understanding of Islam as a human, historical and intellectual movement, not as a storehouse of scientific and technical information."[33] The book cast clerics as the enemy: they encouraged acceptance of the unjust status quo. Intellectuals—not clerics—are Islam's true leaders, Shariati argued. Modern scholars must lead Muslims to join the revolutionary wave of Islamic history begun with Abu Zarr and Imam Husayn, the Prophet's grandson who rebelled against another corrupt caliph in 680.[34]

Justice was a core principle in Shariati's thinking. Islamic justice, he wrote, is based on democratic and egalitarian principles. Religious jurists are therefore not infallible, and Muslims must not blindly follow them. Likewise, monarchy is not permitted in Islam. Muslims must elect their imam, or religious leader, based on commitment to justice. Like Qutb, Shariati invoked monotheism *(tawhid)*, to justify his call to rebel against current leaders. Islam permits loyalty only to one God; that is, one standard of justice.[35]

Justice required no less than a complete inversion of the social order. Shariati used the story of Cain and Abel, Adam's sons, to illustrate the point. Islam was sent by God to reverse the consequences of Cain's murder of Abel, he argued. The murder symbolized the agricultural revolution, when humans abandoned their pastoral ways for farms, cities, and governments. Cain, the capitalist landowner and slave master, has ruled the world ever since. He has oppressed the historical heirs of Abel, the egalitarian nomads who shared the world's natural resources, rather than divide them into private property. The motor of Islamic history, as commanded by God, drives toward the correction of this evil and the restoration of equality and justice.

Muslims therefore face a choice, Shariati declared: to stand by, or to join the flow of history. "It is the responsibility of every individual in every age to determine his stance in the constant struggle between the two wings we have described, and not to remain a spectator," he wrote. "The end of time will come when Cain dies and the system of Abel is established anew."[36]

Shariati envisioned that Islamic revolution would produce a guided democracy, where rulers required the consent and consultation of the governed. The constitution would be written by Muslim intellectuals to ensure its adherence to principles of justice. Shariati warned against adopting European-style democracy, where the power of money in elections would favor the wealthy over the poor and conservatives over progressives.[37]

Islamology caused a sensation, much as Qutb's *Social Justice in Islam* had. It won Shariati a job at a prestigious religious institute in Tehran, the Husayniya Ershad, in 1969. Students again flocked to his message that the masses, not "great men," are the prime movers of history. Iranians must defy the false norms of their corrupt era, as the Quran advised: "Verily God does not change the state of a people until they change the state of their own selves."[38]

Shariati's lectures grew steadily more radical, eventually calling for absolute equality against all social hierarchy. Two August 1970 lectures, entitled "Religion against Religion," preached revolt against elderly clerics. Shariati accused them of being polytheists, because they were more loyal to the social system that guaranteed their status than to God. As polytheists, they distort Islam and turn it into what Marx called the opium of the masses in order to justify the status quo. Therefore, he said:

> Our mission is to continue the mission of the divinely appointed prophets who were the rightful prophets, who had arisen from the fabric of the people . . . who confronted the pseudo-priests who were attached, affiliated to, and dependent upon the rich aristocrats.

Do not wait for the priests to offer pseudo-justice, he concluded; we are each responsible for our hungry neighbors, and in Islam, the poor should expect such justice. "Abu Zarr says, 'I am perplexed by a person who finds no bread in his house. How is it that he does not arise against the people with his sword unsheathed?' "[39]

By the autumn of 1971 Tehran was swept up in "Shariati fever." Shariati's lectures became "happenings," the nexus of a new public that debated social justice. Thousands competed to take his courses at the Ershad.[40] In 1972, he revised *Islamology* for a new course to train Tehran intellectuals as a revolutionary vanguard.

Backlash came swiftly. The shah's secret service, SAVAK, called Shariati in for repeated interrogations. Even clerics at his own Ershad institute turned against him. One of its cofounders, Mohamed Motahhari, eventually quit the institute in protest. He defended clerics' leadership, and he would become a key ally of the Ayatollah Ruhollah Khomeini in the 1977–1979 revolution.

Other religious conservatives attacked the Ershad for admitting women to lectures and for giving such a prominent place to a lay preacher. Top clerics issued fatwas condemning Shariati's books. They accused Shariati of errors in scholarship—especially his belief (shared with Sunni Muslims) that the first successor to the Prophet Muhammad, Abu Bakr, had been elected. They insisted on Shii orthodoxy, that God had chosen Ali, not Abu Bakr, as the Prophet's successor. There was therefore no scriptural basis for an Islamic democracy, they argued.

Shariati began receiving death threats. He responded by radicalizing further. In February 1972, he publicly praised revolutionary guerrillas, the Mojahedin-e Khalq. Founded at Tehran University in 1965, the Mojahedin also drew inspiration from Abu Zarr, the Algerian National Liberation Front (FLN), and the PLO. Islam is a sacred duty to fight oppression, they believed. They argued that revolution would come only through armed revolt, that the shah would never accept change peacefully. Some Mojahedin traveled to Fatah's camps in Lebanon and Jordan for training. They launched their first attack, on a Tehran police station, in the spring of 1972, shortly after Shariati's endorsement. SAVAK quickly captured and killed most of the Mojahedin's leaders. But they soon began recruiting a second generation at the Ershad.[41]

That summer, Shariati staged the Abu Zarr play in Tehran and called upon Ershad's first graduating class to turn ideas into action, through public education and armed struggle. "No blood is ever shed in vain," he assured them, "and death in a righteous and just cause never leads to extinction."[42]

SAVAK finally shut down the Ershad institute in November 1972. But as Shariati had proclaimed, the Ershad's "ball of fire" had already been thrown onto a stack of wood. While Shariati slipped out of Tehran to avoid arrest, his books were being read all over Iran. To admirers, Shariati was a homegrown intellectual who forged a true knowledge of the Iranian self and so liberated the Iranian spirit.[43] To critics, he was a near heretic.

Under pressure from conservative clerics, the regime finally arrested Shariati in September 1973. He spent eighteen months in Komiteh prison, mostly in solitary confinement. After his release in March 1975, he fled to Europe under a false passport. But SAVAK prevented members of his family from following him.

On June 21, 1975, shortly after reaching England, Shariati died of a massive heart attack at age forty-one. He was buried in an elaborate funeral in Damascus, at the shrine of Zeinab, the sister of Imam Husayn.[44]

Two years later, the first protests of the Iranian Revolution broke out. It would be wrong to credit Shariati alone as the inspiration for the revolution. He was merely the most prominent of dozens of revolutionaries and thinkers who laid the basis for popular revolt against the monarchy. Shariati, like Qutb, inspired a generation of underground activists with the message that common believers can understand the Quran and can act on its call to justice. But followers of Shariati and Qutb did not necessarily read their texts as intended. They took license to forge revolution as they saw fit. In ways both

Students at Tehran University hold posters of Ali Shariati (left), former prime minister Mohammed Mossadeq (center), and history lecturer Hashem Aghajari (right) and shout at police during a December 7, 2002, rally at Tehran University. The rally was one of many that year held to pressure the government for liberal reforms. Shariati remained a potent political symbol of revolution against clerical government.

(© Reuters/CORBIS)

violent and peaceful, in the name of Islamic justice, they would oust the shah in Iran and challenge military rule in Egypt. Comparison between Iran and Egypt reveals the differing effects of similar messages in the two countries.

SHARIATI'S MESSAGE AND THE 1979 IRANIAN REVOLUTION

"The works of Shariati were essential to the revolution," remarked one of its most conservative leaders, Ayatollah Beheshti.[45] Throughout Iran in 1978, protesters raised Shariati's portrait high above their many marches alongside pictures of Ayatollah Khomeini. Far from the Ershad's auditorium, they had heard Shariati's call for Islamic justice and now they saw Khomeini as the figurehead of the new order. Demonstrators rarely distinguished between the two men's ideas.[46]

By the end of the year, hundreds of thousands were marching in Tehran and other cities. Women, poor rural migrants, civil servants, and industrial workers joined the students and Mojahedin. Deaths mounted as security forces shot marchers, and the crowds shouted, "Death to the Shah!" After Mohammad Reza Shah fled in January 1979, Khomeini staged a dramatic return from exile. It was only then that the anticlerical supporters of Shariati, and the millions who marched with them, learned of Khomeini's plan to build a regime run by the ayatollahs.

The Iranian Revolution is considered one of the great revolutions of the modern era, along with the French in 1789 and the Russian in 1917. In all three, popular movements ousted their monarchs and replaced them with republics. In all three, revolutionaries aimed to remake society, not just government. Like its predecessors, Iran's revolution was begun by moderate liberals. The 1973 oil boom had raised their expectations for prosperity. But by 1978 Iranians suffered from inflation, a housing shortage and mass unemployment. Disappointed professionals and university students protested first against torture and censorship. They called to restore the 1906 constitution and its guarantees of free speech and assembly. As in 1906, the shah responded with brutal repression.

Revolutionary Islam was the spark that lit the flame of revolt. "The rhythm of the revolution was set by the clerical revolutionaries rather than by students," writes sociologist Charles Kurzman.[47] Religious symbols marked key moments in the escalation of protest, beginning in October 1978 with a funeral procession for Khomeini's son, who had died under mysterious circumstances. The next round of protest was sparked by a newspaper article in which the shah's regime accused Khomeini of being a traitor. Khomeini, the highest-ranking cleric in Iranian Shi'ism, had been exiled to Iraq after leading protests against the shah in 1963. In response to the libelous article, religious students mounted demonstrations in January 1978. Several were shot and killed. Through the spring, students and the radical ayatollahs staged repeated forty-day memorials for the martyrs. In September, workers swelled the ranks of protests and staged a general strike.

Protest reached a climax in December 1978, when more than 2 million flooded Tehran's streets during the holiday marking Imam Husayn's martyrdom at the hands of Caliph Yazid in 680. Revolutionaries used popular passion plays to stir popular feeling. They were influenced by Shariati's depiction of Imam Husayn as the consummate Muslim. The politicization of martyrdom no doubt emboldened many ordinary citizens to face the shah's guns.

Symbols alone, however, did not make the revolution. Equally critical was Islamists' strategy. They unified students and clerics under Khomeini's banner to build a movement strong enough to depose the shah. Within weeks of the first marches, Khomeini's followers built a clerics' network of 9,000 mosques, student followers, and bazaar merchants who contributed funds. Khomeini worked from exile in the holy city of Najaf in Iraq. Followers smuggled cassette tapes of his speeches across the border to Iran. And Shariati's archrival at the Ershad, Ayatollah Motahhari, became Khomeini's agent in Tehran.

Khomeini's strategic position ensured that his ideas would compete with Shariati's when Iranians established the Islamic Republic in 1979. Both men viewed monarchy as unjust and un-Islamic. But Khomeini, as leader of the religious establishment, did not share Shariati's anticlericalism. Quite the contrary, in 1970 he published *Governance of the Jurist*, which argued that clerics should run the state themselves. In his view, the highest-ranking ayatollah should wield supreme power and all members of parliament should be vetted for their knowledge and respect of Islamic law. This was a radical break with all previous Shi'ite writing on government.

Most demonstrators in 1978 knew nothing of Khomeini's book. It had been banned in Iran. They viewed Khomeini simply as the virtuous alternative to the shah—a trade of the "turban for the crown."

Some scholars argue that Khomeini deliberately hoodwinked Iranians in his speeches, which embraced democracy and borrowed Shariati's language about a revolution for the oppressed.[48]

By February, when the shah's army finally surrendered, it was clear that 1979 would not be a replay of 1906. Islam had become the dominant language of the revolution. Religious students inspired by Shariati had gained control of university campuses, the most important rallying space. Even Marxists had begun using Islamic language to rally workers to the revolution. Islamic dress for women became a primary visual symbol of opposition to the shah. By January 1979, women who marched without Islamic head covering were attacked and beaten.[49]

Following French and Russian precedents, Iran's revolutionary coalition unraveled after it deposed the monarch. When Khomeini arrived by Air France jet on February 1, 1979, he was not yet in full control of the revolution. Iranians ignored his call for peace and took up arms against the military. They threw Molotov cocktails and put

The Iranian Revolution reached a peak with anti-shah demonstrations like this one on December 10, 1978. By then, the image of the exiled Ayatollah Ruhollah Khomeini towered over the crowds as a symbol of a virtuous alternative to the monarchy. Few protesters, however, knew about Khomeini's plan for a government by clerics.

(AP Photo/Michel Lipchitz)

up barricades to block the arrival of royal reinforcements, and so forced the army's surrender on February 11.[50]

Khomeini still felt the need to reassure revolutionary leaders, so he did not immediately seek clerical control of government.[51] In coming weeks, however, he built a formidable base of power in the new Islamic Republic Party (IRP) and in the Revolutionary Council, a transitional government. By March, the party and council enabled Khomeini to stage-manage a referendum on the future government. The ballot simply asked Iranians if they wished to replace the monarchy with an Islamic republic. Khomeini blocked the effort of nonclerical Islamists to offer a third choice: democracy.

Khomeini's personal charisma was a second important advantage to the clerical faction. Without Shariati, Khomeini was the sole unifying personality of the revolution. Khomeini appealed especially to the traditional merchants and the urban poor, mostly migrants from villages where folk religion thrived. He spoke slowly with gravitas and used phrases that stirred popular millenarianism. (Many Iranians believed a savior comes every 100 years, and the revolution coincided with the year 1400 in the Islamic calendar.) Pious people called Khomeini "Imam," a reverential title reserved for God's highest representatives on Earth. Posters portrayed Khomeini as a bearded prophet, with a holy glow around him.[52]

Even with these advantages, it took Khomeini's camp more than two years to defeat its opponents. The first stage in the contest came in the summer and fall of 1979, when the constitution was debated and adopted. In June, liberal Islamists drew up a constitution based on the strong presidency and separation of powers in the French Fifth Republic. In heated debates, Marxists argued for greater commitments to social welfare. Kurds wanted strong guarantees of minority rights. Liberals fatefully bowed to Islamist pressure to hold elections for a constituent assembly. Khomeini's supporters easily won a majority, and the Ayatollah Beheshti personally chaired the constituent assembly. The proposal for a government of clerics was first debated publicly only in the fall of 1979.[53]

Even then, the outcome was not a foregone conclusion. Dissident voices raised concerns about a theocracy. Khomeini's "governance of the jurists" was finally approved because of his uncanny ability to exploit opportunity. In early November 1979, the Iranian hostage crisis erupted. Religious students stormed the American embassy after the deposed shah was admitted into the United States for cancer treatment. The students fanned fears of an American-led counterrevolution, as in 1953. Khomeini publicly supported the student occupation against the demands of the liberal prime minister, who resigned. Taking advantage of the public's anxiety, Khomeini rushed a vote on the theocratic constitution. He declared anyone who voted "no" against clerical government an agent of Satan and American imperialism. Khomeini's constitution won with 99 percent of the vote. However, a large number of voters—4 million—abstained.[54]

The Islamic Republic of Iran was not a replica of Khomeini's vision in *Government of the Jurist*. The constitution reflected months of debate and compromise, and combined the rule of Islamic law and Khomeini's supreme jurist with an elected president, parliament, and local councils and the separation of powers found in the French republic.[55] And in the mixed anticolonial, liberal, Marxist, and Islamic discourses of revolution, it promised Iranian citizens justice. Article 2 promised a government that "secures equity, justice, political economic, social, and cultural independence, and national solidarity." Article 3 obliged the state to promote "spiritual virtues based on faith and piety," to "struggle against all forms of vice and corruption," to offer free education and promote science, to expel imperialism and all foreign influence, to eliminate "all forms of tyranny," and to strengthen "Islamic brotherhood and cooperation among the people."[56]

There was still political wiggle room for nonclerics. The next eighteen months, until June 1981, became an extended face-off between Khomeini's power as supreme jurist of Islamic law and the president's power based on the sovereignty of the people. In the end, the unelected jurist proved more powerful than the elected president.

This second stage of the revolutionary contest began with the Islamic Republic of Iran's first presidential election, in January 1980. It was more democratic than the one in 1923 that made Mustafa Kemal Ataturk the first president of the Turkish Republic. Khomeini, worried about the opposition, insisted that the president be a noncleric. Abol Hasan Bani Sadr won the election with 75 percent of the vote. Bani Sadr had been Khomeini's personal assistant and had flown back to Tehran with him on the same jet. Since February 1979, he had become a popular member of the Revolutionary Council by promoting equality and the dissolution of the state's centralized power. He broke with Khomeini in November over the constitution, because he believed it vested too much power in the supreme jurist.[57]

Bani Sadr tried, and failed, to translate his huge electoral majority into presidential power. He began his term with initiatives to reorganize government and to negotiate with the Americans on the hostage crisis. He won the support of liberal clerics like Shariati's father and of Marxist students. Hard-line clergy, however, blocked the reforms and undermined negotiations with populist campaigns to support the hostage-takers. In the summer of 1980, the IRP gained control of parliament and mounted a witch-hunt for traitors based on files taken from the American embassy. Hard-liners also secured power of the judiciary to silence critics on television and in the press.

The tide turned against Bani Sadr in November, when thugs destroyed the Shariati religious center in Mashhad. Protests in support of Bani Sadr erupted. Liberal senior clerics publicly raised doubts about the legitimacy of the supreme jurist. Khomeini struck back with force. After he withdrew his support from Bani Sadr, parliament cut funding for the president's office and moved to impeach him.[58]

Bani Sadr left office in June 1981, and the revolution moved to its third stage. Battle moved into the streets, as the Mojahedin waged a virtual armed revolt against the clerics. Ayatollah Beheshti was killed with seventy others when their IRP conference was bombed at the end of June. In a virtual reign of terror, Khomeini's forces eliminated the Mojahedin, the communists, and all other opponents. Over the next four years, revolutionary courts sentenced 8,000 to death (compared to just 497 from February 1979 to June 1981).[59] The toll in lives exceeded the last months of the shah's rule. The populace rallied to support the government, however, after Saddam Hussein's Iraqi army started a border fight in 1980. The Iran-Iraq War lasted eight years, long enough to consolidate the theocratic regime. "Khomeini had obtained constitutional powers unimagined by the shahs," wrote historian Ervand Abrahamian.[60]

When Khomeini died in 1989, the Islamic Republic bore little resemblance to Shariati's revolutionary vision. It had built its own coercive security force and imposed many restrictions on citizens. Opposition parties were suppressed. Women were officially forced to wear full Islamic veiling and banned from serving as judges in court. They successfully battled initial rollbacks in women's education and employment, as well as changes in family law that reduced the marriage

age, permitted polygamy, and limited women's right to divorce.[61] While the state expanded subsidies to the poor, it did not restructure the economy to redistribute wealth. Oil profits flowed to the centralized power of a state whose three branches were now controlled by clerics. The turbans had won all the riches of the crown.

The Iranian Revolution broke the country's long embrace of liberal constitutionalism, the dominant model of justice since 1906. But the outcome was by no means dictated by Islam. From the rise of Shariati in the 1960s, Islam had become a rich and complex idiom for political debate. As Marxists, liberals, and cultural conservatives entered into the new revolutionary arena, Islam's symbols and its system of authority reshaped their political views. That has not meant that Iranians have come to accept Khomeini's government of jurists. Reform efforts under President Mohammad Khatami (1997–2005) and in the 2009 Green Revolution demonstrated wide support for revising the 1979 constitution. Many Iranians remain committed to their predecessors' constitutionalism and have not fully rejected a liberal commitment to popular—rather than divine—sovereignty.

In the meantime, the Islamic Republic of Iran has influenced politics in neighboring countries, especially Egypt. Iran's revolution boosted the hopes of Muslim Brothers who had only recently been released from prison. As in Iran, Islam became a political arena unto itself, host to a multiplicity of discourses unheard of in Banna's day and unhinged from Qutb's *Milestones*.

SADAT'S ASSASSINATION AND ISLAMIC REVOLUTION IN EGYPT

In 1977—just as protests first erupted in Iran—Islamists in Cairo gathered 50,000 Egyptians in front of Abdin Palace, President Sadat's official residence. In a public prayer, they called on Sadat to govern according to God's revelation and to inaugurate the reign of justice.[62] Months before, another crowd had surged upon the palace to protest a cut in food subsidies. This time, as police fired upon them, the protestors chanted in the name of those who "go to bed hungry":

> You who will rule in the name of right and religion
> You who rules us from Abdin,
> Where is the right? Where is the religion?[63]

In 1881, on that same square in front of Abdin Palace, Urabi had confronted Khedive Tawfiq with the demand for a constitution. Like Urabi, Islamists in 1977 opposed authoritarian rule and sought fair elections to parliament. And like Urabi, they demanded rule of law and equal rights of citizens. Unlike Urabi, they claimed that justice in government can come only through Islamic law.

Islamists enacted a veritable social revolution in Egypt between 1975 and 2000. While they failed to Islamize the state, they succeeded in transforming society—far more than the Iranian Revolution did.[64] In 1975, Marxist students and secular Arab socialists dominated Egyptian politics and media. By the early 1990s, religious programming dominated radio and television, most women wore religious head coverings, and the secular left had virtually disappeared. Even the army and the ruling National Democratic Party published Islamic magazines. Some 20,000 new private mosques were built to meet demand for an Islam free from state control.

Islamic norms were no longer the counterculture of an underground vanguard. Egypt's middle classes publicly embraced them. Women and children—not just men—were invited to the public prayer in 1977. Most women wore religious dress, but not to symbolize a return to their former, domestic seclusion. They, like men, embraced Islam as a civic duty. Their veils accompanied their entry into jobs outside the home and social activity that aimed to make Egyptian society healthier, more prosperous, and more just.[65]

In striking contrast to the movements led by Khomeini or Banna, Islamism in late twentieth-century Egypt was virtually leaderless. It proliferated through multiple, layered movements. Fragmentation was in part a result of Islamism's populist mandate: all ordinary Muslims were duty-bound to promote good and fight evil. Fragmentation was also a response to the state's authoritarianism. When Nasser died from a heart attack in September 1970, Sadat imposed a new tyranny in the name of capitalism, not socialism.

With little free space to speak or organize, opposition movements had few options. Leftists kept a crumbling foothold on university campuses but failed to reach far beyond their base of students and labor unions. Religious activists moved into spaces beyond the state's control, in mosques and religious institutes. Through charities, they built local networks. Access to meeting spaces in every community gave Islamists an advantage over the Left.

Islamists prevailed over socialists and liberals also because of state policy. Sadat promoted Islamist student movements as a strategy to destroy leftists on campus. He expected Islamists to support his re-orientation of Egypt's economy to private property and the capitalist market. For these reasons, he released hundreds of Muslim Brothers from prison in the early 1970s.

Many ex-convicts refused to follow Sadat's capitalist script; nor did they exactly follow Qutb's script. Their agendas reflected reread-ings and creative misreadings of *Milestones*, as well as influence from the Third Worldism that had inspired the PLO's guerrillas and terror-ists. Their embrace of violence was partly an adaptation to the lack of space for political action and partly a response to the state's own vio-lence. Neither gunfire nor charity, however, could replicate in Egypt the political success of Islamists in Iran.

Militant Qutbism was disowned by leaders of the MB in the late 1960s. They circulated refutations of *Milestones* in prison and then published them collectively under the title *Preachers not Judges*.[66] While the text did not condemn Qutb directly, it undermined the very foundation of his jeremiad—that is, his call to fallen Muslims to return to the ideals of the Prophet's generation. *Preachers not Judges* insisted that seventh-century Arabia was no utopia and that the Prophet was a fallible human being. Muslims in the Prophet's day and ever since have never achieved perfect Islam. Therefore, Muslims today cannot be said to have fallen out of perfection; nor were they apostates. *Preachers not Judges* argued that Muslims must now strive, as they have always done, to improve their under-standing of Islam by using their God-given power of human reason. It also argued, against Qutb, that Muslims did not have to prove their faith with acts—and most definitely not with violent revolt against the state. MB leaders demonstrated their faith instead by publishing a magazine, *The Call,* and lobbying parliament to adopt Islamic law.

Independent of the MB, university students built a grassroots Islamic movement. By the mid-1970s, they had won seats on the powerful na-tional student unions (a stepping-stone used by Abu Iyad in the 1950s). They also began running in elections to lead powerful national associa-tions of lawyers, doctors, engineers, and other professionals. They then built a network of private mosques, schools, and clinics throughout

Egypt. These attracted recruits especially in the new suburbs of Cairo, where young university graduates struggled to establish a middle-class life.

The student Islamists found a constituency among Egyptians hurt by Sadat's liberal economic opening. Workers in government and public sector industry saw their jobs and pay slashed. In 1975, 40,000 workers went on strike. In 1977, the food riots in Cairo spread to towns all along the Nile. Rioters targeted symbols of the new bourgeoisie's consumerism, like luxury cars and nightclubs. In their eyes, Sadat's free trade regime reversed Nasser's revolution and undermined social justice.[67]

By 1990, Islamism had replaced socialism and liberalism as the dominant political idiom. The student movement merged with the MB, while al-Azhar university, citadel of establishment Islam, became a friendly ally. Top scholars at al-Azhar did not, however, seek political power as their counterparts in Iran did. There would be no Khomeini in Egypt. The movement was led by just the vanguard of educated lay Muslims that Qutb—and perhaps Shariati—had hoped for.

In the crooks and crannies of social life no longer controlled by Egypt's impoverished state, the Islamist network created what Carrie Rosefsky Wickham has called an alternative political sphere.[68] Parallel to the official political sphere—where the state had rolled back its commitment to social welfare—Islamists created a new public arena supported by their networks of mosques, clinics, schools, and mutual aid societies. It was financed in part by remittances from migrant workers in the Persian Gulf monarchies. Saudi Arabia's government also made direct grants to Islamist projects. In the early 1990s, when Egypt was hit by an earthquake and massive flooding, the Islamist network—not the state—came to people's aid.

The Islamist sphere in Egypt had by then jumped its boundaries to inspire a cultural revolution. Television preacher Shaykh Muhammad Sharawi, for example, hosted a popular Friday show from the 1970s to the 1990s. With an al-Azhar degree, he repackaged traditional scholarship in the colloquial and chatty manner that appealed to moderate Islamists. In contrast to reformers, his gentle persuasion aimed to save individuals, not remake society. Most famously, Sharawi convinced movie actresses to quit their careers and return to God. Meanwhile, cultural icons of the Nasser era fell out of public favor: the official newspaper *Al-Ahram,* for example, stopped serializing Naguib Mahfouz's novels.[69]

Islamists also began to enter politics. Candidates who sympathized with the movement won thirty parliamentary seats in the late 1980s. In contrast to Egypt's military regime fattened on neoliberalism, they offered voters civic virtue: "the image of a moral community" where "merit—both moral/spiritual and practical professional—would be justly acknowledged and rewarded."[70] Political virtue would reign, they promised, after Islamic law became the sole basis of government. And they also promised a fairer distribution of wealth. They seemed to embody the spirit of gradual moral reform preached by Banna a half century before.

All Islamists did not abandon revolutionary goals, however. Radical ideas persisted under the radar and reappeared in times of stress. Student groups, for example, discarded Qutb's most revolutionary tactics, but they still quoted *Milestones* about reviving an ideal Muslim society. And while Sharawi gave advice on life's everyday problems, his alter ego in the radical world gave fire-and-brimstone sermons that condemned the state. Shaykh Kishk, an al-Azhar graduate like Sharawi, had spent time in Nasser's prisons and carried the scars of torture. His sermons, peppered with references to sex and bodily functions, packed Cairo's Source of Life Mosque every Friday. All over the city, his stentorian voice was heard, spilling from cassette players in taxis, fruit juice stands, and doormen's kiosks. Kishk skillfully skirted censors as he humorously maligned Sadat's regime as un-Islamic, warned against Western morals, and criticized the Camp David Accords.[71]

A spate of prison memoirs also reminded Egyptians of the state's violence toward pious martyrs. Zaynab Ghazali, the female Islamist leader who had smuggled *Milestones* out of prison, published *Return of the Pharaoh* in 1974. She described how prison guards had unleashed dogs on her, subjected her to water torture, and left her for long periods without food or a blanket. Another ex-convict, Muhammad Ali Qutb, published a hagiography of his martyred brother. Against *Preachers Not Judges,* he argued that Qutb had never passed judgment on others, nor excommunicated Muslims en masse. He had simply revealed that Islam preached "permanent revolution" against stagnation, corruption, slavery, and tyranny, so that "all people are equal and none is better than another except though piety."[72]

Still other Islamists put Qutb's revolutionary rhetoric into practice. Their call to overthrow the military dictatorship gained a hearing in the late 1970s, as social and economic inequality worsened.[73]

One such activist was Shukri Mustafa, a thirty-five-year-old former university student from Asyut, a major city south of Cairo. He first learned about Qutb in prison, where he landed after Nasser's 1965 mass arrest of Muslim Brothers. Upon his release by Sadat in 1971, Mustafa returned to Asyut university for a degree in agronomy and founded the Society of Muslims (SM). The SM obeyed Qutb's call to withdraw from corrupt society and create a separate, truly Islamic community. Mustafa dressed as the first Muslims were said to do: with a black robe, beard, and shaved head. He accepted only the word of the Quran, rejected all Islamic scholarship, and discouraged Muslims from attending state mosques. He also pledged to destroy the anti-Islamic state, once the SM was strong enough. By 1976, Mustafa had recruited 2,000 members in Asyut and Cairo slums. He became famous for attracting young couples too poor to wed. With the help of migrant workers' remittances from the Persian Gulf, he provided newlyweds with cheap apartments.

The SM imploded amidst a flurry of bad press. Lurid stories appeared about parents frantically searching for runaway daughters. When a former cabinet minister publicly scorned SM members as ignorant heretics, Mustafa responded rashly. He kidnapped the offending minister and demanded that the state release prisoners, investigate corruption, and pay ransom. When the state refused, he murdered the minister. Mustafa's trial and execution dominated newspaper headlines at the same time as Sadat's trip to Jerusalem. The two items were linked in the view of Islamists who opposed peace negotiations with Israel.[74]

Also prominent among the new Islamist revolutionaries was an electrician named Mohammad Abd al-Salam al-Farag. He preached at a private mosque in a Cairo suburb of rural migrants, where few homes had running water or electricity. Like Mustafa, Farag was self-taught in religion. He scorned Islamist students who focused on social work. There can be no justice, Farag preached, under an infidel state.[75] And since the fall of the Ottoman caliphate in 1924, all states have been un-Islamic. "There is no doubt whatever that the false gods of this earth will disappear only at sword-point," Farag wrote. "Today's rulers are apostates from Islam, nourished at the table of colonialism, be it Crusader, Communist, or Zionist."[76]

Farag led a militant group called al-Jihad (Holy War) that recruited not only rural migrants, but also university students and older professionals like Abbud al-Zumur, a thirty-five-year-old air force officer, and Ayman al-Zawahiri, a doctor (and a future leader of al-Qaeda). Farag preached that jihad is the sixth pillar of Islam—and that establishment clerics had hidden this duty from Muslims. His 1981 booklet, *The Hidden Duty*, went beyond Qutb's *Milestones* to argue that the overthrow of the Egyptian state is Muslims' top priority.

These ideas exploded into violence in the summer of 1981, when riots broke out between Muslims and Christians in a Cairo suburb. Al-Jihad was active in the neighborhood. It viewed Copts as a Christian fifth column, who sold out Egypt to foreigners. Violence also broke out in Asyut, which had a large Coptic minority.[77]

In response to the riots, Sadat's regime finally broke with its pro-Islam policies and defended secular nationalism as the glue of Egyptian unity. It publicly condemned Islamist pamphlets that banned Muslims' association with all Christians. But it also condemned the Copts for being provocative. On September 3, 1981, Sadat dismissed the Coptic pope and five bishops and then ordered the mass arrest of 3,000 people, including politicians, lawyers, journalists, students and more than 1,500 Islamists, including the MB's leader, Umar Talmasani, and Shaykh Kishk.[78]

The broad, indiscriminate sweep of arrests caused public outrage. A member of Farag's group, who was an army officer, was appalled to learn that his own brother had been arrested. He decided to act. In late September, the officer presented al-Jihad leaders in Cairo with a plan to attack Sadat at his moment of glory: the October 6 parade to celebrate Egypt's victory against Israel in the 1973 war. Inspired by the recent Iranian Revolution, al-Jihad leaders hoped the murder would trigger a popular uprising.

"I am Khalid al-Islambuli, I have killed Pharaoh, and I do not fear death!" Lieutenant Islambuli yelled, after jumping from a parade tank to shoot Sadat in the reviewing stand. His cry was broadcast across Egypt on live television. To many viewers, his was the voice of the popular will. To the regime, it was a shock to learn that militant Islamism had infiltrated the officer ranks of the military.[79]

The assassination of Sadat did not spark the revolution that the al-Jihad group had hoped for. The military quickly stepped in to secure the republic under the rule of Vice President Hosni Mubarak, a war hero. Sadat's funeral was subdued, in contrast to the emotional crowds that had carried Nasser's coffin to its grave. Islambuli and Farag were tried and executed within six months. Militant Islamists were arrested in another massive sweep, which included Zawahiri. He would spend several years in prison before fleeing Egypt to promote Islamic revolution in Afghanistan.

Given the public's ambivalent mood, Mubarak's regime dared not suppress Islamism altogether. At first, it offered an olive branch to peaceful Islamic reformers. The MB was permitted to enter members in elections, but not as a legal party. They affiliated with other parties and formed a coalition with Labor and Liberal politicians, or ran as independents. This was how they won a notable presence of thirty-six seats in parliament. The regime held the line on legislation, however. In 1985 it quashed a proposal to make Islamic law the sole basis of Egyptian government.

In 1990 the Mubarak regime backtracked, out of fear of Islamists' growing influence. It rigged the elections to ensure Islamists' defeat, leaving parliament with even fewer opposition deputies than it had in 1979. State agents assassinated the leader of the Gamaa (Islamic Group), the most powerful Islamist organization in southern Egypt.

The 1990 crackdown ignited an eight-year insurgency. One reason was that since 1981 Islamists had grown powerful enough to resist. A second reason was that the state's crackdown discredited the moderate MB and played into the hands of militants. "As the formal inclusion of the Muslim Brotherhood during the 1980s turned into outright political exclusion in the early 1990s, the Gamaa and Islamic Jihad felt vindicated," scholars observed. Abbud al-Zumur, now al-Jihad's leader, mocked the MB for playing along with the regime's charade. It had never intended to include Islamists in government, he said: "Whereas France, Italy and Germany permit the formation of a religious party, Egypt is proud of the fact that it doesn't permit such a party."[80]

State violence fueled outrage and support for Islamic revolt. In 1991, a Gamaa pamphlet complained of members' "torture and torture of their wives and their mothers that has become a daily habit in police stations."[81] In 1992, the regime sent 16,000 troops to "liberate" the Cairo suburb of Imbaba from Islamists. Similar invasions occurred in Asyut and other cities. The regime also revived military courts and adopted a shoot-to-kill policy. By 1997 nearly 50,000 people were arrested. Popular support for Islamists ebbed only after the Gamaa massacred fifty-eight tourists and four Egyptians in November 1997 at a Pharaonic temple in Luxor.

Islamist violence in Egypt arose not simply from ideology, but as a specific response to the state's brutal bouts of repression in 1981 and 1990. Only then did militants gain support from other activists and the wider population. As we have seen, the leaders of the MB and student Islamists have vigorously opposed violent revolution. It is also noteworthy that the methods of militant Islamists appear to have been inspired by non-Islamists: Mustafa's kidnapping of a minister mimicked PLO tactics; suicide attacks had been pioneered in Sri Lanka.

The timing and method of Islamic violence casts doubt on arguments that Islamism is inherently violent. The identities of militants also undercuts assumptions that they are motivated by tribal ethics of revenge or by the psychological disorientation of peasants new to modern urban life. Both Islambuli and Zawahiri of al-Jihad came from upper-class families. Islamism in Egypt was not the rage of the ignorant; rather, it was a response to their exclusion from political participation with brutal methods of surveillance, arrest, and torture.

As the air cleared in 1998, more Egyptians than ever agreed with Islamists that the entire system was unjust.

Islamism gained appeal precisely at the moment when confidence in the post-independence states ebbed. Nasserism died when the Arabs met defeat in the 1967 war against Israel. When the shah celebrated 2,500 years of monarchy in 1971, he alienated Iranians by glorifying pre-Islamic Persia with oil riches enjoyed by few. Islam became the matrix for new visions of justice and by the 1990s had replaced liberalism and socialism as the hegemonic political idiom.

These movements were rooted in those of the early twentieth century. After World War I, rulers cast out Islam as the antithesis of modernity and justice. As seen in Chapter 6, Egypt's MB emerged in response to states and elite classes that used European modernity as a weapon to justify their dominance in societies struggling to recuperate from the war. The poor and the pious were by definition excluded from the elitist halls of government. The Cold War aggravated popular alienation. The shah, like monarchs in Iraq, Jordan, and the Persian Gulf, used American aid to fight back challenges to their rule. Arab socialists lost their claims to justice in the 1960s, as Nasser and the Baathists in Iraq and Syria used Soviet weapons to insulate their regimes from popular dissent.

Islamism may also be understood as the historical response to the dislocation of religious authority after World War I. First, Turkey's abolition of the caliphate destabilized hierarchies of authority in the post-Ottoman world, opening a space for Islamic populism. Second, the expansion of public education created a literate audience for Banna's tracts and for his message that individual believers must read the Quran for themselves. The first Islamist movements attracted a following with programs of individual spiritual renewal. Later, with tracts like *Milestones* and *Islamology*, Islamism emerged as a powerful, alternate model of social and political justice.[82]

Islamism may also be seen as a response to the failure of liberal constitutionalism to establish equality under rule of law, in both Qajar Iran and the late Ottoman empire. After World War I, the pain of defeat and the expansion of European rule undermined the claims of secular justice. Minorities were seen as pawns of Great Powers, used against Muslim majorities. At its most militant, Islamism identified unbridled capitalism with Christianity and economic fairness with Islam. It became an ideology of rigid cultural boundaries that was exclusionary as Kemal's Turkish nationalism. Christians, Jews, and other religious minorities have fared poorly in the Middle East since the 1970s.

Islamists' struggle for justice was not, however, essentially violent. Many scholars doubt that Qutb directly ordered the overthrow of the state that Islambuli and al-Jihad attempted. And while Shariati offered *Islamology* as a handbook to Mojahedin guerrillas, Iranians inspired by him eventually toppled the shah peacefully. Terror, torture, and mass violence came only later, as the Khomeini faction battled its former revolutionary comrades for control of government.

As the comparison between Egypt and Iran suggests, Islamism was a malleable movement, not a fixed idea. In both Egypt and Iran, Islamists agreed that Islam opposes tyranny and that justice requires Islamic law. But conditions in each country produced opposite outcomes. While Islamism inspired a political revolution in Iran, it has not evidently made Iranian society more pious. And while Egyptian Islamists failed to achieve a political revolution, they have transformed and sacralized society.[83]

The international Islamic terrorism that spread in the late 1990s was a by-product of these domestic battles over the nation-state. It was a nihilistic mutation of the revolutionary violence embraced by the 1950s Third Worldists, just as the random terror of Abu Nidal was a perversion that delinked Palestinian violence from any constructive political aim. In the mid-1980s, al-Jihad member Zawahiri met the exiled Saudi Islamist Osama bin Laden. They founded al-Qaeda (The Base), which gained notoriety for the attacks on the World Trade Center and Pentagon on September 11, 2001. They justified their attack on infidels as a pillar of Islamic faith and duty. Al-Qaeda unhinged the pursuit of jihad from Qutb's aim to construct a just, Islamic state. It borrowed the method of suicide terrorism from non-Muslims in Sri Lanka.[84] And like Abu Nidal, al-Qaeda gained virtually no popular following in their home countries.

The diffusion of Islamism inside Egypt, by contrast, mirrored methods of nonviolent insurrection in other parts of the world. Decentralized movements, linked by an umbrella organization like the African National Congress or the MB, are more resilient under authoritarian regimes.[85] The leaderless model of political mobilization also met some success in the first Palestinian Intifada of 1987–1991. It is this sort of movement that reappeared in the twenty-first century. The Arab Spring recombined the repertoires of liberal constitutionalism, socialism, and Islamism to challenge post Cold War dictators.

11

WAEL GHONIM OF EGYPT

The Arab Spring and the Return of Universal Rights

As in Egypt in 1881 and Iran in 1906, the "Arab Spring" revolutions of 2011 began when citizens suddenly and collectively refused to accept the tyranny of their regime. Like their predecessors, the 2011 revolts soon assembled broad coalitions of political groups around a unifying demand for constitutional government. The century-old hope to gain justice through universal principles revived, but now in a vernacular deeply rooted in Middle Eastern experience.

On December 17, 2010, a street vendor in Tunisia set himself afire after a government official harassed him. For years, officials had demanded bribes and confiscated the cart he used to sell fruits and vegetables. There were no real jobs in his town, as in most of Tunisia. That December day, the official confiscated the vendor's scales because he lacked a permit. When the local governor refused to hear his complaint, the man yelled, "You'll see me or I'll burn myself!" And then he did. As he lay dying in a hospital, protests by his family, labor unions, and on the Internet launched a revolution. Tunisians began with calls for jobs and soon turned on the regime's corruption and tyranny. Confirming general suspicion, a Wikileaks report provided evidence that President Zine El Abidine Ben Ali had amassed a fortune at public expense during his twenty-three years of rule. Nonviolent protest grew daily and within a month, on January 14, 2011, Ben Ali fled to Saudi Arabia.

That same day, a thirty-year-old Egyptian computer geek typed the word "revolution" on his Facebook page for the first time. In the previous six months, he had attracted 300,000 friends to his page, named "We Are All Khaled Said" for another young Egyptian who had been beaten to death by police. A page friend wrote: "Once upon a time Egypt was a model for Arab people everywhere. If only we could turn back time, to the Urabi and the July revolutions." The page administrator, Wael Ghonim, decided to give a new name to the event planned for January 25. That day, a holiday in memory of police who died fighting British troops in 1952, would now be called: "January 25: Revolution Against Torture, Poverty, Corruption and Unemployment."[1]

Egyptians ousted their president in a mere eighteen days. Soon afterward, Arabs in Libya, Syria, Yemen, and Bahrain rose up against their dictators. In Libya, protest triggered foreign intervention and a civil war that ended that October, when President Muammar Qaddafi was killed. In Syria, mass protests broke out across the country after police tortured children for writing antiregime graffiti on the walls of Deraa, a town south of Damascus. The Syrian army put down the protests brutally, and by year's end had killed an estimated 5,000 citizens. Revolts in Bahrain and Yemen met similarly brutal repression.

The Arab Spring emerged out of a global shift in political and economic power at the dawn of the twenty-first century, with the rise of China and the European Union, and the marginalization of most of the Arab world that did not profit from oil. In a way, the revolts that rolled across the Arab world in 2011 were like those of the turn of the seventeenth century, when Mustafa Ali wrote his memo on Egypt to the sultan. Back then, the rise of capitalist Europe had disrupted the Ottoman economy with inflation and new trade routes. Just as Mustafa Ali called for the end of tyranny and the restoration of justice, so Arabs have risen to condemn the Cold War-era dictatorships that persisted twenty years after the Berlin Wall fell. They have also complained that their leaders have done little to redress the mass unemployment of youth, while a thin layer of elites profited from globalization.

As seen earlier, Arabs had turned against Arab socialism after their governments' defeat in the 1967 war with Israel. They reacted not only to the dishonor of defeat, but also to the meager fruits of socialists' programs of nationalization and land reform. Islamic groups filled the political breach, building a social net that the states could not. In the shadow of their police states, they built a civic order separate from the state, based on an alternate model of justice.

But the possibility of revolution had seemed distant, as the states kept prisons filled with Islamists, labor organizers, and human rights activists. Arabs had watched the shah of Iran fall, only to be replaced by authoritarian ayatollahs. In the summer of 2009 they witnessed the failure of Iranians to challenge the ayatollahs' power in the Green Revolution. They also watched, by contrast, the success of the Justice and Development Party in Turkey, which represented religious democrats opposed to the enduring power of secular Kemalist elites and the army in politics.

The Arab Spring of 2011 was therefore both improbable and long in the making. History will one day offer a clearer picture of why mass revolt broke out then. We can, however, by way of conclusion to this book, offer a historical perspective that reveals the Arab Spring's continuity with past protest, and its novelty. Like previous waves of collective protest, the Arab Spring was born of unity among once-disparate groups: Islamists joined with workers' unions and with liberal and secular groups, even some government officials. And as in nearly all protests since the late nineteenth century, consensus was built on shared demands for constitutional government—the rule of law, representation, and limits on executive power. Finally, as in the past, international factors both helped to shape protest and to determine its impact. As always, activists were quick to borrow strategies from abroad and to exploit opportunities opened by shifts in international relations.

The Arab Spring was most novel in that it produced no clear leaders. Not so much leader*less,* it was leader*ful.* Many small groups coordinated the protests. Second, the Arab Spring was—at the start—avowedly nonviolent. In these two respects it recalls the minor tradition of protest in the Middle East exemplified in Iran's 1906 revolution, with its camps and boycotts, in the Iraqi Communist Party (ICP), and in Palestine, with Akram Zuayter's Gandhian civil disobedience in the 1920s and most remarkably in the first Intifada of 1987–1991. Far from accidental, leaderless nonviolence was a conscious strategy adopted in 2011 by dissidents who had seen every past effort to dislodge dictatorship fail.

This chapter focuses on just one of the ongoing Arab Spring struggles, the January 25 revolution in Egypt. While Egypt's is not more important or exemplary than the other Arab revolts, its particular experience resonates profoundly with the region's past struggles for justice. Most striking is how 2011 recouped the grassroots methods and the constitutional aims of the pre-World War I era. In a sense, the Arab Spring has reprised the struggle interrupted by the world wars and Cold War of the twentieth century. Rebels revived older, universal discourses of justice like human rights and liberal constitutionalism. These had given way after 1918 to local discourses of a separate justice—national, Islamic, and Arab. In almost Hegelian fashion protest came full circle to a synthesis of the universal and the local in Egyptian demands for full sovereignty, democracy, and bread under an elected Islamic government.

From Misfortune to Injustice

Ghonim was by no means the leader of the Egyptian revolution of 2011, despite media efforts to portray him as such. His memoir cannot therefore be read in the same spirit we have read the memoirs of Halide Edib, Akram Zuayter, Hasan al-Banna, Akram al-Hourani, Abu Iyad, or Sayyid Qutb. He would not want us to read it as the road map of the revolution. Ghonim repeats again and again that he is no hero, just an ordinary Egyptian. And therein lay the "zen" of Tahrir Square: ordinary citizens who had never been activists gathered to demand that their president leave. There had been protests with similar demands for years, but never on this scale. In early wintry weeks of 2011, some 15 million Egyptians joined the protests. How and why?

Ghonim's memoir gives the beginning of an answer. He was not in fact an ordinary Egyptian. With degrees in computer engineering and marketing, he had taken a job in Dubai for Google. Like most Egyptians, however, he had long been unhappy with the state of affairs in Egypt. He was too shy and too risk-averse to join protests, but he had recently created a Facebook page for the newest hope in Egyptian politics, Mohamed ElBaradei. Winner of the 2005 Nobel Peace Prize, ElBaradei had retired as director of the International Atomic Energy Agency (IAEA) and returned to Egypt to run for president against Hosni Mubarak. ElBaradei had spoken eloquently in his Nobel lecture on the need to shelter families from the new threats brought by globalization. But in Egypt, his campaign seemed to stall under the old threat of tyranny.

Then, on June 8, 2010, Ghonim saw a photo of Khaled Said on Facebook. Said was a twenty-eight-year-old, underemployed computer programmer with a reputation for drug use and a desire to emigrate to the United States. For reasons that remain obscure, he had been pulled from his chair at an Internet café in Alexandria. Plainclothes police officers hauled him to the street and beat him to death, in public. Said's head was misshapen, bashed in. His jaw dislocated. "I was sitting in my small study in Dubai, unable to control the tears flowing from my eyes," Ghonim wrote. "For me, Khaled Said's image offered a terrible symbol of Egypt's condition. I could not stand by passively in the face of such grave injustice."[2]

Two days later, Ghonim created the "We Are All Khaled Said" Facebook page. His first text entry was: "Today they killed Khaled Said. If I don't act for his sake, tomorrow they will kill me." In two minutes, 300 Facebook users joined the page. Text 2: "People, we became 300 in two minutes. We want to be 100,000. We must unite against our oppressor." In one hour, 3,000 joined. Text 3: "Egyptians, my justice is in your hands." Ghonim wrote in the first-person voice, in colloquial Egyptian dialect. His was not the formal voice of the regime, but the voice of the ordinary Egyptian. His education in marketing had taught him how to draw empathy. On the first day, 36,000 joined his page.

When police claimed that Said died of a drug overdose, Ghonim urged page members to action. An opposition group, called the April 6 Youth Movement for the anniversary of mass strikes in 2008, tried to stage a protest. But the government immediately shut it down. Then a We Are All Khaled Said member suggested a "Silent Stand." To evade police, protesters could randomly converge on a chosen spot. Ghonim amplified the call for a Silent Stand. In two days, the following Friday, members should stand on the waterfront in Alexandria, and on the Nile in Cairo, wearing black, and pray hand in hand for Khaled Said.

The plan was to avoid physical confrontation, Ghonim explained. He was influenced by Gandhi and other nonviolence advocates who reasoned that violent protest would only play into the government's hands. The government would always wield greater means of violence

than the people. Nonviolent actions carried out by a leaderless multitude, by contrast, are difficult for police to confront and stop.

Ghonim liked the idea of a leaderless movement. ElBaradei had so
far disappointed him and he did not want to be chained to ineffec-
tual leaders any more. "It was change, not individuals, that could
unite Egyptians," he wrote. "The response was phenomenal."[3] More
than 100,000 joined the page in the intervening two days. Hundreds
arrived Friday evening on Alexandria's waterfront—Reuters claimed
8,000 stood there silently, reading a Quran, a Bible, or listening to a
sermon on headphones. But security police swarmed the Nile waterfront. Few had managed to gather in Cairo.

"Many people will think, 'So what? What have you gained?'"
Ghonim wrote on the Facebook page. "Here are our gains: a strong
message that we are a united group of Egyptians who care for one
another. . . . We will expose and scandalize anyone who attempts to
torture an innocent person."[4]

By year's end the Facebook page had 300,000 members—most of
them under thirty years old and with no political experience. In the
wake of the November 2010 elections—the most corrupt in recent
history—Ghonim promoted another event. Opposition groups met in
December to protest the electoral fraud. They then decided to schedule
a mass protest for January 25, a new bank holiday in honor of Egypt's
police. On that date in 1952, dozens of police had died in a conflict
with British troops at Ismailia, which led eventually to the revolution in
July. In 2011, the organizers reasoned, large numbers of Egyptians
would be free to join a protest that day—not to honor police, but to
protest against the police state. Ghonim proposed that they make a
more precise point: that the police who died in 1952 had been betrayed
by Gamal Abdel Nasser's oppressive tyranny. Just as Egyptians today
had been betrayed by policies of Anwar Sadat and Mubarak that
handed the nation to the rich. Egyptians must protest against this, the
real cause of tyranny and alienation, he wrote on the Facebook page.

"We ceased to feel for the poor. And this is where the poor people's
statement of 'This is not our country, it's theirs' comes from ('theirs'
referring to the regime and the rich businessmen around it)," Ghonim
wrote. "Jan 25 must be a day for the common striving citizen who is
unable to make a living. . . . I am taking to the street on Jan 25. . . .
And I am ready to die a martyr because it is necessary for our country
to change."[5]

Interest in the January 25 protest exploded after Ben Ali fled Tunisia on January 14. This was when the word "revolution" caught on. With barely a week left to plan, Ghonim made contact with other opposition groups to agree on a location and a strategy. He e-mailed Ahmed Maher, a leader of the April 6 movement, who proposed that Tahrir Square be the meeting point of multiple marches from the different parts of Cairo. Ghonim also contacted the "Ultras," politically motivated soccer fans, who also signed on.

Ghonim flew to Cairo on January 23 and issued the final marching orders on the Facebook page: "Everything You Need to Know about Jan25." The page advised protesters to remain peaceful; carry only an ID card, pocket money, and an Egyptian flag; do not block traffic, and bring friends. Ghonim even hoped that honest police might join the demonstration in honor of police martyrs of 1952, who "offered a model of sacrificing one's life for one's homeland." Finally, the page reminded protesters that the goals of the revolution were to end silence and despair and to fight against the poverty, corruption, high infant mortality, and poor health that plagued Egyptians. Specifically, marchers should demand that the government: 1) ease poverty and unemployment; 2) annul the emergency law (imposed in 1967); 3) fire the minister of the interior, Habib el-Adly; 4) set a two-term limit on the presidency. Accordingly, protesters should stick to the agreed-upon chants: "Long live Egypt!" and "Bread, Freedom, Dignity!" and "Raise Your Voice Up High; With Injustice We Will Not Comply!"[6]

Ghonim signed off and headed to Tahrir Square with his brother. They had to battle police to get there. "We could not believe our eyes," he wrote. Thousands of Egyptians crowded the square, mostly ordinary citizens. Some told Ghonim they had heard of the march from the Facebook page. The largest contingent had come from the poor neighborhood of Shubra. They chanted all afternoon and evening. But that night, police were ordered to clear the square. They attacked the crowd brutally. "Peaceful! Peaceful!" protesters yelled. But in the onslaught, their nonviolent philosophy broke down. Protesters pulled up stones from the pavement and threw them at the police. By dawn, Tahrir Square was clear, but the activists were euphoric.

Fear of the state had been broken. And the revolution had a new goal: to oust Mubarak. "We Don't Want Him" became the leading chant three days later, at a second demonstration dubbed the "Friday of Anger."

Ghonim did not attend that protest. On Thursday evening, January 27, he was kidnapped by police outside of a restaurant and thrown into jail without charges. He spent twelve days alone and blindfolded, interrogated repeatedly. Egyptian security police accused him of being a traitor, an American Central Intelligence Agency (CIA) agent who aimed to undermine Egypt. His interrogators, Ghonim recalled later, really seemed to believe that the protests were a foreign conspiracy. Or did they? Officials in Syria, Libya, Bahrain, and Yemen also blamed protests on foreign subversion—and on drugs.

Outside of Ghonim's prison cell, the revolution built momentum in Tahrir Square. Facebook was no longer the revolution's primary site. Protesters realized that they had captured the ear of the state only by claiming urban territory. As long as they occupied Tahrir Square, they had leverage to demand Mubarak's resignation. Elsewhere in Egypt, protests mobilized more than 15 million citizens, out of a population of 82 million. In sheer scale, January 25 was unprecedented.

The April 6 Youth Movement was one of the leading organizers. On January 18, a founder of the movement, Asmaa Mahfouz, had posted a passionate video calling all Egyptians to join the January 25 protest. "If we still have honor, if we want to live in dignity on this land, we have to go down on January 25," she told the camera, in a stark, black-and-white video:

> Whoever says it's not worth it because there will be only a handful of people, I want to tell him you are the reason for this. Yes, you are the reason. You are a traitor like the president or any security cop who beats us in the streets. Your presence with us will make a big difference! . . . Don't be afraid of the government, fear none but God. God says He will not change the condition of the people unless they change what is in themselves.[7]

Mahfouz, like Ghonim, appealed to Egyptians in a language of humiliation and honor—captured in the popular slogan, "Bread, Freedom, Dignity!" For too many years, Egyptians had bowed down before their brutal state. The shared feeling of humiliation inspired a new sense of community. Emotions, not ideas, were what drew Egyptians to Tahrir Square, observed political scientist Ellis Goldberg.[8]

Mahfouz's video also drew upon April 6 Youth Movement training in nonviolent protest. Since its first protests in support of workers' strikes in April 2008, the movement had trained in nonviolent methods with Serbs who had ousted Slobodan Milosevic in 2000. It had even adopted the Serbian group Otpor's logo, a white fist on a black background.[9] The movement did not display the fist at Tahrir Square, in keeping with the spirit of nonpartisan protest. Several other groups had helped to organize the January 25 protests, including the Kefaya! (Enough!) movement of intellectuals and college professors, ElBaradei's Movement for Change, and the Revolutionary Socialists Movement.

The April 6 Youth Movement also teamed, most importantly, with the Muslim Brotherhood (MB). The latter's younger wing acted in defiance of their elders, who shunned any confrontation with police after suffering decades of brutal imprisonment.[10] But the younger wing proved to be extremely effective. It helped to recruit thousands of protesters after mosque prayers for the Friday of Anger. Young Muslim Brothers also proved crucial in defending the square against police attacks. With the April 6 Youth Movement and the other groups, they set up clinics, passed out vinegar and masks to protect against tear gas, and built barricades and checkpoints to keep out the regime's thugs.

The January 28 protest was a huge success: at least 80,000 people filled Tahrir Square, four times the number on January 25.[11] Not all protesters made it into the square; some sources estimated 300,000 protesters throughout Cairo that day. Police stations were burned, as was the headquarters of the ruling National Democratic Party (NDP), near Tahrir Square. Some believed the government set the fire, to burn incriminating documents.[12] Once again police in full riot gear besieged the protest with tear gas and water cannons, but the protesters held their ground until the army arrived late at night to keep the peace. Exhausted, the police backed off.

"When the first tanks came into Tahrir, we did not know whether we could trust the army," recalled Hatem Mo'men, owner of a fast food chain. "We were letting them through and to me this meant that we, the people, were giving the army the right to enter the square. Every tank had at least thirty, maybe forty demonstrators on board. . . . It was we, the people, who gave the army its legitimacy."[13]

Participants describe the same euphoria of revolution that Edib felt in 1908 Istanbul and that participants in the first Intifada described.

Wael Ghonim helped to mobilize 100,000 Egyptians to occupy Cairo's Tahrir Square with the Facebook page titled "We Are All Khaled Said" that he launched in memory of a young man beaten to death by police. Here he speaks to the crowd in Tahrir Square on February 8, 2011, three days before the demonstrations forced President Hosni Mubarak to resign.
(© Khaled El Fiqi/epa/Corbis)

The world was turned upside down as old and young, male and female, rich and poor embraced, sang, and dressed each other's bandages. It was the diversity of the crowd that gave it power. Not just young men, but Egyptians from all walks of life came, as Mahfouz had invited them to do, to defy the regime's claim that protest was merely a foreign plot.

"You felt you were in utopia," said Dr. Umaima Kamel, an ophthalmologist and member of the MB. She and hundreds of other women went to Tahrir Square every day. The number of overtly religious Egyptians grew each day, too. "On Tuesday, February the 1st, I met Sheikh Emad Effat in the square," recalled Najah Nadi, a student at the religious al-Azhar university. "I asked him about our class at al-Azhar, and he said, 'The lesson is right here.' "[14]

"There was a suspension of norms about social segregation," recalled Nadia Kamel, a leftist filmmaker who spent all eighteen days in Tahrir Square. "You shake hands with someone different from you, who says, 'Welcome aboard!' I have been hugged by so many women muhaggabat [with religious scarves] in the square."[15]

"There was zero sexual harassment, zero verbal harassment—there was so much respect, because people were focused on one goal," recalled Fatma Ghaly, who worked in her family's jewelry store.[16] "I think for the first time in their lives, they began to feel that this country was theirs."

Following the lead of organizers well versed in the methods of non-violence, protesters refused negotiation and kept their demands simple. "Irhal!" (Leave!) was the most common chant. But as days passed, the crowds began to improvise and to invent a new language of justice.

Tahrir Square was part Woodstock, part political laboratory for a new Egypt. "It was a direct democracy," recalled Nadia Kamel. "People would line up to take the mike and tell of their relations with the regime . . . inventing chants," she said. "People would accept or reject the slogans."[17]

A ten-story banner was unfurled on an apartment building facing Tahrir Square. Titled "Our Demands" and signed "Egypt's Youth," it began with the call for Mubarak's overthrow and demanded the dissolution of the legislature, end of the state of emergency, a transitional unity government, election of a parliament to revise the constitution and supervise a presidential election, and court trials for those who killed demonstrators and stole the nation's wealth.[18]

Nightly television talk shows became a crucial revolutionary forum, because television reached far more Egyptians than Facebook did. On the night of February 1, Amr Bassiouny was in Tahrir Square when a film crew invited him to bring his friends to appear on a popular talk show that night. It was a week after the protests had begun, Bassiouny noted, and mainstream television was still clueless. As the cameras began to roll, the host turned to Bassiouny and asked, "So what do you call this?" Bassiouny simply replied, "A revolution."[19] From that night, Bassiouny and others were invited to inform the public about this new thing, the revolution.

On February 2, Mubarak made a television speech promising reform. Numbers at Tahrir Square began to dwindle and frustration rose.

Remarkably, the crowd opted to maintain its nonviolence. "We had discussions, 'Maybe we should become violent,'" Nadia Kamel recalled. "People feared they would be left to rot in Tahrir, that Mubarak just ignored them." Only spectacular acts of violence would make their presence felt, they argued. "But then the next day, more women, kids, and wheelchairs appeared in the square. They blocked violence."[20]

Ghonim's appearance on a television talk show came at a critical moment. It was the night of February 7, the day he was released from prison. Tahrir Square was still at low tide. Mubarak had won much sympathy by portraying himself as a well-meaning "old man" in his television speech. Then police scared the public away. The day after the speech, February 2, NDP thugs attacked Tahrir Square with horses and camels, killing more than 600 and injuring 5,000. Egyptians, first hopeful and then fearful, were at the crossroads of their revolution.

Ghonim gave a raw, emotional interview. He began by expressing his regrets to the parents of martyrs who had died in Tahrir Square. "I am no hero. I was asleep for 12 days. The heroes were the ones in the streets," he told the host. "We are not traitors," he repeated, almost obsessively "We love Egypt." As the host showed photographs of young Egyptian men who had been killed by police, Ghonim bowed his head and sobbed. "I'm sorry, but it's not our fault," he said. "It's the fault of everyone who held onto power." And he ran from the stage.[21]

The next day, February 8, women, children, and people in wheelchairs filled Tahrir Square. Nadia Kamel and other activists believed they came because of Ghonim's interview. "This is the biggest march we have had," wrote Pierre Sioufi on his Facebook page that evening. He had observed Tahrir Square every day from his apartment above the square. Some observers credited Ghonim's television appearance with reviving the revolution.[22]

It was the crowd, not a media-made hero, that finally brought down Mubarak. On February 10, Mubarak appeared on television for a third time. Again he refused to resign—and said he would only delegate power temporarily to the vice president. Tahrir Square exploded in anger. Activists announced a march to the presidential palace the next day, February 11. Fearing bloodshed, military leaders stepped in. The Supreme Council of Armed Forces (SCAF) met without the president's permission and decided that Mubarak must go.

Mubarak had been at Sadat's side the day he was shot in 1981 and had ruled under emergency laws for the thirty years since. As Mubarak slipped out of Cairo with his family, Vice President Omar Soliman announced on television that SCAF would manage the country's affairs. SCAF promptly promised to lift emergency laws, hold elections, and support a transition to democracy. After eighteen days and 846 deaths across Egypt, Tahrir's revolutionaries joyously danced in the square, and then cleaned it up before leaving.[23] "Congratulations, Egypt!" Ghonim wrote on the We Are All Khaled Said page. "This is the historical movement we have been longing to witness."[24]

Ghonim portrayed the January 25 Revolution as a spontaneous outburst of Egyptians fed up with the humiliations of a police state and the injustices of mass unemployment. However, his memoir omits two critical ingredients. First, Egyptians had been refining techniques of protest against Mubarak's police state for a decade. Workers had learned that simple and concrete demands (rather than broad political claims) brought real gains. Second, Kefaya!'s professionals, the April 6 Youth Movement, and other groups had developed a repertoire of street politics by experimenting with circuitous ways of organizing mass demonstrations. They learned their lessons in "safe" protests that did not threaten the regime: in support of the second Intifada in Palestine and against the American invasion of Iraq.[25]

The January 25 demonstration exploded into revolution because it fused three sectors of protest—neighborhoods, workplaces, and professional associations, according to political scientist Mona El-Ghobashy. The Khaled Said murder in June 2010 and the corrupt November elections triggered the fusion of the three groups. Then two events primed them for protest: the bombing of a Coptic church on January 1, 2011, and the ouster of the Tunisian president on January 14. "By the time January 25, 2011 arrived, there was local resonance for the planned national 'day of rage' in virtually every corner of Egypt," El-Ghobashy noted. Kefaya!, the Lawyers' Association, the Wafd, and Ghad opposition parties, ElBaradei's National Association for Change, and the April 6 Youth Movement put into practice all the lessons of street politics they had learned to fill Tahrir Square and at police stations and public squares across Egypt, despite orchestrated police efforts to block their paths. On January 28, the MB, the leftist Tagammu Party, and the Nasserists also joined. Behind the seeming anarchy on television was a highly tuned strategy.

"Grand processions of thousands upon thousands of people in every province made their way to the abodes of the oppressive forces that controlled their lives," El-Ghobashy notes. "When crowds reached town and city centers, they encircled police stations, provincial government buildings, and the NDP headquarters, the triad of institutions emblematic of the regime. The syncopated chorus that had traveled from Sidi Bouzid in Tunis now shook the Egyptian earth: 'The people . . . want . . . to overthrow the regime!' "[26]

Also at work behind the multiple marches was a handbook of nonviolent protest that had traveled around the world, from Massachusetts, to Burma, to Serbia, and to Egypt. Gene Sharp, a political scientist at the Albert Einstein Institution in Boston, wrote *From Dictatorship to Democracy* in 1993 at the request of an exiled Burmese democrat. By the late 1990s, democratic activists in Indonesia, Serbia, and Ukraine translated and circulated it. Soon afterward, Arabic and Persian translations appeared. The book distills practical lessons from the movements Sharp studied that battled Nazi and communist rule in Germany and Eastern Europe. The first lesson was never to meet dictatorship with violence, because states will always wield superiority in violent conflict. The second lesson was that foreign powers are unreliable allies, especially if the internal freedom movement is weak. The third lesson was that a strong, united movement can wear down a dictatorship. But the fourth lesson was never negotiate. It is here, Sharp observed, that Egyptians stumbled.

"A major mistake was made by the opposition in Egypt," Sharp observed a year after demonstrators joyously departed Tahrir Square. "Mubarak said 'I'll resign if you put the military in control.' . . . They agreed."[27] Egyptians had handed power to Mubarak's military henchmen, the same military that had ruled since 1952. While Tunisians successfully negotiated with their smaller military for civilian control of government by the end of 2011, Egyptians had to return to the streets to finally oust SCAF in the summer of 2012.

THE REVOLUTION CONTINUES?

The year 2011 mirrored the grassroots Urabi revolution of 1881–1882, which historian Juan Cole called "a multitude of revolutions taking place simultaneously."[28] Business executives joined college professors, shop owners, and urban workers, along with women, children, and the disabled. As in 1882, they united against a corrupt despot and demanded constitutional government.

The year 2011 also resembled Egypt in the heady days of protest before 1952, not only by way of its memorial to policemen who had died then. In the late 1940s, inflation and unemployment also fueled contempt for a corrupt leader. The monarchy's regime of nepotism was blamed for the army's disastrous defeat in the 1948 war. Multiple movements waged strikes, boycotts, and protests for justice. Their collective mobilization abruptly ended when Nasser's Free Officers overthrew the king in July 1952. Activists in Tahrir Square expressed anger more at Nasser than at Farouk. Echoing Qutb, Ghonim called the Nasser regime "the worst repression in our modern history."[29]

Ghonim quit ElBaradei's campaign because he distrusted the cult of a leader and favored the more steady virtue of the collective people. He was not alone. "There is a conscious antipathy to leaders," said Khaled Fahmy, an Egyptian historian who participated at Tahrir Square. "We don't want leaders, we don't want heroes, like Nasser, Sadat or Saddam. We don't want to entrust our history to them."[30]

As the MB had learned in the 1980s, Tahrir Square's activists in 2011 recognized that people power must be cultivated against state power, deeply and slowly. They aimed for a more fundamental revolution in values. "The revolution happens every day, in every conversation we have, with every strike," Nadia Kamel said in an interview in December 2011.

"The revolution's goal is to revive a civilization, like the Abbasid caliphate (of the 9th century), based on liberal values," said Joe Rizk, a Tahrir Square veteran who founded a think tank called the New Republic. For him, the highest priority was to dismantle Mubarak's security apparatus. Only then might Egyptians rebuild civil society, an independent media, and an independent judiciary. Rizk and the youth activists of Tahrir returned to Tahrir repeatedly through 2011 and early 2012 to keep pressure on SCAF to demilitarize the state.[31]

The Muslim Brotherhood took another tack. Against the leftists and secularists of Tahrir Square, it engaged SCAF's agenda for elections and constitutional reform. It could do so because, unlike the secular parties, the MB had national networks in place, built since the 1980s. The movement could no longer be disabled, as it had been back then, by the arrest and execution of leaders.

"In the 1960s, they [the government] were trying to destroy [us] completely. Now that is impossible. There are more roots than anyone can completely pull out from the streets," said Mohamed Morsi, a sixty-year-old former engineering professor who would become the MB's 2012 presidential candidate.[32] It was on this deep social base that the MB chose to challenge Sharp's dictum never to negotiate with dictators until "they seek personal safe passage to an international airport."[33]

In March 2011, SCAF held a referendum asking Egyptians whether to abolish the constitution immediately or hold elections first based on a few constitutional reforms. At the head of SCAF's committee on constitutional reform stood Tareq El-Bishri, who had written a history thesis on how the military stole the 1952 revolution. He was sympathetic to the MB's demand to hold early elections. It was an open secret that voting "yes" on the referendum was a vote for the MB. The MB prevailed with a 77 percent majority favoring elections first. The 23 percent who dissented were largely the youth groups and leftist parties in Cairo, those who had launched the Tahrir Square revolution.[34]

Samer Soliman, a member of the Social Democratic Party, disagreed with Tahrir Square revolutionaries who boycotted the parliamentary elections of November 2011–January 2012. The party decided to run candidates as part of the Egyptian Bloc, which advocated a secular national government. Many of Egypt's Coptic Christian minority also supported its inclusive program. "Our goal is a constitutional guarantee of basic rights for all citizens," said Soliman.[35] Like many youth and liberals, Soliman looked back nostalgically to the cosmopolitan, pre-Nasser era of parliamentary politics, Saad Zaghlul and the Wafd Party.

Islamists also embraced constitutional goals, denying that they intended to exclude non-Muslims from politics. "The Revolution taught us we are all equal," Mohamed Beltagy told an election rally in a rural town north of Cairo. "We want a real president, a real parliament, with the power to monitor every security institution, including the military council." Beltagy is among the minority of young liberals in the MB.[36] Other moderate Islamists founded splinter parties, outside of the MB's Freedom and Justice Party. These included Hatem Azzam, founder of the small, right-of-center Civilization Party.

"We have three goals: bread, freedom, and social justice," said Azzam, a veteran of Tahrir Square who won a parliamentary seat in November 2011 from Maadi, a district south of Cairo. "We don't consider ourselves an Islamic party," he said. Egyptians of all faiths share the same values about social justice, the thirty-nine-year-old businessman vowed. "I got into politics because of the poor," he explained. "Five years ago, I was driving my daughter to school one day, and I saw a little girl of the same age, going into the garbage. . . . I can't live in a place where my neighbors are eating from the garbage."[37]

Essam el-Arian, the MB's spokesman, dismissed charges that Islamists had hijacked the revolution. He also denied that Islamic law would harm Coptic Christians. "Sharia law is accepted by most Egyptians, even Copts," he declared. "Sharia law means citizenship, under the umbrella of . . . equality and liberty in the Egyptian interpretation."[38]

In November 2011, however, SCAF proved the Tahrir Square skeptics right. Just before the parliamentary elections were to begin, it declared that any future constitution must exempt the military from civilian budgetary oversight. SCAF's leader, Field Marshal Mohamed Hussein Tantawi, also refused to confirm the date for presidential elections, raising fears that there would be no transition to civilian rule at all. Rizk, Nadia Kamel, Azzam and many others rushed back to Tahrir Square. In a bloody confrontation with police on November 19–20, forty-three people were killed. "November was the second wave of the revolution," said Rizk.

Fatma Abdel Halim, a translator from Maadi, brought medical supplies and food. "This is the street of death, don't go here!" men yelled to her, as she arrived at Mohamed Mahmoud Street, which leads out of the square. Rubber bullets were shot right at protesters heads, and many lost an eye. "I think it was revenge for the police who were attacked on January 28," Halim said. The gas police used to clear the square made her ill for two days.[39]

Soliman agreed that Tahrir Square was the revolution's trump card. "In the new political system, street politics is important," he said in December 2011. "Only after the protests two weeks ago did SCAF agree to a presidential election in June."[40]

Graffiti written on the government building that towers over Tahrir Square, the Mogamma, tell the story. Written across its doorways (depicted as the gates of hell in Egyptian satire) were phrases like: "Down with the thieving military council! No submission, no SCAF, no harassment." "#1 Facebook message from people to SCAF: Irhal! Leave! You will not crush our revolution!" Beautifully painted images of martyrs dominated the wall: Sally Zahrain, Khaled Said, Ahmed El-Bassiony, Mina Daniel, Sayyid Bilal.

In December, the ancient Institute of Egypt, established by the French after Napoleon Bonaparte's 1798 invasion, was burned down in another round of violence, during the parliamentary elections. Police had tried to oust occupiers from their tents in front of the cabinet building, located near the institute. They rained stones and bullets on unarmed protesters in the middle of the night. By morning, crowds returned to Tahrir Sqaure. As violence escalated, an al-Azhar shaykh and a medical student were killed. A video of police stripping a woman, and dragging her across the pavement, went viral on the Internet and international media.

Dr. Umaima Kamel of the MB was wary of playing into SCAF's hands. Like most of the MB's old guard, she did not go down to Tahrir Square in December. "I think it is an artificial event to distract people from the democratic way," she said.[41] She feared that SCAF would use violence as an excuse to cancel elections.

Miraculously, the parliamentary elections proceeded. On election day for Giza, a section of Cairo, women lined up outside of a school had waited six hours to vote. Dressed in headscarves and popular clothing styles, they cheerfully stated their intentions to vote for the MB's Freedom and Justice Party; the Nour Party, of Salafist religious conservatives; the MB's reformist spinoff, the Wasat Party; and only occasionally, the secular Egyptian Bloc. "We need a strong shoulder to take on the responsibility of rebuilding Egypt," said a woman in a blue scarf. "The Freedom and Justice are strong." Another woman said she used to stay home on election day. Not today. "We are happy because we are voting with our own free will!"[42]

"There are two themes to this election campaign, observed Samer Shehata, a political scientist. "The issues are SCAF and the constitution, and the fact that people wait on line for five hours to get butagaz (gas for cooking). Only the Islamists link these two themes."[43] He had just attended an election rally where conservative Salafists announced they were manufacturing and distributing the precious gas tanks. Salafi Islamists are more traditional than the MB, heirs to the rigid militants of the 1970s. Like the MB, they used their experience in poor relief to good effect in the election campaign. For the many Egyptians who suffered from unemployment, Islamists were the only credible group who could deliver the "bread" in the revolutionary slogan.

Islamists were also a safe choice for voters who sought "freedom." In the view of common citizens who didn't read daily newspapers, Islamists were most likely to be honest and least likely to be former regime "wolves" running in sheep's clothing. Many Egyptians worried about former NDP officials gaining office again.

As for "social justice," Egyptians remained divided. "I voted for the Kutla (Egyptian Bloc), because of the Copts," said Rowaida Saad El-Din, a Muslim professional. She did not believe the promises of Islamists like Azzam and El-Arian that Christians would enjoy justice under an Islamic state.[44]

As predicted, the Democratic Alliance, headed by the MB's Freedom and Justice Party, won 47 percent of the 498 seats in the People's Assembly. To the surprise of many, Salafi Islamists won 24 percent, while the Egyptian Bloc won less than 10 percent. The Revolution Continues Party, favored by the hardcore youth of Tahrir Square, won just seven seats, with less than 2 percent of the vote. El-Arian hailed the elections as the fulfillment of the revolution, "the building of a real democratic system, after getting rid of—almost—the repressive dictatorship."[45]

Tahrir Square youth groups begged to differ. Days after the election results were posted, they announced demonstrations on the January 25 anniversary against SCAF and continued censorship and police brutality. In protest, ElBaradei dropped out of the presidential race and Wael Ghonim started a new group, Masrena (Our Egypt), to maintain pressure on SCAF to hold the presidential election in June.

Tarek Osman, an Egyptian journalist, worried that the MB had sat on the fence too long. They proclaimed constitutional values but did not condemn the intolerance and violence of right-wing Salafists.[46] His fears played out in the spring of 2012, as the Freedom and Justice Party tried to pack a constituent assembly with its members. Opponents banded together to scuttle the assembly. "I remain optimistic," said Amr Hamzawy, one of a bloc of twenty-seven liberal members of parliament. "Islamists may not continue to benefit from their prior advantage, as people will see they don't deliver."[47]

The historian Fahmy was also not depressed by what he called a temporary victory for the counterrevolution. He compared the Arab Spring to the 1848 revolutions that swept Europe. They, too, were accompanied by a very strong counterrevolutionary current. "They paid off generations later," he remarked, as their democratic ideals germinated in Europe's political soil.[48]

The presidential primary and election held in May and June 2012, however, so dispirited Tahrir activists like Fatma al-Halim, that they refused to vote. The plurality of candidates in the May presidential primary marginalized liberals and reformers. The two top vote-getters, with only about 25 percent of the vote each, were the MB's Morsi, and the Mubarak regime's last prime minister, Ahmed Shafik. Balloting was overshadowed, once again, by SCAF's preemptive efforts. Not only did SCAF reserve to itself power over all military matters, but its allies on the high court also dissolved the parliament on grounds that some (MB) candidates ran as independents even though they had party affiliations.

Ghonim, along with a faction of the April 6 Youth Movement, publicly backed Morsi because a vote for Shafik would effectively end the revolution. "Our stand isn't with the Brothers," he said. "Our stand is with legitimacy; our stand is with democracy." When SCAF delayed the ballot count, rumors ran that it was skewing results for Shafik or cutting a deal with the MB. Crowds of 100,000 or more again filled Tahrir Square to demand results and civilian government. Morsi was declared the winner with barely 52 percent of the vote. Turnout was also 52 percent, much lower than during the parliamentary elections the previous winter.

"The first elected civilian Egyptian president in the history of modern Egypt. The revolution continues," Ghonim tweeted, triumphantly. However, analysts noted that a huge majority of Coptic Christian voters had chosen Morsi's opponent out of fear of Islamist rule.

"There is no such thing called an Islamic democracy," Morsi declared after his victory was confirmed. "There is democracy only. . . . The people are the source of authority." To demonstrate that he represented all Egyptians, Morsi resigned from the MB. In his televised victory speech, he made assurances of equality between men and women and between Muslims and Christians, who represent 10 percent of the population. "Egypt is for all Egyptians; all of us are equals

Supporters of presidential candidate Mohamed Morsi protest in Tahrir Square, June 21, 2012. The Supreme Council of Armed Forces, Egypt's interim military rulers, delayed publishing election results that would eventually place Morsi in office as the first elected president of the Egyptian republic, and as head of a Muslim Brotherhood government, a dream of Hasan al-Banna in 1939. Note the symbol used on Morsi's campaign poster: the balance, for justice.
(© Mohamed Messara/epa/Corbis)

in terms of rights. All of us also have duties towards this homeland," he declared.[49]

Morsi's language may have been a calculated political lie, but it also reflected the development of Islamic political thought in the last two decades. The MB had moved away from the purism of Qutb to promote a hybrid view of Islamic civic virtue and popular sovereignty. And in a move that surprised many, Morsi demonstrated his independence from the military by forcing Tantawi to resign as minister of defense in August. While many Egyptians continued to suspect that Morsi had cut a deal with the military, by September Morsi's approval rating reached 80 percent.[50]

Stormy deliberations on a new constitution continued through the fall of 2012. Constituent assembly debate revolved around the role of Islamic law. Salafis wanted language making Islamic law the main source of law, but the majority insisted on language for Article 2 stipulating that only "the *principles* of Islamic law are the main source of legislation." The word "principles" is a wedge against the theocratic authority of Iranian clerics. It gives wiggle room for interpretation to non-religious scholars. The Muslim Brotherhood campaigned against Salafis, urging voters to approve the constitution in the December 2012 referendum. Tahrir activists opposed the draft, because it made only incremental revisions to the 1971 constitution. The January 25 revolution had mandated, they claimed, a diminution of presidential and military power.[51] The draft won approval in the national election, but it was rejected by a majority in the Cairo district.

NARRATIVES AND MEMORY

The stories of these and the many other Egyptians who made the January 25 Revolution are yet unfinished. They, like all of the activists who have filled these pages, have woven self-narratives to promote an ideal of justice against the claims of opponents. They are no doubt creative counterpoints to historical fact. But accuracy is not the point. Their narratives form the warp and weave of collective memory and political imagination in the Middle East. Stories like Ghonim's, told on television, drove citizens to action.

Stories of former activists have also been retold—especially now that Egyptians, Tunisians, Syrians, and other Arabs as well as Iranians and Turks have revived the century-old project of constitutionalism. The telling of the stories is contentious, however, as different parties claim the mantle of the past, or fashion a new mantle from old cloth.

In Egypt, for example, supporters of the 1952 revolution had rescued Colonel Ahmad Urabi from oblivion and built a monumental tomb in his honor. In Nasser's era, Urabi became a political locus for retrieving national authenticity (in his peasant origins) and for glorifying the army. Urabi's story was revived again in 2011, along with Zaghlul's, but now to recall a past constitution stolen from the people. In a new twist, however, they shared space in the collective memory with Hasan al-Banna. Unlike later Islamists, as we have seen, he did not reject the forms of liberal, constitutional government—and had in fact run for parliament himself.

In postwar Iraq, both General Abdul Karim Qasim and Comrade Fahd have been remembered as tolerant, honest, and caring leaders from a pre-Baath Party golden era.[52] A 2001 official catalogue of communist martyrs featured Fahd as the first and most noble communist condemned to death. It also featured Fahd's slogan, "A Free Homeland and a Happy People."[53] Every year since 1959, the ICP has held a memorial on February 14, Communist Martyrs' Day.[54] And the Freedom Monument has been reclaimed by communists and others as a symbol of justice lost. In January 2004, hundreds of Iraqis gathered to clean and restore it after decades of neglect. It is now a "media forum" and a focal point for political demonstrations by the full range of political groups active in post-Baathist Iraq.[55]

In Syria, public memory of Hourani was suppressed for more than four decades. But as civil war exploded in Syria in 2011, a new website devoted to his memory appeared, with excerpts from his memoir. It lamented that Hourani was buried in exile on a lonely hill in Jordan and compared him to the seventh-century Islamic revolutionary, Abu

The Freedom Monument, built in Baghdad's Tahrir Square in 1961, has again become a rallying point for demonstrators after the fall of the Baath regime. Shown here is a demonstration marking the evacuation of American military forces on December 16, 2011. The woman's placard announces that they are among the Iraqis who reject foreign occupation and who in solidarity have won their liberation, sovereignty, and independence. The picture is of a man lost, presumed dead, in 2006.

(Kyodo via AP Images)

Zarr (whom Ali Shariati also revered): "May Allah have mercy on Abu Zarr, he walks alone, dies alone, and will be resurrected alone." The site extols Hourani's democratic socialism against the oppressive socialism of the current Syrian regime. Interestingly, the site emphasized Hourani's links to the Rifai Sufi order and suggested that his father had contracted his fatal illness in 1915 while distributing food to Armenian refugees.[56]

Many Syrian rebels look back nostalgically to the 1950s as a brief period of democracy. Some blame Hourani for squandering that moment. Radwan Ziadeh, spokesperson for the Syrian National Council, believes Hourani's links to the military poisoned civilian politics and set the stage for the 1963 Baath Party coup. However, Ziadeh has worked with Hourani's daughter, Fida Akram al-Hourani, who was imprisoned in 2007 for her human rights activities.[57]

Equally ambivalent are Palestinians' memories of their defeated leaders, Musa Kazim Pasha and Abu Iyad. Musa Kazim's generation was condemned by activists long before historian Rashid Khalidi blamed him for putting Palestinians into a political "iron cage." Abu Iyad's memory is clouded by the disappointing history of Fatah since his death and by his association with terrorism. His memory fades like the Fatah wall mural in Gaza City, showing his face alongside those of Yasser Arafat and Khalil al-Wazir. The images linger even as governance in Gaza has passed over to Fatah's rivals in the Hamas movement.

In Iran, the revolutionary regime honored Shariati with little more than a postage stamp. Anti-Khomeini dissidents have since revived his memory as a symbol of justice betrayed. Student protesters in 2004, for example, waved Shariati's photograph along with that of Mossadeq (as seen in the photo reproduced in Chapter 10).

In Turkey, too, images of past activists are the currency of political contestation today. Kemalists had honored Edib in official textbooks only as a comrade of Ataturk. They appropriated her as a symbol of his modernity and feminism, while suppressing her role as his liberal critic. Today, the Justice and Development (AK) Party has revived interest in Edib precisely because she refused to choose between modernity and Islam and because she joined the first party to defeat the Kemalists, the Democrat Party. Secular intellectuals expressed dismay at the popularity of her recent biography by Ipek Calislar. Soli Ozel, a Turkish political scientist, problematizes the tendency of secularists to identify the AK Party as simply Islamist, reactionary, and provincial. The party represents a novel fusion, he argues, between Islamic culture and modern enterprise. It is led by businessmen from Anatolia's central provinces who have finally achieved inclusion in Turkish politics, eighty years after the republic was established.[58]

In Israel, David Ben-Gurion, like Ataturk, is ubiquitously memorialized as the nation's founder. The aging patriarch of the Labor Party, Shimon Peres, published a loving memoir/biography of Ben-Gurion in 2011.[59] Critics are marginalized, even as they try to disentangle Ben-Gurion's ideals from the legacy of his militant rival, Menachem Begin. Avraham Burg, former Labor Party Speaker of the Knesset, for example, wrote a 2012 editorial for the *New York Times*, "Israel's Fading Democracy," in which he called Israelis back to Ben-Gurion's original Zionist ideals. "With the elevation of religious solidarity over and above democratic authority, Israel has become more fundamentalist and less modern, more separatist and less open to the outside world."[60]

Foreign news media have portrayed the Arab Spring as the new dawn of democracy in the Middle East, but Arabs speak of democratic restoration, not discovery. They are calling upon deep political tradition and a collective memory of constitutionalism denied. As I set out to write this book, I had expected to find a deep gap in political history. Books like Albert Hourani's *Arabic Thought in the Liberal Age* suggested that constitutionalism died in the Middle East after 1939. While the intellectuals whom Hourani studied may have abandoned liberalism, my research has shown that constitutional goals continued to motivate ordinary people to action after 1940.

While liberals like Edib were tarred as captives of the false universalism of imperialist Europe, democrats today in the Middle East ground their claims to rights, justice, and freedom in homegrown custom. The April 6 Youth Movement leader, Asmaa Mahfouz, wore a headscarf in her January 25 video but spoke as an equal to her male viewers. Palestinians who launched the first Intifada did so by reviving memories of their previous revolts. But they also shared a language of justice with peoples across the world that they simply could not have articulated in the days of World War I.

In a sense we are seeing justice, once interrupted, now retrieved. More than a century ago, opponents of absolute monarchy united in the belief that imposing constitutional controls on the sultan, shah, and khedive would secure their national sovereignty. During World War I, their faith in constitutionalism as a means for securing sovereignty collapsed. The overthrow of King Faysal's constitutional government by the French republic was a shocking betrayal. The war and its "peace to end all peace"[61] interrupted the progress toward constitutional government in the Middle East.

Constitutions written after World War I were imposed from above: by Kemal in Turkey and Reza Shah in Iran, and by French and British occupiers in Lebanon, Syria, Iraq, and Egypt in the 1920s. They were discarded in the Arab socialist revolutions of the 1950s and 1960s. Lebanon's 1926 constitution collapsed under the weight of its own French-era contradictions into sectarian civil war in the 1970s.

"As in much of the Third World, constitutions in the Arab world have long been instruments of rule, rather than instruments of restraint on arbitrary state power," observed El-Ghobashy.[62] Weak constitutions were not the product of a lack of modernity, backward culture, or faith in Islam. They were a product of the Middle East's porous political systems, vulnerable to foreign interference since the days of Russia's Peter the Great and Napoleon's invasion of Egypt in 1798. Only in the late 1940s, as historian William Roger Louis has shown, did the British begin to consider ruling in cooperation with popular political movements in Egypt. Until then, their ambassador worked tirelessly to exclude them from power.[63]

Turkey and Iran provide a telling contrast to the Arab colonies. They escaped direct European rule after World War I, and constitutionalism remained a popular ideal in the 1940s and 1950s, lifting both the Democrat Party and Mohammed Mossadeq's National Front to power. The differing fate of liberal constitutionalism in each country is explained in part by foreign influence: the Turks fell on the right side of the Cold War, joined the North Atlantic Treaty Organization, and were given space to engage in a rough transition to democracy. After the 1960 coup, Turks retained full sovereignty and were able to recast their constitution and return to civilian rule. In Iran, however, geopolitics worked against democratic transition. Iran attracted foreign interest because of its oil, and as in 1911 foreign intervention led to the suspension of the 1906 constitution when Mossadeq was overthrown with the help of the CIA. It was a betrayal on the scale of France's overthrow of Faysal in 1920: Iranians like Shariati rejected liberalism as a false universal ideal deployed by a perfidious West.

In some ways, Arabs' and Iranians' turn toward indigenous traditions of justice nurtured a powerful new political repertoire that has permitted the return to universal models of rights and representation in the Green Revolution and the Arab Spring. Constitutionalism has finally been detached from its former associations with Westernization, secularism, and elitism. As articulated now through indigenous human rights programs, labor unions, and Islamic movements, constitutionalism has once again claimed a populist and authentic mantle. Ghonim's Facebook messages were received not as the superior wisdom of a technocratic elite, but rather as a vernacular and Muslim demand for human justice.

If the Arab Spring leaves nothing more, it will leave a legacy that dispels an old and hardy prejudice that Middle Eastern peoples love despotism and that they act according to a peculiar logic based on alien and anti-Western values. But if the Arab Spring is to bear fruit, it will be because foreign powers abandon the kinds of interventions practiced in the colonial and Cold War eras. In his June 2012 victory speech, Egyptian president Morsi called on voters to unite in a national revival. Such a revival, he warned, also required security forces to defend Egypt's sovereignty and a new balance of power among nations.[64] As Woodrow Wilson and Edib also understood, the restoration of justice in the Middle East depends now, as it has for more than 200 years, on justice in the region's relationship with foreign powers.

CHRONOLOGY

1453	Ottomans conquer Constantinople, establishing an empire in Europe and Asia
1520–1566	Sultan Suleyman the Lawgiver (the Magnificent) reigns over Ottoman empire at the zenith of its territorial expansion
1599	Mustafa Ali travels to Egypt and calls on the sultan to restore justice there
1774, 1792	Ottoman defeats by Russia signal need for reforms under Sultan Selim III
1798	Napoleon Bonaparte invades Egypt
1839	Sultan Abdulmecid proclaims the Gulhane decree, a bill of rights inaugurating the Tanzimat reform era
1856	Imperial decree grants equal rights to non-Muslims in the Ottoman empire
1858	Peasants in Mount Lebanon invoke the Tanzimat in revolt against feudal lords
1876	Midhat Pasha and Young Ottomans lead a constitutional revolt; first Ottoman parliament elected
1878	Sultan Abdulhamid II suspends constitution after defeat by Russia
1881–1882	Colonel Ahmed Urabi leads a constitutional revolution in Egypt
1906–1911	Constitutional revolution in Iran
1908–1912	The Young Turks restore Ottoman constitution; Halide Edib begins career as a Turkish nationalist writer
1914–1918	World War I: Ottomans ally with Central Powers; Armenians driven from Anatolia in virtual genocide; Arab Revolt launched from Mecca against Ottoman Rule; Lord Balfour, Britain's foreign minister, promises a Jewish homeland in

	Palestine; Iran remains under the influence of Entente powers, Russia and Britain
1919	Greek army occupies Western Anatolia; Halide Edib makes a famous speech at Sultanahmet, rallying Turks to defend their homeland; Egyptian revolution against British protectorate
1920	Treaties of San Remo and Sevres partition Ottoman lands among Entente powers; revolts in Anatolia, Syria, Iraq
1921–1922	Musa Kazim Pasha leads a Palestinian delegation to London
1923	Republic of Turkey declared after Turks win war against Greece; Egyptian constitution grants partial independence
1925–1927	Great Syrian Revolt against French mandatory rule
1927	Yusuf Salman Yusuf (Comrade Fahd) founds a communist party in southern Iraq
1928	Hasan al-Banna founds the Muslim Brotherhood in Ismailia, Egypt
1936–1939	Palestinian Arab Revolt
1947	Baath Party founded in Damascus
1948	The Wathbah uprising against British military presence in Iraq; War in Palestine, as British relinquish mandate; David Ben-Gurion proclaims the State of Israel
1949	Hasan al-Banna assassinated in Cairo; Comrade Fahd hanged in Iraq; Coups in Syria begin five years of military rule; Sayyid Qutb publishes *Social Justice in Islam*
1950	Halide Edib elected to the Turkish parliament in the Democrat Party's first defeat of the ruling party founded by Mustafa Kemal Ataturk
1950–1951	Akram al-Hourani's Arab Socialist Party organizes peasant revolt in Syria
1952	Free Officers' coup launches the July Revolution in Egypt
1953	Coup in Iran overthrows Prime Minister Mohammed Mossadeq
1958–1961	Syria and Egypt merge to form the United Arab Republic
1958	Coup led by General Abd al-Karim Qasim overthrows Iraqi monarchy
1959	Fatah movement founded by Abu Iyad, Yasser Arafat, and Khalil Wazir in Kuwait
1963	Baath Party coups in Iraq and Syria; Abdul Karim Qasim murdered
1964	Sayyid Qutb publishes *Milestones,* handbook for Islamic revolution
1967	Israel defeats Arab states in the June war

1968	Ali Shariati publishes *Islamology*, a call for Islamic revolution in Iran
1969	Fatah takes command of the Palestine Liberation Organization (PLO); Yasser Arafat elected president
1970–1971	PLO leaders are expelled from Jordan in Black September War; Gamal Abdel Nasser dies
1972	Black September terrorists kidnap and kill Jewish athletes at Munich Olympics
1973	October war launched by Egypt against Israel
1974	Yasser Arafat gives "gun and olive branch" speech at United Nations
1977	Egyptian president Anwar Sadat makes a plea for peace in Jerusalem, leading to Camp David Accords of 1979
1979	Iranian revolution ousts the shah and establishes the Islamic Republic of Iran
1981	Anwar Sadat assassinated by members of the Islamist al-Jihad group
1982	Israeli invasion expels Abu Iyad, Yasser Arafat, and PLO leadership from Lebanon
1987	Intifada uprising begins against Israeli occupation of Palestinian territories
1988	PLO renounces terror, recognizes Israel, calls for peace negotiations for two separate states, Arab and Jewish, in Palestine
1990–1998	Islamic insurgency against regime of Egyptian president Hosni Mubarak
1993	Oslo Accords signed by PLO chairman Yasser Arafat and Israeli prime minister Yitzhak Rabin, enabling formation of a Palestinian provisional government
1996	Yasser Arafat establishes Palestinian Authority in West Bank and Gaza after Yitzhak Rabin's assassination (1995)
2000	Second Intifada begins in response to Israeli settlement of West Bank and Gaza
2001	Al-Qaeda terror attacks on World Trade Center and Pentagon in United States
2003	United States and allies occupy Iraq, topple Baathist regime
2009	Green Revolution challenges clerical ruling establishment in Iran
2011	Arab Spring breaks out in Tunisia, Egypt, Libya, Syria, Yemen, and Bahrain
2012	Mohamed Morsi, a Muslim Brotherhood leader, elected president in Egypt; Civil war begins in Syria

NOTES

Introduction

1. Andreas Tietze, ed. and trans., *Mustafa 'Ali's Description of Cairo of 1599* (Vienna: Verlag der Österreichischen Akademie der Wissenschaften, 1975), 25.

2. See my own study in *Colonial Citizens: Republican Rights, Paternal Privilege and Gender in French Syria and Lebanon* (New York: Columbia University Press, 2000), 92–100, 117–126; and Marilyn Booth, *May Her Likes Be Multiplied: Biography and Gender Politics in Egypt* (Berkeley: University of California Press, 2001).

3. Eric Foner, *The Story of American Freedom* (New York: W. W. Norton, 1999).

4. Judith N. Shklar, *The Faces of Injustice* (New Haven: Yale University Press, 1990).

5. Michael J. Sandel, *Justice: What's the Right Thing to Do?* (New York: Farrar, Straus and Giroux, 2009), 29.

6. Amartya Sen, *The Idea of Justice* (Cambridge: The Belknap Press of Harvard University Press, 2009), vii.

7. Edward Said, *Orientalism* (New York: Vintage, 1979).

8. L. Carl Brown, *International Politics and the Middle East: Old Rules, New Game* (Princeton: Princeton University Press, 1984).

9. Nancy Fraser, *Justice Interruptus: Critical Reflections on the "Postsocialist" Condition* (New York: Routledge, 1997).

1. Mustafa Ali

1. Cornell H. Fleischer, *Bureaucrat and Intellectual in the Ottoman Empire: The Historian Mustafa Ali (1541–1600)* (Princeton: Princeton University Press, 1986), 146. The reference to the ode to Mehmed III is on p. 153.

2. Fleischer and Piterberg defend the value of Mustafa Ali's historical analysis; Schmidt doubts any historical basis in his writings; Abou-El-Haj also reads his work as polemic. See Fleischer, *Bureaucrat and Intellectual,* 300–306; Jan Schmidt, *Pure Water for Thirsty Muslims: A Study of Mustafa Ali's Kunhu l-ahbar* (Leiden: Het Oosters Instituut, 1991), 106–107, 111–138, 201; Rifaʿat ʿAli Abou-El-Haj, *Formation of the Modern State: The Ottoman Empire Sixteenth to Eighteenth Centuries* (Albany: SUNY Press, 1991), 28; Suraiya Faroqhi et al., eds., *An Economic and Social History of the Ottoman Empire, vol. 2: 1600–1914* (Cambridge: Cambridge University Press, 1997), 553; Gabriel Piterberg, *An Ottoman Tragedy: History and Historiography at Play* (Berkeley: University of California Press, 2003), 35–45.

3. André Raymond, *Cairo: City of History,* trans. Willard Wood (Cairo: The American University in Cairo Press, 2001), 225; Faroqhi et al., *Economic and Social History of the Ottoman Empire,* 440; Madeline C. Zilfi, *The Politics of Piety: The Ottoman Ulema in the Postclassical Age (1600–1800)* (Minneapolis: Bibliotheca Islamica, 1988), 150.

4. Nelly Hanna, *In Praise of Books: A Cultural History of Cairo's Middle Class, Sixteenth to Eighteenth Century* (Syracuse: Syracuse University Press, 2003), 85.

5. Andreas Tietze, ed. and trans., *Mustafa ʿAli's Description of Cairo of 1599* (Vienna: Verlag der Österreichischen Akademie der Wissenschaften, 1975), 25. See also Fleischer, *Bureaucrat and Intellectual,* 304. Tietze notes that Mustafa Ali mistakenly dated his first visit to 1578; it took place in 1568.

6. Tietze, *Description of Cairo,* 72, 74.

7. Ibid., 80.

8. Ibid., 81.

9. Called the *daire-i adliye* in Ottoman Turkish. See Linda Darling, *Revenue Raising and Legitimacy: Tax Collection and Finance Administration in the Ottoman Empire 1560–1660* (Leiden: E. J. Brill, 1996), 283.

10. Fleischer, *Bureaucrat and Intellectual,* 262. I have altered the order of phrases for clarity.

11. Cornell Fleischer, "Royal Authority, Dynastic Cyclism, and 'Ibn Khaldunism' in Sixteenth-Century Ottoman Letters," *Journal of Asian and African Studies* 18, nos. 3–4 (1983): 198–220; Colin Imber, *Ebu's-suʾud: The Islamic Legal Tradition* (Stanford: Stanford University Press, 1997); Linda T. Darling, "Islamic Empires, the Ottoman Empire and the Circle of Justice," in S. A. Arjomand, ed., *Constitutional Politics in the Middle East* (Portland, OR: Hart Publishing, 2008), 11–23. An earlier Circle of Justice emphasized Islamic law over royal authority. See Serif Mardin, *The Genesis of Young Ottoman Thought* (Princeton: Princeton University Press, 1962), 100–101.

12. Lucette Valensi, *The Birth of the Despot* (Ithaca: Cornell University Press, 1993); Edward Seymour Forster, trans., *The Turkish Letters of Ogier*

Ghiselin de Busbecq, Imperial Ambassador at Constantinople 1554–1562 (Oxford: Oxford University Press, 1927).

13. Imber, *Ebu's-su'ud*, 65–97.

14. Andreas Tietze, ed. and trans., *Mustafa 'Ali's Counsel for Sultans of 1581*, 2 vols. (Vienna: Verlag der Österreichischen Akademie der Wissenschaften, 1979–1982), 1:21.

15. Ibid., 1:18 and 2:21.

16. Fleischer, "Royal Authority," and *Bureaucrat and Intellectual*, 8, 290–292.

17. Halil Inalcik, "The Ottoman Decline and Its Effect upon the Reaya," in Henrik Birnbaum and Speros Vryonis Jr., eds., *Aspects of the Balkans: Continuity and Change* (The Hague: Mouton, 1972), 338–354.

18. Amnon Cohen, *Jewish Life under Islam* (Cambridge, MA: Harvard University Press, 1984), 223; Judith Tucker, *In the House of the Law: Gender and Islamic Law in Ottoman Syria and Palestine* (Berkeley: University of California Press, 1998), 179–186; Leslie Peirce, *Morality Tales: Law and Gender in the Ottoman Court of Aintab* (Berkeley: University of California Press, 2003), 375–389.

19. Peirce, *Morality Tales*, 1–15, 86–125, 177, 276–310.

20. Uriel Heyd, *Studies in Old Ottoman Criminal Law* (Oxford: Clarendon Press, 1973), 264; Richard van Dülmen, *Theatre of Horror: Crime and Punishment in Early Modern Germany*, trans. Elizabeth Neu (Cambridge: Polity Press, 1990).

21. Heyd, *Ottoman Criminal Law*, 11, 114, 119 (laws III: 62, 64, 65, 92), 260–264, 299–307.

22. Tietze, *Counsel for Sultans*, 1:36–37, 40, 71–78.

23. Heyd, *Ottoman Criminal Law*, 272–273.

24. Ibid., 313.

25. Tietze, *Description of Cairo*, 56, 81.

26. Tietze, *Counsel for Sultans*, 1:19.

27. Tietze, *Description of Cairo*, 81. Mustafa Ali warned that Arabs would introduce "oppression and injustice" to the empire's heartland (Tietze, *Counsel for Sultans*, 1:80). See also Piterberg, *An Ottoman Tragedy*, 172–181; Jane Hathaway, "The *Evlad-i Arab* ('Sons of the Arabs') in Ottoman Egypt: A Rereading," Colin Imber and Keiko Kiyotaki, eds., *Frontiers of Ottoman Studies*, vol. 1 (London: I. B. Tauris, 2005), 203–216.

28. Tietze, *Counsel for Sultans*, 2:92.

29. Fleischer, *Bureaucrat and Intellectual*, 298, 301–302.

30. Tietze, *Counsel for Sultans*, 1:46.

31. Fleischer, "Royal Authority," 203–211; Lewis V. Thomas, *A Study of Naima*, ed. Norman Itzkowitz (New York: New York University Press, 1972), 65–79; Abou-El-Haj, *Formation of the Modern State*, 23–25, 41–43.

32. Tietze, *Counsel for Sultans*, 2:108.

33. Michael Cook, *Commanding Right and Forbidding Wrong in Islamic Thought* (Cambridge: Cambridge University Press, 2001). Cook's *Forbidding Wrong in Islam* (Cambridge: Cambridge University Press, 2003) summarizes his argument that in the medieval era scholars, not ordinary believers, enforced the injunction.

34. See also Abou-El-Haj, *Formation of the Modern State,* 13.

35. Perry Miller, *The New England Mind: From Colony to Province* (Cambridge: Harvard University Press, [1953] 1981), 27–39; Sacvan Bercovitch, *The American Jeremiad* (Madison: University of Wisconsin Press, 1978).

36. I draw on Cornell Fleischer, Rifa'at 'Ali Abou-El-Haj, and Norman Itzkowitz for my ideas on the advice tradition.

37. Haim Gerber, *State, Society, and Law in Islam: Ottoman Law in Comparative Perspective* (Albany: State University of New York Press, 1994), 174–182; Fariba Zarinebaf-Shahr, "Ottoman Women and the Tradition of Seeking Justice in the 18th Century," in Madeline C. Zilfi, ed., *Women in the Ottoman Empire* (Leiden: E. J. Brill, 1997), 253–263.

38. Darling, *Revenue Raising,* 283–299.

39. Tucker, *In the House of the Law,* 180; Fariba Zarinebaf-Shahr, "Women, Law, and Imperial Justice in Ottoman Istanbul in the Late Seventeenth Century," in Amira El Azhary Sonbol, ed., *Women, the Family, and Divorce Laws in Islamic History* (Syracuse: Syracuse University Press, 1996), 81–95; Amnon Cohen, *The Guilds of Ottoman Jerusalem* (Leiden: E. J. Brill, 2000), 15, 17, 18, 21. For the sixteenth century see Peirce, *Morality Tales;* Amy Singer, *Palestinian Peasants and Ottoman Officials* (Cambridge: Cambridge University Press, 1994), 28–29, 119–124; and Cohen, *Jewish Life under Islam,* 110–139, 223.

40. Tietze, *Description of Cairo,* 37; Ralph S. Hattox, *Coffee and Coffeehouses: The Origins of a Social Beverage in the Medieval Near East* (Seattle: Dept. of Near Eastern Languages and Civilization, University of Washington, 1985), 29–45, 72–82, 92–130; Nelly Hanna, *Making Big Money in 1600: The Life and Times of Ismail Abu Taqiyya, Egyptian Merchant* (Syracuse: Syracuse University Press, 1998), 71–81; Raymond, *Cairo,* 209; and "Quartiers et mouvements populaires au Caire au XVIIIe siècle," in P. M. Holt, ed., *Political and Social Change in Modern Egypt* (London: Oxford University Press, 1968), 104–116.

41. Darling, *Revenue Raising,* 290–293; Fleischer, *Bureaucrat and Intellectual,* 154–168; Karen Barkey, *Bandits and Bureaucrats: The Ottoman Route to State Centralization* (Ithaca: Cornell University Press, 1994), 123–132.

42. Halil Inalcik with Donald Quataert, eds., *An Economic and Social History of the Ottoman Empire, 1300–1914,* vol. 1 (New York: Cambridge University Press, 1994), 415–419, 433–489; Gabriel Baer, *Fellah and Townsman in the Middle East* (London: Frank Cass, 1982), 310.

43. Rhoads Murphey, "Mustafa Safi's Version of the Kingly Virtues as Presented in His *Zübdet'ül Tevarih*, or Annals of Sultan Ahmed 1012–1023 A/H./1603–1614 A.D.," in Imber and Kiyotaki, *Frontiers of Ottoman Studies*, 5–25.

44. Abou-El-Haj, *Formation of the Modern State*, 29–33, 79–89.

45. Bernard Lewis, "Ottoman Observers of Ottoman Decline," *Islamic Studies* 1 (1962): 77.

46. Piterberg, *An Ottoman Tragedy*, 23–27.

47. Zilfi, *Politics of Piety*, 23–40, 129–159; Imber, *Ebu's-su'ud*, 93–94; Cohen, *Guilds of Jerusalem*, 50–59; Katib Chelebi, *The Balance of Truth*, trans. G. L. Lewis (London: George Allen, 1957), 60–62.

48. Robert Dankoff, *An Ottoman Mentality: The World of Evliya Celebi* (Leiden: E. J., Brill, 2004), vii–xiv, 48–82, 106–114.

49. Thomas, *Study of Naima*, 94–95, 106–110; Rifa'at 'Ali Abou-El-Haj, *The 1703 Rebellion and the Structure of Ottoman Politics* (Leiden: Nederlands Institut, 1984), reprinted as an ACLS Humanities E-book, 2008, pp. 3–10, http://quod.lib.umich.edu/cgi/t/text/text-idx?c=acls;cc=acls;view=toc;idno=heb00852.0001.001 (accessed November 15, 2012).

50. Thomas, *Study of Naima*, 77–79; Abou-El-Haj, *Formation of the Modern State*, 43–45. Bernard Lewis in "Ottoman Observers of Ottoman Decline," agrees that "moral courage" derived from the belief that cycles of decline were not inevitable.

51. Thomas, *Study of Naima*, 78.

52. Walter Livingston Wright Jr., trans. and ed., *Ottoman Statecraft: The Book of Counsel for Vezirs and Governors (Nasaih ul-vuzera vel-umera) of Sari Mehmed Pasha, the Defterdar* (Westport, CT: Greenwood Press, [1935] 1971), 64–66, 117–118.

53. Rhoads Murphey, course lectures on Ottoman history, Columbia University, Fall 1990.

54. Bruce McGowan, "The Age of the Ayans, 1699–1812," in Faroqhi et al., *Economic and Social History of the Ottoman Empire*, vol. II 639; Norman Itzkowitz, preface in Thomas, *Study of Naima*, viii; Roger Owen, *The Middle East in the World Economy 1800–1914* (New York: St. Martin's Press, 1981), 1–23; Abraham Marcus, *The Middle East on the Eve of Modernity: Aleppo in the Eighteenth Century* (New York: Columbia University Press, 1988); Abou-El-Haj, *Formation of the Modern State*, 11–18 (synopsis of debates).

55. On state power see Barkey, *Bandits and Bureaucrats*, and Abou-El-Haj, *Formation of the Modern State*, 1–18, 58–60. For skepticism of state capacity see Piterberg, *An Ottoman Tragedy* and review by Carter Vaughn Findley, *American Historical Review* (April 1996): 533. Haim Gerber argues that fair land tenure policies mitigated peasant revolt in *The Social Origins of the Modern Middle East* (Boulder, CO: Lynne Rienner, [1987] 1994). On

demographic causes of seventeenth-century unrest see Jack A. Goldstone, *Revolution and Rebellion in the Early Modern World* (Berkeley: University of California Press, 1991).

56. Ariel Salzmann, *Tocqueville in the Ottoman Empire* (Leiden: E. J. Brill, 2004), 11, 122–175; Abou-El-Haj, *Formation of the Modern State*; Faroqhi et al., *Economic and Social History of the Ottoman Empire*, vol. II 415–417, 433–438; Zilfi, *The Politics of Piety.*

57. Volney quoted in Faroqhi et al., *Economic and Social History of the Ottoman Empire*, vol. II 692.

58. Dick Douwes, *Ottomans in Syria: A History of Justice and Oppression* (New York: I. B. Tauris, 2000) 152–187, 211–217; McGowan in Faroqhi et al., *Economic and Social History of the Ottoman Empire*, 637–758; Salzmann, *Tocqueville*, 150–163. The state revenue figures are from McGowan in Faroqhi et al., *Economic and Social History of the Ottoman Empire*, vol. II 714.

59. John Obert Voll, *Islam: Continuity and Change in the Modern World* (Boulder, CO: Westview Press, 1982), 39–62, 86; Gamal El-Din El Shayyal, "Some Aspects of Intellectual and Social Life in Eighteenth-century Egypt," in Holt, *Political and Social Change*, 117–132.

60. Natana DeLong-Bas, *Wahhabi Islam: From Revival and Reform to Global Jihad* (Oxford: Oxford University Press, 2004), 1–92, 193–226; David Dean Commins, *The Wahhabi Mission and Saudi Arabia* (New York: I. B. Tauris, 2006), 7–39.

61. DeLong-Bas, *Wahhabi Islam*, 25–26, 246–248. For alternate views on Wahhab's tolerance and jihad see Madawi Al-Rasheed, *A History of Saudi Arabia* (Cambridge: Cambridge University Press, 2002), 14–23, and David Commins, "Traditional Anti-Wahhabi Hanbalism in Nineteenth-Century Arabia," in Itschak Weismann and Fruma Zachs, eds., *Ottoman Reform and Muslim Regeneration* (London: I. B. Tauris, 2005), 81–96.

62. Kenneth M. Cuno, *The Pasha's Peasants: Land, Society, and Economy in Lower Egypt, 1740–1858* (Cambridge: Cambridge University Press, 1992), 17–47.

63. Abou-El-Haj, 25, appendix D; Benedict Anderson, *Imagined Communities* (New York: Verso, [1983] 2006), 49–63.

64. Raymond, *Cairo*, 196, 202–225.

65. Gabriel Baer, "Popular Revolt in Ottoman Cairo," in his *Fellah and Townsman in the Middle East* (London: Frank Cass, 1982), 225–252; Raymond, *Cairo*, 238–239, 272–273.

66. Baer, *Fellah and Townsman*, 253–254, 285, 291, 296, 298, 301, 308; Cuno, *Pasha's Peasants*, 86–96.

67. Shmuel Moreh, trans., *Napoleon in Egypt: Al-Jabarti's Chronicle of the French Occupation* (Princeton: Markus Wiener, 1993), 19–22.

68. Ibid., 83.

69. Ibid., 83–85.

70. Ibid., 85–95. See also Juan Cole, *Napoleon's Egypt* (New York: Palgrave MacMillan, 2007), 197–211; Thomas Philipp and Moshe Perlmann, eds., *Abd al-Rahman al-Jabarti's History of Egypt*, 4 vols. (Stuttgart: Franz Steiner Verlag, 1994), 3:38–48.

71. Quote from Jabarti in Afaf Loutfi El Sayed, "The Role of the *'ulama'* in Egypt during the Early Nineteenth Century," in Holt, *Political and Social Change*, 273.

72. Baer, "Popular Revolt," 246–247; Afaf Lutfi Al-Sayyid Marsot, *Egypt in the Reign of Muhammad Ali* (Cambridge: Cambridge University Press, 1984), 36–59.

73. Caroline Finkel, *Osman's Dream: The Story of the Ottoman Empire 1300–1923* (New York: Basic Books, 2006), 389–412. Quote on p. 394.

74. Salzmann, *Toqueville in the Ottoman Empire*, 187; Finkel, *Osman's Dream*, 413–425; Mardin, *Genesis of Young Ottoman Thought*, 134–149; Bernard Lewis, *The Emergence of Modern Turkey* (London: Oxford University Press, 1968), 69–76.

75. Niyazi Berkes, *The Development of Secularism in Turkey* (New York: Routledge, [1964] 1998), 94–95, 147; Mardin, *Genesis of Young Ottoman Thought*, 149–162; Seyfettin Ersahin, "The Ottoman Ulema and the Reforms of Mahmud II," *Hamdard Islamicus* 12, no. 2: 19–40; Frederick F. Anscombe, "Islam and the Age of Ottoman Reform," *Past and Present* 208 (August 2010): 159–189.

76. Anscombe, "Islam and the Age of Ottoman Reform," 183; Butrus Abu-Manneh, *Studies on Islam and the Ottoman Empire in the 19th Century (1826–1876)* (Istanbul: Isis Press, 2001), 59–97.

77. Roderic H. Davison, *Reform in the Ottoman Empire 1856–1876* (Princeton: Princeton University Press, 1963), 36–37.

78. Akram Fouad Khater, *Sources in the History of the Modern Middle East* (Boston: Houghton Mifflin, 2004), 12–14.

79. Berkes, *Development of Secularism in Turkey*, 144; Mardin, *Genesis of Young Ottoman Thought*, 175–189.

80. Abou-El-Haj, *Formation of the Modern State*, 65, 70.

81. Salzmann, *Tocqueville in the Ottoman Empire*; Stanford J. Shaw and Ezel Kural Shaw, *History of the Ottoman Empire and Modern Turkey*, vol. 2 (New York: Cambridge University Press, 1977), 58–61.

82. Abu-Manneh, *Studies on Islam*, 71. Abu-Manneh, Inalcik, and Mardin emphasize internal origins, against the European origins cited by Shaw and Berkes.

83. Abu-Manneh, *Studies on Islam*, 84; Lewis, *Emergence of Modern Turkey*, 105–108.

84. Abu-Manneh, *Studies on Islam,* 86.

85. Mardin, *Genesis of Young Ottoman Thought,* 203; Abu-Manneh, *Studies on Islam,* 85; Davison, *Reform in the Ottoman Empire,* 39.

86. Abu-Manneh, *Studies on Islam,* 91, translating the phrase *ilan-i adalet.*

87. Quoted in Mardin, *Genesis of Young Ottoman Thought,* 157.

88. Ibid., 157, 162; Caglar Keyder, *State and Class in Turkey* (New York: Verso, 1987).

89. Lewis, *Emergence of Modern Turkey,* 107.

2. Tanyus Shahin of Mount Lebanon

1. Antun Dahir al-Aqiqi, manuscript translated in Malcolm H. Kerr, *Lebanon in the Last Years of Feudalism, 1840–1868* (Beirut: American University of Beirut, 1959), 44–45; Marwan Buheiry, "The Peasant Revolt of 1858 in Mount Lebanon: Rising Expectations, Economic Malaise, and the Incentive to Arm," in Tarif Khalidi, ed. *Land Tenure and Social Transformation in the Middle East* (Beirut: American University of Beirut, 1984), 291–301.

2. Kerr, *Lebanon in the Last Years,* 141 n. 2. Letter from Shahin to the people of Jubail, dated April 3, 1860; conversation with historian Abdulrahim Abuhusayn of the American University in Beirut, November 5, 2012.

3. Caesar Farah (*The Politics of Interventionism in Ottoman Lebanon, 1830–61* [New York: I. B. Tauris, 2000], 585) argues 3,600–4,000 Christians died. Others estimate 10,000–12,000 dead. See Leila Fawaz, *An Occasion for War* (Berkeley: University of California Press, 1995), 226; Samir Khalaf, *Civil and Uncivil Violence in Lebanon* (New York: Columbia University Press, 2004), 96.

4. Ussama Makdisi, *The Culture of Sectarianism* (Berkeley: University of California Press, 2000), 96–101, 105, 115–117.

5. Roderic H. Davison, *Reform in the Ottoman Empire 1856–1876* (Princeton: Princeton University Press, 1963), 52–83 (quote is from p. 57); Serif Mardin, *The Genesis of Young Ottoman Thought* (Princeton: Princeton University Press, 1962); Butrus Abu-Manneh, *Studies on Islam and the Ottoman Empire in the Nineteenth Century (1826–1876)* (Istanbul: Isis Press, 2001), 97, 125.

6. Buheiry, "Peasant Revolt of 1858," 296; Charles Issawi, *The Fertile Crescent 1800–1914* (New York: Oxford University Press, 1988), 48–51; Roger Owen, *The Middle East in the World Economy 1800–1914* (New York: I. B. Tauris, 1993), 91–99, 153–167.

7. Dominique Chevallier, "Aux origines des troubles agraires libanais en 1858," *Annales* 14, no. 1 (January–May 1959), 35–64; James C. Scott, *The Moral Economy of the Peasant* (New Haven: Yale University Press, 1977), 182–187.

8. Chevallier, "Aux origines des troubles," 58–64.

9. Henry H. Jessup, *Fifty-Three Years in Syria*, vol. 1 (Reading, UK: Garnet, [1910] 2002), 164–165; Buheiry, "Peasant Revolt of 1858," 296–298.

10. Summary based on Yehoshua Porath's critical reading of documents published after 1860 by Jouplain, Hattuni, Aqiqi, Ismail, Dufferin, Poujoulat, and others in "The Peasant Revolt of 1858–1861," *Asian and African Studies* 2 (1966): 77–157.

11. Kerr, *Lebanon in the Last Years*, 21–22; Makdisi, *Culture of Sectarianism*, 107, 115.

12. Kerr, *Lebanon in the Last Years*, 21–25, 49, 123–127.

13. Ibid., 117, 148–150.

14. Ibid., 97–99. Kerr infers that the "benevolent decrees" mentioned in the second article refer to the Hatt-i Humayun of 1856.

15. Ibid., 103.

16. Ibid., 112, 114, 123–126, 128–129, 133–135.

17. Ibid., 112.

18. Ibid., 104, 107.

19. Ibid., 110–111.

20. Ibid., 114–115, 118–119, 136–138; Porath, "The Peasant Revolt of 1858–1861," 105–109.

21. Kerr, *Lebanon in the Last Years*, 139.

22. Ibid., 116–117.

23. Ibid., 141, note 2.

24. Ibid., 143–144.

25. Khalaf, *Civil and Uncivil Violence*, preface and chapter 4.

26. Fawaz, *Occasion for War*, 46, 51, 211 on Church plot to expel the Druze; 22–24, 39–42, 68–73, 100 on resentment of Maronite wealth and privilege; 47–50 on low level sectarian violence.

27. Farah, *Politics of Interventionism*, 542–585, 702–744; Abdulrahim Abuhusayn, "An Ottoman against the Constitution: The Maronites of Mount Lebanon and the Question of Representation in the Ottoman Parliament," in Jorgen Nielsen, ed., *Religion, Ethnicity and Contested Nationhood in the Former Ottoman Space* (Boston: E. J. Brill, 2012), 89–114.

28. Ussama Makdisi, "Corrupting the Sublime Sultanate: The Revolt of Tanyus Shahin in Nineteenth-Century Ottoman Lebanon," *Comparative Studies in Society and History* 42, no. 1 (January 2000), 194, 196.

29. Makdisi, *Culture of Sectarianism*, 106–107.

30. Scott, *Moral Economy of the Peasant*, 167, 184; see also Dipesh Chakrabarty, *Habitations of Modernity* (Chicago: University of Chicago Press, 2002), chapters 1, 6, 9.

31. Alex Havemann, "The Impact of Peasant Resistance on 19th-Century Mount Lebanon," in F. Kazemi and J. Waterbury, eds., *Peasants and Politics*

in the Modern Middle East (Miami: Florida International University Press, 1991), 85–100. See also Khalaf, *Civil and Uncivil Violence*, 83, 94.

32. Davison, *Reform in the Ottoman Empire*, 61.

33. Ibid., 58.

34. Farah, *Politics of Interventionism*, 541, 731.

35. Davison, *Reform in the Ottoman Empire*, 100–106; Abu-Manneh, *Studies on Islam*, 125–129.

36. Davison, *Reform in the Ottoman Empire*, 108; Farah, *Politics of Interventionism*, 724.

37. Fawaz, *Occasion for War*, 132–140.

38. Kerr, *Lebanon in the Last Years*, 145–148.

39. Engin Akarli, *The Long Peace: Ottoman Lebanon 1861–1920* (Berkeley: University of California, 1993).

40. Mardin, *Genesis of Young Ottoman Thought*, 281 (quote from Mustafa Fazil Pasha).

41. Ibid., 105, 301.

42. Robert Devereux, *The First Ottoman Constitutional Period: Study of the Midhat Constitution and Parliament* (Baltimore: The Johns Hopkins University Press, 1963), 35–53, 80–85.

43. Ibid., 113.

44. Ibid., 138–144. Note: Devereux counts the number of deputies as variously 130 and 129; Abuhusayn, "An Ottoman Against the Constitution," 93–94.

45. Ibid., 186–221.

46. Midhat Pasha, "The Past, Present, and Future of Turkey," *The Nineteenth Century* vol. 3 no. 16 (June 1878): 992–993.

47. Ariel Salzmann, "Citizens in Search of a State: The Limits of Political Participation in the Late Ottoman Empire," in C. Tilly and M. Hanagan, eds., *Extending Citizenship, Reconfiguring States* (Lanham, MD: Rowman & Littlefield, 1999), 37–66.

48. Selim Deringil, *The Well-Protected Domains: Ideology and the Legitimation of Power in the Ottoman Empire, 1876–1909* (London: I. B. Tauris, 1998) 11, 115, 166–176.

3. Ahmad Urabi and Nazem al-Islam Kermani

1. Ahmad Urabi, *The Defense Statement of Ahmad Urabi,* trans. Trevor Le Gassick (Cairo: American University in Cairo Press, 1982), 32–33.

2. David S. Landes, *Bankers and Pashas: International Finance and Economic Imperialism in Egypt* (Cambridge, MA: Harvard University Press, 1958), 69.

3. John T. Chalcraft, *The Striking Cabbies of Cairo* (Albany: State University of New York Press, 2005), 47; Joel Beinin, *Workers and Peasants in the Modern Middle East* (New York: Cambridge University Press, 2001), 44–70.

4. Charles Kurzman, *Democracy Denied 1905–1915: Intellectuals and the Fate of Democracy* (Cambridge, MA: Harvard University Press, 2008).

5. Nader Sohrabi, *Revolution and Constitutionalism in the Ottoman Empire and Iran* (Cambridge: Cambridge University Press, 2011).

6. Juan R. I. Cole, *Colonialism and Revolution in the Middle East* (Cairo: The American University in Cairo Press, 1999), 3–22.

7. Abd al-Munim Ibrahim al-Jamii, trans. and ed., *Mudhakkirat al-Zaim Ahmad Urabi* (Cairo: Dar al-Kutub wa al-Wathaiq al-Qawmiya, 2005), 1:6–16.

8. Urabi, *Defense Statement*, 18.

9. Al-Jamii, *Mudhakkirat al-Zaim Ahmad Urabi*, 1:97.

10. Khaled Fahmy, *All the Pasha's Men* (Cairo: American University in Cairo Press, 2002); Ehud Toledano, *State and Society in Mid-Nineteenth Century Egypt* (Cambridge: Cambridge University Press, 1990), 181–195; P. J. Vatikiotis, *A History of Modern Egypt*, 4th ed. (Baltimore: The Johns Hopkins University Press), 72–73.

11. Urabi, *Defense Statement*, 19.

12. Landes, *Bankers and Pashas*, passim; Vatikiotis, *History of Modern Egypt*, 73–89, 101–105; Marsot, *A History of Egypt*, 2nd ed. (New York: Cambridge University Press, 2007), 80–83.

13. AbdelAziz EzzelArab, "The Experiment of Sharif Pasha's Cabinet (1879): An Inquiry into the Historiography of Egypt's Elite Movement," *International Journal of Middle East Studies* 36 (2004): 561–589.

14. Benedict Anderson, *Imagined Communities* (New York: Verso [1983] 2006), 49–68; Cole, *Colonialism and Revolution*, 110–132, 190–212.

15. Wilfred Blunt, *Secret History of the English Occupation of Egypt* (New York: Knopf, 1922), 370.

16. Urabi, *Defense Statement*, 18.

17. Ibid., 8–10, 20, 22–23.

18. Charles Kurzman, *Modernist Islam, 1840–1940: A Sourcebook* (New York: Oxford University Press, 2002), 39.

19. Ibid., 53, from Muhammad Abduh, *Laws Should Change* (Cairo, 1881).

20. Juan Cole, "New Perspectives on Sayyid Jamal al-Din al-Afghani in Egypt," in Rudi Matthee and Beth Baron, eds., *Iran and Beyond* (Costa Mesa, CA: Mazda, 2000), 13–34; Nikki R. Keddie, *Sayyid Jamal ad-Din Al-Afghani: A Political Biography* (Berkeley: University of California Press, 1972), 10–32, 81–128.

21. Cole, "New Perspectives on Sayyid Jamal al-Din al-Afghani," 31; Blunt, *Secret History*, 368.

22. Alexander Schölch, *Egypt for the Egyptians! The Socio-Political Crisis in Egypt, 1878–82* (Oxford: Ithaca Press, 1981), 153–160; Blunt, *Secret History*, 375–379.

23. Trevor Le Gassick, introduction to Urabi, *Defense Statement*, 24.

24. Al-Jamii, *Mudhakkirat al-Zaim Ahmed Urabi,* 1:299; Schölch, *Egypt for the Egyptians,* 160–170.

25. Le Gassick in Urabi, *Defense Statement,* 10–11.

26. Schölch, *Egypt for the Egyptians,* 160, 170. "A just and lawful regime" translates as "hukuma shuriya adila" in Arabic.

27. J.A.M. Caldwell, *Dustur: A Survey of the Constitutions of the Arab and Muslim* States (Leiden: E. J. Brill, 1966), 24–26; Nathan J. Brown, *Constitutions in a Nonconstitutional World* (Albany: State University of New York Press, 2002), 26–29. See Arabic text in al-Jamii, *Mudhakkirat al-Zaim Ahmed Urabi;* English text in Blunt, *Secret History.*

28. Urabi, *Defense Statement,* 25.

29. Schölch, *Egypt for the Egyptians,* 180–186.

30. Ibid., 245; Cole, *Colonialism and Revolution,* 238–239.

31. Urabi, *Defense Statement,* 29.

32. Cole, *Colonialism and Revolution,* 237.

33. Schölch, *Egypt for the Egyptians,* 250–253; Cole, *Colonialism and Revolution,* 253–259.

34. Cole, *Colonialism and Revolution,* 247; Schölch, *Egypt for the Egyptians,* 270–293. Schölch estimates that 250, not 400, notables assembled.

35. Urabi, *Defense Statement,* 42.

36. John Ninet, *Lettres d'Egypte 1879–1882,* Anouar Louca, ed. (Paris: Editions CNRS, 1979), 194–196; Blunt, *Secret History,* 285–291; Cole, *Colonialism and Revolution,* 241–249.

37. Yvonne Haddad, "Muhammad Abduh: Pioneer of Islamic Reform," in Ali Rahnema, ed., *Pioneers of Islamic Revival* (Atlantic Highlands, NJ: Zed, 1994), 30–63.

38. Cole, *Colonialism and Revolution,* 249–268.

39. Blunt, *Secret History,* 282–283.

40. Urabi, *Defense Statement,* 42.

41. Blunt, *Secret History,* 374.

42. Ninet, *Lettres d'Egypte,* 200; Blunt, *Secret History,* 292–342.

43. The Earl of Cromer, *Modern Egypt* (London: MacMillan and Co., 1908), 322, 324, 326.

44. "Al-Adala al-Ingliziyya [English Justice]," in Jamal al-Din al-Afghani and Shaykh Muhammad Abduh, *al-Urwah al-Wuthqa* (Beirut: Dar al-Kitab al-Arabi, 1980), 358.

45. Muhammad Abduh, "The Theology of Unity" (1897) in Kurzman, *Modernist Islam,* 54–60; Jacques Berque, *Egypt: Imperialism and Revolution,* trans. Jean Stewart (New York: Praeger, 1972), 214–220.

46. Schölch and Cole disprove old views that Urabi merely staged a coup. See also Thomas Mayer, *The Changing Past: Egyptian Historiography of the Urabi Revolt 1882–1983* (Gainesville: University of Florida Press, 1988).

47. Mayer, *Changing Past*, 5–27.

48. Afsaneh Najmabadi, *The Story of the Daughters of Quchan* (Syracuse: Syracuse University Press, 1998), 61–62; Sohrabi, *Revolution and Constitutionalism*, 289–299.

49. Abdul-Hadi Hairi, *Shiism and Constitutionalism in Iran* (Leiden: E. J. Brill, 1977).

50. Bayat's argument about the tactical use of religion is more persuasive than Afary's view that Islam posed an absolute threat to democracy. See Mangol Bayat, *Iran's First Revolution: Shi'ism and the Constitutional Revolution of 1905–1909* (New York: Oxford University Press, 1991); Janet Afary, *The Iranian Constitutional Revolution, 1906–1911* (New York: Columbia University Press, 1996); Najmabadi, *Daughters of Quchan;* Ervand Abrahamian, *Iran between Two Revolutions* (Princeton: Princeton University Press, 1982). My thinking on religion and popular political consciousness is influenced by E. P. Thompson's *The Making of the English Working Class* (New York: Penguin, [1963] 1991); and Dipesh Chakrabarty's discussion of Indian labor history in *Provincializing Europe: Postcolonial Thought and Historical Difference* (Princeton: Princeton University Press, 2000), 72–96.

51. Najmabadi, *Daughters of Quchan*, 4–7.

52. Abrahamian, *Iran between Two Revolutions*, 76–80.

53. Tabatabai quoted in Bayat, *Iran's First Revolution*, 127; Sohrabi, *Revolution and Constitutionalism*, 342–343.

54. Mangol Bayat, "The Tale of the Quchan Maidens as an 'Originator' Event of the Constitutional Revolution," *Comparative Studies of South Asia, Africa and the Middle East* 25, no. 2 (2005): 400–401.

55. Abrahamian (*Iran between Two Revolutions*, 83–85) says 14,000 gathered there; Bayat (*Iran's First Revolution*, 130) says 13,000–20,000; Afary (*Iranian Constitutional Revolution*, 55) says 14,000.

56. Sohrabi, *Revolution and Constitutionalism*, 344–349; Afary, *Iranian Constitutional Revolution*, 53–60.

57. Bayat and Afary follow Ahmad Kasravi in emphasizing the role of nonclerics. See Ahmad Kasravi, *History of the Iranian Constitutional Revolution* (Tehran, 1940–1943) [in Persian]. I thank Suad Jafarzadeh for her translations.

58. Nazem al-Islam quotes from Bayat, *First Iranian Revolution*, which quotes Muhammad Nazem al-Islam Kirmani, *Tarikh-e Bidari-ye Iraniyan/History of the Awakening of the Iranians*, 3 vols. (Tehran: Bonyad Farhang-e Iran, 1967).

59. Nazem al-Islam Kermani, *Tarikh-i bidariye Iraniyan* [History of Iranians' awakening], Ali Akbar Sirjani, ed. (Tehran: Peikan Publishing, 1997), 2:138–142. I thank Leila Piran for her translations. See also Bayat, *Iran's First Revolution*, 58–60.

60. Abrahamian, *Iran between Two Revolutions*, 79–80; Afary, *Iranian Constitutional Revolution*, 42.

61. Bayat, *Iran's First Revolution*, 73.

62. Ibid., 128.

63. Abrahamian, *Iran between Two Revolutions*, 76–80.

64. Bayat, *Iran's First Revolution*, 142.

65. Said Amir Arjomand, *The Turban for the Crown* (New York: Oxford University Press, 1988), 37–39.

66. Said Amir Arjomand, "Islam and Constitutionalism since the Nineteenth Century: The Significance and Peculiarities of Iran," in S. A. Arjomand, ed., *Constitutional Politics in the Middle East* (Portland, OR: Hart Publishing, 2008), 37.

67. Nikki R. Keddie, *Modern Iran: Roots and Results of Revolution* (New Haven: Yale University Press, 2003), 68; Sohrabi, *Revolution and Constitutionalism*, 354–356.

68. Afary, *Iranian Constitutional Revolution*, 99–109.

69. Kermani, *Tarikh-i bidari*, 38–45.

70. Najmabadi, *Daughters of Quchan*, 61–113; quotes from pp. 40, 109.

71. Some historians argue that they should have deposed the shah in December 1907. See Bayat, *Iran's First Revolution*, 213–214; Afary, *Iranian Constitutional Revolution*, 134.

72. Abrahamian, *Iran between Two Revolutions*, 92–96; Bayat, *Iran's First Revolution*, 232–234, 253–258; Afary, *Iranian Constitutional Revolution*, 102.

73. Afary, *Iranian Constitutional Revolution*, 258–259.

74. Quoted in Bayat, *Iran's First Revolution*, 157; Afary, *Iranian Constitutional Revolution*, 219–220, 253–254, 269–271.

75. Afary, *Iranian Constitutional Revolution*, 272, 311–313.

76. Ibid., 42–43.

77. Bayat, *Iran's First Revolution*, 74.

78. Afary, *Iranian Constitutional Revolution*, 43; Bayat, *Iran's First Revolution*, 234.

79. Kermani, *Tarikh-i bidari*, 143, 198, 238.

80. Bayat, *Iran's First Revolution*, 236, 258.

81. Afary, *Iranian Constitutional Revolution*, 328–339.

82. Morgan Shuster, *The Strangling of Persia* (New York: The Century Co., 1912), 204.

83. Linda T. Darling, "Islamic Empires, the Ottoman Empire and the Circle of Justice," and Arjomand, "Islam and Constitutionalism," both in Arjomand, *Constitutional Politics in the Middle East*, 29–32, 33–44.

84. Arjomand, "Islam and Constitutionalism," 44.

85. Midhat Pasha, "The Past, Present, and Future of Turkey," *The Nineteenth Century* vol. 3 no. 16 (June 1878): 992–993.

86. Kurzman, *Democracy Denied,* 15–20.

4. Halide Edib, Turkey's Joan of Arc

1. Halide Edib, *The Turkish Ordeal: Being the further memoirs of Halide Edib* (New York: Century Co., 1928), 27.

2. For current scholarly debates on the Armenian genocide, in which nearly a million Armenians were murdered in 1915–1916, see Ronald Grigor Suny, Fatma Müge Göçek, and Norman M. Naimark, eds., *A Question of Genocide: Armenians and Turks at the End of the Ottoman Empire* (New York: Oxford University Press, 2011). For a debate on use of the term "genocide" see Paul Boghossian, "The Concept of Genocide," *Journal of Genocide Research* 12, nos. 1–2 (2010): 69–112.

3. Wilson's speech to Congress, January 8, 1918, is available at www.ourdocuments.gov/doc.php?flash=true&doc=62 (accessed July 18, 2011).

4. Edib, *Turkish Ordeal,* 30–34.

5. Inci Enginun, *Halide Edib Adivarin Eserlerlinde Dogu ve Bati Meselesi* (Istanbul: Dergah Yayinlari, 1995), 54; Ipek Çalişlar, *Halide Edib: Biyografisine Sigmayan Kadin* (Istanbul: Everest Yayinlari, 2010), 171–173.

6. Edib, *Turkish Ordeal,* 23.

7. Elizabeth Frierson, "Women in Late Ottoman Intellectual History," in Elisabeth Ozdalga, ed., *Late Ottoman Society: The Intellectual Legacy* (New York: RoutledgeCurzon, 2005), 135–161.

8. Halide Edib, *Memoirs of Halide Edib* (New York: Century Co., 1926), 197.

9. Hans-Lukas Kieser, *A Quest for Belonging: Anatolia beyond Empire and Nation (19th–21st Centuries)* (Istanbul: Isis Press, 2007), 20–28.

10. Edib, *Memoirs,* 95.

11. Ibid., 213.

12. Erik J. Zürcher, *The Young Turk Legacy and Nation Building* (New York: I. B. Tauris, 2010), 26–40.

13. Stanford Shaw and Ezel Kural Shaw, *History of the Ottoman Empire and Modern Turkey,* vol. 2 (New York: Cambridge University Press, 1977), 275–278. Joyful election crowds: Edib, *Memoirs,* 271–272.

14. Edib, *Memoirs,* 260.

15. Ahmed Emin, "The Development of Modern Turkey as Measured by Its Press," *Studies in History, Economics & Public Law* 59 (1914): 127. Statistics on 1913 periodicals are on p. 119.

16. Edib, *Memoirs,* 270–271.

17. Halide Salih, "The Future of Turkish Women," *The Nation,* October 24, 1908, p. 149, cited in Rehan Nishanyan, "Early Years of the Young Turk

Revolution (1908–1912) as Reflected in the Life and Works of Halide Edib" (MA thesis, McGill University, 1990), 30–33.

18. Edib, *Memoirs*, 274–275. On Islamic activists see Shaw and Shaw, *History of the Ottoman Empire*, 278.

19. Shaw and Shaw, *History of the Ottoman Empire*, 282.

20. Erik J. Zürcher, *Turkey: A Modern History*, 3rd ed. (New York: I. B. Tauris, 2004), 99–103; M. Şükrü Hanioğlu, *Preparation for a Revolution: The Young Turks, 1902–1908* (New York: Oxford University Press, 2001), 5–6, 40–42, 138–188, 279–288.

21. Edib, *Memoirs*, 208–210.

22. Nishanyan, "Early Years of the Young Turk Revolution," 34–38, 61–78; Emel Sönmez, "The Novelist Halide Edib Adivar and Turkish Feminism," *Die Welt des Islams* 14, no. 1/4 (1973): 84, 90–93; Elif Gozdasoglu Kucuka-lioglu, "The Representation of Women as Gendered National Subjects in Ottoman-Turkish Novels (1908–1923)," *Journal of Gender Studies* 16, no. 1 (March 2007): 8–9.

23. Hülya Adak, "Intersubjectivity: Halide Edib (1882–1964) or the Ottoman/Turkish (Woman) as the Subject of Knowledge" (PhD thesis, University of Chicago, 2001), 87–139.

24. Sönmez, "Novelist Halide Edib Adivar," 81–115; Nishanyan, "Early Years of the Young Turk Revolution"; Deniz Kandiyoti, "Slave Girls, Temptresses, and Comrades: Images of Women in the Turkish Novel," *Feminist Issues* (Spring 1988): 35–49; Azade Seyhan, "Is Orientalism in Retreat or in for a New Treat? Halide Edip Adivar and Eine Sevgi Ozdamar Write Back," *Seminar* 41, no. 3 (September 2005): 209–225.

25. Nishanyan, "Early Years of the Young Turk Revolution," 72–125.

26. Adak, "Intersubjectivity," 127–129.

27. See the introduction to the 2005 Gorgias Press reprint of *Memoirs of Halide Edib*, ix.

28. Edib, *Memoirs*, 321.

29. Halide Salih, "Mehasin-i Okuyan Kardeşlerime," *Mehasin* 6 (Subat 1324): 418–421, as quoted in Tulay Keskin, "Feminist/Nationalist Discourse in the First Year of the Ottoman Revolutionary Press (1908–1090): Readings from the Magazines of *Demet, Mehasin,* and *Kadin* (Salonica)" (MA thesis, Bilkent University, 2003), 72.

30. Hanioğlu, *Preparation for a Revolution*, 3–27, 82–129; Hamit Bozarslan, "Le Prince Sabahaddin (1879–1948)," *Schweizerische Zeitschift fur Geschichte* 52 (2002): 287–301.

31. Edib, *Memoirs*, 331.

32. Kieser, *Quest for Belonging*, 422.

33. Edib, *Memoirs*, 335, 338.

34. Mustafa Aksakal, *The Ottoman Road to War in 1914* (Cambridge: Cambridge University Press, 2008).

35. Ronald Grigor Suny, "Writing Genocide: The Fate of the Ottoman Armenians," in Suny et al., *Question of Genocide*, 15–41; Edward J. Erickson, *Ordered to Die: A History of the Ottoman Army in the First World War* (Westport, CT: Greenwood Press, 2001), 210–211; Hikmet Özdemir, *The Ottoman Army 1914–1918: Disease and Death on the Battlefield* (Salt Lake City: University of Utah Press, 2008), 119–133.

36. Edib, *Memoirs*, 386–388, 431–471; Edib, *Turkish Ordeal*, 14–18.

37. Edib, *Memoirs*, 375.

38. Letter to Crane, September 16, 1919. Crane Family Papers and Charles Crane Papers, box 4, folder 5, Bakhmeteff Archive, Columbia University Rare Book and Manuscript Library. Hereafter "Crane Papers."

39. Kieser, *Quest for Belonging*, 49; Caleb Frank Gates, *Not to Me Only* (Princeton: Princeton University Press, 1940), 249–263.

40. M. Zekeria, "Turkey's Fiery 'Joan of Arc'; Her Double Role as Leader," *New York Times*, November 26, 1922, p. 112; Gates, *Not to Me Only*, 249–254; Nur Bilge Criss, *Istanbul under Allied Occupation 1918–1923* (Boston: E. J. Brill, 1999), 52–55.

41. Zekeria, "Turkey's Fiery 'Joan of Arc.' "

42. Kieser, *Quest for Belonging*, 426.

43. Criss, *Istanbul under Allied Occupation*, 94–114.

44. Calislar, *Halide Edib*, 174–195; Zurcher, *Turkey*, 138–139. Available at http://tr.wikisource.org/wiki/Misak-i Milli (accessed September 2, 2011).

45. Edib, *Turkish Ordeal*, 65–124.

46. Inginun, 58; Ryan Gingeras, *Sorrowful Shores: Violence, Ethnicity and the End of the Ottoman Empire, 1912–1923* (New York: Oxford University Press, 2009); Zürcher, *Young Turk Legacy*; M. Şükrü Hanioğlu, *Ataturk: An Intellectual Biography* (Princeton: Princeton University Press, 2011).

47. Edib, *Turkish Ordeal*, 142.

48. Letter from Ankara to Crane, May 24, 1920. Crane Papers.

49. Edib, *Turkish Ordeal*, 187, 261–276, 284–310, 367.

50. Ibid., 381.

51. Hanioğlu, *Ataturk*, 48–67, 226–232.

52. Ibid., 187–188; Hülya Adak, "National Myths and Self-Na(rra)tions: Mustafa Kemal's *Nutuk* and Halide Edib's *Memoirs* and *The Turkish Ordeal*," *The South Atlantic Quarterly* 102, no. 2/3 (Spring/Summer 2003), 509–527.

53. Clark, *Twice a Stranger*, xi–xvii, 40–64.

54. Zekeria, "Turkey's Fiery 'Joan of Arc.' "

55. Çalişlar, *Halide Edib*, 294–295.

56. Halide Edib, *The Shirt of Flame* (New York: Duffield & Co., 1924), 145. Edib herself translated the 1922 Turkish original, *Ateshten Gömlek*.

57. Çalişlar, *Halide Edib*, 306; Yaprak Zihnioglu, *Kadinsiz Inkilap* (Istanbul: Metis Yayinlari, 2003). English-language sources on Turkish feminism are rare. See Deniz Kandiyoti, "End of Empire: Islam, Nationalism and Women in

Turkey," in Kandiyoti, ed., *Women, Islam and the State* (Philadelphia: Temple University Press, 1991), 22–47; Elif Gozdasoglu Kucukalioglu, "The Historical Roots of the Women's Movement," paper given at the Turkey at the Crossroads: Turkey, Turkish Women and the State Conference, Bodrum, Turkey 2005. Available at http://pages.towson.edu/ncctrw/summer%20institutes/Papers-Website/Kucukalioglu%2005.pdf (accessed October 9, 2012).

58. Çalişlar, *Halide Edib,* 310–313.

59. Ibid., 314–315. See Erik Jan Zürcher, *Political Opposition in the Early Turkish Republic: The Progressive Republican Party 1924–25* (Leiden: E. J. Brill, 1991), 138–145, for the manifesto of the Progressive Republican Party.

60. Zürcher, *Political Opposition in the Early Turkish Republic* and Zürcher, *Turkey,* 168–169; Feroz Ahmad, "The Progressive Republican Party, 1924–25," in his *From Empire to Republic* (Istanbul: Bilgi University Press, 2008), 239–260.

61. Hanioğlu, *Ataturk,* 109–117, 133–145.

62. Çalişlar, *Halide Edib,* 323–329, 334.

63. Zürcher, *Turkey,* 175.

64. Edib, *Turkish Ordeal,* 407. These paragraphs draw heavily on Adak, "Intersubjectivity," 200–215.

65. Zekeria, "Turkey's Fiery 'Joan of Arc' "; Robita Forbes, "Two Women Contend for a New 'Eden' in the East," *New York Times,* February 7, 1926, pp. 9, 22.

66. Russell B. Porter, "New Turkey Lauded at Williamstown," *New York Times,* August 4, 1928, p. 3.

67. Çalişlar, *Halide Edib,* 344–400.

68. Ibid., 409–418.

69. *Aksham,* September 8, 23, 27, and 30, 1939.

70. Çalişlar, 410, 419–421. Halide Edib, *The Clown and His Daughter* (London: George Unwin, 1935).

71. Adak, "Intersubjectivity," 210–217.

72. See her *Aksham* columns from February 2, 1944, to December 27, 1949.

73. Zürcher, *Turkey,* 213.

74. Ibid., 214–215. On the democratic transition see Kemal H. Karpat, *Turkey's Politics: The Transition to a Multi-Party System* (Princeton: Princeton University Press, 1959), 137–195, 223–242; John M. VanderLippe, *The Politics of Turkish Democracy: Ismet Inönü and the Formation of the Multi-Party System, 1938–1950* (Albany: State University of New York Press, 2005); Barin Kayaoğlu, "Strategic Imperatives, Democratic Rhetoric: The United States and Turkey, 1945–52," *Cold War History* 9, no. 3 (August 2009): 321–345.

75. "Election Law Passed," *Aksham,* March 2, 1950.

76. Çalişlar, *Halide Edib*, 448–449.

77. Caglar Keyder, *State and Class in Turkey* (New York: Verso, 1987); Ahmet Emin Yalman, *Turkey in My Time* (Norman: University of Oklahoma Press, 1956), 246–247.

78. Çalişlar, *Halide Edib*, 451–452.

79. Law 5816 Against Insult to Ataturk, July 25, 1951, set jail terms for public insult of the memory of Ataturk.

80. *Mor Salkimli Ev* (Istanbul: Ozgur Yayinlari, 1996) was first published in book form in 1963 after serialization in *Yeni Istanbul* in 1955. *The Turkish Ordeal* was published in Turkish in 1962 as *Turku'un Atesle Imtihani*. On self-censorship see Çalişlar, *Halide Edib*, 498–499.

81. Karpat, *Turkey's Politics*, 430. Much of this paragraph is drawn from this book.

82. Calislar, *Halide Edib*, 460–461; "Siyasi Vedaname," *Cumhuriyet*, 5 Ocak 1954 ["Farewell to Politics," *Republic*, January 5, 1954].

83. Baki Tezcan, "Lost in Historiography: An Essay on the Reasons for the Absence of a History of Limited Government in the Early Modern Empire," *Middle Eastern Studies* 45, no. 3 (May 2009): 477–505; Erol Köroğlu, "The Enemy Within: Aka Gunduz's *The Star of Dikmen* as an Example of Turkish National Romances," in Jale Parla and Murat Belge, eds., *Balkan Literatures in the Era of Nationalism* (Istanbul: Istanbul Bilgi University Press, 2009), 77–90.

5. David Ben-Gurion and Musa Kazim in Palestine

1. Ohannes Pacha Kouyoumdjian, *Le Liban à la veille et au début de la guerre: Mémoires d'un gouverneur, 1913–1915* (Paris: Centre d'histoire arménienne contemporaine, 2003).

2. Engin Akarli, *The Long Peace: Lebanon 1861–1920* (Berkeley: University of California Press, 1993); Akram Khater, *Inventing Home: Emigration, Gender and the Middle Class 1870–1920* (Berkeley: University of California Press, 2001).

3. Kouyoumdjian, *Le Liban*, 70–73, 85–88, 92–97, 133, 137–139, 144–151, 162–165.

4. Kouyoumdjian, *Le Liban*, 174; Aram Andonian, ed., *The Memoirs of Naim Bey* (Newtown Square, PA: The Armenian Historical Research Association, 1964 repr.), 9–10.

5. Kouyoumdjian, *Le Liban*, 111.

6. Ibid., 177.

7. Ibid., 184–185.

8. Ronald Grigor Suny, "Writing Genocide: The Fate of the Ottoman Armenians," in Ronald Grigor Suny, Fatma Müge Göçek, and Norman M. Naimark, eds., *A Question of Genocide: Armenians and Turks at the End of the*

Ottoman Empire (New York: Oxford University Press, 2011), 15–41. For an opposing view see M. Hakan Yavuz, "Contours of Scholarship on Armenian-Turkish Relations," *Middle East Critique* 20, no. 3 (Fall 2011): 231–251.

9. Vahakn N. Dadrian, *The History of the Armenian Genocide* (Providence, NJ: Berghahn Books, 1995), 179–181, 209, 221.

10. Andonian, *Memoirs of Naim Bey,* 3–4; Taner Akçam, *The Young Turks' Crime against Humanity* (Princeton: Princeton University Press, 2012), 125–226; Uğur Ümit Üngör, *The Making of Modern Turkey* (New York: Oxford University Press, 2011), 55–106.

11. Dadrian, *History of Armenian Genocide,* 222–225.

12. Andonian, *Memoirs of Naim Bey,* 8; Keith David Watenpaugh, *Being Modern in the Middle East* (Princeton: Princeton University Press, 2006), 124.

13. Armenian General Benevolent Union, *The Armenian General Benevolent Union: One Hundred Years of History,* vol. 1: *1906–1940,* ed. Raymond H. Kevorkian and Vahe Tachjian, trans. G. M. Goshgarian (Cairo, 2006), 63.

14. Nora Arissian, "The Armenian Genocide in the Syrian Press," in Richard Hovannisian, ed., *The Armenian Genocide: Cultural and Ethical Legacies* (New Brunswick, NJ: Transaction Publishers, 2007), 303–307.

15. Linda Schilcher, "The Famine in Syria 1915–1918," in J. Spagnolo, ed., *Problems of the Modern Middle East in Historical Perspective* (Reading, UK: Ithaca Press, 1992), 229–258.

16. Bedross Der Matossian, "The Armenians of Palestine 1918–48," *Journal of Palestine Studies* 41, no. 1 (Autumn 2011): 29–30; Conde de Ballobar, *Jerusalem in World War I* (New York: I. B. Tauris, 2011), 80; Salim Tamari, *Year of the Locust: A Soldier's Diary and the Erasure of Palestine's Ottoman Past* (Berkeley: University of California Press, 2011), 142; Hagop Arsenian and Arda Arsenian Ekmekji, "Surviving Massacre: Hagop Arsenian's Journey to Jerusalem, 1915–1916," *Jerusalem Quarterly* 49 (Spring 2012): 26–42.

17. Erez Manela, *The Wilsonian Moment: Self-Determination and the International Origins of Anticolonial Nationalism* (New York: Oxford University Press, 2007), 3–13, 63–75; Lerna Ekmekcioglu, "Surviving the New Turkey: Armenians in Post-Ottoman Istanbul (1918–1935)," unpublished book manuscript.

18. "Bolsheviki Seize State Buildings, Defying Karensky," *New York Times,* November 8, 1917, p. 1, and "Britain Favors Zionism: Balfour Gives Cabinet View in a Letter to Rothschild," *New York Times,* November 9, 1917, p. 3.

19. Shabtai Teveth, *Ben-Gurion: The Burning Ground, 1886–1948* (Boston: Houghton-Mifflin, 1987), 114.

20. Ibid., 3–38.

21. Robert Blobaum, "The Politics of Antisemitism in Fin-de-Siècle Warsaw," *Journal of Modern History* 73, no. 2 (June 2001): 275–306; David Vital, *Zionism: The Crucial Phase* (Oxford: Clarendon Press, 1987), 35–65; Anita

Shapira, *Land and Power: The Zionist Resort to Force, 1881–1948* (New York: Oxford University Press, 1992), 1–52.

22. David Ben-Gurion, "In Judea and Galilee," in Ben-Gurion, *Rebirth and Destiny of Israel* (New York: Philosophical Library, 1954), 5; Teveth, *Ben-Gurion,* 117.

23. Shapira, *Land and Power,* 62.

24. Teveth, *Ben-Gurion,* 44–51; Zachary Lockman, *Comrades and Enemies: Arab and Jewish Workers in Palestine, 1906–1948* (Berkeley: University of California Press, 1996), 1–110.

25. Ben-Gurion, "In Judea and Galilee," 22; Teveth, *Ben-Gurion,* 63.

26. Teveth, *Ben-Gurion,* 90.

27. Ibid., 96.

28. Yair Auron, *The Banality of Indifference: Zionism and the Armenian Genocide* (New Brunswick, NJ: Transaction Publishers, 2000), 162–179 (quote on p. 325); Teveth, *Ben-Gurion,* 106.

29. David Ben-Gurion, "Earning a Homeland," *Rebirth and Destiny of Israel,* trans. M. Nurock (New York: Philosophical Library, 1954), 3–6.

30. Jehuda Reinharz, *Chaim Weizmann: The Making of a Statesman* (New York: Oxford University Press, 1993), 1–59.

31. Vital, *Zionism,* 89–162, 211–235; Shapira, *Land and Power,* 83.

32. *The Letters and Papers of Chaim Weizmann, vol. 7-A,* Leonard Stein, ed. (Jerusalem: Israel Universities Press, 1975), 81–83, 114–115; Jonathan Schneer, *The Balfour Declaration* (New York: Random House, 2010), 333–346; Jehuda Reinharz, "The Balfour Declaration and Its Maker: A Reassessment," *Journal of Modern History* 64 (September 1994): 455–499; Tom Segev, *One Palestine, Complete,* trans. Haim Watzman (New York: Henry Holt, 2000), 36–43. Other scholars discount Weizmann's role. See Charles D. Smith, "The Invention of a Tradition: The Question of Arab Acceptance of the Zionist Right to Palestine during World War I," *Journal of Palestine Studies* 22, no. 2 (Winter 1993): 59 n.8.

33. A facsimile of Balfour's note to Rothschild may be found at: www.mfa.gov.il/MFA/Peace+Process/Guide+to+the+Peace+Process/the+Balfour+Declaration.htm

34. Isaiah Friedman, *The Question of Palestine* (New Brunswick, NJ: Transaction Publishers, 1973), 283.

35. Teveth, *Ben-Gurion,* 114–117. Ben-Gurion also appeared in the *New York Times* in "Peace Army for Palestine," April 27, 1917, p. 11.

36. David Ben-Gurion, *Letters to Paula,* trans. Aubrey Hodes (Pittsburgh: University of Pittsburgh Press, 1971), 34, letter of September 17, 1918; Shimon Peres and David Landau, *Ben-Gurion: A Political Life* (New York: Schocken/Random House, 2011), 29.

37. Teveth, *Ben-Gurion,* 132–134.

38. Ben-Gurion, *Letters to Paula,* 44, letter of March 3, 1919.

39. Teveth, *Ben-Gurion,* 220–238; Peres and Landau, *Ben-Gurion,* 38–40.

40. Ben-Gurion, *Rebirth and Destiny,* 47–48.

41. Benny Morris, *Righteous Victims: A History of the Zionist-Arab Conflict, 1881–2001* (New York: Vintage, 2001), 105.

42. "Sees Great Future for Jew and Arab," *New York Times,* December 12, 1917, p. 5.

43. Abigail Jacobson, *From Empire to Empire: Jerusalem between Ottoman and British Rule* (Syracuse: Syracuse University Press, 2011), 164–166. Variation on quote in Morris, *Righteous Victims,* 91.

44. Adam LeBor, *City of Oranges: An Intimate History of Arabs and Jews in Jaffa* (New York: W. W. Norton, 2007).

45. Michelle Campos, *Ottoman Brothers* (Stanford: Stanford University Press, 2010).

46. Teveth, *Ben-Gurion,* 96.

47. Doreen Ingrams, *Palestine Papers: 1917–1922: Seeds of Conflict,* (London: J. Murray, 1972) 33, quoting Public Record Office document, FO 406/40.

48. Rashid Khalidi, *The Iron Cage: The Story of the Palestinian Struggle for Statehood* (Boston: Beacon Press, 2006), 96.

49. Ilan Pappe, *The Rise and Fall of a Palestinian Dynasty: The Husaynis 1700–1948* (Berkeley: University of California Press, 2010), 111.

50. Population data is conflicting and inaccurate. See Jacobson, *From Empire to Empire,* 3–5, 22–52; Baruch Kimmerling and Joel Migdal, *Palestinians: The Making of a People* (Cambridge, MA: Harvard University Press, 1994), 25–26, 71; Rashid Khalidi, *Palestinian Identity* (New York: Columbia University Press, 1997), 59–61; Roberto Mazza, *Jerusalem from the Ottomans to the British* (New York: I. B. Tauris, 2009), 30–45.

51. Reprinted in Ann Mosely Lesch, *Arab Politics in Palestine, 1917–1939* (Ithaca: Cornell University Press, 1979), 85–86. Alternate translation in Y. Porath, *The Emergence of the Palestinian-Arab National Movement 1918–1929* (London: Frank Cass, 1974), 60–61.

52. Doreen Ingrams, *Palestine Papers,* 30–32: quoting from Public Record Office documents, FO 371/3383 and 371/3395.

53. Pappe, *Rise and Fall,* 127–139; Jacobson, *From Empire to Empire,* 22–52.

54. Translation of a French-language leaflet in George Antonius, *The Arab Awakening* (Safety Harbor, FL: Simon Publications, [1939] 2011), 435–436.

55. Jacobson, *From Empire to Empire,* 153–155; Muhammad Y. Muslih, *The Origins of Palestinian Nationalism* (New York: Columbia University Press, 1988), 158–163.

56. Muslih, *Origins of Palestinian Nationalism,* 178–185; Jacobson, *Empire to Empire,* 156–157; Porath, *Emergence,* 40, 42, 71.

57. United States Department of State, *Foreign Relations of the United States. Paris Peace Conference* (Washington, DC: U.S. Government Printing Office, 1919), Vol. III, 889–894 and Vol. IV, 164–170.

58. Isaiah Friedman, *The Question of Palestine, 1914–1918* (New York: Schocken Books, 1973), 325, and 292–308 on Jewish reactions; J. M. N. Jeffries, *The Balfour Declaration* (Beirut: The Institute for Palestine Studies, 1967).

59. Petition from Muslim and Christian delegates of Jerusalem, June 16, 1919. King-Crane Commission Digital Collection, http://dcollections.oberlin.edu/u?/kingcrane,2453 (accessed July 13, 2012).

60. Ibid. Recommendations of the King-Crane Commission with regard to Syria-Palestine and Iraq (August 29, 1919). Available at http://unispal.un.org/UNISPAL.NSF/0/392AD7EB00902A0C852570C000795153 (accessed July 13, 2012).

61. Porath, *Emergence,* 62. Shapira, *Land and Power,* 109.

62. Porath, *Emergence,* 100–101; Morris, *Righteous Victims,* 94–97; Lesch, *Arab Politics,* 201–204; Pappe, *Rise and Fall,* 196–202.

63. Porath, *Emergence,* 107–109, 125; Pappe, *Rise and Fall,* 208.

64. Porath, *Emergence,* 140–145; Pappe, *Rise and Fall,* 220–222.

65. "Correspondence with the Palestine Arab Delegation and the Zionist Organisation 1922," www.gwpda.org/1918p/palestine_zionist_1922.html (accessed July 14, 2012); "British White Paper of 1922," http://avalon.law.yale.edu/20th_century/brwh1922.asp (accessed July 18, 2012).

66. Pappe, *Rise and Fall,* 223–224.

67. Sahar Huneidi, "Was Balfour Policy Reversible? The Colonial Office and Palestine, 1921–23," *Journal of Palestine Studies* 27, no. 2 (Winter 1998): 23–41.

68. Morris, *Righteous Victims,* 107–108.

69. Najib Nasser, "Tasfiya al-Hisaab," *Al-Karmil,* June 19, 1927. Reproduced with comment in Qustandi Shomali, "Nagib Nassar l'intransigeant 1873–1948," *Revue d'études Palestiniennes* 2 (Winter 1995): 80–90.

70. Teveth, *Ben-Gurion,* 372–373; Segev, *One Palestine,* 304–311.

71. Morris, *Righteous Victims,* 112–122; Lesch, *Arab Politics,* 209–211; Segev, *One Palestine,* 314–327.

72. Public Record Office, "Extension of Imperial Preference to Palestine 1921–1931," CO 733/211/5, Musa Kazem Husseini to High Commissioner, September 18, 1931, Gale Publishing online archive, "Arab-Israeli Relations 1917–1970," 49–54. Available at www.gale.cengage.com.

73. Weldon C. Matthews, *Confronting an Empire, Constructing a Nation: Arab Nationalists and Popular Politics in Mandate Palestine* (London: I. B. Tauris, 2006), 122–134, 171.

74. Akram Zuayter, *al-Harakat al-wataniyah al-filastiniyah 1935–1939* (Beirut: Muassasat al-Dirasat al-Filastiniya, 1980).

75. Matthews, *Confronting an Empire*, 119–122.

76. Mark Tessler, *A History of the Israeli-Palestinian Conflict* (Bloomington: Indiana University Press, 1994), 170.

77. Matthews, *Confronting an Empire*, 68–74, 84–94, 123–124.

78. Ibid., 210–219; Lesch, *Arab Politics*, 214–215. The photo of Musa Kazim being beaten is in Walid Khalidi, *Before Their Diaspora: A Photographic History of the Palestinians, 1876–1948* (Washington, DC: Institute for Palestine Studies, 2010), 110.

79. Khalidi, *Iron Cage*, 88.

80. Pappe, *Rise and Fall*, 258; Lesch, *Arab Politics*; Porath, *Emergence*, 136.

81. Philip Mattar, *The Mufti of Jerusalem* (New York: Columbia University Press, 1988), 33–49.

82. Norman Bentwich, *For Zion's Sake: A Biography of Judah L. Magnes* (Philadelphia: The Jewish Publication Society of America, 1954), 178.

83. Menahem Kaufman, ed., *The Magnes-Philby Negotiations, 1929* (Jerusalem: The Magnes Press, 1998), 50–54.

84. David Ben-Gurion, *My Talks with Arab Leaders* (New York: Third Press, 1973), 18–21.

85. Morris, *Righteous Victims*, 122, 139–144.

86. Zuayter, *al-Harakat al-wataniyah*, 1, 14, 23–24; Matthews, *Confronting an Empire*, 171–195, 239, 243.

87. Zuayter, *al-Harakat al-wataniyah*, 41.

88. Lesch, *Arab Politics*, 216–221; Matthews, *Confronting an Empire*, 247–254; Morris, *Righteous Victims*, 130–132.

89. Zuayter, *al-Harakat al-wataniya*, 82–83, 92–93. The phrase for civil disobedience in Arabic is *asiyaan al-madani*.

90. Zuayter, *al-Harakat al-wataniyah*, 107–112.

91. Ted Swedenburg, *Memories of Revolt* (Minneapolis: University of Minnesota Press, 1995), 32.

92. Shapira, *Land and Power*, 275–281.

93. Robert Lansing, *The Peace Negotiations* (New York: Houghton-Mifflin, 1921), chapter 13. Available at www.gutenberg.org/cache/epub/10444 (accessed July 14, 2012); Senator William E. Borah's November 19, 1919, speech on the League of Nations is in Robert C. Byrd, *The Senate 1789–1989: Classic Speeches 1830–1993*, vol. 3, Wendy Wolff, ed. (Washington, DC: U.S. Government Printing Office), 569–573.

94. The March 1919 article from *Der Jude* is translated in Martin Buber, *A Land of Two Peoples*, Paul Mendes-Flohr, ed. (Chicago: University of Chicago Press, 1983), 39–41. I thank Sam Brody for introducing me to the pacifists of Brith Shalom.

95. Judith N. Shklar, *The Faces of Injustice* (New Haven: Yale University Press, 1990), 41.

96. Piotr Wróbel, "Jewish Warsaw before the First World War," *Polin Studies in Polish Jewry*, vol. 3 special issue, "The Jews in Warsaw," Antony Polonsky, ed. (Portland, OR: The Littman Library of Jewish Civilization, 1988): 156–187; Joshua D. Zimmerman, *Poles, Jews, and the Politics of Nationality* (Madison: University of Wisconsin Press, 2004), 126–190; Stephen D. Corrsin, *Warsaw before the First World War* (Boulder, CO: East European Monographs, 1989), 78–109; Ezra Mendelsohn, *Zionism in Poland* (New Haven: Yale University Press, 1981), 1–36.

97. Shapira, *Land and Power,* 60–82, 173–186. See p. 191: "the public regarded the ideas advocated by Brith Shalom . . . as an act bordering on treason."

98. Gilbert Aschar, *The Arabs and the Holocaust* (New York: Metropolitan Books, 2009), 35–50, 65–71, 104–121, 158–162.

6. Hasan al-Banna of Egypt

1. Anwar Sadat, *Revolt on the Nile* (New York: J. Day, 1957), 31–32, 48–50.

2. "Memorandum of Conversation between Shaikh Hassan Al Banna and Philip W. Ireland, First Secretary of Embassy," August 27, 1947. Document 833.00/8–2947, National Archives and Records Administration, College Park, Maryland. Hereafter "Memorandum of Conversation between Shaikh Hassan Al Banna and Philip W. Ireland." I thank Samer Shehata for alerting me to this document.

3. Albion Ross, "Moslem Brotherhood Leader Slain as He Enters Taxi in Cairo Street," *New York Times*, February 13, 1949, p. 1; "Assassin's Shot Fatal to Moslem Chieftain," *Los Angeles Times,* February 13, 1949, p. 13.

4. Gamal al-Banna, personal interview, Cairo, May 16, 2008. For a negative view of Banna see Gudrun Kraemer, *Hasan al-Banna* (New York: Oneworld, 2010); for a positive view see Brynjar Lia, *The Society of the Muslim Brothers in Egypt: The Rise of an Islamic Mass Movement 1928–1942* (Reading, UK: Ithaca Press, 1998).

5. Abd al-Fattah M. El-Awaisi, "Emergence of a Militant Leader: A Study of the Life of Hasan Al-Banna: 1906–1928," *Journal of South Asian and Middle Eastern Studies* 23, no. 1 (Fall 1998): 51.

6. Ellis Goldberg, "Peasants in Revolt: Egypt 1919," *International Journal of Middle East Studies* 24 (1992): 261–280; M. W. Daly, ed., *The Cambridge History of Egypt,* vol. 2 (New York: Cambridge University Press, 1998), 248–251; Donald M. Reid, "Political Assassination in Egypt, 1910–1954," *The International Journal of African Historical Studies* 15, no. 4 (1982): 628.

7. Hasan al-Banna, *Memoirs of Hasan Al Banna Shaheed,* trans. M. N. Shaikh (Karachi: International Islamic Publishers, 1981), 82. I have modified the translation for accuracy and idiom. See the Arabic edition: Hasan

al-Banna, *Mudhakkirat al-dawah wa al-daiyah* (Beirut: al-Maktab al-Islami, 1974), 27.

8. Izhak Musa Husaini, *The Moslem Brethren: The Greatest of Modern Islamic Movements* (Beirut: Khayats, 1956), 34. (Translation of 1952 Arabic original.)

9. Banna, *Memoirs,* 60.

10. Ibid., 84; Husaini, *Moslem Brethren,* 3.

11. Banna, *Memoirs,* 74; Heather J. Sharkey, *American Evangelicals in Egypt: Missionary Encounters in the Age of Empire* (Princeton: Princeton University Press, 2008), 96–148.

12. Banna, *Memoirs,* 109–111.

13. Ibid., 109–110.

14. Şükrü Hanioğlu, *Ataturk: An Intellectual Biography* (Princeton: Princeton University Press, 2011), 147–158; Nilüfer Göle, *The Forbidden Modern: Civilization and Veiling* (Ann Arbor: University of Michigan Press, 1997).

15. Malcolm H. Kerr, *Islamic Reform: The Political and Legal Theories of Muhammad Abduh and Rashid Rida* (Berkeley: University of California Press, 1966), 155–158.

16. Al-Shaykh Muhammad Rashid Rida, *Al-Khalifa* (al-Zahra al-Ilam al-Arabi, 1988); Mahmoud Haddad, "Arab Religious Nationalism in the Colonial Era: Rereading Rashid Rida's Ideas on the Caliphate," *Journal of the American Oriental Society* 117, no. 2 (April–June 1997): 253–277.

17. Banna, *Memoirs,* 113.

18. Ibid., 119; Richard P. Mitchell, *The Society of the Muslim Brothers* (New York: Oxford University Press, 1993), 5–6.

19. Jacques Berque, *Egypt: Imperialism and Revolution,* trans. Jean Stewart (New York: Praeger, 1972), 395.

20. Afaf Lutfi al-Sayyid Marsot, *Egypt's Liberal Experiment: 1922–1936* (Berkeley: University of California Press, 1977), 73–110.

21. Lia, *The Society of the Muslim Brothers in Egypt,* 53–75.

22. Banna, *Memoirs,* 124–126, 140.

23. Ibid., 127–129.

24. Ibid., 141–142; Mitchell, *The Society of the Muslim Brothers,* 8.

25. Banna, *Memoirs,* 156–157.

26. Johannes J. G. Jansen, "Hasan Al-Banna's Earliest Pamphlet," *Die Welt des Islams* 32 (1992): 257.

27. Husaini, *Moslem Brethren,* 11; Lia, *The Society of the Muslim Brothers in Egypt,* 60–72; Banna, *Memoirs,* 160–167.

28. Husaini, *Moslem Brethren,* 36.

29. Ihsan Abd al-Qaddus, "Al-Rajl alathi yatbihi nisf al-milyun," in As-sam Faris, ed., *Al-Imam al-Shahid Hasan al-Banna bi-aqlam muasirihi wa talamidhatih* (Amman: Dar Ammar, 2006), 134, 225.

30. Husaini, *Moslem Brethren*, 34.

31. Ziad Munson, "Islamic Mobilization: Social Movement Theory and the Egyptian Muslim Brotherhood," *The Sociological Quarterly* 42, no. 4 (Autumn 2001): 500–504.

32. Mitchell, *The Society of the Muslim Brothers*, 185, 193–194.

33. Lia, *The Society of the Muslim Brothers in Egypt*, 93–152.

34. Hasan al-Banna, "Nahwa al-Nur," in his *Majmuat Risail al-Imam al-Shahid Hasan al-Banna* (Beirut: Dar al-Nahhar, 1965), 166. The translation is my own. See also "Toward the Light," in *Five Tracts of Hasan Al-Banna (1906–1949)*, trans. Charles Wendell (Berkeley: University of California Press, 1978): 104. Wendell mistakenly dated the letter at 1947, when it was republished in an anthology. The 1936 date is mentioned by Banna in his *Mudhakkirat al-daawah*, 218–219, and in Mitchell, *The Society of the Muslim Brothers*, 15.

35. Banna, "Nahwa al-Nur," 168, 176–177; Wendell, *Five Tracts*, 106–107, 113.

36. Banna, "Nahwa al-Nur," 190–191; Wendell, *Five Tracts*, 124–125.

37. Banna, *Mudhakkirat al-dawah*, 217–218.

38. Mitchell, *The Society of the Muslim Brothers*, 234–236.

39. Frantz Fanon, *The Wretched of the Earth*, trans. Richard Philcox (New York: Grove Press, 2004), 8. Original French text published in 1961. William Roger Louis, *The British Empire in the Middle East 1945–1951* (Oxford: Clarendon Press, 1984), 226–231.

40. Banna, "Nahwa al-Nur," 180–181; Wendell, *Five Tracts*, 116, 119–120. The verses of the Quran cited were 49:13 and 49:10.

41. Beth Baron, *Egypt as a Woman* (Berkeley: University of California Press, 2005), 207–213; Leila Ahmed, *Women and Gender in Islam* (New Haven: Yale University Press, 1992), 189–202; Margot Badran, *Feminism in Islam* (Oxford: Oneworld, 2009).

42. Lia, *The Society of the Muslim Brothers in Egypt*, 235–247.

43. Ibid., 239–240; Mitchell, *The Society of Muslim Brothers*, 11–12, 328–329.

44. Lia, *The Society of the Muslim Brothers in Egypt*, 250–251.

45. Ibid., 249

46. Banna, *Memoirs*, 260. The speech was reprinted in the MB's weekly magazine, *Al-Nadhir*, on February 7, 1939, but not reprinted as a pamphlet until after Banna's death.

47. Hasan al-Banna, "Risalat al-mu'tamar al-khamis" [Message from the Fifth Congress], in *Majmuat*, 237–297.

48. Ibid., 256.

49. Ibid., 256, 258.

50. Ibid., 273.

51. Ibid., 296; Kraemer, *Hasan al-Banna*, 52–53.

52. Banna, *Memoirs*, 270–286.

53. Lia, *The Society of the Muslim Brothers in Egypt*, 260–267.

54. Afaf Lutfi Al-Sayyid Marsot, *A History of Modern Egypt*, 2nd ed. (New York: Cambridge University Press, 2007), 118–119; P. J. Vatikiotis, *The History of Modern Egypt*, 4th ed. (Baltimore: The Johns Hopkins University Press, 1991), 348–352.

55. Lia, *The Society of the Muslim Brothers in Egypt*, 256–271.

56. Husaini, *Moslem Brethren*, 92; Mitchell, *The Society of the Muslim Brothers*, 289–291; Joel Beinin and Zachary Lockman, *Workers on the Nile* (Princeton: Princeton University Press, 1987), 363–388.

57. Banna, *Memoirs*, 140.

58. The unit was named the Special Section *(al-nizam al-khass)* by the MB. Outsiders gave it the more sinister name of Secret Apparatus *(al-jihaz al-sirri)*. See Mitchell, *The Society of the Muslim Brothers*, 30.

59. Sadat, *Revolt on the Nile*, 48–49.

60. Gamal al-Banna, personal interview, Cairo, May 16, 2008.

61. Mitchell, *The Society of the Muslim Brothers*, 206.

62. Ibid., 48–49, 53–54.

63. Banna, *Memoirs*, 119–120.

64. Reid, "Political Assassination in Egypt," 632–636; Vatikiotis, *History of Modern Egypt*, 365–366.

65. "Memorandum of Conversation between Shaikh Hassan Al Banna and Philip W. Ireland."

66. Berque, *Egypt*, 600–604, 624–625, 652–654.

67. Ibid., 657.

68. Husaini, *Moslem Brethren*, 19–21; Mitchell, *The Society of the Muslim Brothers*, 37–52.

69. Mitchell, *The Society of the Muslim Brothers*, 58–71.

70. Rifaat al-Said, of the leftist Tagammu Party, is a prominent critic of Banna. See his *Hasan al-Banna: mata, kayfa, wa limatha?* [Hasan al-Banna: When, how, and why?] (Cairo: al-Ahali, 1990) and *Hasan al-Banna al-shaykh al-musallah* [Hasan al-Banna, the armed shaykh] (Cairo: Akhbar al-Yawm, 2004).

71. Robert O. Paxton, "The Five Stages of Fascism," *The Journal of Modern History* 70, no. 1 (March 1998): 1–23.

72. In 1942 the American minister Alexander Kirk supported British ambassador Miles Lampson's view that the king refused to declare war out of pro-Axis sympathy, not out of anticolonial nationalism. See *Foreign Relations of the United States 1942, The Near East and North Africa*, vol. 4 (Washington, DC: U.S. Government Printing Office, 1942), 63–70.

73. Louis, *British Empire*, 238–264; John Voll, "US Policy toward the Unity of the Nile Valley, 1945–1952," in Israel Gershoni and Meir Hatina,

eds., *Narrating the Nile: Politics, Cultures, Identities* (Boulder, CO: Lynne Rienner, 2008), 96–103; Peter Hahn, "National Security Concerns in US Policy toward Egypt, 1949–1956," in *The Middle East and the United States,* David W. Lesch, ed. (Boulder, CO: Westview Press, 2007), 75–78.

74. Joel Beinin, *The Dispersion of Egyptian Jewry* (Berkeley: University of California Press, 1998), 66–71.

75. Mitchell, *The Society of the Muslim Brothers,* 328.

76. Ziad Munson, "Islamic Mobilization: Social Movement Theory and the Egyptian Muslim Brotherhood," *The Sociological Quarterly* 42, no. 4 (Autumn 2001): 500–507; Selma Botman, *The Rise of Egyptian Communism, 1939–1970* (Syracuse: Syracuse University Press, 1988).

7. Comrade Fahd

1. According to historian Aziz Sbahi, who participated in the Wathbah, journalists chose the term to signify an important political event that fell short of a revolution. Telephone interview at his Ontario, Canada, home, April 3, 2009.

2. Hanna Batatu, *The Old Social Classes and the Revolutionary Movements of Iraq* (Princeton: Princeton University Press, 1978), 545.

3. Batatu, *Old Social Classes,* 33, 44–57, 274, 333–361; Charles Tripp, *A History of Iraq,* 2nd ed. (New York: Cambridge University Press, 2000), 108–131; Samira Haj, *The Making of Iraq 1900–1963* (Albany: State University of New York Press, 1997), 32–34.

4. "1,000,000 Take Part in Procession," *Iraq Times,* April 19, 1959, p. 3.

5. Joe Stork, "The Soviet Union, the Great Powers and Iraq"; Abdul-Salaam Yousif, "The Struggle for Cultural Hegmony during the Iraqi Revolution,"; and Sami Zubaida, "Community, Class and Minorities in Iraqi Politics," all in Robert A. Fernea and William Roger Louis, eds., *The Iraqi Revolution of 1958* (New York: I. B. Tauris, 1991), 95–105, 172–210.

6. Malik Saif, oral history quoted in Tareq Y. Ismael, *The Rise and Fall of the Communist Party of Iraq* (New York: Cambridge University Press, 2008), 63.

7. Baha ud-Din Nuri, known as Basim, was a Kurd who led the party until his arrest in 1953. The quote is from his 1992 memoir, translated in Ismael, *The Rise and Fall,* 44.

8. Walter Z. Laqueur, *Communism and Nationalism in the Middle East* (New York: Frederick A. Praeger, 1956), 189; Rami Ginat, "Soviet Policy towards the Arab World," *Middle Eastern Studies* 32, no. 4 (October 1996): 321–335; J. D. Hargreaves, "The Comintern and Anti-Colonialism: New Research Opportunities," *African Affairs* 92 (1993): 255–261; Jaan Pennar, "The Arabs, Marxism and Moscow: A Historical Survey," *Middle East Journal* 22, no. 4 (Autumn 1968): 433–447. Batatu (*Old Social Classes,* 985–986) is more skeptical of an American connection.

9. Yusuf Salman Yusuf, *Kitabat al-Rafiq Fahd* (Baghdad: al-Tariq al-Jadid, 1976), 473–474.

10. Zaki Khairi, introduction to Yusuf, *Kitabat al-Rafiq Fahd*, 6–7.

11. Gökhan Çetinsaya, *Ottoman Administration of Iraq, 1890–1908* (New York: Routledge, 2006), 1–3, 147–151. Of the 3 million Iraqis in 1920, more than half were Shii Arabs. See Charles Tripp, *A History of Iraq*, 2nd ed. (New York: Cambridge University Press, 2000), 31; The 1947 census counted 4.5 million total population: 51 percent Shi'i Arabs; 20 percent Sunni Arabs; 18 percent Sunni Kurds; 7 percent non-Muslims. See Batatu, *Old Social Classes*, 40.

12. Reidar Visser, *Basra, the Failed Gulf State* (Münster, Germany: Lit Verlag, 2005), 66–69.

13. Tripp, *A History of Iraq*, 40–45.

14. Visser, *Basra,* 120–125.

15. Written communication from Aziz Sbaiti, June 26, 2009. Sbaiti argued that Batatu's description of the meetings with Pyotr Vasili are drawn from unreliable British intelligence records.

16. Haj, *The Making of Iraq,* 3–39, 57–61, 70–71; Marion Farouk-Sluglett and Peter Sluglett, "Labor and National Liberation: The Trade Union Movement in Iraq, 1920–1958," *Arab Studies Quarterly* 5, no. 2 (Spring 1983): 139–147.

17. Quoted in Batatu, *Old Social Classes,* 368, quote from Abd al-Rahman al-Kawakibi, *Tabai al-Istibdad* [*The Attributes of Tyranny*] (Cairo, 1900), 71–72.

18. Quoted in Batatu, *Old Social Classes,* 370.

19. Ibid., 428–429.

20. Ibid., 429.

21. Freya Stark, *Baghdad Sketches* (New York: Dutton, 1938), 18, 113.

22. Freya Stark, *Beyond Euphrates* (London: J. Murray, 1951), 103.

23. Farouk-Sluglett and Sluglett, "Labor and National Liberation," 147–151.

24. Ismael, *Rise and Fall,* 20–24; Batatu, *Old Social Classes,* 431–433.

25. Joseph Sassoon, *Economic Policy in Iraq, 1932–1950* (New York: Routledge, 1987), 21–29; Stephen Helmsley Longrigg, *Iraq, 1900 to 1950* (London: Oxford University Press, 1953), 247–255, 269; Tripp, *History of Iraq,* 81–107.

26. Salim Tamari, "Najati Sidqi (1905–79): The Enigmatic Jerusalem Bolshevik," *Journal of Palestine Studies* 32, no. 2 (Winter 2003): 79–94; Hargreaves, "The Comintern and Anti-Colonialism," 255–261; Pennar, "The Arabs, Marxism and Moscow," 433–437.

27. Batatu, *Old Social Classes,* 492.

28. Yusuf, *Kitabat al-Rafiq Fahd,* 466. Irina had saved two letters and a watch from Yusuf. In a 1973 photo (ibid., 471) of Irina with her daughter

Susan, and two grandchildren, Susan bears a striking resemblance to her father (ibid., 468).

29. Batatu, *Old Social Classes,* 509. See also Kazim Habib and Zahdi al-Dawudi, *Fahd wa al-haraka al-wataniya fi al-Iraq* [Fahd and the Nationalist Movement in Iraq] (Beirut: Dar al-Konooz al-Adabiya, 2003), 456–486.

30. al-Rafiq Sarim, introduction to Fahd's "Hizb Shuyui, Laa Ishtiraqiya Dimuqratiya" [A communist party, not democratic socialism], in Yusuf, *Kitabat al-Rafiq Fahd,* 23, 28, 30.

31. Batatu, *Old Social Classes,* 496.

32. Yusuf, *Kitabat al-Rafiq Fahd,* 37, 55, 65, 66.

33. Ismael, *Rise and Fall,* 31.

34. Batatu, *Old Social Classes,* 512–515; Ismael, *Rise and Fall,* 27–29. Ismael dates this meeting to February 1944.

35. Batatu, *Old Social Classes,* 416–417, 493–494, 502, 520–521; Abbas Shiblak, *Iraqi Jews: A History of Mass Exodus* (London: Saqi, 2005), 36; Sassoon, *Economic Policy in Iraq,* 3–4.

36. Batatu, *Social Origins,* 515–519.

37. "A Free Homeland and a Happy People: Our National Cause," booklet of 52 pages issued by the Iraqi Communist Party (ICP), April 1945, translation as enclosure to dispatch 783 of June 21, 1945, American Legation, Baghdad. Confidential U.S. State Department Central Files, Iraq, 1945–1949, Mi 788, box 1.

38. Loy W. Henderson to Secretary of State, January 31, 1945 (890G.00/1–3145). Confidential U.S. State Department Central Files, Iraq, 1945–1949, Mi 788, box 1.

39. Sami Michael, interviewed in *Forget Baghdad,* documentary film by Samir (Arab Film Distribution, 2002). Michael was forced to flee Iraq in 1946 and became a well-known writer in Israel.

40. Aziz Sbahi, *Uqud min Tarikh al-Hizb al-Shuyui al-Iraqi* (Dimashq: Manshurat al-Thiqafa al-Jadida, 2002), 304.

41. Batatu, *Old Social Classes,* 608, 653–656.

42. Orit Bashkin, *New Babylonians: A History of Jews in Modern Iraq* (Stanford: Stanford University Press, 2012), chapter 4. The 1947 census counted 113,000 urban Jews and 4,000 rural ones. See Batatu, *Old Social Classes,* 40.

43. Batatu, *Old Social Classes,* 651; Shiblak, *Iraqi Jews,* 36, 61, 79–84.

44. Batatu, *Old Social Classes,* 481–482, 645–646; quote is on p. 645.

45. Ibid., 616–622.

46. Zohair Jazairy, personal interview, Washington, DC, August 8, 2008.

47. Tareq Ismael, telephone interview, February 5, 2009.

48. Schoenrich to Secretary of State, January 21, 1946 (890G.00B/1–2146); Moose to Secretary of State, January 23, 1947 (890G.00B/1–2347); Moreland to Secretary of State, June 21, 1945 (890G.00/6–2145). Confidential U.S. State Department Central Files, Iraq, 1945–1949, Mi 788, box 1.

49. "Mustalzamat Kifahna al-Watani," in Yusuf, *Kitabat al-Rafiq Fahd*, 217–233; on its popularity see Khairi's introduction to Yusuf, *Kitabat al-Rafiq Fahd*, 13, and Sbahi, *Uqud min Tarikh al-Hizb*, 286–290, 294–302, 305–308; Orit Bashkin, *The Other Iraq: Pluralism and Culture in Hashemite Iraq* (Stanford: Stanford University Press, 2009), 52–104; Eric Davis, *Memories of State: Politics, History, and Collective Identity in Modern Iraq* (Berkeley: University of California Press, 2005), 55–98.

50. Interviews of Sami Michael and Moussa Houri in *Forget Baghdad*; Batatu, *Old Social Classes*, 531–532; ICP, *Shuhada' al-Hizb, Shuhada' al-watan* (Beirut: Dar Konooz, 2001), 13, 15.

51. Batatu, *Old Social Classes*, 533, 624.

52. Ibid., 533–536; Sbahi, *Uqud min Tarikh al-Hizb*, 311–315.

53. Batatu, *Old Social Classes*, 537–538; Sasson Somekh, *Baghdad Yesterday: The Making of an Arab Jew* (Jerusalem: Ibis, 2007), 123–124.

54. Orit Bashkin, *The Other Iraq*, 101.

55. Sbahi, *Uqud min Tarikh al-Hizb*, 318.

56. Ibid., 318–319; Tareq Ismael, telephone interview, February 5, 2009.

57. Batatu, *Old Social Classes*, 608.

58. Yusuf, *Kitabat al-Rafiq Fahd*, 463; Batatu, *Social Origins*, 544.

59. Sbahi, *Uqud min Tarikh al-Hizb*, 331. Aziz al-Hajj, who later left the party, argues that Fahd exerted little influence in the Wathbah. See his *Al-Shahada lil-Tarikh* (London: Al-Rafid Publishing, 2002), 100–102.

60. Sassoon, *Economic Policy in Iraq*, 14, 70–73.

61. Batatu, *Old Social Classes*, 551.

62. Ismael, *Rise and Fall*, 39; Batatu, *Old Social Classes*, 553.

63. The foregoing descriptions of January 27 events by Husni and al-Hajj are found in al-Hajj, *Al-Shahada lil-Tarikh*, 99–103.

64. Sbahi, *Uqud min Tarikh al-Hizb*, 341.

65. Batatu, *Old Social Classes*, 552–557.

66. Somekh, *Baghdad, Yesterday*, 136; Abdul-Salaam Yousif, "The Struggle for Cultural Hegemony during the Iraqi Revolution," in Fernea and Louis, *Iraqi Revolution of 1958*, 174.

67. Sbahi, *Uqud min Tarikh al-Hizb*, 338.

68. Ibid., 342–361.

69. In addition to Sbahi cited above, this account draws on Batatu, *Old Social Classes*, 625–627; Haj, *Making of Iraq*, 94–96, 99–103.

70. Haj, *The Making of Iraq*, 103.

71. Sbahi, *Uqud min Tarikh al-Hizb*, 374, and interview, April 3, 2009.

72. Shuhada al-Hizb, *Shuhada al-Watan* (Beirut: Hizb al-Shuyui al-Iraqi, 2001), 39; Tripp, *History of Iraq*, 122–128. Sbahi, *Uqud min Tarikh al-Hizb*, 403–407; Jasim Haddad, "His Royal Hanging . . . ," *al-Mada* (online newspaper) 6:1465, March 26, 2009, p. 12, www.almadapaper.net.

73. Batatu, *Old Social Classes*, 568–569; United States National Archives (USNA). Confidential U.S. State Department Central Files, Iraq 1945–1949, Mi 488/2, 890G.00B/2–1749, "Trials by Court Martial of Iraqi Communists . . . Baghdad, Feb. 17, 1949," with translations of official press release and *Al-Shaab* newspaper.

74. Ismael, *Rise and Fall*, ix–x.

75. USNA, Confidential U.S. State Department Central Files, Iraq 1945–1949, Mi 488/2, 890G.00B/3–1449, "Police Chief's Statement on Communist Movement in Iraq," Baghdad, March 14, 1949. Quotes interview with Police Chief Ali Khalid in *Iraq Times*.

76. Yousif, "Struggle for Cultural Hegemony," 175–177; Batatu, *Old Social Classes*, 569, 454. For a critical assessment of communism's hegemony see Eric Davis, "History for the Many or History for the Few? The Historiography of the Iraqi Working Class," in Zachary Lockman, ed., *Workers and Working Classes in the Middle East* (Albany: State University of New York Press, 1994), 271–301.

77. Laqueur, *Communism and Nationalism in the Middle East*, 202; Fernea and Louis, *Iraqi Revolution of 1958*, 48, 54, 142.

78. Bashkin, *The Other Iraq*, 103–111.

79. Batatu, *Old Social Classes*, 802.

80. Elie Kedourie, *Arabic Political Memoirs and Other Studies* (London: Cass, 1974), 179–181.

81. Norman Daniel, "Contemporary Perceptions of the Revolution in Iraq on 14 July 1958," in Fernea and Louis, *Iraqi Revolution of 1958*, 10–12, 22–24.

82. Uriel Dann, *Iraq under Qassem: A Political History, 1958–1963* (New York: Praeger, 1969), 29.

83. Kanan Makiya, *The Monument* (Berkeley: University of California Press, [1991] 2004), 78–88; Abd al-Rahman Munif, "The Monument of Freedom," *MIT Electronic Journal of Middle East Studies* 7 (Spring 2007): 117–155.

84. Johan Franzen, *Red Star over Iraq* (New York: Columbia University Press, 2011), 92–96; Batatu, *Old Social Classes*, 806.

85. Batatu, *Old Social Classes*, 837–842; Dann, *Iraq under Qassem*, 4, 22, 28–29, 40–42.

86. Batatu, *Old Social Classes*, 808–890, and Marion Farouk-Sluglett and Peter Sluglett, *Iraq since 1958: From Revolution to Dictatorship* (London: I. B. Tauris, [1987] 2003), 1–84.

87. Dann, *Iraq under Qassem*, 210–225, 237–241.

88. Ibid., 225–233, 250; Batatu, *Old Social Classes*, 866–909, 951, 958; Haj, *Making of Iraq*, 111–139.

89. Farouk-Sluglett and Sluglett, *Iraq since 1958*, 54–56, 63–64.

90. Haj, *Making of Iraq*, 111–127; Farouk-Sluglett and Sluglett, *Iraq since 1958*, 74–75.

91. Dann, *Iraq under Qassem*, 315. Dann cites Hajj from *World Marxist Review* (November 1963): 36–43.

92. Quote in *New York Times* cited by Haj in *Making of Iraq*, 191 n.61; "Fulbright Says West Has No Policy on 'Most Dangerous' Crisis in Iraq," *Washington Post*, April 29, 1959; Tripp, *History of Iraq*, 142–162; Nathan J. Citino, "Middle East Cold Wars: Oil and Arab Nationalism in U.S.-Iraqi Relations, 1958–1961," in Kathryn C. Statler and Andrew L. Johns, eds., *The Eisenhower Administration, the Third World, and the Globalization of the Cold War* (Lanham, MD: Rowman & Littlefield, 2006), 245–269; Carol R. Saivetz, "The Soviet Union and the Middle East, 1956–1958," in Fernea and Louis, *Iraqi Revolution of 1958*, 221–244; Dann, *Iraq under Qassem*, 233.

93. "Introduction" and Carol R. Saivetz, "The Soviet Union and the Middle East, 1956–1958," in Louis and Owen eds., *A Revolutionary Year*, 1–13, 221–244; Haj, *Making of Iraq*, 34; Batatu, *Old Social Classes*, 33, 48–49.

94. Batatu, *Old Social Classes*, 974–982; Farouk-Sluglett and Sluglett, *Iraq since 1958*, 84.

95. Batatu, *Old Social Classes*, 983–989; Farouk-Sluglett and Sluglett, *Iraq since 1958*, 85–86.

96. Geoff Eley, *Forging Democracy: The History of the Left in Europe, 1850–2000* (New York: Oxford University Press, 2000).

97. Joel Beinin, *Workers and Peasants in the Modern Middle East* (New York: Cambridge University Press, 2001), 114–141; Batatu, *Old Social Classes*, 321.

8. Akram al-Hourani and the Baath Party in Syria

1. Akram al-Hourani, *Mudhakkirat Akram al-Hourani*, 4 vols. (Cairo: Maktabat Madbuli, 2000), 2:1420.

2. Stephanie Cronin, "Resisting the new state: the rural poor, land and modernity in Iran, 1921–1941," in S. Cronin, ed. *Subalterns and Social Protest* (New York: Routledge, 2008), 141–170; Ted Swedenburg, "The Role of the Palestinian Peasantry in the Great Revolt (1936–1939)," in Edmund Burke III and Ira M. Lapidus, eds., *Islam, Politics and Social Movements* (Berkeley: University of California Press, 1988), 169–203.

3. Doreen Warriner, *Land Reform and Development in the Middle East* (New York: Oxford University Press, 1962), 7–13; Joel Beinin, *Workers and Peasants in the Modern Middle East* (New York: Cambridge University Press, 2001), 117–122; Farhad Kazemi and John Waterbury, *Peasants and Politics in the Modern Middle East* (Miami: Florida International University Press, 1991); Joel Gordon, *Nasser's Blessed Movement* (Cairo: The American Uni-

versity in Cairo Press, 1996), 19–31, 58–62; Jacques Berque, *Egypt: Imperialism and Revolution* (New York: Praeger, 1972), 662–670.

4. Dietrich Rueschemeyer, Evelyne Huber Stevens, and John Stephens, *Capitalist Development and Democracy* (Chicago: University of Chicago Press, 1992), 40–78, 269–302; David Waldner, personal interview, July 10, 2009, Washington DC.

5. Jonathan P. Owen, "Akram al-Hourani: A Study of Syrian Politics, 1943–1954" (PhD diss., Johns Hopkins University, 1992), 289–290.

6. James A. Reilly, *A Small Town in Syria: Ottoman Hama in the Eighteenth and Nineteenth Centuries* (New York: Peter Lang, 2002), 29.

7. Izz al-Din Diyab, *Akram al-Hurani . . . kama arifuhu* (Beirut: Bisan, 1998), 15–24; Dick Douwes, *Ottomans in Syria: A History of Justice and Oppression* (New York: I. B. Tauris, 2000), 152–187, 211–217; Reilly, *Small Town in Syria*, 93–116, 124–138.

8. Douwes, *Ottomans in Syria*; Hanna Batatu, *Syria's Peasantry, the Descendants of Its Lesser Notables, and Their Politics* (Princeton: Princeton University Press, 1999), 40.

9. Owen, "Akram al-Hourani," 9–10.

10. Hourani, *Mudhakkirat*, 1:68; Sami al-Jundi quoted in Hamdan Hamdan, *Akram al-Hurani . . . Rajil lil-Tarikh* (Beirut: Bayyan, 1996), 16.

11. Hourani, *Mudhakkirat,* 1:190–199. Hourani omitted mention that the SSNP leader, Antun Saadeh, adopted fascist symbols and methods.

12. Diyab, *Akram al-Hurani*, 25–42.

13. Ibid., 5, 42. Sami al-Jundi corroborates Diyab's view in his *Al-Baath* (Beirut, 1969), 62–63, cited by Nabil M. Kaylani, "The Rise of the Syrian Baath, 1940–1958: Political Success, Party Failure," *International Journal of Middle East Studies* 3 (1972): 7–9.

14. Hourani, *Mudhakkirat,* 1:245.

15. Ibid., 1:256–257; Batatu, *Syria's Peasantry,* 124–125.

16. Eid al-Fitr is the Muslim holiday ending the fasting month of Ramadan. On the campaign and election see Hourani, *Mudhakkirat,* 1:255–267.

17. Hourani, *Mudhakkirat,* 1:269; Philip S. Khoury, *Syria and the French Mandate* (Princeton: Princeton University Press, 1987), 254–261, 417–422, 598–604.

18. Owen, "Akram al-Hourani," 50–51; Joshua M. Landis, "Nationalism and the Politics of Za'ama: The Collapse of Republican Syria, 1945–1949" (PhD diss., Princeton University, 1997), 190; Gordon H. Torrey, *Syrian Politics and the Military 1945–1958* (Columbus, OH: Ohio State University Press, 1964), 81; Patrick Seale, *The Struggle for Syria: A Study in Post-War Arab Politics, 1945–1958*, new ed. (New Haven: Yale University Press, 1987), 31–33.

19. John F. Devlin, *The Baath Party: A History from Its Origins to 1966* (Stanford, CA: Hoover Institution Press, 1976), 14–15.

20. Ibid., 25; Patrick Seale, *Asad: The Struggle for the Middle East* (Berkeley: University of California Press, 1988), 30–37.

21. Owen, "Akram al-Hourani," 52–53.

22. Landis, "Nationalism," 193–210.

23. Seale, *Struggle for Syria,* 30.

24. Hourani, *Mudhakkirat,* 1:808–809.

25. Ibid., 1:809.

26. Owen, "Akram al-Hourani," 39–41; Seale, *Struggle for Syria,* 38–39; Batatu, *Syrian Peasantry,* 127.

27. Landis, "Nationalism," 322–324; Seale, *Struggle for Syria,* 33–34; Hourani claims there was no violence to justify army intervention in *Mudhakkirat,* 1:859–863.

28. Miles Copeland, *The Game of Nations* (London: Weidenfeld and Nicolson, 1969), 34–43; Douglas Little, "Cold War and Covert Action: The United States and Syria, 1945–1958," *Middle East Journal* 44, no. 1 (Winter 1990): 51–56.

29. Seale, *Struggle for Syria,* 42–45; Tabitha Petran, *Syria* (New York: Praeger, 1972), 96; Owen, "Akram al-Hourani," 65–70; Landis, "Nationalism," 344–357; Torrey, *Syrian Politics,* 139 n.3.

30. Owen, "Akram al-Hourani," 93–100; Diyab, *Akram al-Hurani,* 53. See also Hourani's defense of Rashid Ali in *Mudhakkirat,* 1:865, and Copeland (*Game of Nations,* 43) on the U.S. ambassador's belief that the coup would jump-start democracy in Syria.

31. Hourani, *Mudhakkirat,* 884, 2:1028.

32. Batatu, *Syria's Peasantry,* 6, 29, 41, 62–63. 67–68; Seale, *Asad,* 44.

33. Hourani, *Mudhakkirat,* 1:885–886; Petran, *Syria,* 98; Owen, "Akram al-Hourani," 79; Batatu, *Syria's Peasantry,* 86–87.

34. Hourani, *Mudhakkirat,* 2:1087, 1090.

35. Sibai, like Hasan al-Banna in Egypt, favored republicanism. Unlike Banna, he was attracted to socialist ideas. He renamed the Syrian Brotherhood the Islamic Socialist Front.

36. Hourani, *Mudhakkirat,* 2:1100–1120; Petran, *Syria,* 98; Seale, *Struggle for Syria,* 76–86. Seale believed soldiers who claimed that Hourani proposed the coup; Hourani denied it in a 1971 interview with Petran; Owen ("Akram al-Hourani," 81–92) agrees with Petran.

37. Naziha al-Homsi, *al-Jinnah al-Daiya* (2003), 36–38; Owen, "Akram al-Hourani," 78–79.

38. Hourani, *Mudhakkirat,* 2:1189.

39. Owen, "Akram al-Hourani," 86–92; Batatu, *Syrian Peasantry,* 111, 124–129.

40. Seale, *Asad,* 43.

41. Diyab, *Akram al-Hurani,* 54–55.

42. Ibid., 58–60.

43. Owen, "Akram al-Hourani," 113–115. Quote is from *al-Fayha*, excerpted in a July 5, 1950, report by an American diplomat. Hourani, *Mudhakkirat*, 2:1198–1199.

44. Batatu emphasizes this point in *Syria's Peasantry*, 126.

45. Hourani, *Mudhakkirat*, 2:1210–1224.

46. Batatu, *Syria's Peasantry*, 124–130 (quote on p. 128 is from a 1985 interview with Batatu); Devlin, *Baath Party*, 57; Seale, *Asad*, 41–44.

47. Steven Heydemann, *Authoritarianism in Syria* (Ithaca: Cornell University Press, 1999), 49; Petran, *Syria*, 99–100; Seale, *Struggle for Syria*, 93–97.

48. *Al-Nasr*, October 30, 1950, quoted in Hourani, *Mudhakkirat*, 2:1192.

49. Hourani, *Mudhakkirat*, 2:1315–1340.

50. Seale, *Struggle for Syria*, 120; Heydemann, *Authoritarianism in Syria*, 66; Petran, *Syria*, 101. Batatu (*Syrian Peasantry*, 128) claims the ASP had 10,000 members. Other estimates were as low as 1,500.

51. Albion Ross, "Landlords of Syria Launch Protest against Bill to Curb New Holdings," *New York Times*, August 9, 1951, p. 8; Owen, "Akram al-Hourani," 152–153.

52. *Al-Hawadith*, September 19, 1951, quoted in Hourani, *Mudhakkirat*, 2:1423.

53. Batatu (*Syria's Peasantry*, 128) estimated the crowd at 40,000; the editor of *Al-Hawadith* estimated it at 10,000. See Hourani, *Mudhakkirat*, 2:1423.

54. Hourani, *Mudhakkirat*, 2:1420–1422.

55. Warriner, *Land Reform*, 101–103, 108–109.

56. al-Homsi, *al-Janna al-Daiya*, 61, 75.

57. David Waldner, *State Building and Late Development* (Ithaca: Cornell University Press, 1999), 74–94; Warriner, *Land Reform*, 109–112; Heydemann, *Authoritarianism in Syria*, 30–54.

58. Seale, *Struggle for Syria*, 176; Hourani, *Mudhakkirat*, 2:1475–1496.

59. Batatu, *Syria's Peasantry*, 142.

60. Devlin, *Baath Party*, 2, 13, 25.

61. Hourani, *Mudhakkirat*, 2:1594–1595.

62. Seale, *Struggle for Syria*, 176–177; Heydemann, *Authoritarianism in Syria*, 51–54; Hourani, *Mudhakkirat*, 2:1631–1637.

63. Itzchak Weismann, "The Politics of Popular Religion: Sufis, Salafis, and Muslim Brothers in 20th-Century Hamah," *International Journal of Middle East Studies* 37 (2005): 50–54.

64. Hourani, *Mudhakkirat*, 2:1642.

65. Ibid., 1675; Seale, *Struggle for Syria*, 182–185. Heydemann (*Authoritarianism in Syria*, 75) says nineteen Baath seats; Seale (*Struggle for Syria*, 182–185) says twenty-two seats; Petran (*Syria*, 108) says sixteen seats.

66. Heydemann, *Authoritarianism in Syria*, 51–54.

67. Kaylani, "The Rise of the Syrian Baath," 17–18.

68. Petran, *Syria*, 113.

69. Hourani, *Mudhakkirat*, 3:1923–1924.

70. Seale, *Struggle for Syria*, 219–220.

71. Ibid., 263–282.

72. Sam Pope Brewer, "Syria Reported Forming a Cabinet," *New York Times*, December 31, 1956, p. 3; Hanson W. Baldwin, "Syria: Middle East Proving Ground," *New York Times Magazine*, February 3, 1957, p. 178.

73. Salim Yaqub, *Containing Arab Nationalism* (Chapel Hill: University of North Carolina Press, 2004), 119–135.

74. Hourani, *Mudhakkirat*, 3:2345–2346, 2386–2387, 2430–2432, 2445–2453; Seale, *Struggle for Syria*, 283–306; Yaqub, *Containing Arab Nationalism*, 147–180; Douglas Little, "Cold War and Covert Action: The United States and Syria, 1945–1958," *Middle East Journal* 44, no. 1 (Winter 1990): 51, 69–74; David W. Lesch, "The 1957 American-Syrian Crisis: Globalist Policy in a Regional Reality," in David W. Lesch, ed., *The Middle East and the United States* (Boulder, CO: Westview Press, 2007), 106–116.

75. Hourani, *Mudhakkirat*, 3:2456–2464.

76. Ibid., 3:2526, 2543.

77. Ibid., 3:2532.

78. Ibid., 4:2802–2817, 2845–2853.

79. Devlin, *Baath Party*, 28–37; Batatu, *Syria's Peasantry*, 142; Hourani, *Mudhakkirat*, 2:1597.

80. Hourani, *Mudhakkirat*, 4:3047.

81. Mohammad Ali Atassi, personal interview, Washington, DC, July 2009. See the English homepage of the Hourani website launched in 2011: http://akram-alhourani.com/index_EN.htm. Translation is altered to follow that of Sahih, at: http://corpus.quran.com/translation.jsp?chapter=33&verse=23.

82. Seale, *Asad*, 47–48.

83. Anecdotal evidence from multiple unrelated sources, including Syrian historian Joshua Landis, May 2009.

84. Seale, *Struggle for Syria*, 40.

85. Ghassan al-Imam, "Autobiographies: Is Staying Silent Better Than Telling Lies?" *Asharq Alawsat Online*, July 7, 2005, www.aawsat.com/english/news.asp?section=2&id=725 (accessed March 3, 2010).

86. Owen, "Akram al-Hourani," 1–10.

87. Kaylani, "Rise of the Syrian Baath," 7.

9. Abu Iyad

1. David Hirst, *The Gun and the Olive Branch* (New York: Harcourt Brace Jovanovich, 1977), 333.

2. United Nations 2283rd General Plenary Meeting, November 13, 1974, paragraph 62. Available at http://unispal.un.org/unispal.nsf/udc.htm (accessed January 17, 2011).

3. "Israel Honors Her Dead at Tel Aviv Airport Rite," *New York Times,* September 8, 1972, p. 12; *Jerusalem Post,* September 8, 1972, p. 3. *New York Times* editorials on September 6 and 7 also referenced Hitler. Israel's oldest daily newspaper, *Haaretz,* used the phrase "murderous organization" in these first days. Prime Minister Golda Meir also referenced the Holocaust, in Simon Reeve, *One Day in September* (New York: Faber and Faber, 2000), 131–132.

4. Abou Iyad, *Palestinien sans patrie: Entretiens avec Eric Rouleau* [Abu Iyad: A Palestinian without a country] (Paris: Fayolle, 1978), 8–17. Other editions: Abu Iyad, *Filastini bi-la huwiyah: liqaat maa al-katib Arik Rulu,* trans. Nasir Muruwwah (Muassassat al-Shuhada al-Filastiniyah, 1979); Abu Iyad with Eric Rouleau, *My Home, My Land,* trans. Linda Butler Koseoglu (New York: Times Books, 1981). I have primarily used the English translation, with reference to the French original.

5. Janet L. Abu-Lughod, "Demographic Characteristics of the Palestinian Population: Relevance for Planning Palestine Open University," unpublished manuscript, Paris, UNESCO, June 30, 1980. Available at unesdoc.unesco.org /images/0008/000822/082220eb.pdf (accessed September 9, 2011).

6. Abu Iyad with Rouleau, *My Home, My Land,* 3.

7. Ibid., 4.

8. Rochelle A. Davis, personal interview, Georgetown University, December 8, 2010; Rochelle A. Davis, *Palestinian Village Histories: Geographies of the Displaced* (Stanford: Stanford University Press, 2010); Ghassan Kanafani, "Returning to Haifa," in *Palestine's Children,* trans. Barbara Harlow and Karen E. Riley (Boulder, CO: Lynne Reinner, 2000), 149–196; Isabelle Humphries and Laleh Khalili, "Gender of Nakba Memory," in Ahmad H. Sadi and Lila Abu-Lughod, eds., *Nakba: Palestine 1948 and the Claims of Memory* (New York: Columbia University Press, 2007), 222.

9. Abou Iyad, *Palestinien sans patrie,* 32.

10. Frances S. Hasso, "Modernity and Gender in Arab Accounts of the 1948 and 1967 Defeats," *International Journal of Middle East Studies* 32 (2000): 491–510.

11. Adam LeBor, *City of Oranges: An Intimate History of Arabs and Jews in Jaffa* (New York: W. W. Norton, 2007), 48–61; Michelle U. Campos, *Ottoman Brothers: Muslims, Christians, and Jews in Early 20th-Century Palestine* (Stanford: Stanford University Press, 2011).

12. Abu Iyad with Rouleau, *My Home, My Land,* 9.

13. Haim Levenberg, *The Military Preparations of the Arab Community in Palestine, 1945–1948* (London: Frank Cass, 1993), 127.

14. Abu Iyad with Rouleau, *My Home, My Land*, 9.

15. Levenberg, *Military Preparations*, 240.

16. Abu Iyad with Rouleau, *My Home, My Land*, 12.

17. William B. Ziff, *The Rape of Palestine* (New York: Longmans, Green and Co., 1938), 475.

18. Menachem Begin, *The Revolt* (Los Angeles: Nash Publishing, [1948] 1972), 41.

19. "Golda Meir Scorns Soviets," *Washington Post and Times Herald,* June 16, 1969, p. A15.

20. Mahmoud Darwish, *Journal of an Ordinary Grief,* trans. Ibrahim Muhawi (Brooklyn: Archipelago Books, 2010), 129. (Original Arabic edition published in Beirut, 1973.)

21. Hasan Khalil Husayn, *Abu Iyad, Salah Khalaf: safahat majhulah min hayatihi* (Amman, 1991), 43, 108; Dawud Ibrahim, *Salah Khalaf, al-muallim al-muharib: hayatahu, nidalahu, istashadahu.* Batulat filastiniya series no. 2. (Jerusalem: Abu Arafa, 1991), 12, 21.

22. Abu Iyad with Rouleau, *My Home, My Land*, 15–16.

23. Alan Hart, *Arafat: A Political Biography,* 4th ed. (Bloomington: Indiana University Press, 1989), 25–38, 67–68, 86–88; Andrew Gowers and Tony Walker, *Behind the Myth: Yasser Arafat and the Palestinian Revolution* (New York: Olive Branch Press, 1992), 13–15.

24. Ibrahim, *Salah Khalaf,* 8; Abu Iyad with Rouleau, *My Home, My Land,* 34.

25. Gowers and Walker, *Behind the Myth,* 26; Yezid Sayigh, *Armed Struggle and the Search for State: The Palestinian National Movement, 1949–1993* (New York: Oxford University Press, 1997), 84–86.

26. Gowers and Walker, *Behind the Myth,* 26; Sayigh, *Armed Struggle,* 84–88; Abu Iyad with Rouleau, *My Home, My Land,* 33; Michael C. Hudson, "Developments and Setbacks in the Palestinian Resistance Movement, 1967–1971," *Journal of Palestine Studies* 1, no. 3 (Spring 1972): 78.

27. Helena Cobban, *The Palestinian Liberation Organisation: People, Power, Politics* (New York: Cambridge University Press, 1984), 16.

28. Abu Iyad with Rouleau, *My Home, My Land,* 40.

29. Ibrahim, *Salah Khalaf,* 7, 20–21; Husayn, *Abu Iyad,* 28, 42–43, 50–72, 109; Abou Daoud with Gilles du Jonchay, *Palestine: De Jérusalem à Munich* (Paris: Anne Carrière, 1999), 150–151.

30. Abu Iyad with Rouleau, *My Home, My Land,* 35; Sayigh, *Armed Struggle,* 119–122.

31. Hart, *Arafat,* 160–174; Cobban, *Palestinian Liberation Organisation,* 33.

32. Sayigh, *Armed Struggle,* 147, 161–193 (Sayigh dates the invasion to August 28); Cobban, *Palestinian Liberation Organisation,* 36–38; Shaul

Mishal, *The PLO under Arafat: Between Gun and Olive Branch* (New Haven: Yale University Press, 1986), 8–10.

33. Alain Gresh, *The PLO: The Struggle Within*, trans. A. M. Berrett, rev. ed. (London: Zed, 1988), 14–20.

34. Abou Iyad, *Palestinien sans patrie*, 99–100; Sayigh, *Armed Struggle*, 178–179.

35. Abu Iyad with Rouleau, *My Home, My Land*, 59; Cobban, *Palestinian Liberation Organisation*, 48; Husayn, *Abu Iyad*, 120–125; Sayigh, *Armed Struggle*, 179–184, 195–209.

36. Hirst, *Gun and the Olive Branch*, 306–307; Sayigh, *Armed Struggle*, 147, 183.

37. Husayn, *Abu Iyad*, 93–96, 109, 115, 128–129.

38. Eric Rouleau, preface to Abou Iyad, *Palestinien sans patrie*, 10.

39. Abou Iyad, *Palestinien sans patrie*, 104–105; Sayigh, *Armed Struggle*, 179–180.

40. Husayn, *Abu Iyad*, 105–107.

41. Ibid.; Abou Daoud with du Jonchay, *Palestine*, 235–236.

42. Quoted from *Al-Hadaf*, September 13, 1969, in Sayigh, *Armed Struggle*, 214. Sayigh argues the violence was due to factional rivalry.

43. Abou Iyad, *Palestinien sans patrie*, 108–109.

44. The Palestine Liberation Movement, Fateh, *A Dialogue with Fateh* (1972), p. 11. Translation of Spring 1969 interview with an unnamed Fateh leader who identified himself as the one who named Arafat as chief of Fatah. That was Abu Iyad.

45. Cobban, *Palestinian Liberation Organisation*, 11–14, 25–26.

46. Wendy Pearlman, "Spoiling Inside and Out: Internal Political Contestation and the Middle East Peace Process," *International Security* 33, no. 3 (Winter 2008/2009): 79–109; Hudson, "Developments and Setbacks," 64–84; Mirko Aksentijevic, "Reflections on the Palestinian Resistance," *Journal of Palestine Studies* 2, no. 1 (Autumn 1972): 111–119. On troop strength see Sayigh, *Armed Struggle*, 263.

47. Sayigh, *Armed Struggle*, 174–183; Hirst, *Gun and the Olive Branch*, 306–307; Hishaam D. Aidi, *Redeploying the State* (New York: Palgrave MacMillan, 2009), 1.

48. Husayn, *Abu Iyad*, 131–132.

49. Sayigh, *Armed Struggle*, 260–263; Abu Iyad with Rouleau, *My Home, My Land*, 81.

50. Abu Iyad with Rouleau, *My Home, My Land*, 94–95.

51. Abu Iyad claims Wasfi al-Tal ordered the action and that 3,000 died. Sayigh (*Armed Struggle*, 279–281) claims al-Tal did not give the order and that only 250 died.

52. Sayigh, *Armed Struggle*, 292–299.

53. Abu Iyad with Rouleau, *My Home, My Land,* 97–98; Abou Daoud with du Jonchay, *Palestine;* Sayigh, *Armed Struggle,* 306–310.

54. Abu Iyad with Rouleau, *My Home, My Land,* 106. Further references to Munich are drawn from pp. 106–112.

55. Jamal al-Gashey, interview in *One Day in September,* directed by Kevin Macdonald (Passion Pictures, 1999); Alex P. Schmid and Janny de Graaf, *Violence as Communication: Insurgent Terrorism and the Western News Media* (London: Sage, 1982), 1–17, 30–31.

56. Anat N. Kurz, *Fatah and the Politics of Violence: The Institutionalization of a Popular Struggle* (Portland, OR: Sussex Academic Press, 2005), 68; Pearlman, "Spoiling Inside and Out," 79–109.

57. Abou Daoud with du Jonchay, *Palestine,* 85, 136, 169–174, 203–205, 533–537, 706; "Jordan Says Captive Concedes Al Fatah is Black September," *New York Times,* March 25, 1973, p. 14; Patrick Seale, *Abu Nidal, Gun for Hire* (New York: Random House, 1992) 84–85 (1990 interview).

58. Abou Daoud with du Jonchay, *Palestine,* 575–580.

59. Ibid., 622–627.

60. "U.N. General Assembly Approves Debate on International Terrorism," *Jerusalem Post,* September 25, 1972, p. 4. These two paragraphs are based on a review of all three newspapers dated September 6 through October 5, 1972.

61. "Not the Way to Fulfill Hope," *Al-Quds,* September 6, 1972, p. 1 [in Arabic].

62. "Victims of the Munich Crime: Innocent Athletes and Reputation of a Just Cause," *Al-Ittihad,* September 8, 1972, p. 1.

63. Abd al-Karim Abu al-Nasr, "The Avengers," and Samir Atallah, "The Black September Olympics," *Al-Nahar,* September 8, 1972, p. 9; "'Palestine Munich' to 'Palestine-Lebanon-Syria,'" *Al-Nahar,* September 9, 1972, p. 1.

64. Abou Daoud with du Jonchay, *Palestine,* 637, 640–644, 687.

65. Reeve, *One Day in September,* 131–155.

66. Begin, *The Revolt,* 60 and 134; Rouleau, preface in Abou Iyad, *Palestinien sans patrie,* 16–17.

67. Idith Zertal, *Israel's Holocaust and the Politics of Nationhood* (New York: Cambridge University Press, 2005), 115–127, 182–190.

68. Repeated in David G. Dalin and John F. Rothmann, *Icon of Evil: Hitler's Mufti and the Rise of Radical Islam* (New York: Random House, 2008), 103; Benny Morris, *Righteous Victims* (New York: Vintage, 1999), 514.

69. Fateh, *Dialogue with Fateh,* 62–72; Gilbert Ashcar, *The Arabs and the Holocaust,* trans. G. M. Goshgarian (New York: Metropolitan Books, 2009), 166–168, 225–226, 239.

70. Yehoshafat Harkabi, *Arab Attitudes to Israel* (Jerusalem: Israel Universities Press, 1972), 8; Kurz, *Fatah and the Politics of Violence,* 30; Ashcar, *Arabs and Holocaust,* 225, 230.

71. Interview with Khaled al-Hassan, Kuwait, April 1989, in Gowers and Walker, *Behind the Myth*, 107.

72. Abu Iyad with Rouleau, *My Home, My Land*, 135.

73. Rosemary Sayigh, *Palestinians: From Peasants to Revolutionaries*, new ed. (New York: Zed Books, 2007), 196–197.

74. Sayigh, *Armed Struggle*, 334–335.

75. "Interview . . . in *Monday Morning*, May 29, 1978," *Journal of Palestine Studies* 7, no. 4 (Summer 1978): 206–207.

76. Abu Iyad with Rouleau, *My Home, My Land*, 137.

77. Hart, *Arafat*, 380.

78. "The Speech of Yasser Arafat," *Journal of Palestine Studies* 4, no. 2 (Winter 1975): 181–192.

79. Pearlman, "Spoiling Inside and Out," 91; Sayigh, *Armed Struggle*, 344–345, 349–358.

80. Sayigh, *Palestinians*, 187–196.

81. Abu Iyad with Rouleau, *My Home, My Land*, 222–223.

82. Rex Brynan, "PLO Policy in Lebanon: Legacies and Lessons," *Journal of Palestine Studies* 18, no. 2 (Winter 1989): 48–70; Hirst, *Gun and the Olive Branch*, 398–408; Sayigh, *Armed Struggle*, 508; Morris, *Righteous Victims*, 509–515; Avi Shlaim, *The Iron Wall* (New York: W. W. Norton, 2001), 396.

83. Sayigh (*Armed Struggle*, 545) counts 17,285 Arab dead and 368 Israeli soldiers dead. Benny Morris (*1948* [New Haven: Yale University Press, 2008], 406–407) counts 5,800 Israeli dead in 1948, up to 12,000 Palestinian dead, and 2,000 other Arab deaths.

84. Rashid Khalidi, *Under Siege: P.L.O. Decisionmaking during the 1982 War* (New York: Columbia University Press, 1985), 67–97; Sayigh, *Armed Struggle*, 522–543.

85. Amnon Kapeliouk, *Arafat l'irreductible* (Paris: Fayard, 2004), 212.

86. Estimates range from 800 (Israeli) to 3,500. Sources: Sayigh (*Armed Struggle*, 539) cites an International Red Cross estimate of 1,500 dead, revised upward to 2,750; Gowers and Walker, *Behind the Myth*, 214; Hirst, *Gun and the Olive Branch*, 428.

87. Seale, *Abu Nidal*, 39–42; "A New Road for PLO," *Journal of Palestine Studies* 14, no. 2 (Winter 1985): 219–222 (reprint of December 7, 1984, interview of Abu Iyad by Scott McLeod in the *New Statesman*).

88. Ibrahim Abu-Lughod, "Flexible Militancy: A Report on the Sixteenth Session of the Palestine National Council, Algiers, February 14–22, 1983," *Journal of Palestine Studies* 12, no. 4 (Summer 1983): 28.

89. McLeod, "A New Road for PLO," 219–222. See also interview with Abu Iyad in "Israel Does Not Open a Single Door," *US News & World Report*, December 15, 1986, p. 38; Emile F. Sahliyeh, *The PLO after Lebanon War* (Boulder, CO: Westview Press, 1986), 196–202; Sayigh, *Armed Struggle*, 577.

90. Karma Nabulsi, "Abu Iyad," *Independent,* January 18, 1991.

91. Sahliyeh (*PLO after Lebanon,* 165) reports 92 percent approval rating in 1983; Eric Rouleau, in "The Future of the PLO," *Foreign Affairs* 62 no. 1 (Fall 1983), 154, reports the same percentage in a July 1983 poll; Sayigh (*Armed Struggle,* 591) reports 74 percent approval rating in 1986.

92. Zeev Schiff and Ehud Yaari, *Intifada,* trans. Ina Friedman (New York: Simon & Schuster, 1991), 20.

93. Sayigh, *Armed Struggle,* 607–624; Sari Nusseibeh, *Once upon a Country* (New York: Farrar, Straus, and Giroux, 2007), 264–286.

94. Mary Elizabeth King, *A Quiet Revolution: The First Palestinian Intifada and Nonviolent Resistance* (New York: Nation Books, 2007); Schiff and Yaari, *Intifada,* 31, 340.

95. Sayigh, *Armed Struggle,* 608.

96. Ibid., 608, 619–622; "Abu Iyad Says PLO Wants to Launch Political Initiative: We Have to Declare Independence," Voice of Palestine, Algiers, 6 October 1988, from *BBC Summary of World Broadcasts,* October 8, 1988; "Fatah Leader Abu Iyad on Plan to Escalate Palestinian Uprising," *BBC Summary of World Broadcasts,* November 8, 1988.

97. Edward Said, "Intifada and Independence," *Social Text* 22 (Spring 1989): 34.

98. Ibid., 23–32.

99. Sayigh, *Armed Struggle,* 623–624; Alan Cowell, "Arafat Will Press Diplomatic Effort," *New York Times,* December 19, 1988, p. A13.

100. Telephone interview with Robert Pelletreau, January 31, 2011. "Fatah's Salah Khalaf Gives Details of Recent Meetings with US Ambassador in Tunis," *BBC Summary of World Broadcasts,* June 30, 1989.

101. "Salah Khalaf, Address (via Video Tape) to the International Center for Peace in the Middle East, Jerusalem, 22 February, 1989," in *Journal of Palestine Studies* 18, no. 4 (Summer 1989): 153; "Abu Iyad Breakthrough" and "Abu Iyad Speaks in Jerusalem—on Video," *Jerusalem Post,* February 23, 1989.

102. Clinton Bailey, "Arafat Cannot Negotiate Peace," *New York Times,* March 8, 1989, p. A31. Abu Iyad's speech was excerpted in an op-ed on the same page: "Israel and Arafat Can Talk."

103. Salah Khalaf, "Lowering the Sword," *Foreign Policy* 78 (Spring 1990): 92–93.

104. Seale, *Abu Nidal,* 44, 91–178; Hart, *Arafat,* 41; Susan Hattis Rolef, "Israel's Policy toward the PLO," in Avraham Sela and Moshe Maoz, ed., *PLO and Israel: From Armed Conflict to Political Solution, 1964–1994* (New York: St. Martin's, 1997), 268.

105. Mona Ziade, "Arafat in Tight Spot over Gulf Crisis," Associated Press, August 19, 1990.

106. Telephone interview on October 26, 2012, with William B. Quandt, a Brookings Institution scholar in Tunis that summer.

107. Tom Segev, *The Seventh Million* (New York: Henry Holt, 1991), 505.

108. Seale, *Abu Nidal*, 312; interview with Quandt, October 26, 2012.

109. Michael Wines, "The Man behind Munich," and Youssef M. Ibrahim, "Two Ranking Aids to Arafat Are Slain by Gunman in Tunis," *New York Times*, January 15, 1991, pp. A12 and A1, respectively; "Sure Losers: The Palestinians," *New York Times*, January, 21, 1991, p. A16. Yoram Hazony, "A Life Passed in Terror," *Jerusalem Post*, January 16, 1991. Jonathan C. Randal, "Document Suggests Abu Nidal Was behind Slaying of Arafat Aide," *Washington Post*, July 23, 1991, p. A17.

110. Husayn, *Abu Iyad*, 6. The daughters were named Iman, Jihad, and Aliya. Abu Iyad also had two sons, Iyad and Ziyad.

111. Husayn, *Abu Iyad*, 175, 177, 181.

112. World Bank data on Palestinian population in the West Bank and Gaza available at www.google.com/publicdata/explore (accessed 10/11/11). Refugee statistics for November 1993 available at www.mideastweb.org/mref ugees.htm (accessed 10/11/11).

113. Kapeliouk, *Arafat*, 294; "PLO Chairman's Address to the Opening Session of the 20th PNC Conference," Radio Monte Carlo [in Arabic], September 23, 1991, from *BBC Summary of World Broadcasts*, September 25, 1991.

114. Edward Said, "The Morning After," *The London Review of Books*, 15, no. 20 (October 21, 1993): 3.

115. Avi Shlaim, "Ehud Barak," *London Review of Books* 23, no. 2 (January 25, 2001): 9–29.

116. Zeev Schiff, "Israeli Death Toll in Intifada Higher Than Last Two Wars," *Haaretz*, August 24, 2004.

117. Abu-Lughod, "Flexible Militancy," 31–36.

118. Abu Iyad with Rouleau, *My Home, My Land*, 147.

119. Michael Mann, *The Dark Side of Democracy: Explaining Ethnic Cleansing* (New York: Cambridge University Press, 2005), 1–10.

10. Sayyid Qutb and Ali Shariati

1. Roger Owen and Şevket Pamuk, *A History of Middle East Economies in the Twentieth Century* (Cambridge: Harvard University Press, 1999), 97–103.

2. Anouar Abdel-Malek, *Egypt: Military Society* (New York: Random House, 1968).

3. Sayyid Qutb, *Milestones* (New Delhi: Islamic Book Service, 2002), 7. Arabic original: Sayyid Qutb, *Maalim fi al-tariq* (Cairo and Beirut: Dar al-Shuruq, 1982), 5.

4. "Port Huron Statement of the Students for a Democratic Society, 1962," available at www.campusactivism.org/server-new/uploads/porthuron .htm (accessed December 27, 2011).

5. Qutb, *Milestones*, 8; Qutb, *Maalim al-Tariq*, 6–7.

6. Sayyid Qutb, *A Child from the Village*, trans. John Calvert and William Shepherd (Syracuse: Syracuse University Press, 2004), 113–124.

7. Adnan Musallam, *From Secularism to Jihad: Sayyid Qutb and the Foundation of Radical Islamism* (Westport, CT: Praeger, 2005), 95.

8. John Calvert, *Sayyid Qutb and the Origins of Radical Islamism* (New York: Columbia University Press, 2010), 125.

9. Sayyid Qutb, *Social Justice in Islam*, trans. John B. Hardie and Hamid Algar (Oneonta, NY: Islamic Publications International, 2000), 19; Calvert, *Sayyid Qutb*, 105–106, 125–126.

10. Qutb, *Social Justice*, 19–35, 44.

11. Ibid., 68; Calvert, *Sayyid Qutb*, 131–135.

12. Calvert, *Sayyid Qutb*, 139–179.

13. Musallam, *From Secularism to Jihad*, 139.

14. Calvert, *Sayyid Qutb*, 179–185.

15. Musallam, *Secularism to Jihad*, 145–146.

16. Ibid., 150; Calvert, *Sayyid Qutb*, 194. Much of the paragraph is taken from Calvert.

17. William Shepard, "The Development of the Thought of Sayyid Qutb as Reflected in Earlier and Later Editions of 'Social Justice in Islam,'" *Die Welt des Islams* 32, no. 2 (1992): 204–207.

18. Qutb, *Milestones*, 10–11.

19. Ibid., 11–12.

20. Ibid., 18.

21. Ibid., 30.

22. Ibid., 57. On Islam's right see pp. 74–75.

23. Ibid., 89.

24. Ibid., 59–73, 76.

25. Barbara H. E. Zollner, *The Muslim Brotherhood: Hasan Hudaybi and Ideology* (New York: Routledge, 2009), 43; Musallam, *Secularism to Jihad*, 168–169.

26. Salah Abd al-Fattah Khalidi, *Sayyid Qutb: min al-milad ila al istishhad* (Beirut: Dar al-Qalam, 1991), 372–401.

27. Musallam, *Secularism to Jihad*, 169–170; Calvert, *Sayyid Qutb*, 256–259.

28. Ali Rahnema, *An Islamic Utopian: A Political Biography of Ali Shariati* (New York: I. B. Tauris, 1998), 14.

29. Ibid., 35–56.

30. Translation modified by the author from "And Once again Abu Dharr Part 1," www.shariati.com/english/abudhar/abudhar1.html (accessed November 8, 2011).

31. Rahnema, *Islamic Utopian*, 84–86.

32. Ibid., 176–189.

33. "Islamology: The Basic Design for a School of Thought and Action Part 1," www.shariati.com/english/islam/islam1.html (accessed November 8, 2011).

34. "Islamology: The Basic Design for a School of Thought and Action Part 4," www.shariati.com/english/islam/islam4.html (accessed November 8, 2011); and Rahnema, *Islamic Utopian,* 191–201.

35. Ali Shariati, "The World-View of Tauhid," from *Islamology* 1 (1968): 46–56, in Shariati, *On the Sociology of Islam,* trans. Hamid Algar (Oneonta, NY: Mizan Press, 1979), 82–87.

36. Ali Shariati, "The Philosophy of History: Cain and Abel," *Islamology* 1 (1968): 68–85, in *On the Sociology of Islam,* 97–110.

37. Yann Richard, "Contemporary Shii Thought," in Nikki R. Keddie, *Modern Iran: Roots and Results of Revolution,* updated ed. (New Haven: Yale University Press, 2006), 200–205; Ervand Abrahamian, *The Iranian Mojahedin* (New Haven: Yale University Press, 1992), 111–113, 195–199.

38. Ali Shariati, "Approaches to the Understanding of Islam," first two lectures at Ershad, October 1968, in Shariati, *On the Sociology of Islam,* 39–69.

39. Ali Shariati, *Religion vs. Religion,* trans. Laleh Bakhtiar (Chicago: ABC International Group, 2003), 60, 62; Rahnema, *Islamic Utopian,* 249–250.

40. Rahnema, *Islamic Utopian,* 265, 280.

41. Abrahamian, *Iranian Mojahedin,* 87–100, 126–140.

42. Rahnema, *Islamic Utopian,* 296.

43. Shariati not only followed Fanon and Aimé Césaire, whom he studied in Paris, but he also anticipated the postcolonial ideas of Latin Americans. See, for example, Walter Mignolo, *Local Histories/Global Designs* (Princeton: Princeton University Press, 2000). For a critical view see especially Hamid Dabashi, *Theology of Discontent: The Ideological Foundation of the Islamic Revolution in Iran* (New Brunswick, NJ: Transaction Publishers, 2008), 102–146. He calls Shariati's views "Marxism Islamicized."

44. Rahnema, *Islamic Utopian,* 330–335, 363–377.

45. Abrahamian, *Iranian Mojahedin,* 105.

46. Keddie, *Modern Iran,* 200, 206–207, 226.

47. Charles Kurzman, *The Unthinkable Revolution in Iran* (Cambridge, MA: Harvard University Press, 2004), 149.

48. Ervand Abrahamian, *Khomeinism* (Berkeley: University of California Press, 1993); Keddie, *Modern Iran,* 234; Kurzman, *Unthinkable Revolution;* Said Amir Arjomand, *The Turban for the Crown* (New York: Oxford University Press, 1989); Asef Bayat, *Street Politics* (New York: Columbia University Press, 1997).

49. Kurzman, *Unthinkable Revolution,* 149–152.

50. Ibid., 154–162; Arjomand, *Turban for the Crown,* 126–127.

51. Keddie, *Modern Iran,* 240.

52. Arjomand, *Turban for the Crown*, 100–102; Abrahamian, *Khomeinism*; Mehdi Abedi and Michael M. J. Fischer, "An Iranian Village Boyhood," in Edmund Burke III and David Yaghoubian, eds., *Struggle and Survival in the Modern Middle East* (Berkeley: University of California Press, 2006), 237–252.

53. Shaul Bakhash, *Reign of the Ayatollahs* (New York: Basic Books, 1986), 75–83.

54. Arjomand, *Turban for the Crown*, 139; Keddie, *Modern Iran*, 248–249; Ervand Abrahamian, *A History of Modern Iran* (New York: Cambridge University Press, 2008), 168–169.

55. Bakhash, *Reign of the Ayatollahs*, 52–91; Abrahamian, *History of Modern Iran*, 162–169.

56. "The Islamic Constitution of Iran," excerpted in Kemal H. Karpat, ed., *Political and Social Thought in the Contemporary Middle East* (New York: Praeger, 1982), 512–516.

57. Keddie, *Modern Iran*, 209–210; Bakhash, *Reign of the Ayatollahs*, 96.

58. Bakhash, *Reign of the Ayatollahs*, 138–165; Keddie, *Modern Iran*, 242–253.

59. Keddie, *Modern Iran*, 253; Abrahamian, *History of Modern Iran*, 181.

60. Abrahamian, *History of Modern Iran*, 164.

61. Parvin Paidar, *Women and the Political Process in Twentieth-Century Iran* (New York: Cambridge University Press, 1995), 265–355.

62. Gilles Kepel, *Muslim Extremism in Egypt* (Berkeley: University of California Press, 1984), 145.

63. Raymond William Baker, *Sadat and After* (London: I. B. Tauris, 1990), 128–130.

64. Asef Bayat, *Making Islam Democratic: Social Movements and the Post-Islamist Turn* (Stanford: Stanford University Press, 2007), 16–48.

65. Carrie Rosefsky Wickham, *Mobilizing Islam: Religion, Activism, and Political Change in Egypt* (New York: Columbia University Press, 2002); Bayat, *Making Islam Democratic*; Saba Mahmood, *The Politics of Piety: The Islamic Revival and the Feminist Subject*, 2nd ed. (Princeton: Princeton University Press, 2005).

66. The book was published under the name of Hasan al-Banna's successor, Hasan al-Hudaybi. See Barbara H. E. Zollner, *The Muslim Brotherhood: Hasan al-Hudaybi and Ideology* (New York: Routledge, 2009). The following draws on her analysis of *Preachers not Judges* on pp. 64–145, and on Gilles Kepel, *Muslim Extremism in Egypt* (Berkeley: University of California Press, 1985), 61–63.

67. John Waterbury, *The Egypt of Nasser and Sadat* (Princeton: Princeton University Press, 1983), 207–231, 354–361; Raymond William Baker, *Egypt's Uncertain Revolution under Nasser and Sadat* (Cambridge, MA: Harvard University Press, 1978), 165–169.

68. Wickham, *Mobilizing Islam*, 6–18, 178–180, 202–203.

69. Jacquelene G. Brinton, "Preaching Islamic Renewal: Shaykh Muhammad Mitwalli Sharawi and the Syncretization of Revelation and Contemporary Life" (PhD diss., University of Virginia, 2009); Tarek Osman, *Egypt on the Brink*, rev. ed. (New Haven: Yale University Press, 2011), 86–87, 93–97.

70. Wickham, *Mobilizing Islam*, 160.

71. Kepel, *Muslim Extremism in Egypt*, 129–156, 172–190.

72. Muhammad Ali Qutb, *Sayyid Qutb—al-Shahid al-Azal* (Cairo: al-Mukhtar al-Islami, 1974), 1–2, 141–143; Zainab al-Ghazali, *Return of the Pharaoh*, trans. Mokrane Guezzou (Leicester: The Islamic Foundation, 1994), 50.

73. Waterbury, *Egypt of Nasser and Sadat*, 228–231, 366–370; Owen and Pamuk, *A History of Middle East Economies in the Twentieth Century*, 135–146; Osman, *Egypt on the Brink*, 136–139; Baker, *Egypt's Uncertain Revolution*, 150–151, 245.

74. Kepel, *Muslim Extremism*, 70–102, 110–116; Patrick D. Gaffney, *The Prophet's Pulpit* (Berkeley: University of California Press, 1994), 80–112.

75. Anthony Shadid, *Legacy of the Prophet* (Boulder, CO: Westview Press, 2001), 75–79; Roxanne L. Euben and Muhammad Qasim Zaman, eds., *Princeton Readings in Islamist Thought* (Princeton: Princeton University Press, 2009), 325. (I have paraphrased them here.)

76. As quoted in Kepel, *Muslim Extremism*, 195–197. See an alternative extract in Euben and Zaman, *Princeton Readings*, 327–345.

77. Kepel, *Muslim Extremism*, 156–171; Gaffney, *Prophet's Pulpit*, 251–262.

78. Waterbury, *Egypt of Nasser and Sadat*, 359–364; Mohamed Heikal, *Autumn of Fury: The Assassination of Sadat* (New York: Random House, 1983), 227–241.

79. Kepel, *Muslim Extremism*, 192, 204–207; Heikal, *Autumn of Fury*, 242–255.

80. Mohammed M. Hafez and Quintan Wiktorowicz, "Violence as Contention in the Egyptian Islamic Movement," in Quintan Wiktorowicz, ed., *Islamic Activism: A Social Movement Theory Approach* (Bloomington: Indiana University Press, 2004), 75. These paragraphs are drawn largely from their chapter (pp. 61–88), and from Kepel, *Muslim Extremism*, 241–257.

81. Hafez and Wiktorowicz, "Violence as Contention," 79.

82. Gaffney, *Prophet's Pulpit*, 80–112, 268. For a broader historical view on the rise and decline of legal authority in Islam see Richard Bulliet, *Islam: The View from the Edge* (New York: Columbia University Press, 1995).

83. Bayat, *Making Islam Democratic*, 16–41.

84. Robert A. Pape, "The Strategic Logic of Suicide Terrorism," *American Political Science Review* (July 14, 2003): 20–32; Euben and Zaman, *Princeton Readings*, 432.

85. Kurt Schock, *Unarmed Insurrections: People Power Movements in Nondemocracies* (Minneapolis: University of Minnesota Press, 2005), 142–153.

11. Wael Ghonim of Egypt

1. Wael Ghonim, *Revolution 2.0: The Power of the People Is Greater Than the People in Power* (Boston: Houghton Mifflin Harcourt, 2012), 135–136. For consistency, I have changed the spelling of Urabi from the book's transliteration, "Oraby."

2. Ghonim, *Revolution 2.0,* 59; Amro Ali, "Saeeds of Revolution: De-Mythologizing Khaled Saeed," *Jadaliyya,* www.jadaliyya.com/pages/index/5845/saeeds-of-revolution_de-mythologizing-khaled-saeed (accessed August 5, 2012).

3. Ghonim, *Revolution 2.0,* 74.

4. Ibid., 80, 106–108.

5. Ibid., 146–148.

6. Ibid., 166, 169.

7. "Meet Asmaa Mahfouz and the blog that Helped Spark the Revolution," *YouTube.com,* www.youtube.com/watch?v=eBg7O48vhLY&lr=1 (accessed February 9, 2012).

8. Paper delivered at the Middle East Studies Association, Washington, DC, December 2, 2011.

9. Interview with April 6 Youth Movement leader Ahmed Maher on Al-Jazeera, "Egypt: Seeds of Change," February 9, 2011. Available at www.youtube.com/watch?v=QrNzOdZgqN8 (accessed February 24, 2011).

10. Hazem Kandil, "The Revolt in Egypt," interview in *The New Left Review* 68 (March–April 2011): 17–55.

11. Kandil, "The Revolt in Egypt," 17–25.

12. Hatem Rushdy, ed., *18 Days in Tahrir: Stories from Egypt's Revolution* (Hong Kong: Haven Books, 2011), 100.

13. Rushdy, *18 Days in Tahrir,* 103, 106.

14. Ibid., 187.

15. Nadia Kamel, personal interview in Cairo, December 14, 2011.

16. Rushdy, *18 Days in Tahrir,* 151–152.

17. Nadia Kamel, interview, December 14, 2011.

18. Karima Khalil, ed., *Messages from Tahrir: Signs from Egypt's Revolution* (Cairo: The American University in Cairo Press, 2011), 50–51.

19. Rushdy, *18 Days in Tahrir,* 132.

20. Nadia Kamel, personal interview, Cairo, December 14, 2011.

21. Dream TV interview with Mona al-Shazly, February 7, 2011. Available at www.guardian.co.uk/world/video/2011/feb/08/egypt-activist-wael-ghonim -google-video (accessed February 7, 2012).

22. Nadia Kamel, personal interview, Cairo, December 14, 2011; Sioufi quote in Rushdy, *18 Days in Tahrir,* 251; Jeremy Brown, BBC report from Tahrir Square, February 8, 2011; Steven A. Cook, *The Struggle for Egypt* (New York: Oxford University Press, 2012), 290–292.

23. Abdel Monem Said Aly, "State and Revolution in Egypt: The Paradox of Change and Politics," Brandeis University Crown Center for Middle East Studies, Crown Essay 2 (January 2012), 42–50; death toll cited by Egyptian government report of April 19, 2011: *Tahrir al-nihai lil-lajna al-tahqiq wal-taqsa al-haqaiq bishan al-ahdath allati waqibat thawrat 25 yanayir 2011* [Fact-finding national commission about the January 25 Revolution: final report], 8.

24. Ghonim, *Revolution 2.0,* 290.

25. Asef Bayat, "The Arab Street"; Paul Schemm, "Activist Dissent and Anti-War Protests in Egypt"; and Joel Beinin, "The Working Class and the Popular Movement in Egypt," in Jeannie Sowers and Chris Toensing, eds., *The Journey to Tahrir* (New York: Verso, 2012), 82–83, 85–106.

26. Mona El-Ghobashy, "The Praxis of the Egyptian Revolution," in Sowers and Toensing, *Journey to Tahrir,* 21–40; quotes on pp. 26, 35.

27. Gene Sharp, interview with Tim Franks on *HARDtalk,* BBC World Service, February 2, 2012. See also Gene Sharp, *From Dictatorship to Democracy,* 4th ed. (East Boston, MA: The Albert Einstein Institution, 2010).

28. Juan R. I. Cole, *Colonialism and Revolution in the Middle East: Social and Cultural Origins of Egypt's Urabi Movement* (Cairo: American University in Cairo Press, 2000), 20.

29. Ghonim, *Revolution 2.0,* 29. See also Aly, "State and Revolution in Egypt," 59.

30. Khaled Fahmy, personal interview, Cairo, December 14, 2011.

31. Joe Rizk, personal interview, Cairo, December 13, 2011.

32. Quoted in Samer Shehata and Joshua Stacher, "The Muslim Brothers in Mubarak's Last Decade," in Sowers and Toensing, *Journey to Tahrir,* 176.

33. Sharp, *From Dictatorship to Democracy,* 11.

34. Kandil, "The Revolt in Egypt," 22–26.

35. Samer Soliman, personal interview, American University in Cairo campus, December 11, 2011.

36. Robert F. Worth, "Egypt's Human Bellwether," *New York Times Magazine,* January 19, 2012. Available at www.nytimes.com/2012/01/22/magazine /mohamed-beltagy-future-of-egypt.html?pagewanted=all&_r=0 (accessed November 14, 2012).

37. Hatem Azzam, personal interview, Maadi, December 15, 2011.

38. Essam El-Arian, interview with Stephen Sackur on *HARDtalk*, BBC World Service, April 1, 2011. Available at http://news.bbc.co.uk/2/hi/programmes/hardtalk/default.stm (accessed February 6, 2012).

39. Fatma Abdel Halim, personal interview, Cairo, December 15, 2011.

40. Samer Soliman, personal interview, Cairo, December 12, 2011.

41. Dr. Umaima Kamel, personal interview, Moqattam, December 16, 2011.

42. Personal interviews in front of the Umm al-Muminin school in the al-Haram district, Cairo, December 14, 2011.

43. Samer Shehata, personal interview, Cairo, December 11, 2011.

44. Rowaida Saad Eddine, personal interview, Cairo, December 16, 2011.

45. Essam El-Arian, "Egypt Is the True Victor in this Election," *Guardian .co.uk,* November 30, 2011, www.guardian.co.uk/commentisfree/2011/nov/30/egypt-victor-election-democracy (accessed October 10, 2012). For election results see "Egypt's Islamist Parties Win Elections to Parliament," www.bbc.co.uk/news/world-middle-east-16665748 (accessed August 6, 2012).

46. Tarek Osman, *Egypt on the Brink*, rev. ed. (New Haven: Yale University Press, 2011), 251–254.

47. Amr Hamzawy, discussion at the Carnegie Endowment for International Peace, May 4, 2012.

48. Khaled Fahmy, personal interview, Cairo, December 13, 2011.

49. CNN Wire Staff, "Muslim Brotherhood's Morsi declared Egypt's New President," June 24, 2012. Available at http://wtvr.com/2012/06/24/muslim-brotherhoods-morsi-declared-egypts-new-president/ (accessed November 14, 2012), includes Ghonim and Morsi quotes; Muhammad Shukri, "Mursi Faces Challenge to Bring Copts on side," *BBC.co.uk,* July 1, 2012, www.bbc.co.uk/news/world-middle-east-18634891 (accessed August 5, 2012); "Egypt President Mursi's First Speech: Key Quotes," *BBC.co.uk,* June 25, 2012, www.bbc.co.uk/news/world-middle-east-18577334 (accessed August 5, 2012). Full speech of June 24, 2012, available (in Arabic) at www.youtube.com/watch?v=CRZ6VphJrXE&feature=related (accessed October 10, 2012).

50. Ahmad Shokr, "And the Winner Is . . . ," and Zaynab Abul-Magd, "Interpreting the Coup," *Egyptian Independent,* July 24 and July 1, 2012, respectively.

51. Tarek Radwan, "Moderates and Liberals Double-down on the Constitution," *Atlantic Council,* September 28, 2012, at www.acus.org; Muhammad Abdel Kader, "Egypt's Salafists, Brotherhood at Odds over Constitution Draft," *al-Monitor.com,* October 17, 2012 (translation of October 16 article from *al-Masry al-Youm* by Joelle El-Khoury); Kareem Fahim and Mayy El Sheikh, "Egyptian Court Declines to Rule on the Legality of Drafting a New Constitution," *New York Times,* October 24, 2012. An English translation of the October 15 draft constitution may be found at http://dailynewsegypt.com/2012/10/16/translation-of-the-released-constitutional-draft-part-1/.

52. Kazim Habib and Zahdi al-Dawudi, *Fahd wa al-Haraka al-Wataniya fi al-Iraq* (Beirut: Dar al-Konooz al-Adabiya, 2003), 10.

53. Tareq Ismael, telephone interview, February 5, 2009. See also Ismael, *The Rise and Fall of the Communist Party of Iraq* (New York: Cambridge University Press, 2008), ix, and Aziz Sbahi, *Uqud min Tarikh al-Hizb al-Shuyui al-Iraqi* (Dimashq: Manshurat al-Thiqafa al-Jadida, 2002), 408.

54. See "Iraqi CP Commemorates 'Communist Martyr's Day,'" *Iraqi Letter*, http://iraqiletter.blogspot.com/2009/02/on-communist-martyrs-day-14th-february.html (accessed October 10, 2012); and www.almadapaper.net/sub/03–1465/17.pdf

55. Khalid al-Taie, "Baghdad's al-Tahrir Square Becomes an Open Media Forum," *Al-Shorfa*, December 29, 2010, http://mawtani.al-shorfa.com/en_GB/articles/iii/features/iraqtoday/2010/12/29/feature-02 (accessed August 7, 2012); and Ned Parker and Raheem Salman, "In Baghdad, Weekly Day of Rage Is a Low-Key Event," *Los Angeles Times*, May 14, 2011, http://articles.latimes.com/print/2011/may/14/world/la-fg-iraq-protests-20110514 (accessed August 7, 2012). Also based on personal interviews with Zohair al-Jazaery, an Iraqi judge, Washington, DC, August 28, 2008, and Stephen Negus of the *Financial Times*, March 31, 2009; and an Iraqi blogger who recalled his father's regular visits to the monument in "Between Salim's Freedom and Kahramana's Jars Hide All My Personalities," http://saminkie.blogspot.com/search?q=freedom+monument (accessed October 10, 2012).

56. "Akram Al-Hourani," http://akram-alhourani.com/index_EN.htm (accessed August 7, 2012).

57. Radwan Ziadeh, personal interview, Washington, DC, January 2009. He later became spokesperson for the Syrian National Council.

58. Soli Özel, personal interview, Istanbul, June 2011; Ipek Çalışlar (Edib's biographer), personal interview, Istanbul, June 2011; Huseyin Aydin (former associate of Erdogan), personal interview, Washington, DC, June 2011.

59. Shimon Peres and David Landau, *Ben-Gurion: A Political Life* (New York: Schocken Books, 2011).

60. Avraham Burg, "Israel's Fading Democracy," *The New York Times*, Aug. 5, 2012.

61. David Fromkin, *A Peace to End All Peace: The Fall of the Ottoman Empire and the Creation of the Modern Middle East* (New York: Holt, 2001).

62. El-Ghobashy, "Unsettling the Authorities," 125–126.

63. William Roger Louis, *The British Empire in the Middle East 1945–1951* (Oxford: Clarendon Press, 1984), 226–264.

64. Full speech of June 24, 2012, available (in Arabic) at www.youtube.com/watch?v=CRZ6VphJrXE&feature=related (accessed October 10, 2012).

FURTHER READING

Introduction

Readers seeking an introduction to modern Middle Eastern history will find the following books useful: Caroline Finkel, *Osman's Dream: The History of the Ottoman Empire* (New York: Basic Books, 2005); James L. Gelvin, *The Modern Middle East: A History* (New York: Oxford University Press, 2005); Nikki R. Keddie, *Modern Iran: Roots and Results of Revolution* (New Haven: Yale University Press, 2006).

Two collections offer a broad view of other Middle Eastern histories written "from below." I found early inspiration in Edmund Burke III and David Yaghoubian, eds., *Struggle and Survival in the Modern Middle East*, 2nd ed. (Berkeley: University of California Press, 2005). A more recent and more scholarly volume is: Stephanie Cronin, ed., *Subalterns and Social Protest: History from Below in the Middle East and North Africa* (New York: Routledge, 2008). Asef Bayat has contributed much to a new view of the politics of everyday resistance in his *Street Politics: Poor People's Movements in Iran* (New York: Columbia University Press, 1997) and *Life as Politics: How Ordinary People Change the Middle East* (Stanford: Stanford University Press, 2010).

For introductions to Islam and justice see Khaled Abou El Fadl, *The Place of Tolerance in Islam* (Boston: Beacon Press, 2002); Mohammed Arkoun, *Rethinking Islam* (Boulder, CO: Westview Press, 1994); Karen Armstrong, *Islam: A Short History* (New York: Random House, 2002); Michael Cook, *Forbidding Wrong in Islam* (Princeton: Princeton University Press, 2003); Linda T. Darling, *A History of Social Justice and Political Power in the Middle East: The Circle of Justice from Mesopotamia to Globalization* (New York: Routledge, 2012); Majid Khadduri, *The Islamic Conception of Justice* (Baltimore: The Johns Hopkins University Press, 1984); Lawrence Rosen, *The Justice of Islam* (New York: Oxford University Press, 2000);

394

and Abdulaziz Sachedina, *The Islamic Roots of Democratic Pluralism* (New York: Oxford University Press, 2001).

On theories of justice and the history of social movements see Joel Beinin and Frederic Vairel, eds., *Social Movements, Mobilization, and Contestation in the Middle East and North Africa* (Stanford: Stanford University Press, 2011); John Rawls, *Justice as Fairness: A Restatement* (Cambridge: Harvard University Press, 2001); Michael J. Sandel, *Justice: What's the Right Thing to Do?* (New York: Farrar, Straus, and Giroux, 2009); Amartya Sen, *The Idea of Justice* (Cambridge: Harvard University Press, 2009); Judith N. Shklar, *The Faces of Injustice* (New Haven: Yale University Press, 1990); and Sidney G. Tarrow, *Power in Movement: Social Movements and Contentious Politics,* 3rd ed. (New York: Cambridge University Press, 2011).

Chapter 1

There is just one biography of Mustafa Ali of Gallipoli in English: Cornell H. Fleischer, *Bureaucrat and Intellectual in the Ottoman Empire: The Historian Mustafa Âli (1541–1600)* (Princeton: Princeton University Press, 1986). Several of Mustafa Ali's texts have been translated by Andreas Tietze and are listed in the notes to Chapter 1. On the Circle of Justice see Darling, *A History of Social Justice,* cited in the Introduction above.

On the *nasihatname* tradition see Rifa'at 'Ali Abou-El-Haj, *Formation of the Modern State: The Ottoman Empire Sixteenth to Eighteenth Centuries* (Albany: SUNY Press, 1991). I have borrowed the concept of jeremiad from historians of American politics and religion. Prominent and recent works on the topic include Sacvan Bercovitch, *The American Jeremiad* (Madison: University of Wisconsin Press, 1978) and John D. Carlson and Jonathan H. Ebel, *From Jeremiad to Jihad: Religion, Violence and America* (Berkeley: University of California Press, 2012).

A good introduction to Egyptian history is Afaf Lutfi Al-Sayyid Marsot, *A History of Egypt,* 2nd ed. (New York: Cambridge University Press, 2007). Introductory works that reflect current scholarship on the Ottoman Tanzimat are sorely lacking in English. For an introduction, see Erik Jan Zürcher, *Turkey: A Modern History,* 3rd ed. (New York: I. B. Tauris, 2004). The classic on Turkish intellectual history is Şerif Mardin, *The Genesis of Young Ottoman Thought* (Syracuse: Syracuse University Press, 2000). For a newer view, stressing indigenous roots of reform see Butrus Abu-Manneh, *Studies on Islam and the Ottoman Empire in the 19th century (1826–1876)* (Istanbul: Isis Press, 2001).

Chapter 2

The primary source for Tanyus Shahin's peasant revolt is Malcom H. Kerr, *Lebanon in the Last Years of Feudalism, 1840–1868* (Beirut: American

University of Beirut, 1959). For a general introduction to the history of labor in the Middle East see Joel Beinin, *Workers and Peasants in the Middle East* (New York: Cambridge University Press, 2001). The classic work on how and why peasants rebel is James C. Scott's *The Moral Economy of the Peasant* (New Haven: Yale University Press, 1976).

An overview of Lebanese history may be found in Fawwaz Traboulsi, *A History of Modern Lebanon* (Ann Arbor, MI: Pluto Press, 2007). On the origins of sectarian violence see Ussama Makdisi, *The Culture of Sectarianism: Community, History and Violence in Nineteenth-Century Ottoman Lebanon* (Berkeley: University of California Press, 2000). For details on the 1860 massacres see Leila Tarazi Fawaz, *An Occasion for War: Civil Conflict in Lebanon and Damascus in 1860* (Berkeley: University of California Press, 1995). An optimistic perspective on the sectarian relations after 1861 is found in Engin Akarli's *The Long Peace: Ottoman Lebanon, 1861–1920* (Berkeley: University of California Press, 1993).

Chapter 3

A translation of Ahmed Urabi's testament is available in Trevor Le Gassick, ed., *The Defense Statement of Ahmed Urabi* (Cairo: American University in Cairo Press, 1982). For a recent analysis of the revolution see Juan R. I. Cole, *Colonialism and Revolution in the Middle East* (Cairo: The American University in Cairo Press, 1999). For the oppressive conditions in the Egyptian military see Khaled Fahmy, *All the Pasha's Men* (Cairo: American University in Cairo Press, 2002).

A broad introduction to the movements that contributed to Iran's constitutional revolution is Janet Afary, *The Iranian Constitutional Revolution, 1906–1911* (New York: Columbia University Press, 1996). For the revolution from Nazem al-Islam's perspective see Mangol Bayat, *Iran's First Revolution: Shi'ism and the Constitutional Revolution of 1905–1909* (New York: Oxford University Press, 1991). Afsaneh Najmabadi gives a novel view of how the revolution invented new repertoires of political meaning in *The Story of the Daughters of Quchan* (Syracuse: Syracuse University Press, 1998).

A recent collection of essays on Middle Eastern constitutionalism is S. A. Arjomand, ed., *Constitutional Politics in the Middle East* (Portland, OR: Hart Publishing, 2008). Charles Kurzman has published two books that place both constitutional revolutions in a broader intellectual and global framework: *Modernist Islam, 1840–1940: A Sourcebook* (New York: Oxford University Press, 2002) and *Democracy Denied 1905–1915: Intellectuals and the Fate of Democracy* (Cambridge, MA: Harvard University Press, 2008). A classic on Arab intellectuals is Albert Hourani's *Arabic Thought in the Liberal Age, 1798–1939* (New York: Cambridge University Press, 1983). For an introduction to Jamal al-Din al-Afghani's thought see Nikki R. Keddie, *An Islamic Response to Imperialism: Political and Religious*

Writings of Sayyid Jamal ad-Din "al-Afghani" (Berkeley: University of California Press, 1983).

Chapter 4

Halide Edib's first memoir is widely available in two editions. The facsimile of the 1926 original is *Memoirs of Halide Edib* (Piscataway, NJ: Gorgias Press, 2004). A new edition with an introduction by Sibel Erol is *House with Wisteria: Memoirs of Turkey Old and New* (New Brunswick, NJ: Transaction, 2009).

For background on the political transition from empire to republic see Zürcher, *Turkey: A Modern History*, cited above, 3rd ed., and Şükrü Hanioğlu, *Ataturk: An Intellectual Biography* (Princeton: Princeton University Press, 2011).

Chapter 5

For recent debates on the Armenian genocide see Ronald Grigor Suny and Fatma Müge Göçek, eds., *A Question of Genocide: Armenians and Turks at the End of the Ottoman Empire* (New York: Oxford University Press, 2011), and M. Hakan Yavuz, "Contours of Scholarship on Armenian-Turkish Relations," *Middle East Critique* 20, no. 3 (Fall 2011): 231–251. Keith David Watenpaugh gives a vivid picture of politics and society in Aleppo after the war in *Being Modern in the Middle East: Revolution, Nationalism, Colonialism and the Arab Middle Class* (Princeton: Princeton University Press, 2006).

The literature on the Palestinian conflict is vast and contentious. Common overviews include Benny Morris, *Righteous Victims: A History of the Zionist-Arab Conflict, 1881–2001* (New York: Vintage, 2001) and Charles D. Smith, *Palestine and the Arab-Israeli Conflict*, 7th ed. (New York: Bedford/St. Martin's, 2009). A readable introduction to the history of the Palestine mandate is Tom Segev, *One Palestine, Complete* (New York: Henry Holt, 2000).

The classic biography of David Ben-Gurion is Shabtai Teveth, *Ben-Gurion: The Burning Ground, 1886–1948* (Boston: Houghton-Mifflin, 1987). A more recent biography by his political heir is Shimon Peres and David Landau, *Ben-Gurion: A Political Life* (New York: Schocken/Random House, 2011). For two opposing views of Zionism in mandate Palestine see Anita Shapira, *Land and Power: The Zionist Resort to Force, 1881–1948* (Stanford: Stanford University Press, 1992) and Gabriel Piterberg, *The Returns of Zionism: Myths, Politics and Scholarship in Israel* (New York: Verso, 2008).

The following three books evoke the daily lives of Palestinians in the late Ottoman period and early years of the British mandate: Salim Tamari, *Year of the Locust: A Soldier's Diary and the Erasure of Palestine's Ottoman Past* (Berkeley: University of California Press, 2011); Rashid Khalidi, *Palestinian Identity* (New York: Columbia University Press, 1997); and Walid Khalidi, *Before Their Diaspora: A Photographic History of the Palestinians, 1876–1948*

(Washington, DC: Institute for Palestine Studies, 2010). The classic study of the Palestinian revolt of 1936–1939 is Ted Swedenburg, *Memories of Revolt* (Minneapolis: University of Minnesota Press, 1995).

Chapter 6

For an introductory biography of the Muslim Brotherhood's founder see Gudrun Kraemer, *Hasan al-Banna* (New York: Oneworld, 2010). Distressingly, translations of Banna's speeches and memoir are out of print and difficult to find outside of academic libraries: Hasan al-Banna, *Memoirs of Hasan Al Banna Shaheed*, M. N. Shaikh, trans. (Karachi: International Islamic Publishers, 1981) and *Five Tracts of Hasan Al-Banna (1906–1949)*, Charles Wendell, trans. (Berkeley: University of California Press, 1978). A good translation of his most important essay, "Toward the Light," is published in Roxan L. Euben and Muhammad Qasim Zaman, *Princeton Readings in Islamist Thought* (Princeton: Princeton University Press, 2009), 49–78.

For the history of the Muslim Brotherhood in Egypt, the following two books are essential reading: Brynjar Lia, *The Society of the Muslim Brothers in Egypt: The Rise of an Islamic Mass Movement 1928–1942* (Reading, UK: Ithaca Press, 1998), and Richard P. Mitchell, *The Society of the Muslim Brothers* (New York: Oxford University Press, 1993). For context in Egyptian politics and society of the era see Marsot's *Egypt*, cited under Chapter 1 above; Arthur Goldschmidt, Amy J. Johnson, and Barak A. Salmoni, eds., *Re-Envisioning Egypt 1919–1952* (New York: The American University in Cairo Press, 2005), and the novel by Naguib Mahfouz, *Palace Walk* (New York: Anchor, 2011).

Chapter 7

There are no biographies or translated texts of Yusuf Salman Yusuf (Comrade Fahd) in English, but there are several histories of the Iraqi Communist Party. The most authoritative is Hanna Batatu, *The Old Social Classes and the Revolutionary Movements of Iraq* (Princeton: Princeton University Press, 1978). More accessible introductions include Tareq Y. Ismael, *The Rise and Fall of the Communist Party of Iraq* (New York: Cambridge University Press, 2008), and Johan Franzen, *Red Star over Iraq* (New York: Columbia University Press, 2011). The Iraqi Communist Party also maintains an English language website: www.english.iraqicp.com/english.html.

For an introduction to Iraqi history see Charles Tripp, *A History of Iraq*, 2nd ed. (New York: Cambridge University Press, 2000), and Marion Farouk-Sluglett and Peter Sluglett, *Iraq since 1958: From Revolution to Dictatorship*, reprint of 1987 original (London: I. B. Tauris, 2003). Sasson Somekh evokes the intercommunal life of Baghdad in his *Baghdad, Yesterday: The Making of an Arab Jew* (Jerusalem: Ibis Editions, 2007). In a similar vein, a documentary film on Jewish Iraqi communists who emigrated to Israel after 1948 includes valuable (subtitled) historical interviews: *Forget Baghdad: A Film by Samir* (Arab Film Distribution, 2006).

Chapter 8

We have no biography of Akram al-Hourani, or texts from him, in English. The most accessible introduction to Syrian history in the mid-twentieth century is Patrick Seale's biography of Hafez al-Asad, *Asad: The Struggle for the Middle East* (Berkeley: University of California Press, 1988). The early chapters evoke the world of rural poverty, colonialism, and radical politics that animated Hourani. Seale's older book is a dense and indispensable analysis of how Syrian politics was overwhelmed by regional rivalries in the 1950s: *The Struggle for Syria: A Study in Post-War Arab Politics, 1945–1958*, new ed. (New Haven: Yale University Press, 1987).

For background on Syrian politics between 1920 and 1946 see Philip S. Khoury, *Syria and the French Mandate* (Princeton: Princeton University Press, 1987), and Elizabeth Thompson, *Colonial Citizens: Republican Rights, Paternal Privilege, and Gender in French Syria and Lebanon* (New York: Columbia University Press, 2000). On the Baath Party see Nikolaos van Dam, *The Struggle for Power in Syria: Politics and Society under Asad and the Ba'th Party* (New York: I. B. Tauris, 1996). For a political scientist's view on how the Syrian state became a dictatorship see Steven Heydemann, *Authoritarianism in Syria* (Ithaca: Cornell University Press, 1999). Hanna Mina's novel, *Fragments of Memory* (Northampton, Mass: Interlink, 2004) is perhaps the most powerful depiction of peasant poverty in the 1920s and 1930s. It should be coupled with Hanna Batatu, *Syria's Peasantry, the Descendants of Its Lesser Notables, and Their Politics* (Princeton: Princeton University Press, 1999).

Chapter 9

The literature on Palestine and Israel is so vast that this list can only provide the briefest introduction. Abu Iyad's memoir is still available from used booksellers: Abu Iyad with Eric Rouleau, *My Home, My Land*, Linda Butler Koseoglu, trans. (New York: Times Books, 1981). For a portrait of his home city of Jaffa see Adam LeBor, *City of Oranges: An Intimate History of Arabs and Jews in Jaffa* (New York: W. W. Norton, 2007). A recent study of Palestinian refugees' memories is Rochelle A. Davis, *Palestinian Village Histories: Geographies of the Displaced* (Stanford: Stanford University Press, 2010). For an unconventional but vivid portrait of Gazan refugees in the 1950s see Joe Sacco's historically grounded *Footnotes in Gaza: A Graphic Novel* (New York: Metropolitan Books, 2009). For a classic Palestinian account of diaspora see the fiction of Ghassan Kanafani, spokesman for the Popular Front for the Liberation of Palestine: *Palestine's Children* (Lynne Rienner, 2000) and *Men in the Sun* (Washington, D.C.: Three Continents, 1998). The groundbreaking academic study of the Palestinians' expulsion is Benny Morris, *The Birth of the Palestinian Refugee Problem Revisited* (New York: Cambridge University Press, 1988). This argument is condensed and placed into historical context in Morris's *Righteous Victims,* cited under Chapter 5 above.

The best single study of Fatah and the Palestine Liberation Organization (PLO) in their foundational years remains Helena Cobban, *The Palestinian Liberation Organisation: People, Power, Politics* (New York: Cambridge University Press, 1984). For a more accessible and pessimistic history of Palestinian nationalist movements, see Rashid Khalidi, *The Iron Cage: The Story of the Palestinian Struggle for Statehood* (Boston: Beacon Press, 2006). The authoritative volume on the PLO's resort to violence is Yezid Sayigh, *Armed Struggle and the Search for State: The Palestinian National Movement, 1949–1993* (New York: Oxford University Press, 1997). A standard journalistic account of the Munich massacre is Simon Reeve, *One Day in September* (London: Faber & Faber, 2001). A 1999 documentary by the same name but directed by Kevin Macdonald is a more careful study, with compelling interviews.

To complement Morris's *Righteous Victims,* the best book on the Palestine-Israel conflict from a leftist viewpoint remains David Hirst, *The Gun and the Olive Branch* (New York: Harcourt Brace Jovanovich, 1977), which was reprinted by Nation Books in 2003. Another standard book, and good read, from a regional viewpoint is Avi Shlaim, *The Iron Wall: Israel and the Arab World* (New York: W. W. Norton, 2001). For Palestinian and Israeli experiences of violence see Sari Nusseibeh, *Once upon a Country* (New York: Farrar, Straus, and Giroux, 2007), and David Grossman, *To the End of the Land* (New York: Vintage, 2011).

Chapter 10

Translations of texts by Sayyid Qutb and Ali Shariati are plentiful. Qutb's memoir is available in English as *A Child from the Village,* John Calvert and William Shepherd, trans. (Syracuse: Syracuse University Press, 2004). His two major texts are *Milestones* (New Delhi: Islamic Book Service, 2002) and *Social Justice in Islam,* trans. John B. Hardie and Hamid Algar (Oneonta, NY: Islamic Publications International, 2000). The best scholarly biography is John Calvert, *Sayyid Qutb and the Origins of Radical Islamism* (New York: Columbia University Press, 2010).

For a detailed biography of Shariati see Ali Rahnema, *An Islamic Utopian: A Political Biography of Ali Shari'ati* (New York: I. B. Tauris, 1998). Anthologies of his lectures include *On the Sociology of Islam,* Hamid Algar, trans. (Oneonta, NY: Mizan Press, 1979) and *What Is to Be Done?*, ed. Farhang Rajaee (Houston: Institute for Research and Islamic Studies, 1986).

On the Iranian Revolution see Nikki R. Keddie, *Modern Iran: Roots and Results of Revolution,* updated ed. (New Haven: Yale University Press, 2006); Ervand Abrahamian, *Khomeinism* (Berkeley: University of California Press, 1993); and Charles Kurzman, *The Unthinkable Revolution in Iran* (Cambridge: Harvard University Press, 2004).

Asef Bayat's comparison of Islamism in Egypt and Iran provides an important insight into how political context shapes ideas, and vice versa. It is included in his *Making Islam Democratic: Social Movements and the Post-Islamist Turn* (Stanford: Stanford University Press, 2007), 16–48. On the expansion of mainstream Islam in Egypt see Carrie Rosefsky Wickham, *Mobilizing Islam: Religion, Activism, and Political Change in Egypt* (New York: Columbia University Press, 2002). For a more accessible, journalistic view of Egyptian Islamism in comparison with other Islamic movements see Anthony Shadid, *Legacy of the Prophet* (New York: Basic Books, 2002). For more scholarly comparative approaches see Quintan Wiktorowicz, ed., *Islamic Activism* (Bloomington: Indiana University Press, 2004). A useful anthology of texts by Islamists is Euben and Zaman, *Princeton Readings in Islamist Thought,* cited under Chapter 6 above.

Chapter 11

Wael Ghonim's memoir, *Revolution 2.0: The Power of the People Is Greater Than the People in Power* (Boston: Houghton Mifflin Harcourt, 2012), is a good introduction to young people's frustrations that fed into the revolution. Two readable introductions to recent Egyptian politics are Tarek Osman, *Egypt on the Brink*, rev. ed. (New Haven: Yale University Press, 2011), and Jeannie Sowers and Chris Toensing, eds., *The Journey to Tahrir* (New York: Verso, 2012). For a broader view, a readable journalists' synthesis of the Arab Spring is Lin Nouiehed and Alex Warren, *The Battle for the Arab Spring* (New Haven: Yale University Press, 2012). Another useful source for scholarly commentary on news trends is the *Jadaliyya* website: www.jadaliyya.com.

INDEX